August 28, 1998.

To John,

With deep appreciation
for your help with my new
U.Va. Center for Governmental
Studies,
　Every good wish,

Larry.

Also by Larry J. Sabato

Dirty Little Secrets

Dirty Little Secrets

★ ★ ★

The Persistence of Corruption in American Politics

LARRY J. SABATO

AND

GLENN R. SIMPSON

TIMES 𝕿 BOOKS

RANDOM HOUSE

ISBN: 0-8129-2499-1

Manufactured in the United States of America

9   8   7   6   5   4   3   2

First Edition

Sabato: To the memory of my father, N. J. Sabato—
a proud patriot and model citizen

Simpson: For Mary

Foreword

The most disturbing trend in American public life today is found in the answers to a poll question asked regularly by the Roper organization: Do you think you can trust the government in Washington to do what is right most of the time?

In 1964, 76 percent of Americans polled answered yes. Today, that number has plunged to an abysmal 19 percent.

The implications are profound. The federal government is not some alien outpost that can be viewed by Americans with bemused detachment. It is how we organize and define ourselves as a nation; it *is* us. Countless books have been written about the effects of low self-esteem among children. Why should low self-esteem in a nation be any less of a concern?

The symptoms of the disease are easy enough to discern. At their most extreme, they lead to events like the bombing of a federal building in Oklahoma City, or the shooting of government employees. But even more disturbing are the more subtle effects—the erosion of public spiritedness, the distrust of national rules and information that emanate from Washington, the lack of confidence in our ability to address problems at a national level. As trust in government declines, the nastiness of national politics rises, with the rewards going not to those who appeal to the best in Americans, but to those who are best able to exploit the cynicism and distrust. Some of the most thoughtful, most public-spirited American politicians are simply choosing to leave the stage: Senator Bill Bradley of New Jersey, Senator Nancy Kassebaum of Kansas, Senator Sam Nunn of Georgia. Others, like General Colin Powell, ignore the call to step on the stage.

Clearly, something must be done. But what? Many of the events that have contributed to the free fall in public trust over the past three decades are irreversible: the assassination of a president, the loss of thousands of lives in a war the nation could not understand, the humiliation of Watergate. Other causes are economic: the result of two decades of stagnant wages and a slowdown in the growth of living standards. To successfully address those complex economic problems, the nation will need strong national leadership; but strong national leadership will only be possible when the leaders regain the trust of the people.

In *Dirty Little Secrets,* Larry Sabato and Glenn Simpson suggest a place to begin: the reform of the political system. Their book provides a catalog of the corruption prevalent in modern American politics. It is different from the sort of corruption that prevailed a half century ago. Big city bosses and bag men making payoffs are gone. But in their place is a new and toxic combination of technology and money that may undermine the system—and confidence in the system—even more. The tale that Sabato and Simpson have to tell is eye-opening; it is also deeply disturbing.

The book is the result of an unusual but fortunate pairing of talents. Larry Sabato has established himself as one of the most perceptive and peripatetic figures in the field of political science, and Glenn Simpson is rapidly becoming one of the most respected investigative journalists in Washington. Political scientists and journalists rarely collaborate; the former fear the latter lack intellectual rigor, while the latter fear the former are captives of the ivory tower. But Sabato deserves credit for recognizing that the investigative skills of a talented journalist could add greatly to the understanding of political science; and Simpson deserves credit for understanding the importance of the analytical skills of the academic.

The result is a powerful, path-breaking book that should become must reading for anyone trying to understand American politics.

Since completing work on this book, Glenn Simpson has joined the Washington bureau of the *Wall Street Journal.* It has been a pleasure working with such a fine journalist; and it has been an education learning what Sabato and Simpson have unearthed about the workings of our political system. Many Americans cried out for political reform in the elections of 1992 and 1994, but so far they have gotten little. Perhaps this book will prompt a more thorough debate in 1996 and lead to real reform.

Alan Murray,
Washington Bureau Chief,
Wall Street Journal

Preface and Acknowledgments

This book is an unusual undertaking—not so much for its subject matter but for the rare partnership that brought it about. This is one of the few American books ever jointly authored by a political scientist and a journalist.[1]

It is odd that our two professions have not been twinned more frequently, since academics and journalists are interested in many of the same political phenomena. But there is tension between our professions, and each group is critical of the other's standards and practices. To an academic, the journalist often seems sensationalistic, inclined to play to "the masses," sloppy and error-prone because of time pressures, and too much the generalist to develop real expertise. To a journalist, the academic frequently appears long-winded and pompously ponderous, insufferably slow to reach an unqualified conclusion, ridiculously specialized, and concerned only with his or her reputation among a tiny group of elite peers.

There is some truth in both critiques. Although the two professions do run on parallel tracks, they arrive at separate destinations. Political scientists prefer to observe the political system from a discreet distance, "objectively" describing and quantitatively classifying their observations in lectures and journal articles. Journalists yearn to be in the thick of the brawl, holding public officials accountable by publicizing the hidden deals, the waste, and the frauds.

Yet political scientists and journalists have vital goals in common. We both want to uncover the truth about our system of government, to teach others what we have learned, and to improve the process through public enlightenment. So, by way of an experiment, one political scientist and one journalist have merged methods, reaching a compromise in approach and writing style, to produce this book. The political scientist has brought to the task a theoretical and historical framework, plus the study of practical politics and a prescriptive bent. The journalist has added his ability to unearth the facts beneath the appearance, the better to target and tailor proposed reforms.

Melding the methods and standards of these two distinct professions has not always been easy, but we are satisfied with the results, and we hope that this project will encourage others in political science and journalism to join forces. Of course, our colleagues and all our other readers must judge the fruitfulness of this exotic hybrid.

On the road to publication we have received extraordinary help that must be acknowledged here. This study was financed in part through the generosity of the Schumann Foundation, the Joyce Foundation, and the Barbara and Robert Stuart Foundation. We wish to thank in particular John Moyers, executive director of the Florence and John Schumann Foundation; Lawrence H. Hansen, vice president of the Joyce Foundation; and Trevor Potter, former chairman of the Federal Election Commission, for their confidence in us and the financial arrangements that helped to make this book possible.

We have also benefited enormously from the solid research of administrative assistants throughout the development of this book. At the top of the list is Charles H. Woodcock, a graduate student at the University of Virginia and our project manager and senior research associate. Chuck's dedication to this project was truly exceptional, and he was more our colleague than assistant. Day after day (or should we say, late night after late night), he persevered as our jack of all trades—topflight administrator, interviewer, researcher, idea-generator, and editor. We could not have done it without him, and we will always be grateful for his efforts.

University of Virginia graduate student Lawrence Schack, who assisted Chuck Woodcock, accomplished his assigned tasks skillfully and thoroughly. He took many burdens on his shoulders, always cheerfully, and we are in his debt. Washington-based free-lancer Lawrence Binda's keen interviewing skills and writing talents were key as well. Working with coauthor Simpson, Larry penned the first draft of the sections on congressional fraud and political dirty tricks. David H. Kaefer, who received his B.A. from the University of Virginia in May 1995, was a crack researcher on voter fraud; he prepared voluminous background data on several of the case studies featured in chapter 10, as well as expertly helping Chuck Woodcock in a wide range of tasks. Chuck and Dave formed the original core of "Team Corrupt" at the University of Virginia, and we acknowledge with hearty thanks the devoted work of the other members: graduate students Rick Mayes and Bob Ritter, and undergraduates Alvar Soosaar, Sean Serpe, Christopher Keene, Jennifer Miller, Jason Johnson, Joel Young, and Sandra Rao. We watched these remarkable young people set a modern record for all-nighters, and we were dazzled by their talents and delighted by their unflagging dedication. As a consequence, we can now formally confirm what our readers have probably already suspected: the denigrating commentary one hears about Generation X is malarkey.

Also deserving special mention for their help in many forms are University of Virginia administrative assistant Nancy Rae; Robert Balkin, publisher and editor-in-chief of *The Hotline;* Judy Birckhead; Elizabeth Breeden; Weldon and Mildred Cooper; Greg Jenkins; Amy Keller; Jay Martin; Betty Shepard; our intrepid agent Stacey Woolf of Bob Woolf and Associates; Dwayne Yancey of the *Roanoke Times;* the staff at Glenn Simpson's former newspaper, *Roll Call,* whose support made much of this project possible; and all of our 303 interviewees for their time and trouble—they are individually listed in the appendix.

A final, special appreciation is due Peter S. Smith, our patient and thoughtful editor at Times Books, who in a hundred ways has made this a better book and was a genuine pleasure to work with throughout this volume's gestation. Few people outside a publishing house understand how much an especially talented editor can add and how many crises he can skillfully enable authors to overcome. But we understand it because we benefited enormously from Peter's guidance, intervention, and editing genius. We also wish to thank Peter Osnos, publisher of Times Books, for his belief in this project from start to finish and his determination that our book be given the resources it needed. And Alan Murray, Washington Bureau Chief of the *Wall Street Journal,* has our gratitude for both his foreword to this volume and his careful review of, and many useful suggestions for, the manuscript.

Finally, we take full responsibility for all errors that remain in this book, but in view of the tensions that often keep political scientists and journalists at arm's length, we reserve the right to blame one another!

Larry J. Sabato
Charlottesville, Virginia

Glenn R. Simpson
Washington, D.C.

Contents

Dirty Little Secrets

Introduction

The most fundamental and compelling issue on the national need-to-do agenda is political reform. Americans have lost faith in the system that sustains their democracy, believing that it serves special interests more than the general citizenry. Officeholders—most of them—want to do the right things but cannot bring themselves to change a system that, for all its faults, has the redeeming quality of having elected them. Meanwhile, the campaigns that put them into office are sinking ever deeper into a bog of sleaze and slime—a primordial political ooze whose toxicity is increased by new technologies that make voters who are already turned off hate politics all the more intensely.

The voters' disgust and cynicism are easily understood. After all, they have been promised political reform repeatedly—and the promises have been repeatedly broken. Twice in the last four years, citizens have flocked to the polls to vote against business as usual in Washington. At least in the area of political reform, business as usual continued after both elections, even though the established order was supposedly ousted first in 1992 and then in 1994. In 1992, Americans who backed Bill Clinton and the Democrats thought they would get reform, but they did not: Clinton and his heavily Democratic Congress accomplished nothing in the campaign cleanup department. In 1994, Americans who supported Newt Gingrich and the Republicans expected reform, too, but got far less than many had hoped for. Indeed, Gingrich and the GOP, while denouncing Democratic methods of corruption for years, learned from them—and invented new and more perfect forms of corruption. If anyone doubted that both parties benefited from the status quo, the doubt was removed in the months following an especially cynical "photo op" in June 1995. Bill Clinton and Newt Gingrich shook hands for the cameras in New Hampshire to pledge reform, but once again they did not bother to deliver.

The politicians always have a list of excuses at the ready. It is someone else's fault, you know, and you are not to worry, because reform is just around the corner: it is on the schedule for next spring, no—next summer, no—next fall. But the voters are still waiting. The purpose of this book is to force politicians to turn the corner at long last, by providing their bosses, citizens, and the tribunes in the press with the evidence of corruption and the remedies to correct it.

We would like to begin by recalling a few incidents from the 1994 elections, all of them seemingly of strictly local interest. When the definitive history of American politics in the twentieth century is written, none of these stories is likely to merit more than a footnote, if that. But the fact that they are fairly routine may say more about the stubborn persistence of corruption in America than the big stories that will merit the full chapters in that yet-to-be-written volume.

• In nineteen key House races around the country, the Christian Coalition distributed a voter guide that accused Democrats—including Ways and Means Chairman Dan Rostenkowski of Illinois—of "Promoting Homosexuality to Schoolchildren." In tiny print at the bottom of the guide, the coalition said it based this claim on House of Representatives roll call vote number 91. The vote was on an amendment prohibiting the dissemination of obscene material on school grounds and barring the use of federal funds for any educational program set up to promote homosexuality. The Democrats in question all voted *for* the amendment; but in doing so they were also voting against an even stronger competing proposal and thus—in Orwellian fashion—became "promoters" of homosexuality.

• In Tennessee, the state Democratic Party paid out more than

$110,000 to several groups whose actual existence appears to be in doubt. These include a company called American Business Planning, the North Memphis Voters League, the Ninth District Democratic Voters Drive, and the West Tennessee Voter Council. None of the groups was registered with the state as a business or campaign organization. A written request to the Tennessee Democratic Party seeking the most general information about the groups was spurned. Meanwhile, in nearby Georgia, state Democrats sent $30,000 to a firm with no offices that was owned by a black political consultant, Munson Steed. The state party chair defended the legitimacy of the payment but could cite no instance of Steed's work other than the printing of T-shirts.

• In Maine, "pollsters" called residents late in the fall campaign to ask if their opinion of GOP nominee Rick Bennett would change if they knew he had defaulted on $10,000 worth of student loans. In fact, Bennett had consistently met his required monthly payments on his remaining $7,000 balance. In Alaska, similar "pollsters" called voters and falsely asserted that Tony Knowles, Democratic candidate for governor, supported gay marriages and adoptions. "Knowing this, does this make you more or less likely to vote for Tony Knowles?" they asked.

• Shirley Miller, wife of Georgia Governor Zell Miller, discovered that someone with access to the secret code of a business in suburban Seattle had twice perused her credit file on the database of Equifax, a major Atlanta-based credit data clearinghouse. When word got out among Georgia Democrats, two other Democratic candidates for the state legislature soon discovered that their records had been reviewed as well by a local repossession firm, Georgia Recovery Inc. The snooping was eventually traced to a veteran GOP investigator.

• Senator Frank Lautenberg was struggling to win reelection in New Jersey, but he took time away from his state in March for an event in Houston, at which he brought in $45,314. The reason prominent Houstonians showered such largesse on a New Jersey senator? He chaired the appropriations subcommittee that had control over transportation funds the city wanted.

• In Alabama, dozens of absentee ballots were sent by election officials to a phantom post office box and later picked up by an unknown individual. Comatose and incapacitated people somehow voted absentee as well. Throughout California, noncitizens registered and cast votes; a San Francisco man, dead a dozen years ago, voted; and an astonished Kern County woman, while in the voting booth, heard another unknown woman in the line outside request a ballot in her name. In some Texas counties, political activists visited homebound voters and cast ballots for candidates preferred by the activists, not the voters.

The devil, as they say, is in the details. In writing *Dirty Little Secrets,* we spent the bulk of our time looking at the everyday, ordinary, behind-the-scenes business of politics to an extent that the daily media seldom are able to match. The details indeed paint a disturbing picture.

It is an article of faith in Washington that American politics is not nearly as corrupt as it once was. Every time there is a public outcry about a new revelation of influence-peddling, conflict of interest, or financial chicanery, this part of the catechism is intoned anew. The governing elites, and some supportive journalists and analysts, are quick to call the uproar "unwarranted hysteria," an understandable but misguided reaction on the part of the uninformed masses to the sometimes not pretty but necessary practice of politics.

Defenders of our current system point out politicians no longer accept large bags of cash behind closed doors from secret benefactors. The true corruption of old is far worse than the mildly questionable practices that draw complaints in our own time, they say. In fact, our national politics today is supposedly quite clean: there have been very few cases of outright bribery revealed in recent years, and public servants are required by law to abide by strict ethical codes that guard against conflicts of interest and other perceived evils. Granted, the public's anger at politicians and its suspicions about the machinations of the political class have grown ever hotter, but that is explained away by pointing to the excruciatingly intense media coverage that attends an elected official's every foible.

As professional observers of American politics steeped in the conventional wisdom of journalism and academia, we have been among the apologists. There were obvious, ugly excesses in politics, to be sure. But we knew that the vigorous practice of politics had always been a rough-and-tumble business, rarely admired for its elegance but inevitable in a vigorous democracy. The political free market had always encouraged participants to pursue their objectives with little restraint, and it usually rewarded those who went about the task most skillfully, be they legislators seeking re-election or interest groups amassing financial support for favored candidates.

Reformers who complained that the campaign finance system was legalized bribery seemed puritanical idealists who wanted to purify politics out of existence. After all, a large part of politics is cut-throat competition among organized interests, and fundraising and other forms of electioneering currently in disrepute among reformers are the channels by which such competition has always been pursued.

In recent years, however, we have begun to wonder. True enough, the cash bribe has become almost extinct. And after Watergate some reasonably effective reforms were enacted that helped to correct specific ills observed in the Nixon scandals. Our politics *are* cleaner in some respects than they used to be. Yet time and again we have encountered disturbing practices that, upon reflection, can only be labeled corrupt and that cry out for change. The reformers may have been exaggerating campaign finance abuses a decade ago, but as the years since Watergate have ticked by, the situation has indisputably worsened and the influence-peddlers have become increasingly brazen. Indeed, influence-peddling and other corruptions are in some ways more worrisome than they have ever been, because they are now so institutionalized that virtually everyone practices them. The rules of the game, at least as perceived by the players, seem to demand it. Never mind that the *written* rules—our laws and governmental codes of conduct—seem to forbid it. Perhaps the public has sensed it correctly all along: anger stems not from the media's exaggeration of official missteps, but from disgust at genuinely offensive institutionalized behavior that is simply taken for granted as normal and expected by the political class.

An excellent example of this systemic decline was the savings and loan (S&L) debacle of the late 1980s and the subsidiary 1989–91 "Keating Five" scandal in the U.S. Senate. While the S&L matter has virtually vanished from public consciousness (a passing not mourned in Washington), the bills from this $500 billion fiasco will continue to come due for decades. Many explanations have been proposed for why Congress and the executive branch failed to notice the massive fraud and waste occurring in the federally backed S&L system. The issue has been so obscured by the passage of time and the absence of proof in many cases that we will probably never know for certain why it happened.

Perhaps the most convincing reason was offered by two public servants who warned of the catastrophe in advance and tried to stop it: Republican Congressman James Leach of Iowa, now the respected chair of the House Banking Committee, and Edwin Gray, the able former public relations man who was serving as the nation's top savings and loan regulator when much of the disaster took place. Both are convinced that the role of money in politics was the single biggest factor in escalating the savings and loan mess from an expensive mistake into a fiscal catastrophe of titanic proportions. Yet in very few instances was it alleged that campaign or bribery laws were violated, and no congressmen were indicted for corrupt practices. Rather, evidence abounds that oversight of the nation's financial system was corrupted by *legal* campaign contributions.[1]

The Keating Five case, perhaps the most publicized part of the S&L debacle, was a small-scale illustration of this. Charles Keating, a high-flying con man with a dubious business record, persuaded a bipartisan group of five senators to gang up on Edwin Gray and other federal regulators and keep them at bay so that he could go on looting his S&L (to the tune, eventually, of $2 billion). By all appearances, it was not Keating's charm that persuaded the senators to join the battle, but rather his money. Together, the five legislators quietly collected more than $1 million in campaign contributions from Keating.

This was clearly a case of corruption, as bad as or worse than most of the campaign finance abuses of the pre-Watergate era. On several well-documented occasions, the senators had sought—out of the public view—to influence regulators or pass legislation of benefit to Keating. In some instances, these efforts were clearly linked to fundraising efforts by Keating on their behalf.[2] Yet the five legislators felt no legal repercussions from this case: the U.S. Senate Select Committee on Ethics—clearly perplexed by the absence of any evidence suggesting the senators had profited personally—actually absolved most of them of any serious wrong-doing. Only one, Democrat Alan Cranston of California, was formally called to account by the committee, and even that condemnation was purely symbolic.[3] ("Ah, the mutual aid society," Cranston had declared upon meeting his benefactor, Keating.) Two of the remaining four—Democratic Senators Dennis DeConcini of Arizona and Donald Riegle of Michigan—ultimately saw their political careers damaged but were permitted to serve out their terms without any formal institutional punishment. The other two, Republican John McCain of Arizona and Democrat John Glenn of Ohio, were actually reelected. Keating himself went to prison for stealing from his S&L and will remain there well into the next century.

It was murmured at the time that a panel of senators could hardly crucify five of their own for what was merely an extreme example of what takes place every day in Washington. Indeed, the committee members went out of their way to make clear that there was nothing fundamentally improper in senators accepting money from favor-seekers, or in senators aggressively seeking to influence governmental decisions on behalf of anyone deemed a "constituent."[4] For his part, Cranston fairly pointed out that "my actions were not fundamentally different from the actions of many other senators."[5] Cranston said examples of other senators engaging in similar conduct were "plentiful":

> The present system makes it virtually impossible—*virtually impossible*—for a senator to avoid what some will assert is a conflict of interest. There is no Senate rule stating when you can and when you cannot help a contributor. I do not see how one can be formulated. . . . How many of you, after really thinking about it, could rise and declare you have never, ever helped—or agreed to help—a contributor close in time to the solicitation or receipt of a contribution?[6]

Cranston was right.

It is impossible to observe an event such as the S&L debacle up close without developing a gnawing fear (or worse) that a system that allows something like this to happen is seriously ill. Yet in its wake, there was no reform of the laws that permitted it to occur.

Our History of Corruption

Even when scandals have been followed with reforms, inevitably corruption finds a way to thrive in the new environment. The result is that wave upon wave of corruption washes over American democracy, despite all attempts to erect a seawall sufficiently strong to prevent it. Corruption is truly a staple of our Republic's existence, and its durable, undeniable persistence in the face of repeated, energetic attempts to eradicate it is darkly wondrous.[7] During the last century and a quarter of our history, the United States has been shaken to the core by three major scandals: Crédit Mobilier, Teapot Dome, and Watergate.

The cycle of growing corruption often followed by a period of attempted reform is apparent repeatedly over the years. The so-called Gilded Age following the Civil War is a case in point. Greed was the golden rule—he who had the gold ruled—and no scandal of the era better demonstrated that than Crédit Mobilier.[8] This enormous scam took its name from a corporation formed to construct the nation's first transcontinental railroad. An intricate scheme of payoffs, overcharging, and kickbacks inflated the railroad's actual cost from $51 million to $93.5 million, a figure that included both excess profits and massive graft—some of which found its way to Congress. In order to stave off a potential congressional inquiry into stupendous profit, the corporation's directors (including a Massachusetts congressman, Oakes Ames) distributed valuable shares of Crédit Mobilier to ranking legislators. Not long afterward, an unhappy non-congressional stockholder who believed he was being cheated in the enterprise filed suit, and confidential court papers were soon in the hands of the *New York Sun.*

The papers were published during the 1872 presidential campaign, as Republican Ulysses S. Grant was seeking his second term, and the news for the Republicans could not have been worse. The incumbent vice-president Schuyler Colfax, his nominated successor Henry Wilson, Speaker of the House James G. Blaine, and House committee chairmen galore—Republicans all—were credibly accused of accepting bribes. With memories of the Civil War still fresh, however, the GOP-leaning electorate initially chose to believe the denials of the accused, and Republicans easily won the 1872 election. Nevertheless, the opposition's outcry was sufficient to generate a congressional committee investigation. With honest leadership at the committee's helm, the facts began to emerge fully, ruining the careers of many of those involved and irrevocably tainting Grant's administration even though the president was not directly implicated.

Reform efforts at the time consisted mainly of attempts to reclaim the ill-gotten profits from Crédit Mobilier and Union Pacific executives, but even these modest moves failed.[9] However, much as with the S&L scandal more than a century later, the episode greatly deepened the public's cynicism and mistrust of the mix of business and government, helping to pave the way for more successful turn-of-the-century measures to tame big business.

Civic reformers received a much greater boost from the exposure of abuses committed by big-city party machines. Lincoln Steffens and his fellow Progressive "muckrakers" turned up the heat on the bribery and graft foundations of New York City's Tammany Hall and similar machines in St. Louis, Minneapolis, Pittsburgh, Philadelphia, and elsewhere. First in *McClure's* magazine and then in his best selling book, *The Shame of the Cities,* Steffens fueled the Progressive movement's determination to defang the bosses.[10] Some of the Progressives' remedies were on target, effective, and enduring, such as the direct election of U.S. senators and the substitution of broadly based primary elections for boss-controlled nominating conventions. But in the arena of campaign finance corruption, Progressivism was much less successful. In 1907, 1910, and 1911, Congress passed various pieces of campaign finance legislation forbidding corporations and national banks from contributing to congressional and presidential candidates, mandating disclosure of campaign expenditures, and establishing spending limits for House and Senate campaigns. These rules were codified and expanded in the federal Corrupt Practices Act of 1925, the Congress's first comprehensive legislation in the campaign finance field.[11]

Unfortunately, the law sounded better than it read, especially after the courts had finished interpreting it.[12] The spending limits applied only to money expended with the candidate's "knowledge and consent." Disclosure was frequently meaningless because the campaign reports were often unavailable to the public, many substantial costs (such as printing and telephone) were exempted, and there were no audits of any kind. Primary elections were excluded from the law, so that in the South—where victory in the Democratic primary was tantamount to election—the real campaign was hidden from scrutiny. And the corporate and bank contribution ban was easily evaded: shell "educational" organizations were set up to launder corporate money before it was passed on to campaigns, and individual bank officers were simply reimbursed for their generous personal gifts to candidates. It is no accident that in its nearly half-century on the statute books, the Corrupt Practices Act was the basis for *not a single* prosecution.[13]

Shortly before the Corrupt Practices Act was passed, the country was rocked by its greatest scandal since Crédit Mobilier, the so-called Teapot Dome affair,[14] and once again a presidential administration was battered. In 1920, Warren G. Harding, the handsome and stately Republican senator from Ohio, was elected president by the largest majority since the Civil War. His call for a return to "normalcy" (it wasn't a word; he tripped over "normality" in a speech) proved attractive to an America weary of war and the idealistic rigidity of President Woodrow Wilson. But in two and a half years in office, Harding was to prove to be our nation's least competent president and (with U.S. Grant) the worst judge of character in his appointees.

The most infamous of these appointees was Interior Secretary Albert B. Fall of New Mexico, who became the first cabinet officer in history to serve a prison term. Financially destitute when he left his U.S. Senate seat to join Harding's cabinet, Fall was soon in the green, buying cattle and expensive parcels of land around his Western homestead. Even at the time it was obvious he could not have turned things around on a cabinet salary of $12,000 a year. Rather, he sold his office as well as a couple of extremely valuable tracts of land full of crude oil to corporate interests. Then in 1921 Fall cleverly got the unsuspecting Harding to transfer control of oil lands set aside as naval petroleum reserves from the U.S. Navy Department to the Interior Department. Without competitive bidding, he gave drilling rights at Elk Hills, California, to multimillionaire Edward L. Doheny and those at Teapot Dome, Wyoming, to another oil tycoon, Harry F. Sinclair. Everyone but the taxpayers did well. Fall was the beneficiary of about $400,000 in graft ($100,000 from Doheny and approximately $300,000 from Sinclair). Doheny and Sinclair each gained access to tens, maybe hundreds, of millions of dollars in oil; today in our oil-dependent economy, Elk Hills alone is worth perhaps $50 billion.

Alas for Albert Fall, there were other disgruntled oilmen, cut out of the action, to contend with. And conservationists (the predecessors of modern environmentalists) were up in arms about the loss of preserved lands. Democrats in Congress, led by the able Senator Thomas Walsh of Montana, saw an opportunity to recoup power. They were aided in their quest by Fall himself, who had carelessly accepted some of his graft in bonds whose serial numbers could be traced.

In response to a congressional subpoena, Fall first snowed his investigators with tens of thousands of pages and documents in an age before computers and large Senate staffs. But these stalling tactics only slowed the inevitable, and the dogged Walsh gradually tightened the noose around Fall's neck: following a Senate condemnation, Fall was eventually convicted in court and imprisoned.[15] He was not alone in his humiliation. Other Harding appointees, including the attorney general, Harry Daugherty; the secretary of the navy, Edwin Denby; and the head of the Veteran's Bureau, Charles Forbes, were also exposed for their corrupt activities in an administration honeycombed with vice.

Scandal aplenty was stoking the fires of reform, and a new Democratic administration elected in 1924 pledged to clean up the mess seemed a real possibility—until an act of Providence intervened. On August 2, 1923, President Harding expired in San Francisco, probably of a heart attack, while on a cross-country speaking tour. With him died the political culpability for corruption, for surely the Democrats would have made of his own words a 1924 political epitaph: "If Albert Fall isn't an honest man, I'm not fit to be President of the United States!"[16]

The new president, Calvin Coolidge, was a straightlaced New Englander who had been far removed from the shenanigans of

Harding's gang. Within eight months he had cleaned house, forcing out of office the prime offenders besides Fall, who had already resigned as interior secretary in March 1923. Coolidge also appointed two special prosecutors, one Democrat and one Republican, to go after the guilty individuals and regain the oil lands for the public (which they accomplished). Harding's reputation was buried, and many of the dead president's men were ruined. But in the process Coolidge distanced himself from Harding and won a presidential term in his own right in November 1924. Substantive reform efforts then fizzled; while the Corrupt Practices Act passed the following year, it did not really change the established Washington ways of doing business, as we have already reviewed.

In the twentieth century, only Teapot Dome matched in intensity the megascandal of Watergate—the next awful presidential-sized trauma that unfolded from 1972 to 1974. The outlines of Watergate are well known to most Americans: a melange of dirty tricks, including the bugging of the Democratic National Committee (DNC); the misuse of the CIA, FBI, and the IRS; and gross political and governmental improprieties, such as massive, hidden, in-cash contributions to a presidential campaign, all designed to get Richard Nixon reelected president and to get back at Nixon's enemies.[17] Just as in 1872, voters in 1972 chose to ignore early revelations about a corrupt cancer growing on the presidency, giving Nixon another White House term in part because the Democrats had nominated an exceptionally weak candidate, Senator George McGovern. But Nixon and his vice president, Spiro Agnew (caught in an unrelated bribery investigation), were forced to do what U.S. Grant and Schuyler Colfax and Warren Harding had avoided: resign their high offices.

Other than the Nixon and Agnew resignations, the most significant result of Watergate was campaign finance reform. The process of reforming how campaigns were financed actually predated Watergate, with the 1971 passage of the Federal Election Campaign Act (FECA).[18] This act replaced the Corrupt Practices Act, and it tightened reporting requirements substantially, so much so that investigators had an easier time tracking down some aspects of Watergate. (For example, misused campaign funds were the source of payments to the burglars who broke into the DNC headquarters at the Watergate office complex.) But real reform came after Watergate, when

Congress passed amendments in 1974 that elevated FECA to historic importance.[19] Among the most important provisions were various limits on expenditures and contributions: severe limits on what presidential and congressional contenders could spend overall, limits on what wealthy candidates could spend from their own fortunes, limits on what individuals and groups could spend on their own ("independently") to promote favored candidates, and limits on direct contributions to candidates of $1,000 per election for an individual and $5,000 for a political action committee (PAC). The 1974 FECA also maintained and expanded strong disclosure requirements; established an enforcement agency, the Federal Election Commission (FEC); and brought about public funding of presidential general election campaigns via an income-tax checkoff.[20]

Campaign finance reformers were convinced in the mid-1970s that they had created a clean new world for politics, but their high hopes have not been realized. The first blow was struck by the Supreme Court in 1976. In its landmark ruling *Buckley v. Valeo,*[21] the Court eliminated *expenditure* limits as violations of First Amendment rights. This opened the door to unlimited spending by every congressional candidate, by the wealthy from their own pockets, and so-called independent groups and individuals who choose to support or oppose federal candidates without any aid or direction from the candidates or their staffs.[22] After the Court ruling, Congress passed some fix-up amendments to FECA that still did not alter the thrust of the Court's changes.[23] In 1979, Congress made its last successful pass at amending FECA, liberalizing rules affecting state and local party organizations.[24] While helpful to party building, the 1979 changes also opened up a gaping regulatory hole, permitting millions of dollars to be raised and spent on activities affecting federal elections (such as voter registration and get-out-the-vote efforts) without effective contribution limits and in some instances full accounting and disclosure to the Federal Election Commission.

And that is only the beginning of FECA's problems, as many examples in this volume will demonstrate. There are now so many ways to arrange hidden expenditures and off-the-books electoral activities that the true total of money raised and spent for the 1996 presidential candidates will almost certainly be double or even several times the officially reported totals. FECA and the Corrupt Practices Act that preceded it were well-intentioned attempts at reform, but the law of unintended consequences combined with unfavorable judicial decisions rendered them both severely damaged goods. These two laws passed to cure corruption have one other similarity: over time, smart lawyers, clever consultants, and determined candidates have engineered massive loopholes through which heavily laden Brink's trucks have been driven each election season.

This brief sketch of some major incidents in the history of American corruption cannot begin to do justice to the rich variety of our history's corrupt injustices. And it is certainly not comprehensive, for a mere listing of the major and minor flaps about corruption over the last two centuries would by itself be as long as a book; in recent decades alone it would have to include many dozens of episodes.[25] But our discussion can help suggest some tentative hypotheses about the nature of the Republic's corrupt political practices. For one, the cycles and waves of (first) corruption and (then) attempted reform are remarkably predictable—perhaps not as regular as the phases of the moon and the tides, but repeated in a recognizable pattern over the centuries. Interestingly, the government of the United States has suffered through one mega-scandal every fifty years since 1872: Crédit Mobilier (1872–73), Teapot Dome (1923–24), and Watergate (1972–74). The press and public should be on guard around 2023!

Americans today are often thought to be cynical, and well they may be so, given deceptive governmental misadventures such as Vietnam and Watergate. Yet a survey of American history can also suggest an enduring public naiveté: citizens are generally trusting and at first invariably aghast by a specific political perfidy. This naive attitude extends to the reformist impulse that follows any shocking revelation. Even in our current antigovernment age, most Americans have a lasting belief in the legislative quick fix. There is no blight, no problem that cannot be cured with a sweeping statute, especially one that regulates the behavior of politicians without costing taxpayers much (or any) money. In the long run there may be as much or more surprise that the legislative fix does not work as there was at the original offense—which usually leads to a second, and third, round of attempted reform, often just as fruitless in the end.

In addition, in the public's eyes, all corruption is equally bad, but some corruptions are more equal than others. Not every revelation of chicanery affects the citizenry deeply or produces a reformist response. "Bad apple" corruptions—the occasional legislator on the take, such as Dan Rostenkowski—are taken in stride. But whenever corruption touches the core of American political life, especially the presidency and the chief executive's closest advisers,[26] there appears to be a stronger, more immediate public reaction. There may be an executive bias here to match the greater hopes and elevated status with which the public and often the press invests presidents (and governors and mayors). And this may be one reason why corruption in the legislative arena is often tolerated far more, for far longer, before people demand change.

Of course, the public's innocent unworldliness, and its executive bias, certainly cannot alone account for the persistence of corruption. Corrupt practices exist for the same reason that most reform efforts fail. Americans enjoy an exceptionally high degree of freedom thanks to near-absolute constitutional grants of political speech and association. This well-lit frontispiece, however, has a matching dark side: as *Buckley v. Valeo* argued, it is consequently difficult, and in some cases impossible, to regulate political activities closely. Oddly, the Constitution may sometimes guarantee that the law fails. As we discuss more fully in chapter 11, this is a recurrent theme in the history of campaign finance reform efforts, and reasonable remedial plans must take it into account.

One other characteristic of the American people can help to explain the persistence of corruption in U.S. politics. At the core of our self-image is an optimistic belief in progress, in an ever-improving society made better by force of good will, Providence, and hard work. A corollary of the idea of American progress is a disinclination to accept the reality of *regression:* what goes forward can and frequently will slip backward (as our look back at U.S. corruption has shown). High standards must be unceasingly and vigilantly enforced by a people and a press wary of deterioration. Few corrupt practices are ever permanently retired, and whenever citizens think otherwise and let down their guard, a return to the corruption of old is facilitated.

In the following section, we expand a bit on these concepts and draw additional observations and conclusions about corruption's nature, not just from the American experience but from that of human civilization through the ages. If we learn history's lessons well, perhaps we can begin to understand the power and persistence of corruption in the United States—maybe even enough to short-circuit the next mega-scandal. It may not be due until 2023, but in today's supercharged, fast-paced environment, things sometimes arrive ahead of schedule.

The "Principles" of Corruption

> In every government on earth is some trace of human weakness, some germ of corruption and degeneracy, which cunning will discover, and wickedness insensibly open, cultivate, and improve.
> —*Thomas Jefferson,* Notes on the State of Virginia[27]

We have already suggested the outlines of the kinds of corruption we seek to investigate. But before proceeding further, it is important to establish with greater clarity what we mean in this book when we refer to "corruption." Like Jefferson, we recognize the universality of corruption, its inevitability in every regime. Yet the *standards* and *morals* existing in any society affect the perception and reality of corruption, even its very definition. Scholars have argued for centuries about the proper definition and nature of corruption.[28] Those who wish to treat it narrowly see corruption as limited to its most outrageous manifestations: bribery, extortion, and graft. But most who have studied the subject believe corrupt politics extends far beyond these obvious and unquestionable sins, especially in the United States where the press and public tend to demand relative purity in the conduct of governmental and political affairs (even while often cynically expecting the worst from their officials).

The renowned political scientist V. O. Key defined "graft" as "abuse of power for personal *or party* profit" (emphasis added).[29] Corruption is not merely private *personal* gain at public expense; rather, as Key noted, the gain can also be registered on behalf of a political entity, such as a party or political action committee. In fact, corruption is often employed to produce both personal enrichment *and* political control, with the latter normally necessary to achieve the former.

In this volume, we intend to explore both kinds of corruption, the personal and the systemic. And in doing so, we will take a broad view of corruption, regarding it as *significant impairment of integrity in the conduct of public affairs, or unlawful or unethical wrongdoing in the course of campaigning or governing*. This definition, while expansive, is *not* all-encompassing. For example, a fair reading of the definition would not lead to the conclusion that the age-old and still widely accepted practice of patronage is, in and of itself, corrupt.[30] Patronage is clearly legal for at least some governmental positions in every state and nationally; many such appointees are well qualified for their jobs, assisting rather than impairing the work of government; and nothing in their selection would violate the provisions of any reasonable code of ethics. Much depends on the circumstances. If patronage is legal and does not produce incompetent appointees, it would be a stretch to say it is corrupt. But the illegal use of patronage employees to gain unfair advantage in a political campaign *would* be unethical and therefore corrupt. Another example: contrary to much press and interest group commentary, a political action committee is a completely legitimate form of interest-group expression, and the PAC's pooling of individuals' contributions to influence the outcome of election contests is an integral and healthy part of an active democracy.[31] But the evasion of election and tax laws by otherwise legal PACs and foundations *is* corrupt. Throughout this study we will make similar distinctions and repeatedly refer to our definition of corruption to explain our criticism of certain individuals, organizations, and political practices.

Moreover, we will try to do what many critics of the contemporary American political scene do not: distinguish between *real* corruption and *pseudo* corruption—acts improperly labeled corrupt.[32] For example, all incumbent "perks" are not inherently bad, and some are necessary. Members of Congress must be able to communicate with their constituents by mail and other means. The *degree* to which they do so, the *substance* of those missives, and the *timing* of mailings are three factors that separate legitimate from corrupt practices. To condemn the frank in toto is merely to indulge the public's dislike of, and cynicism about, politicians and all their activities. But if the criticism is narrowed to those who spend tax-payers' money with abandon and mail excessively, who use their newsletters and personalized form letters to promote themselves rather than to inform or discuss policy, and who flood the post office with correspondence mainly close to election day, then *real* corruption of incumbent perks is being targeted. We have tried in every chapter of the book to tailor our barbs narrowly, not only out of fairness but because it is a far more effective strategy against corruption. The rhetoric of pseudo corruption may have popular appeal, but it is easily dismissed by those with the power to remedy the real problems. In the realm of reform, exaggeration is the enemy of change, just as the perfect is the enemy of the good. We have attempted to avoid overblown alarmism, as well as insistence on unrealistic perfection in the reforms we propose.

At the same time, we refuse to pretend that all is well, or to avert our eyes when we see unpleasant realities that shake our comfortable, preferred notions about the current state of American democracy. Defenders of the existing state of affairs—not just politicians and political professionals, but also many inside-the-Washington-beltway journalists and pundits—are too inclined to dismiss reformers and their plaints. True enough, some of these reformers are goo-goo ideologues whose purist notions seek to take the politics out of politics. But the chummy status quo crowd is guilty of the greater sin: a refusal to recognize and remedy the corrupt practices that do exist, all the while dismissing mounting proof of those ills with a shrug of the shoulders and an insider's "boys-will-be-boys" wink. We hope to present enough evidence of corruption in this volume to convince all but the most jaded of the necessity for action. While this or that corrupt practice may appear minor in isolation, collectively they are deeply disturbing and proof positive that standards in U.S. politics are on a slippery-slope decline. Moreover, minimizing wrongdoing guarantees it will get worse; the loss of our capacity to feel outrage is one reason corruption creeps upward.

Perhaps not surprisingly, the American people have been more perceptive than the insiders in sensing the deterioration in their politics. Public disgust, anger, and alienation have been steadily mounting, finding expression not just at the polls but in a wide array of grassroots sentiments, from the disturbing militia fringe groups to the broadly based term-limits movement. But neither militias nor term limits will correct the deep-seated defects of American politics, in part because these alleged antidotes attack the symptoms rather than the causes of the country's maladies. Later, we will propose reforms better suited to the real problems that bedevil us. Before the remedies are prescribed, of course, the problems must be described, because as history teaches, an aroused and informed public is an essential requirement to accomplish reformation in any democratic system.

A review of the history of, and the literature about, corruption also yields several other conclusions that will guide our rummage around the cellars and hidden backrooms of American politics:

1. *Corruption has no ideology, no partisan coloration.* Throughout human history, corruption has been a constant, occurring to varying degrees in every kind of nation-state, government, and society.[33] As we will show, both Democrats and Republicans participate in corrupt practices, some of them widespread. Given the nature of competitive politics, when one side adopts a corrupt activity, succeeds at it, and gets away with it, the technique is legitimized and rationalized for use by the other side. Corruption can become so accepted that it is simply a "custom" of politics, often unquestioned by candidates, officeholders, or occasionally even by the press. Illegal activities in New York's Tammany Hall, Chicago's Daley machine, and the Maryland contractors' payoff system for Governors Spiro Agnew (Republican) and Marvin Mandel (Democrat) are but three prominent examples. Another application of this unprincipled principle is that a change of power from one party to another may simply involve a change in machines, with no decrease in the level of corruption. ("Meet the new boss," sang an old rock group, "same as the old boss.") Some of the current practices of incumbent congressmen and the political consulting industry—outlined later in this volume— demonstrate other instances of ingrained, corrupt custom.

2. *While corruption is inevitable and a constant, its precise manifestations are ever changing.* As already mentioned, outright bribery was once the preferred modus operandi of corruption in America, and a lengthy line of scandals can be traced to it:[34] Crédit Mo-

bilier, Teapot Dome, Abscam (a late 1970s law enforcement sting operation in which a phony "Arab sheik" gave some congressmen money in exchange for their official help), and a hundred major embarrassments over the centuries in New Jersey, Louisiana, West Virginia, and sister states. Similarly, elections were often stolen as a matter of course, and appeals to bigotry and racism were standard on the campaign trail, especially in the South. We provide modern examples of some of these corrupt methods, and certain strains (such as election fraud) that may be poised for a comeback. But none of these practices is as widespread today as fifty or a hundred years ago. Instead, new ways and means of corruption have been found, many of them designed to fit loopholes in the election laws or adapted to the dazzling new technologies of election campaigns. These will be our main focus.

3. *Corruption flourishes in secrecy and wherever the people and the press tolerate it.* Cockroaches and dirty campaigners love and live in the dark shadows. When their activities are undisclosed, the corrupters go about their business unimpeded. When the news media decline to explore and investigate suspicious practices, they fail in their most basic responsibilities. When the electorate learns of such practices via the press or other means and tolerates corruption (if only through inaction such as neglecting to punish the perpetrators at the polls), the voters contribute to an environment that nurtures corruption.

4. *A system of government or politics can be at least as corrupting as human nature itself.* We have studied politicians in close proximity for many years, and as much as it may disappoint the cynics, we have not found politicians to be venal *as a class*. While there are a number of individual exceptions, most professional politicians, especially those already in public office, want to do good or seek to do the right thing, *if doing good is an option that does not result in their political demise.* However, if the "normal and customary" practices of campaigning engaged in by both parties are seedy, and if a candidate believes "everybody's doing it, and if I don't do it, I may lose," then most politicians will suspend their ethical codes. They will willingly accept a distasteful means that ensures what they regard as the good and essential end of their

continued power. In other words, otherwise ethical people are put at a disadvantage by a corrupting system and almost forced to do unto others as they are being done to. Strict ethicists will correctly argue that the truly honorable person would not stoop to conquer, whatever the provocation. Yet reasonable reformers must keep in mind that the professional politician has a "power gene" in his or her genetic code that overrides all usual inhibitions to achieve victory or maintain power—and genetic engineering, however advanced it may become, will never be able to change that reality.

5. *Any crusade to eradicate corruption is naive and doomed to failure, but corruption can be controlled and limited.* The political mind is ingenious and the stakes high, and as noted earlier, given our First Amendment freedoms of speech and association in the United States, there can never be an airtight statutory solution to many of the problems we identify in this book. In fact, as the Corrupt Practices Act and the Federal Election Campaign Act show, almost every attempt to revise and "improve" the election laws is guaranteed to create new, unforeseen loopholes that will be exploited in time, bringing discredit upon those very same high-minded reforms. Instead, sunshine is the most powerful disinfectant for corruption, and exposure can force corrupt custom to change by turning the socially or politically acceptable into the unacceptable, utilizing the awesome power of public opinion. We intend to shine light into some dark corners of American politics, and we hope the press and all others who care about America and the American system of government will continue to do so and intensify the luminosity in the years ahead.

Past as Prologue: Corruption Persists

As history has taught us, and as we intend to demonstrate in the balance of this book, it is impossible to simply declare victory over corruption and then move on. The modern successors to American corruptions of old prove as much. The S&L disaster of the 1980s is the direct offspring of Crédit Mobilier, Teapot Dome, and Watergate. The Keating case was not an aberration but a harbinger; in fact, scandal has become so routine that it no longer seems so scandalous. Donations of $1 million or more in obvious protection money from individuals and corporations whose motives are no more noble than Keating's are no longer news. Ambassadorships are still purchased by wealthy campaign contributors as official Washington blithely looks the other way. Corporate welfare clients such as the Archer Daniels Midland company (which depends almost entirely on federal subsidies for its profits) and financiers like Cincinnati billionaire Carl Linder (ex-partner of Charles Keating) cynically lard the coffers of both political parties so that they will come out on top no matter who wins at the polls. If the system is so much cleaner today than it once was, how should we explain such multimillion dollar grotesqueries in contemporary Washington?

If one looks behind the facade, or to the places where it has crumbled away, the view is of a campaign system about as rotten as it has ever been. The once-clear legal standards established in the post-Watergate era have been almost completely eviscerated. To cite but one example, following Watergate, as noted above, a citizen could give no more than $1,000 per election to a single candidate for federal office and only $25,000 in aggregate for a year, while a corporation could directly spend nothing at all. Moreover, there was no legal way to contribute money without publicly disclosing it. Today, these limitations are a joke to the political elite. Millions of dollars change hands between politicians and their individual and corporate supporters, much of it in secret.

While the Federal Election Commission attempts to regulate campaign conduct, it is a captive of its own bipartisan design and has become gridlocked and almost completely overwhelmed. Some political players find legal means to get around the FEC's regulations; others simply violate the rules outright—confident that they are unlikely to be brought to account by the FEC for years (if ever). Even if they are unlucky and are caught, the penalties will be infinitesimally smaller than the political prizes to be gained from violating the law.

The traditional notion of corruption—a public servant using his position to enrich himself personally—is nearly an anachronism. This kind of corruption is increasingly rare, largely because most government officials today are fairly (perhaps generously) compensated. A rank-and-file congressman now earns over $133,000 a year—more than five times the median income of American families. At least sixty-four of the eighty-seven men and women who first joined the U.S. House of Representatives on January 3, 1995, faced not a cut in pay but rather a raise—in many instances a very hefty one.[35] Ordinarily, this could be hailed as a victory for good government, but unfortunately the graft of olden days has not been eradicated so much as superseded—while we have tended to look for corruption in one place, it has removed itself to another.

Alan Cranston, protesting his treatment by the Ethics Committee in the Keating Affair, observed self-servingly, "In every case of financial impropriety considered by the Senate throughout its history, the alleged misconduct was the use of public office for a Senator's *private* profit."[36] Indeed, today corruption is not just a danger of political life, it is an unavoidable component of it. It has become impossible to maintain one's place in the political system without participating in or benefiting from corruption, whether in fundraising, political horsetrading, or campaigning. Perhaps more than ever before, achieving political power consigns a person to a wrenching series of choices. The energy an elected official must expend merely to remain in office is often crushing. The game creates its own rules, almost every one of which demands a price in integrity. The candidate who plays according to the rules of the game places himself at a disadvantage, as he knows his opponent may not allow scruples to stand in the way of victory. "Why should I play by stricter rules than my opponent if it means letting her win?" Today's corruption, in short, is not a matter of bad apples, but a function of operating in a system where integrity has become a handicap.

These are some of the themes that we will examine, and some of the problems we will try to suggest solutions to, in *Dirty Little Secrets*.

To us, it is painfully obvious that there is no single culprit and no simple answers. However, the first step toward curing our system's ills is to frankly acknowledge and catalog what has occurred in recent years. To that end, in the spring of 1994 we embarked on an effort to survey the political landscape during a critically important campaign season and compile an inventory of the system's failings. We sought to pull back the veil on the pivotal 1994 election and to reveal deterioration in the larger political environment. Our goal was and is to give the press and the public hard evidence about the flaws in our process, and some suggestions for realistic reform, in preparation for future campaigns and governments.

Admittedly, we did not anticipate so startling a demonstration of our point of view as the one provided on Election Day 1994. Years of careful organizing by once-obscure forces on the political scene helped to produce a stunning electoral coup. To the shock and amazement of the Washington political elite, the seemingly permanent Democratic majority in the House of Representatives was snuffed out, and Republicans were restored to dominance in the U.S. Senate after eight years in the minority.

The shock and amazement in the media and the political establishment were themselves clear indications of the level to which the system had deteriorated, as well as of the complacency of the elites and the press. In their view, the end of the Democrats' forty-year hegemony was never meant to be. As we will describe in later chapters, the Democrats had built an incumbency protection machine more powerful than any in the nation's history. And they had shared a good many of its secrets with their Republican colleagues. It amounted to a remarkably effective shield against the winds of political change.

But in November 1994 a GOP hurricane proved stronger than the shield. For the first time in the adult lives of most Americans, the political underpinnings of modern American government were washed away by a tidal wave, and the nation's laws would be written by Republicans as of 1995. As a result of the election, key elements of Franklin Delano Roosevelt's New Deal were placed under siege, and aspects of Lyndon Johnson's Great Society were consigned to history's dust bin. The political discourse suddenly veered from universal health care and gay rights to flat tax rates and a sharp cutback in the growth of government.

In the national media and among the political class (particularly the Democratic establishment), responsibility for the fall of the Democratic Congress was primarily laid at the feet of President Bill Clinton—the first Democrat to occupy the White House in a dozen years and the most unpopular newly elected president since polls have been taken.

But while Clinton's woes surely played a critical role, it is far too simplistic to give him all the credit or blame; it is arguable whether his mistakes had to prove so costly for Democrats. After all, Democratic president Jimmy Carter was held in considerable disrepute in 1978, but Democrats kept control of both houses of Congress in midterm elections that year. And in 1980, after a full term, Carter was even more unpopular than Clinton was at midterm; while the Senate went Republican that year, Democrats in the House retained their majority.

The Democrats' mastery of the politics of incumbency in the reform era following Watergate was so complete that even the immensely popular Ronald Reagan could not bring a party majority in both houses into office with him in the election of 1980 or even in his 1984 forty-nine-state reelection landslide. This circumstance—extremely frustrating and infuriating to the Republicans, who had won the presidency time and again—led inevitably to the radicalization of the congressional Republican Party. Through the 1980s and 1990s, GOP House leaders and rank-and-file members grew increasingly impatient and angry with the Democrats' often arrogant rule.

There are many reasons for the Republican congressional ascendance in 1994, not the least the political desires of a majority of voting Americans. Yet the GOP's long-sought victory was abetted by what were, at best, unorthodox new campaign techniques, and at worst, unethical and illegal practices. The Right's adoption and successful execution of many of the Left's tactics enabled Republicans and their allies to develop extraordinary organizational and financial strength by circumventing some of the principal post-Watergate reform laws. The Republicans' new-found tactics are the first act of our story.

PART I

Revolution

A revolution breaks out when all the antagonisms of a society have reached their highest tension.

—*Leon Trotsky, c. 1920*

"The greatest midterm majority sweep of the 20th century," Republican National Committee Chairman Haley Barbour called the 1994 elections. He was exaggerating, but only by half. In the November 1994 elections, Republicans increased their numbers in the House of Representatives by an amazing fifty-two seats, while adding to their Senate ranks by eight, a feat that had not been equaled in almost fifty years.

The American electorate had finally taken the second step in its long-prophesied lurch rightward. The country had lifted one foot with the election of Ronald Reagan in 1980, but only in 1994, fourteen years later, did the voters complete the stride. Whether the election will usher in a new era of Republican dominance at both the congressional and executive levels of national government is of course unknown, but, indisputably, the center shifted. The basic political dynamic that had existed in Washington since the Truman presidency was gone.

In the aftermath of what was quickly dubbed the tsunami, shell-shocked Democrats and a stunned national press corps groped for explanations. The world had changed overnight. Some of the hypotheses put forth were plausible, indeed likely. The election of President Clinton in 1992 left both elected branches of government in Democratic hands for the first time since the Carter presidency, allowing angry voters to focus their wrath on a single party. (Tellingly, following the Carter presidency Republicans seized the Senate but failed narrowly to take the House.) The 1991 redistricting created more competitive legislative districts, undoubtedly boosting Republicans. The conservative elements of the electorate voted more heavily in 1994.[1]

But perhaps the most important factor was that public resentment of what were seen as corrupt and distant Washington political elites had reached a fever pitch. This anger did not come out of nowhere. It first strongly evidenced itself in the 1992 election, when Bill Clinton was swept into office on promises to reform the way business is done in Washington—an upbeat and optimistic and forward-looking message for which the public clearly yearned. It was a tantalizing promise the electorate did not forget. But by 1994, it appeared Clinton had. The Republicans, led by Newt Gingrich—who as we will see had already mastered the rhetoric of reform—stepped into the breach.

Gingrich the Revolutionary

Gingrich had begun his long journey to power in 1974, and his themes then were strikingly similar to his themes in 1994. Yet it took until 1994 for his vision to reach critical mass and convert itself into a Republican majority. The missing ingredient was corruption, and it was missing in two ways. As a political issue that Gingrich could use to discredit the Democratic ancien regime, it took time to ripen. As a political modus operandi, an organizing principle by which Gingrich accumulated and maintained political power, it took time to master.

Gingrich wears the mantle of a revolutionary, and it is not merely a pose. However, the analogy is true in ways Gingrich will never admit. Like Lenin and his fellow October revolutionaries, the Bolsheviks of American politics seized hold in 1994 of a revolution only partly of their own making. Although Gingrich's ability to recognize and capitalize upon the public's reformist impulse was unique, he himself did not create that impulse. But the observation that goes to the heart of the theses of this book is this: like Lenin & Co., Gingrich and his coinsurgents exploited the public's reformist longings in order to obtain power, but once they gained it they failed—indeed hardly even sought—to truly reform the system.

The revolution of 1994 did not come about because of the Contract with America, nor because the electorate desired a balance of power, nor because the Clinton health care plan failed. Rather, it was, in addition to being the product of the public's mounting resentment of Washington, the result of a deliberate and original analysis of contemporary political dynamics by conservative organizers. Beginning in the late 1980s, they copied the tactics of those they viewed as their oppressors, the Democrats: the use of shadow organizations, and the extraction of massive amounts of campaign funds from interests with a stake in governmental decisions. They also invented some entirely new tricks.

The common thread was the evasion of two fundamental principles of modern politics: sunshine and limits. The most important players in 1994, Newt Gingrich and the Christian Coalition, found ways to skirt these bedrock ethical principles, operating largely in secret and observing few restrictions on their campaign activities. While the coalition cannot be said to have conspired with Gingrich, its origins as a potent but frustrated political player are similar to his, and its outlook—that it was fighting a Holy War against the illegitimate dictatorship of the Democratic Party—nearly identical. And like Gingrich, the coalition was willing to stoop to conquer.

Gingrich and the Christian Coalition were also abetted by a reinvigorated national Republican Party leadership intent on aggressive politics at the congressional level. The new Republican Party leaders were perhaps less consequential than Gingrich or the Christian Coalition but nonetheless proved critical in assembling the GOP's House majority and were undeniably more effective and better focused than their predecessors. Like Gingrich and the Christian Coalition, the leadership of the Republican Party evinced a willingness to walk a very fine line and more than occasionally to step over it. To some extent, this "line" is a matter of law: some of what the Republicans and their allies did seems to be legally questionable. Other tactics are in a legal gray area. However thin that line, the new methods of the Christian Coalition, Newt Gingrich, and the Republican Party are indisputably violations of the spirit of laws—of norms and commonly accepted principles. They cannot pass one crucial test: is this how we want our political system to operate? We believe that for the majority of Americans, the answer is an unambiguous "no."

Before we go deeper into our examination of how this line was crossed, it helps to recall precisely what the guidelines are. In the latter half of the 1970s, following passage of campaign reforms in the Federal Election Campaign Act and amendments, the rules of political combat were fairly clear. Political parties could accept no more than $25,000 from a single person, while individual candidates could accept no more than $1,000 from a single person. If an interest group wanted to engage in campaign activities, the members went down to the Federal Election Commission and set up a Political Action Committee. The rules on interest group PACs were also clear: no person could contribute more than $5,000 to a PAC, and no PAC could directly contribute more than $10,000 to a single candidate.

Even more than contribution limits, the defining principle of the new reforms was disclosure. All meaningful political financing activity was to be reported to the Federal Election Commission. As the Justice Department puts it: "The FECA is a 'sunshine' statute. It reflects Congress's belief that the public has a right to know which individuals and organizations support which federal candidates, and in what amounts, so that voters can make informed decisions at the polls."[2]

Yet sunshine, unfortunately, is as inconstant in politics as it is in life.

1

The Education of a House-Wrecker

A revolution is always distinguished by impoliteness.
—*Leon Trotsky*

I n 1973, Newt Gingrich was an ambitious, well-liked thirty-year-old history professor at West Georgia College in Carrollton, Georgia, a small company town in the rural, conservative Piedmont section of Georgia. He had been active in politics since working as a volunteer for Richard Nixon in 1960, and had dropped out of college for a year in 1964 to manage a congressional campaign. While he had made up his mind to become a congressman as a teenager, for more than a decade Gingrich had been content to remain in the background. But after a failed bid for chairman of the West Georgia history department in 1973, Gingrich, in a fashion that would later become his trademark, adjusted his sights radically upward. In 1974, he would run for Congress.

Gingrich's first political opponent was John J. Flynt, a fifty-nine-year-old conservative Democrat in his twentieth year of undistinguished service in the House. Close to the military establishment and corporate America, anti-civil rights and antiunion, Flynt was the embodiment of the old southern Democratic politician who, but for the legacy of the Civil War, would have had no place in a party that had become firmly liberal in both economic and social issues. In that sense and others, Flynt was representative of the Democratic

Party's enduring dominance of Congress. He was ideologically at odds with many of his fellow party members but shared with them an understanding of how to milk the machinery of the House to ensure his seemingly perpetual reelection; a member of the committee on appropriations and its subcommittee on defense spending, he was adept at steering federal largesse to the folks back home.

Few gave the upstart Gingrich much of a chance. The *Atlanta Journal-Constitution* said in December 1973 that he was likely to be "one of the darker dark horses of the 1974 political year."[1] This was particularly the case because of the mushrooming Watergate scandal and a weakening economy. Asked if he expected opposition in the Republican primary, Gingrich joked, "Who else would want to run against a 20-year Democratic incumbent in the year of Watergate during an energy crisis?"[2]

By the fall of that year, he had already assembled a campaign team, despite the fact that the election was more than a year away—an unusual degree of advance planning by the standards of the day. As befit the era and his own character, Gingrich's bid was infused with equal doses of arrogance and idealism. At a September 30, 1973, meeting of the newly formed Gingrich-for-Congress executive committee, the future Speaker of the House "explained that his ultimate goal is to help the country become self-governing, that winning in 1974 with an honest campaign, really honest and not just one which claims to be or talks about being honest, is only a step toward that goal."[3] This account, drawn from the campaign's own internal minutes, does not elaborate on Gingrich's contention that America was not "self-governing" at the time. But other materials from this period indicate that Gingrich believed in—or at least was seeking to tap into—the notion that America's democracy had become dysfunctional, a dictatorship. Why Gingrich believed this, or was willing to say it, is not clear. But the crucible in which such a message was forged was of course Watergate.

Gingrich's "Open and Honest" Campaign

At the time Gingrich was formulating his first campaign strategy, John Dean was giving evidence to the Senate Watergate Committee of the massive political crimes of the Nixon administration. The democratic process ultimately prevailed, yet the notion of a dictatorship in Washington seemed to have captured Gingrich's imagination and stayed with him long after Nixon was gone.

Gingrich argued that the dictatorship was due to the influence of special interests on government. A draft fundraising solicitation, handwritten by Gingrich, stated, "Freedom must be earned by each generation. Have you carried out your part of the burden? Only if *you* help can we eliminate the domination of the special interests!"

Gingrich told his supporters that his own campaign "must be really open and honest" because, among other things, "people have been sweet-talked too often." He laid down basic campaign rules, the first of which was "Honesty in everything," and encouraged the campaign to operate openly, "that is, apply the sunshine law to politics."[4] Another indication of Gingrich's thinking comes from a handwritten draft of a speech Gingrich wrote for himself that year, "America's Real Problems": "I believe America can solve its problems and can build a better future for its children *IF*: We will put aside partisan, mud slinging politics and put America above ambition."[5]

Even though these were the earliest hours of the dawning era of public cynicism about government, Gingrich perceived what kind of new issues might motivate voters. Gingrich was "deeply concerned," one Gingrich campaign pamphlet said, "about the attitudes of the arrogant, out-of-touch politicians in Washington." He was crafting the prototype of the modern anti-Washington campaign, testing a technique and a strategy the awesome power of which he had yet to fully recognize. Attacking the existing power structure as corrupt is not new in American politics, but Gingrich undertook the tactic in a newly aggressive and systematic manner. While his use of scandalmongering to advance himself and his party is fairly well-known, the extent to which it defines his political essence—and the extent to which it is at odds with his own conduct—is virtually unknown to those who were not present at the creation.

"Newt Gingrich promises you a fair and decent campaign with open records of campaign expenses and contributions," the pamphlet went on. "He believes that this race can be a model of the kind of elections America deserves . . . a campaign that will help restore dignity to our cherished electoral process." Certainly these were natural themes for candidates in the year of Watergate, but Gingrich made them the centerpiece of his campaign. In a newsletter to supporters, he said some of the "keynotes" of his campaign were that "people distrust all politicians and don't like incumbents who take their votes for granted," and "the voters are so fed up with dirty tricks and the general mess in Washington that many of them will not even bother to go to the polls."[6] He sharpened his message as the campaign progressed, saying voters were "sick of lawyers and sick of incumbents." His opponent, Flynt, was both.[7]

The professor was just getting started. In the third week of September, with the election just eight weeks away, Gingrich went to the Atlanta press with allegations that Flynt had engaged in an unusual transaction with executives of the Georgia division of Ford Motor Co.[8] Gingrich said he was "amazed and appalled" that Flynt would agree to rent some of his property to Ford, then go to bat for the company in Washington in a dispute over exhaust emission regulations.[9] He dismissed Flynt's explanations that Ford's decision to rent some of his property to a neighbor was not surprising and Ford's expectation of his congressman's help in the emissions fight was legitimate. The arrangement raised "a possible serious breach of ethics," said Gingrich. The Atlanta press gave the story considerable attention, but Flynt continued to shrug it off. Gingrich proceeded to turn up the heat, taking new charges to the press about a Flynt employee who managed the congressman's farm as well as his district office. The employee, Gingrich implied, was being paid with government funds to work on Flynt's farm.[10] His ire increasing, Flynt explained that the district office job was part-time, as was the farm work. It was not an uncommon arrangement for the time, and on its face, there was nothing untoward about it. But Gingrich was on to a larger truth: irrespective of Flynt's guilt or innocence, many congressmen *did* misuse their staff and pad their payrolls. Indeed, just the previous year, Representative J. Irving Whalley had been convicted of taking kickbacks from his staff. Whalley was not the first to do so—J. Parnell Thomas of New Jersey won that distinction in 1949—nor would he be the last. Three years after Whalley's conviction, Wayne Hays resigned when it was revealed that he kept his mistress on his payroll. There were at least three similar cases in the 1970s and have been others since.

At a press conference at the Georgia state Capitol, Gingrich filed the first ethics complaint of his career, calling for the House Committee on Standards of Official Conduct to investigate Flynt's dealings with Ford and his payroll practices, saying the cases "indicate serious breaches of ethical standards."[11] The thirty-one-year-old untenured professor demonstrated a gift for invective and insinuation. "I am not suggesting that Congressman Flynt was bribed or committed an illegal act," Gingrich said slyly. "With the few confused facts we now have, there is no way to determine what his relationship to the Ford Motor Co. was and is."[12] It would be "all too easy to point the finger at an incumbent congressman and blame him for the pervasive impact of special interests. That approach lets all of us off too easily." Added Gingrich, "My opponent is not an evil man. He is simply a typical example of a political system that has lost all sense of morality and ethics."

Notwithstanding his denial that he was "suggesting" illegality, Gingrich then proceeded to suggest in a roundabout way that Flynt had, in fact, been bribed. It was "time that we were honest and admitted that the very system of special interests, lobbyists and hidden payoffs corrupts all but the most honest of men," he declared. Moreover, "Congressmen do not bribe themselves. Someone else has to be involved in this dance of decay, deceit and dishonesty. The huge special interests who dominate Congress have trapped us all in a quicksand of distrust. Huge private corporations and union counterparts dominate our society."

A few weeks later he recited his charges against Flynt at a press conference, then declared, "I would never accuse Mr. Flynt of being a crook, based on this alone. I just want him to step forward and explain these allegations. After all, all three were originally reported by the media: I have only asked him if they are true."[13] This time, in addition to employing the word "crook" to describe his opponent while denying having made an accusation of criminality, Gingrich added a new rhetorical flourish—that he was merely following up on media reports. Later in his career, Gingrich would refine this tactic, periodically citing published reports of various allegations for which, in fact, he had clearly been the primary source.[14]

Despite Gingrich's contention that Flynt and his colleagues were in bed with special interests—which they almost certainly were—Gingrich himself was securing special interest support in his quest to join their club. At a meeting of key leaders of the Gingrich campaign, it was announced that the Communications Workers of America (CWA) had decided to back Gingrich. "This group has 4,000 members in the 6th district and letters about Newt will be sent out to all of them," the campaign minutes recount. "They will also be printing articles about Newt in their newsletters, they are providing telephoners, and they will be sending out a minimum of 10,000 letters for Newt."[15] It is not surprising that a union would back an opponent of Flynt, whom the unions considered a bitter enemy. As the minutes note, "This group [CWA] has never before worked for a Republican candidate in Georgia, but they are working for Newt because they dislike Flynt very much." What is surprising is that the CWA would undertake such extensive efforts on behalf of a Republican, which might not sit well with the group's overwhelmingly Democratic membership or with Gingrich's own supporters, for many of whom unionism was tantamount to socialism. Indeed, antiunionism was so virulent in the sixth congressional district, one long-time resident recalls, that the West Georgia State College student union was forced to change its name to "student assembly" after too many people got the wrong idea.[16]

There was a solution to Gingrich's problem, however: the CWA operated for Gingrich behind the scenes. "They have been very careful to make sure that everything they are doing for Newt is nonreportable as a contribution," the minutes state. Gingrich appears to have been aware of, and assented to, this skulduggery.[17] In addition to voter dislike for unions, Gingrich had other reasons to keep his ties to labor under wraps. On the very day Gingrich was informed of the CWA's decision to back him, he was also told that archconservative Senators Barry Goldwater and James Buckley had written a letter to Republicans on his behalf; they would most likely not have been pleased to learn that they were backing a union man.

There was no real ideological inconsistency in Gingrich's union ties, however; whether Goldwater and Buckley knew it or not, Gingrich was a moderate Republican at the time. The real inconsistency was one of ethics. Accepting covert help from unions was a striking abandonment of the principles Gingrich had laid down at a meeting of the same group of campaign aides just thirteen months before. The watchwords "honesty in everything" and "apply the sunshine law to politics" had been forgotten. But it was not the only departure revealed in the minutes. Section 10 of the minutes, captioned "Attack," records Gingrich proposing that the campaign "find some people to picket Flynt," apparently without revealing the instigatory role of the Gingrich campaign.[18] A staff member proposed recruiting blacks for the job, and Gingrich endorsed the idea. "Newt said he thought it would be good publicity and would be effective with the media and with the public," the minutes record. But Gingrich campaign manager Chip Kahn counseled against the idea, and it was scratched. Gingrich pushed for other covert negative attacks against Flynt as well. "Newt again reminded the group that editors of local papers should be getting letters every week against Flynt and Newt asked people to call in when Flynt is on the radio and ask nasty questions," the minutes state. Gingrich's aggressiveness was evidently such that Kahn felt it dangerous and tried to restrain him. Kahn offered several interjections during the meeting, reminding everyone that in addition to putting out a negative message about Flynt, it was important to put out a positive message about Gingrich.

Former Gingrich campaign manager L. H. "Kip" Carter, a neighbor and West Georgia faculty colleague who later had a bitter falling-out with Gingrich, confirms that subterfuge was a common Gingrich campaign tactic in those days—phony letters-to-the-editor, bogus pickets, secret alliances, planting nasty questions during radio interviews.[19] Though these are tried-and-true tricks of the political underworld and not capital crimes, it is significant how profoundly at odds they were with Gingrich's loudly stated principles. "I have done and will do nothing that has to be kept under lock and key," Gingrich had declared just one year before. "If we are to have honest, responsible government, we must begin with honest, responsible politics. It is impossible to run a closed campaign and then expect to have open government after the election."[20] The gaping contradiction between Gingrich's words and deeds, which was to become a career-long pattern, was beginning to emerge.

The minutes also reflect Gingrich's frustration with the fundraising difficulties of an obscure candidate: "Newt said he was stymied about fundraising and just doesn't have the answer about how to improve it."[21] It was a universal political experience, and one that Gingrich would learn to cope with.

Like many who came before him, Gingrich found a clever way to circumvent the new federal limits on campaign contributions; he persuaded a group of wealthy supporters to make substantial loans to his campaign. While technically legal, the loans were a clear violation of the spirit of the new reforms. Arguably, they amounted to illegal contributions insofar as the financially ailing Gingrich campaign was not creditworthy. That became clear after the election, when Gingrich failed to pay back the loans. Ultimately, almost a decade would pass before Gingrich finally repaid the money, without interest.

Expediency was the true watchword of Gingrich's campaign. Winning required it. "I have run this race as well as I know how," he said. "I have no regrets."[22] Indeed, the redeeming quality of Gingrich's tactics was that they worked, putting Flynt on the defensive for the first election in years. The attacks had worked so well that by late October, Gingrich and many of his campaign staff were convinced that victory was at hand. "Newt said he thinks if the election were held this Tuesday he would win with 52% of the vote," the minutes from a meeting two weeks before the election note. The newspapers agreed. "Most political observers give Gingrich a good chance at taking Flynt's seat," said the *Journal-Constitution* a few days before the election. The dark horse had taken on a new shade.

But in the end the anti-Republican tide of Watergate simply proved too powerful, and on election day Gingrich came up just 2,800 votes short, an excruciatingly thin margin. He had come agonizingly close; there was no question he would run again.

Round Two in Georgia

Gingrich had found an effective formula for running against Jack Flynt, and he was not going to abandon it. The realization that in post-Watergate America ethical attacks could be the political equivalent of nuclear weapons began to flower more fully. Announcing his second bid for Congress in March 1976, Gingrich declared,

> I am running because the special interests dominate our government and have come to believe they own it. They think you and I don't know enough to make decisions. They think

you and I should be told what to do instead of being asked what should be done. They are trying to run America at our expense.

I am running for Congress because I am fed up with politicians, bureaucrats, and special interests who run this country at the expense of working people. . . . My vision is of a country in which Representatives come home often. Where they listen to the citizens back home rather than to special interest lobbyists. Where the Congress makes the laws and the bureaucrats enforce them. Where leaders tell the truth, even when it hurts. Where tough issues are discussed openly. Where complex issues are explained, and not simplified into grotesque sloganeering. Finally, where politics becomes mutual self-government and campaigns are mutual education between the candidate and the voter.[23]

While he portrayed himself as a moderate Republican reformer, this speech's theme is akin to one of Alabama Governor George Wallace's favorites. Like Wallace, Gingrich sensed a powerful mood in the electorate, a sense of resentment at Washington and the elites residing there.

In the 1970s, Democrats had just begun to insulate themselves from political competition. Following the 1976 election, recalls former GOP campaign operative Steven Stockmeyer, the Republicans investigated what they considered at the time an odd phenomenon: the failure of their party to win back many of the traditionally Republican congressional seats that had been won by Democrats in the anti-Watergate wave two years before. "We were shocked that some of those seats that the Watergate babies took Republicans didn't get back, and so we did some extensive research," he recalled.

We found that the sum and substance of it was that when you asked people why they liked their incumbent or why they voted to re-elect them, the biggest clusters of responses were constituent service and communication. The '74 class was not dumb when they increased newsletters and increased staff allowances and all that stuff. They knew exactly what they were doing. The survey proved them right.[24]

And the seeds of what was to come were already present. Gingrich was not wrong in the thrust of the claims he was making. Congress was awash in scandals at the time. In 1976 alone, Representative Henry Helstoski (Democrat of New Jersey) had been indicted for bribery, Representative Andrew Hinshaw (Republican of California) had been convicted of bribery, Representative James Hastings (Republican of New York) had been indicted for mail fraud and kickbacks, and Representative James Jones (Democrat of Oklahoma) had pleaded guilty to failing to report a campaign contribution. In 1978, the massive Koreagate influence-peddling scandal broke (thirty-one members of Congress were implicated), as well as a host of unrelated scandals, including several indictments and an investigation of Georgia's own senator, Herman Talmadge (Democrat). In retrospect, the public's receptivity to Gingrich's message is not at all surprising.

While corruption and reform then were clearly going to remain a big part of his campaign, for most of the spring, Gingrich's emphasis was on other matters. Once again, however, as the battle wore on Gingrich began shifting the terms of the campaign toward ethics issues. This time, his critique began to take on a partisan tone. "The news media continues to uncover more and more congressional corruption every day," he told a group of Young Republicans in late August.[25] "We have seen padded payrolls and falsified travel vouchers, bribery and forgery, all by men we elect to pass our laws and lead this country, and all by powerful members of the Democratic Party."

> The issue in this campaign is not going to be the moral integrity of the White House but the ethics of Congress, and we can take the lead in cleaning up the House and making it a working body again. . . . No one can say that Jerry Ford is not an honest and decent man. It is his congressional opposition that has been caught doing things most of us wouldn't even dream of. The power that is being abused this year is in Congress, not the White House.[26]

Gingrich grew even bolder in his tactics, making ethics the foremost issue in the final weeks. Some seven weeks before the election, he flew to Washington to challenge Flynt, a senior member of the

House Ethics Committee, on his own turf. At a press conference outside the Capitol, Gingrich labeled Flynt's stewardship of the ethics committee "corrupt and incompetent.[27]

> Two years ago the people of the United States breathed a sigh of relief that hopefully the political scandals of this country were over. They sent to Washington the freshest . . . and newest . . . Congress in recent history.
>
> But public hope has decayed. The scandals are not over. The American people have been outraged by repeated abuses of power by members of Congress. Incredible as it may seem, congressional misconduct has become almost commonplace, just another example of politics as usual. The reason is simple. Over the past two years, through one front page scandal after another, the House ethics committee has failed to act. They have made only three feeble moves to correct the abuses, efforts that would seem comic if we were not talking about the U.S. Congress.[28]

Two weeks later, the stunts grew even more extreme. This time, Gingrich took his campaign against Congress to the local federal penitentiary. Even measured against the incivility of today's political discourse, Gingrich's comments are remarkably extreme. "The United States Congress is the guardian of the public trust. Every Congressman has a sacred responsibility to uphold their stewardship of this great nation. But the sorry truth is that there are men serving in the House of Representatives who would better serve in this United States prison. . . . Is it any wonder this country is leaderless when we are literally governed by criminals?"[29]

Despite his merciless battering of Flynt, Gingrich knew he would probably not be elected in 1976. With the governor of Georgia at the top of the Democratic Presidential ticket, the tide would be overpowering. (On Election Day he was happy just to have lost by a few thousand votes.) That did not mean the attacks were without purpose: there would be another election in two years.

Unfortunately for Gingrich, two years was a long time to wait—particularly since he faced the prospect of being unemployed for the next year: because of the campaign, Gingrich had been forced on sabbatical from teaching for the spring semester, and there would be no work in the summer either. "After the '76 election, we didn't have any money, we had debts out the gazoo," recalled his erstwhile friend Carter. "Gingrich wasn't supposed to start teaching again until the fall, and we were in a hell of a fix." Intent on running again, knowing it would be his last chance, but desperate to keep his family afloat, Gingrich turned to a wealthy supporter, Chester Roush, who helped him organize a limited partnership that would finance a novel Gingrich planned to write. The partnership consisted largely of Gingrich campaign contributors who were associated with the largest company in the area, a copper and aluminum wire manufacturer called Southwire. The book was never published, but Gingrich kept the $13,000 that had been raised. Gingrich also arranged to give a paid speech before the local bank—which was owned by the Richards family, the same family that owned Southwire. Carter said the speech, which was about futurism (one of Gingrich's favorite subjects), netted him $2,500, "which sounds like nothing now, but you've got to remember this was 1976, when Newt was making maybe ten or eleven thousand dollars a year. The book thing and that, together, were more than he would have made in a year. Way more. . . . That was a godsend." Gingrich, the foe of special interests, was now in hock to the biggest interest in town.

The Third Time's the Charm

For his third try at Congress, Gingrich once again began gearing up more than a year in advance, holding a fundraising dinner in October of 1977. "In 1974, we had to carry the burden of Watergate and an anti-Republican national tide. Then in 1976, we had to run upstream against the favorite-son presidential sweep. . . . Experts generally agree that without Watergate or Carter, we would have won twice. I stand here tonight to tell you that in 1978 we will win." Once again, Gingrich promised he would run "a positive, issue-oriented" campaign.[30]

The prospect of yet another grueling, bitter fight with Gingrich—a fight he was likely to lose this time—was too much for Jack Flynt. He decided to retire. Thus Gingrich ended up facing Virginia Shapard, a state senator. Despite his pledge to run a clean and positive campaign, Gingrich once again went on the attack. "If you like welfare cheaters, you'll love Virginia Shapard," read one particularly incendiary Gingrich flier. "In 1976, Virginia Shapard voted to table a bill to cut down on welfare cheaters," the flier claimed. "People like Mrs. Shapard, who was a welfare worker for five years, and Julian Bond fought together to kill the bill."[31] Bond was Georgia's best-known black politician at the time, and none too popular in the conservative sixth district. While race-baiting was nothing new in southern politics, Gingrich also hit Shapard for her campaign finances. Despite his own huge fundraising advantage and support from wealthy businessmen, Gingrich denounced Shapard for making loans to her own campaign, claiming she was trying to buy the election. The Gingrich campaign also hinted at improprieties in Shapard's campaign filings.[32] All of this was too much for at least some observers. "We are happy to see a vigorous campaign for Congress waged in the sixth district," opined the *Atlanta Journal-Constitution,* which had backed Gingrich in his previous two contests. "But the Gingrich approach seems to have gone beyond vigor and into demagoguery and plain lying. . . . We regret that his campaign strategy has been of such a low order that we cannot consider extending our support to this third bid for election."

Notwithstanding the criticism from Atlanta, Gingrich was coming on stronger than ever and even managed to increase his surreptitious support among local unions (Shapard was less conservative than Flynt, but her family owned a nonunion mill). In addition to the CWA, Gingrich received aid from the local chapter of the United Auto Workers. Once again, it was all done sub rosa.[33]

Gingrich's strategy had worked: Shapard was on the defensive almost constantly. Gingrich's tactics were validated on Election Day, when he defeated Shapard comfortably, 54 to 46 percent. It seems clear that the truly distinguishing characteristic of his tactics was his use of the ethics issue in all three contests.

The Freshman Who Roared

Perhaps to make up for lost time, upon entering Congress Gingrich immediately began to make a name for himself. In early 1979, after a month in office, Gingrich called for a Democratic congressman who had been convicted of payroll padding, Charles Diggs, to resign from office. If he failed to do so, Gingrich threatened, he would move to have him expelled. "My effort to expel Congressman Diggs, the convicted felon, has been a big project for me so far," Gingrich wrote to a supporter.[34] After only ten months in office, Gingrich then called on the House leadership to resign, saying it had failed to address the country's economic problems.

He also sought to involve himself in building up the Republican Party. An article in the *Atlanta Journal-Constitution* described his plans, saying Gingrich and other young Republicans "are trying to show people that Republicans are the ones who can pull the country out of the mess they say a Democratic Congress has created." That meant "setting up clear 'test votes' so that liberal-voting members of Congress must do so publicly; confronting the majority party more aggressively than traditional congressional courtesy suggests; making it harder for incumbents (who are largely Democrats) to win reelection; and trying to make Republicans less boring."

Back home in Georgia, speaking to a group of Young Republicans, he was even more blunt about his view of how politics should be waged: "I think one of the great problems we have in the Republican Party is that we don't encourage you to be nasty. We encourage you to be neat, obedient, and loyal and faithful and all those Boy Scout words, which would be great around the camp fire, but are lousy in politics."[35]

Displaying his remarkable unconventionality, Gingrich, despite his obvious ambition, also declared that he was "not going to carve out a subcommittee to dominate."[36] It was a striking decision. Congress in the late 1970s had evolved into a subcommittee government; Democrats and Republicans alike perceived subcommittees as the keys to power. Gingrich preferred to pick the lock.

One of his many projects was to organize a mass event on the steps of the Capitol featuring 1980 presidential nominee Ronald Reagan and the Republican candidates for the House and Senate. At the event, Reagan and the other candidates pledged to pursue five key Republican goals, including tax cuts. The pledge was variously called a "Capitol compact" and a "solemn covenant." While the event received a brief spate of media coverage, it was quickly forgotten—by everyone but Gingrich. "That was the dress rehearsal for the Contract with America," said veteran Republican operative Steven Stockmeyer. "That was the forerunner. It was Newt's idea, it was his baby."

Gingrich also became an enthusiastic backer of the new cable network that had been created to cover the House's proceedings. A franked mailing by Gingrich in December 1982 carried an item headlined, "Watch Congress on TV." "Did you know that Congress is televised on cable now? Eleven million American homes and schools are hooked up to C-Span, the network that televises the proceedings of the House of Representatives."

Gingrich stuck to his strategy through his early terms, seeking to confront the Democrats, filing ethics charges against several of them, and promoting a more aggressive and unified campaign style for the party. These efforts did not endear him to party elders; the Atlanta media frequently carried stories on Gingrich's poor relations with his more senior Republican colleagues. But he started to win friends when he scored a major victory in 1984 with his famous goading of Speaker of the House Tip O'Neill by obliquely questioning his patriotism. Gingrich's taunts provoked a rant by O'Neill—televised by C-Span—that resulted in O'Neill being formally disciplined for impugning Gingrich.[37]

To Gingrich, the Democrats were evil dictators. O'Neill was a "thug," and Democrats maintained themselves in power only by cheating. During the 1980s, he developed this message into a mantra. "These people are sick," he said in 1988. "They are destructive of the values we believe in. They are so consumed by their power, by a Mussolini-like ego, that their willingness to run over normal human beings and to destroy honest institutions is unending."[38]

Congress, Gingrich would assert over and over, had become a cesspool of corruption. "I must report to my fellow citizens that this 100th Congress may be the most irresponsible, destructive, corrupt and unrepresentative Congress of the modern era," he said on the floor of the House, before the television cameras, in 1987.[39]

The ability of Democrats to maintain control of the House for so long was suspicious. "It is a little hard to suggest that in a year when a substantial number of Senators in both parties were not being reelected, in a year when governors were not being re-elected and county commissioners and sheriffs were not being re-elected," said Gingrich following the 1986 elections, "that magically, the one place in America that was 98.5 percent effective was the House of Representatives."[40]

The improbably high rate at which incumbents won reelection was "a fundamental insult to the constitutional freedoms of America, and it is nothing more than a game written on Capitol Hill by a left wing party that knows it cannot possibly survive in fair elections in this country, and therefore they cheat every day."[41] As we shall see, Gingrich set out aggressively to expose the Democrats' "cheating," though many would eventually charge that some of his means involved cheating, too.

2

The Old Order

Gingrich's critique of the Democratic Party's ability to dominate Congress was bombastic, outrageous, and close to the mark. By manipulating the system to their advantage, Democrats had essentially squeezed a lot of the democracy out of the system. It is worth looking in some detail at the unique features of the House the Democrats built for themselves during the 1950s, 1960s, and 1970s, which Newt Gingrich and his Republican cadres simultaneously reviled and sought entry to during the 1980s.

Subcommittee government was the foundation. In every session of Congress between 1967 and 1994, roughly half of the Democratic members of the House of Representatives chaired a committee or subcommittee. In the Senate, better than 80 percent of majority party members (during periods of both Republican and Democratic control) were chairmen of these self-contained empires. Particularly in the post-Watergate House Democrats reduced the power of their full committee chairmen and redistributed it to a larger group of subcommittee chairmen. This balkanization of power soon became a central component of the modern interest-group state. Subcommittee chairmen quickly discovered that their newly sovereign status in these regulatory fiefdoms enabled them to extract funds from interest groups. In exchange, the groups expected to receive preferential treatment.

The cumulative effect of several hundred politicians exercising their baronial prerogatives was to insulate the Democratic Party from electoral uncertainty. Routinely during the 1980s, 90 percent or more of those seeking reelection to the House won it; in the early and middle part of this century, the reelection rate rarely went over 80 percent and sometimes dipped to 60 percent. Equally important in perpetuating this ossification were two taxpayer-financed perquisites. Franked mail—the right of each legislator to send correspondence, much of it election related, free of charge, was perfected during the Democrats' forty-year reign. And legislators hired legions of staff members to do their water-carrying; congressional staffs ballooned 500 percent between 1947 and 1994. While Republicans shared in these goodies, it was a Faustian bargain for them, as any pro-incumbent measure that aided individual Republican officeholders also helped to lock in their minority status.

In elections for the House of Representatives, there was another dubious source of Democratic strength during the 1970s and 1980s: redistricting. Because they controlled a disproportionate share of the state capitals, where congressional districts are drawn, Democrats were able to manipulate the district-drawing process in their favor. Academics disagree on how much partisan benefit is gained from "gerrymandering," but politicians generally do not.[1] District lines are among the hardest-fought political prizes.

Laboring for Democrats

However, the most influential factor spanning the entire era was the Democratic Party's symbiotic relationship with organized labor. Labor and the Democrats first came to embrace each other during the New Deal, when Franklin Roosevelt backed a series of acts that allowed trade unions to expand rapidly. The relationship grew ever more intimate during Roosevelt's long tenure and explicitly more campaign-oriented. In 1943, the Congress of Industrial Organizations (CIO) invented the first political action committee, known simply as PAC, which had a full-time staff of 135 employees who set up political organizations down to the precinct level and churned out sophisticated campaign manuals and pamphlets. PAC registered voters, began issuing voting guides, and sought to "educate" the public.[2] Though by law PAC was not to use money from union treasuries in general elections, it raised "voluntary" funds to the tune of more than a million dollars in its early years.

In 1955, when the CIO merged with the more staid American Federation of Labor (AFL), the PAC was replaced by the Committee on Political Education (COPE). One of the AFL-CIO's largest departments, COPE was committed to "bring together the rank-and-file union members in a congressional district to campaign systematically for all Democratic candidates."[3] It provided research, printing, and manpower to candidates in addition to direct cash contributions. COPE proved a political machine of awesome, unmatched power. As COPE director Alexander Barkan put it, "We've got organizations in fifty damn states and it goes right down from the states to the cities. There's no party can match us. . . . Give us ten or fifteen years and we'll have the best political organization in the history of this country."[4] COPE's critics were inclined to agree. As one bitterly noted in 1968, "The only way for a Republican and/or conservative candidate to adequately 'cope with COPE' would be to set up a parallel organization with all of COPE's advantages and resources."[5] It was to be a prophetic statement.

The labor movement became less powerful economically in the 1960s, 1970s, and 1980s as membership declined, but the unions themselves managed to preserve much of their political power by persuading Democrats to allow them to bring public employees into the fold. While the number of union members is roughly the same today as it was in 1963 (about 16.5 million), the character of the membership has changed dramatically. In 1960, 94 percent of all union members were in the private sector and only 6 percent in the public sector. Today, the public labor market makes up 40 percent of the total union population.

The Democrats also protected labor during the campaign reform era of the 1970s when Congress was attempting to limit the power of special interests. The method was a special exemption for labor from limits on so-called in-kind contributions to candidates—contributions in the form of goods or services rather than cash. This gigantic loophole allowed labor to provide Democrats with massive, untold amounts of campaign assistance—and would later prove instructive to mass organizers on the right. A fairly substantial hint of how much extra help Democrats receive from labor can be gleaned from the budget of the National Education Association (NEA), now the nation's largest union with some 2.1 million members. The NEA's PAC contributed about $4 million in the 1994 elections, with 98 percent of it going to Democrats, but this is only a portion of what the group provided. It also allotted $9.8 million to government relations, in contrast to a modest $1.3 million to collective bargaining.[6] The former figure is but one portion of a $25 million budget for "public affairs," which includes all manner of seemingly campaign-related activities, including "political information and advocacy" ($53,000), "legislative and political activity" ($876,000), and "national party participation" ($291,000).[7] Another program, Campaign Assistance to Affiliates ($730,000), helps NEA "secure member support for association-endorsed candidates" and helps state affiliates "establish effective PAC fundraising programs."[8] The goal of its Education and Training program ($395,000) is to "provide affiliates with education and training to increase their capacity and success in political campaigns."[9]

Some of the money goes for lobbying rather than campaigning, but the division is unclear. For example, a $182,000 program called Political Anti-Privatization Activities went to fighting legislative initiatives aimed at privatizing public schools and to opposing "the Radical Right's efforts to win state and local elective offices."[10] The blandly named Affiliate Capacity Development program ($250,000) is intended "to enhance state affiliates' capacity to deliver the association's legislative and political program." Of course, delivering a political program usually involves some degree of electioneering.

Beyond these considerable sums, the NEA has a substantial work force from which to provide in-kind assistance to campaigns. Among other initiatives, the NEA has set up Congressional contact teams in every House district. These precinct-level groups are intended to be primarily lobbying units, but again, any such organization is almost necessarily involved in campaigning.

Across the board, in-kind contributions account for an indeterminate but vast amount of labor political activity, including phone banks, communication with and education of members and families, get-out-the-vote efforts, publicity, printing, mailing services, and even the services of paid union staff, provided to candidates free of charge. For the most part, this assistance is never publicly reported in filings with the Federal Election Commission (FEC) or elsewhere. Federal election law requires unions to report only *partisan* communications funded from the general treasury—those intended to support one candidate or party—to union members and employees, as well as the families of both. The loophole lies in the distinction between what constitutes partisan and nonpartisan communications. Non-partisan activities such as "equal opportunity" candidate appearances, the distribution of incumbent voting records, registration, and get-out-the-vote drives, are *not* reported, but they can easily be utilized in a thinly veiled, partisan manner.

Little or nothing of what the unions do is explicitly illegal, and their strength is based, fundamentally, on their numbers—certainly a democratic recipe for obtaining power. But as almost every Republican politician well knows, unions are hardly monolithic in their voting patterns anymore. Whereas union leaders are overwhelmingly liberal and Democratic, some 40 percent of union members pull the lever for the GOP in many elections. Yet Republicans have been denied the cash and organizational strength that might be their due based on voting patterns. Democrats may now get only 60 percent of union votes, but they get close to 100 percent of union money and organizational support, a statistic that only increased the bitterness of frustrated Republican organizers such as Gingrich. In the 1980s and 1990s, Republicans in Congress offered legislation to democratize the apportionment of union campaign resources. Citing Thomas Jefferson's remark that "to compel a man to furnish contributions of money for the propagation of opinions in which he disbelieves and abhors is sinful and tyrannical," they denounced the use of union dues for campaign activity as "political slavery." Democrats, of course, kept all such legislation safely bottled up.

Other Sources of Democratic Dollars

During the 1970s, Democrats developed other new funding sources: organized and financially potent liberal ideological movements made possible by the emergence of a huge middle class with an unprecedented mass of disposable income. While officially nonpartisan, these movements gravitated toward, and grafted themselves onto, the Democratic Party, becoming important new allies in financing and grassroots campaigning. The most influential of these groups were the entertainment industry, environmental groups, feminist organizations, and the consumer movement.

In the 1960s and 1970s, a sizable and wealthy Hollywood contingent of actors, producers, directors, and writers had become active in the Democratic Party. In the 1970s, Congress drastically revised the rules of campaign finance, enacting new limits on the size of individual contributions and placing meaningful caps on gifts for the first time. No longer could just a few millionaires provide the bulk of a candidate's funds. The new rules thus greatly empowered industries and groups that could produce large numbers of individuals, each willing to donate the new $1,000-per-candidate limit. Hollywood was made to order for such a system.

The environmental and feminist movements, meanwhile, pioneered major technical innovations that multiplied their clout and their ability to help Democratic candidates. Perhaps the most significant of these was the fundraising practice known as "bundling," invented in the early 1980s by an environmental group called the Council for a Livable World. This method circumvents the $5,000 contribution limit on PACs by channeling funds to candidates outside the PAC framework in "bundles" of individual checks. While no single check can be larger than $1,000, there is no limit on the number of checks that can be placed in a bundle. In 1982, while PACs were limited to $5,000 in direct contributions per candidate, the Council for a Livable World was pouring as much as $23,000 into the coffers of a single candidate. Many believed the practice violated the spirit of the Watergate reforms, which had sought to channel organized interest-group activity into limited PAC giving.

But the most important consequence of bundling was the evisceration of the vital post-Watergate reform principle of *disclosure*. Since a group that bundled did not identify precisely the contributions it had sent to candidates, there was no reliable way to track its real influence.

The Council for a Livable World largely dropped from prominence in the mid-1980s (though it is still in operation), but its tactics withstood legal challenges by conservatives and were soon adopted by Emily's List, a highly organized, liberal feminist operation. The group raised $350,000 in 1986, $418,000 in 1988, $973,000 in 1990, $4.4 million in 1992, and $8.2 million in 1994. Unlike some other PACs, Emily's List has never even pretended to be bipartisan. Its charter specifically designated its receipts for pro-choice Democratic women candidates.

Emily's List has been beset by controversy, with reform groups and Republicans decrying its successful evasion of legal limits on contributions. But the group's tactics allowed it to become one of the most successful special-interest fundraising operations in politics. The $8.2 million in gifts gathered by Emily's List in 1994 is only slightly behind the $8.8 million spent that year by the nation's biggest traditional PAC, the Democratic Republican Independent Voter Education Committee, operated by the Teamsters Union.[11] And whereas the Teamsters have millions of members, the members of Emily's List number only in the thousands.

The "trial lawyer" lobby was the other major new financial partner of the Democrats to arise during the 1970s. A product of the consumer movement, trial lawyers make their living bringing suits against companies for economic and physical harm they allegedly cause. As such, they are bitterly opposed to any reform of the country's liability laws and seek to block any such legislation that comes down the pike. Their efforts are usually concentrated on the Senate. Liability reform proposals opposed by the Association of Trial Lawyers of America (ATLA) died by Senate filibuster in 1978, 1986, 1988, 1990, 1992, and 1994. Not surprisingly, then, the trial lawyers have continued to invest most heavily in Senate Democrats.

By 1994, ATLA's PAC was giving $2 million to Democratic candidates and just $132,000 to Republicans. As we shall see, however, looking just at the contributions from ATLA's PAC to the Democrats seriously underestimates the true extent of the trial lawyers' influence over the party: in addition to their generous PAC funding, trial lawyers also concertedly make personal contributions to favored candidates through bundling. Their massive contributions have escaped detection thus far because of the nature of contribution reporting and their particular industry. Unlike corporate names, most law firms are not readily identifiable to a reporter. Thus to find out how much the trial lawyers are giving, a researcher is required to examine a vast number of law firms to determine which are involved primarily in bringing torts. The results of such an examination are eye-popping, however. We found that in 1994 trial lawyers contributed more than $1.46 million to the Democratic Senatorial Campaign Committee alone, and at least another $1.3 million to the Democratic National Committee.[12] Additional untold millions flowed to individual Senate candidates such as Massachusetts Senator Edward Kennedy, who (by our conservative count) took in at least $205,000 from trial lawyers. These numbers are far higher than previously reported.

Yet the raw figures still do not tell the whole story, particularly with regard to the Democratic Senatorial Campaign Committee (DSCC). In the 1994 election, the DSCC received only 308 contributions of $10,000 or more. Of those, at least 80, or 26 percent, were from trial lawyers. Thus one-fourth of the most economically important contributions to the DSCC come from trial lawyers. The overall numbers are also revealing. For the 1994 election, the DSCC raised a total of $9.99 million in itemized individual contributions.[13] Of that amount, trial lawyers provided at least $1.46 million, or 14.6 percent of the total.

The rise of the Democrats' new allies in the 1970s could not have come at a worse time for the Republican Party. For the first two decades of the Democrats' forty-year majority in the House (1954–74), the Democratic Party's advantages in congressional elections were primarily the result of hostility to the GOP in the South left over from the Civil War and, nationally, genuine affection for the party of the New Deal. But by the early 1970s, Republicans had been on the verge of breaking the Democrats' longstanding grip on many districts where voters were more conservative than the party's leaders. This was particularly true in Newt Gingrich's South, where the Democratic Party's dominance had begun to erode seriously in the 1960s as the party took up the civil rights banner.

During the 1950s, the number of southern House seats won by Republicans had remained low, at around 6 percent of the total. Beginning in 1960, however, the Republicans reaped steady gains, so that by 1972, the GOP's share of southern seats had increased to 30 percent.[14] Then in the election of 1974, the Democrats made a Watergate comeback, and they were able to drive the Republicans' share of southern seats back down to 25 percent. The trauma inflicted on the Republican Party by Watergate was fleeting at the national level: by 1980, Ronald Reagan was riding the crest of a major Republican surge. Yet it would be the mid-1990s before the GOP was able to achieve major new gains in its share of southern House seats. Until then, the Democratic Party's money advantage helped its candidates keep winning in the South, ensuring their majority in the House of Representatives.

When Newt Gingrich first ran for Congress, he had railed against the special-interest funded despotism of those in power. When he finally arrived in Congress, he discovered that the system was seductive. It was still an aspect of the tyranny he decried, but it could offer an extraordinary degree of protection from the whims of the electorate. This was why he declared he was not going to carve out a subcommittee to dominate.

An astute student of the machinery of power, Gingrich grasped the centrality of the subcommittee in the existing order. Just as money flowed from union and interest-group coffers into the campaign chests of their ideological allies in the Democratic Party, so too did the thousands of pragmatic lobbies that had business before the House and Senate dispense largesse. The only difference was that lobbyists' gifts had nothing to do with any ideology other than the belief that giving money to committee and subcommittee chairmen is the best way to get what you want out of Congress. Since each chairman is lord and master of his or her own little legislative barony, the opportunities for the writers of laws and those affected by the laws for discovering certain commonalities of interest are usually numerous. How exactly do these fiefdoms work? Who were these barons Gingrich would do so much to demonize during the next decade?

Frank Lautenberg and Bob Carr:
Apostles of the Old Order

Two of Gingrich's colleagues during his rise to power were U.S. Senator Frank Lautenberg of New Jersey and U.S. Representative Robert Carr of Michigan. For most of the time that they served with

Gingrich, Lautenberg and Carr were powerful members of the Democratic ruling class. Obscure on the national scene but well known in Congress, they boasted modest, though not insignificant, legislative achievements. Like the bulk of their Democratic brethren, they eventually held positions as subcommittee chairmen in their respective chambers, posts that gave them a clout greater than junior backbenchers, but decidedly beneath that of the dozen or so committee chairmen and elected leaders in either body. There were 300 others on Capitol Hill just like them. In their respective chambers, Carr and Lautenberg chose to pursue positions of influence on the appropriations committee, and each would eventually come to chair the subcommittee that doled out funds for transportation projects.

Carr's experience in the early 1990s showed what a big difference a subcommittee chairmanship could make to a career politician. As a middle-level member in the 100th Congress (1989–90), Carr had collected a relatively modest $397,000 in campaign contributions, including $150,000 in gifts from individuals, and $208,000 from political action committees.[15] In 1992, after it became clear that he was in line to chair the transportation subcommittee, Carr discovered how well liked he actually was, collecting a total of $1.1 million, including $481,000 from individuals (a 120 percent increase) and $566,000 from political action committees (a 172 percent increase).[16]

Representing a district that was 55 percent Republican and by no means certain to reelect him on the strength of a modest campaign, Carr found support all across the country. Reconstructing the process from Carr's filings with the Federal Election Commission yields an initially inscrutable list of seemingly unrelated backers. On February 12, 1992, for example, he received a bundle of checks for $500 each from a group of thirteen people, twelve of whom gave southern California addresses.[17] There was Theresa Solis from a firm called Obrien-Kreitzberg, Anil Verma from Anil Verma Associates, Delon Hampton from Delon Hampton and Associates, Georgina Kabler from Kabler Construction, Martin Rubin of Parsons Brinkerhoff.

One would have to be a close reader of obscure engineering publications or an aficionado of the Los Angeles construction business to know that all of these contributors had something in common: each had a financial interest in the planned Los Angeles subway. O'Brien-Kreitzberg and Parsons Brinkerhoff are "construction managers" for the project, which is receiving $1.6 billion in federal funds.[18] Delon Hampton Associates is a designer of various subway facilities. Anil Verma Associates was a designer of station interiors, while Kabler Construction also worked on subway interiors.[19]

The $6,500 in contributions, by accident or design, was well-timed, arriving just six days before the House Subcommittee on Transportation Appropriations kicked off its annual series of hearings on transportation funding. When Los Angeles officials appeared to testify about their desperate need for the subway, Carr said he expected "to be a good supporter of rail in Los Angeles. . . . You're friends of mine."[20] The subcommittee and the full committee later came up with $110 million for the project.[21]

Carr next picked up an infusion of $16,000 in late April from the construction and engineering community in Houston, which had gathered to honor Carr at the mansion of Houston mayor Bob Lanier in the exclusive River Oaks neighborhood. The timing of the Houston money was even more propitious than the Los Angeles subway builders' gifts. The funds came into Carr's campaign coffers only five days before Houston officials appeared before the transportation subcommittee to plead for $50 million in transit money. Houston at the time was mired in controversy over newly elected Mayor Lanier's plan to spend the city Transportation Authority's money on completely unrelated projects, which had also raised eyebrows at the Federal Transit Administration.[22] But Carr—who on numerous other occasions adamantly insisted that federal funds be put to the purposes for which they were appropriated—did not seem concerned by the dispute. "The whole Houston metropolitan area is working its way through problems the way they ought to be worked through," Carr gushed. "As long as you keep doing that, you're going to have the support of this committee." The committee recommended $28 million for Houston's bus system.[23]

The pattern continued. On September 15, Carr received $5,750 in contributions from residents of Kentucky, and another $2,000 trickled in on the 17th. Not a single one of these twenty donors was described in Carr's campaign report as having anything to do with Louisville's Standiford Airport, which, at the time the donations were made, was seeking millions of dollars in federal funding to expand its runways. Yet, curiously enough, all twenty stood to benefit financially from the federally funded expansion of the facility, and several actually held top positions running the project.

Frank Lautenberg had gravitated immediately to the appropriations committee upon entering the Senate in 1982. In 1986, when Democrats took control of the Senate for the first time in six years, Lautenberg became chairman of the Appropriations Subcommittee on Transportation, an ideal perch from which to steer federal dollars back to New Jersey.

While he had the luxury of facing the voters only once every six years, Lautenberg lived in a state as precarious as Carr's. Elected by a whisker, he would always live in fear of defeat. In his 1988 reelection bid, Lautenberg was held to an unimpressive 54 percent of the vote, virtually guaranteeing the incumbent would face another major fight in six years. The senator and his staff took the message to heart, hardly pausing before beginning to raise money for 1994.

Fortunately for Lautenberg, fairly early in his career he had happened upon one of those rare, indispensable staff aides who could make all the difference. Eve Lubalin had a keen, indeed exceptional, understanding of politics and politicians. A graduate of Harvard University, Lubalin had been working in the Senate longer than Lautenberg when she accepted a post in his office in 1983. She was also the author of a provocative 1982 doctoral thesis (which had emerged from a stint as a Johns Hopkins University congressional fellow under Senator Birch Bayh in the late 1970s), about the impact of ambition on the behavior of incumbent politicians. Ambition theory, she wrote, "assumes that as politicians go about fulfilling their daily responsibilities and meeting the minimal requirements of their jobs, their first priority will always be to concern themselves with the extent to which their current activities optimize their chances for achieving their office goals."[24] Fundraising, although not specifically discussed in her thesis, certainly qualifies as a significant activity with respect to political goals.

By 1986, she was Lautenberg's top aide. Although her position was financed entirely with taxpayer funds, she quickly took charge of his fundraising operation and never let go. This was not an uncommon arrangement but was ethically questionable: Senate rules discourage official staff from extensive involvement in fundraising, which is supposed to be conducted in the main out of a private office. She would come to be known as a fierce fundraiser, notorious among her staff for faxing order-filled memos late at night.[25] By 1992, Lautenberg had already raised nearly $2 million, half of which had gone into sustaining his campaign operation and half of which he had banked.

By the spring of 1993, the worst fears of Lautenberg's staff were being confirmed: polls showed that only 42 percent of New Jersey voters thought the senator was doing a good job, and most could not cite any specific thing that he had done. The rap was perhaps unfair. Lautenberg was a hard-working senator who looked out for his state and, among other achievements, he could take credit for one of the most popular public health measures in years: a ban on smoking in airplanes. But he had always been overshadowed by his fellow New Jersey senator, Bill Bradley, the former basketball star and respected policy wonk.

Obviously, the good news about Frank Lautenberg was not getting out. Therefore, he could really only do one thing: raise a lot of money to ensure that his message would be heard far and wide.[26] Late in the evening on July 2, 1993, Eve Lubalin sat down and fired off one of her famous memoranda to the Lautenberg campaign staff. Written in raw stream-of-consciousness style with frequent abbreviations ("FRL," for instance, was Frank R. Lautenberg), the memo outlined a series of fundraising gambits, such as sending newspaper clippings to potential contributors about a possible challenge to Lautenberg by popular Republican Tom Kean, the former New Jersey governor, in order to emphasize Lautenberg's dire situation.[27] She also outlined possible strategies for holding fundraising events: "Possible Houston business event—hosted by Continental's CEO Bob Ferguson. Mayor Lanier would possibly join. Need to see if they go together." And "Is American HQ in Dallas? That's another possible."[28]

While the events Lubalin had in mind in this passage did not materialize as planned, her thinking is revealing. Lubalin was suggesting a possible swing through Texas during which Lautenberg could tap three fundraising sources: American Airlines, Continental Airlines, and the handout-hungry Houston mayor Bob Lanier, all of whom would want to help (or at least not antagonize) the powerful chairman of the Senate Appropriations Subcommittee on Transportation.

Lubalin returned to this theme in a comment directed to fundraiser Mimi Walsh: "Mimi—should follow up with Minikes and see when he feels we could move on a Philly business event. Fax him Kean clips 1st and tell him you'll be calling. Can tell him I helped Karen Daroff out with something since dinner and she seems very enthusiastic about helping FRL."[29]

"Minikes" referred to Stephen Minikes, a Washington-based lobbyist for the City of Philadelphia who was seeking federal funding for a major overhaul of the city's dilapidated airport and was also raising funds for Lautenberg. Karen Daroff is a prominent Philadelphia designer who held a contract for redesigning the interiors of the Philadelphia airport. Both had contributed to Lautenberg on June 14, about two weeks before Lubalin's memo was written.[30]

As to the nature of the "something" that Lubalin helped Daroff with, Daroff said she does not remember getting any favors at all from Lautenberg or Lubalin. However, she admitted she was "affected by [Lautenberg's] work on a personal and professional level" and that there was an "indirect" connection between her contribution and her Philadelphia airport contract. Lautenberg has asserted that Lubalin had merely instructed her staff to help Daroff find some phone numbers that were publicly available.[31] A previously undisclosed document, released to the authors under the Freedom of Information Act, shows that on July 9, 1993, six days after Lubalin's memo was written, a letter went out from Lautenberg's office to the Federal Aviation Administration (FAA) urging the FAA to fund the Philadelphia airport project.[32] In addition, Lautenberg's committee, during consideration later that fall of the year's bill providing future transportation funding, approved an unusual provision ordering the FAA to spend an additional $10 million on the Philadelphia airport.[33] Such orders are rare: usually the FAA enjoys discretion in deciding how to spend airport money.

In fairness, Lautenberg had ample reason to support the Philadelphia airport project beyond campaign contributions. Philadelphia is just across the Delaware River from Camden, N.J., and the economic benefits from a rehabilitated airport would spill into his own state. However, there were no such considerations regarding Lubalin's next suggestion: "Mimi/Jen—We need to find out who Nick Forsman is from FRL. Keep this name. I think he is represented by Tom Quinn in town and VERY rich. Just did something nice that made him very $$. He called FRL to thank him."[34]

"Forsman" was Nicholas Forstmann, a principal in one of the top leveraged buyout firms on Wall Street, Forstmann-Little, which controls several billion-dollar companies. He is indeed very wealthy. The "something nice" was apparently Lautenberg's support for a $10 million appropriation for a program with which Forstmann is associated called Cities in Schools.

Confronted with this passage, Lautenberg's staff produced a letter the senator signed backing funding for the program, as well as other documentation supporting their explanation that Lautenberg had not really done anything to make Forstmann rich, contrary to the implication of the memo, but rather had simply endorsed a worthy cause. Among this evidence was a June 22 letter from Forstmann to Lautenberg, containing Forstmann's campaign contribution, which thanked Lautenberg "for your help with Cities in Schools."

Forstmann's firm owns Gulfstream Aerospace, a maker of luxury jet aircraft that has extensive dealings with the Federal Aviation Administration, an agency under the jurisdiction of Lautenberg's subcommittee. Curiously, Forstmann, a deeply conservative Republican, contributed to only one other Democrat that year: Bob Carr, Lautenberg's House counterpart on transportation appropriations. Thus, of the roughly 350 Democratic incumbents on Capitol Hill, Forstmann had chosen to contribute to the two who were most influential on transportation funding—an amazing coincidence, if that was what it was. Carr is a well-documented Gulfstream supporter, having previously helped persuade the FAA to buy a Gulfstream jet.[35]

Further down in the memo, Lubalin again picked up the transportation theme. Stating that Lautenberg would call two lobbyists for fundraising help, she added, "They can draw in DC Board of Trade people—FRL gets transp $$."[36] This was a reference to the fact that the Washington, D.C. Board of Trade, a District of Columbia group backed by local merchants, is a major lobbyist for federal transportation dollars to the District and would likely be interested in helping out the chairman of the Senate Subcommittee on Transportation Appropriations; indeed, perhaps the board would be afraid not to help him.

Still in the same consciousness stream, Lubalin then suggested that multimillionaire Abe Pollin, the owner of the Washington Capitals professional hockey team and the Washington Bullets basketball team, would be likely to help raise money. "FRL has helped him out on a number of things lately and he should be called for an event in this area."[37] Pollin has great economic interest in federally funded projects in the Washington area, such as the local subway system, nearby National Airport, and road projects. But when confronted with Lubalin's reference to Pollin, Lautenberg's staff asserted that none of Lautenberg's help "on a number of things" had to do with transportation policy or any other federal issues in which Pollin had an economic interest. They were able to produce only one thing Lautenberg had done for Pollin—a letter he had written to the Immigration and Naturalization Service (INS) on behalf of a Lithuanian Jew for whom Pollin was seeking to gain political asylum.[38] The circumstances here are inconclusive, as is often the case when money and power mix. Grounds exist to wonder whether the INS letter was the only favor Lautenberg had done Pollin. Lubalin wrote that there had been "a number of things," and Pollin's business interests are deeply entwined with federal decisions. But there is no certain way to answer the question: while Congress has mandated that all federal departments be subject to the Freedom of Information and Government in the Sunshine Acts, requiring all meeting notes and correspondence to be publicly available, it has declined to apply such laws to itself. Even the letter to the INS, however, is somewhat damning. Why is Lubalin soliciting any contributor on the basis of what the senator has done for him—even if that favor is a benign act?

Dollars, Democrats, and Decisions: The Congressional Connection

Carr was only narrowly reelected in 1992, his race having been profoundly affected by a new political mood beginning to sweep the country. While Carr's strategy had been to tout the millions of dollars in economic benefits he had brought home for his constituents, his opponent Richard Chrysler had successfully fought back by labeling Carr part of the old-time, free-spending establishment drunk on perks and pork. Carr survived Chrysler's challenge, but the message from voters was unmistakable, and almost immediately after the election he vowed to push for reform in the federal appropriations process. Over the first few months of 1993, Carr developed new standards. "I intend to hold transportation projects to a standard of investment which the marketplace would recognize, one that makes sure that each is the best possible use of the taxpayer's dollar," the new chairman declared righteously at a March press conference.[39]

By the time he announced this push for reform, Carr's quest for financing for his next campaign had already begun anew. His first foray was south to Florida, to the district of former Democratic Congressman Bill Lehman, who had bequeathed the subcommittee chairmanship to Carr. An initial fundraiser on February 24 in Orlando netted $17,800.[40] While it would be difficult to tell from looking at Carr's campaign filings, most of those who attended had a financial interest in Orlando-area transportation projects. Eduardo Morales, who gave $500, is a structural engineer who works on local airports. Thomas Huestis, another who gave $500, works for a municipal bond firm, Public Financial Management, that advises the Greater Orlando Airport Authority. Egerton Van den Berg and Gordon Arkin are partners at Foley & Lardner, a law firm that represents the Greater Orlando Airport Authority.[41] Dick Batchelor is a lobbyist who represents a local bus system called LYNX as well as the Greater Orlando Airport Authority.[42] Lawyer E. Thom Rumberger works with a contractor for the Greater Orlando Airport Authority. Douglas Prescott works for HNTB, an engineering consulting firm that does work for the Greater Orlando Airport Authority.[43] Several of the contributors also have stakes in federally funded road and rail projects.

Many of these contributors are not shy about admitting that their interest was not in Carr's views on the great issues of the day. Carr, recalled contributor and civil engineer Carl Vargas, "was on the transportation committee, and there were several transportation issues that were important to the state of Florida and we needed to communicate with him. At the time, we were concerned some money may have been cut off for Florida." Added Vargas, "It wasn't a party thing. I'm a Republican."[44]

Carr delivered. On June 25, his committee approved $7 million to pay for forty buses for the LYNX system.[45] The following year brought an even bigger bonanza: $22.5 million for the Orlando International Airport, $6.5 million for a local interstate, $6.7 million for a downtown Orlando streetcar project called OSCAR, and an additional $7 million for LYNX.[46] (Funding for several of these projects was subsequently scaled back significantly by the Senate as part of the usual legislative give-and-take.) The airport grant was highly unusual, the director of the Greater Orlando Airport Authority happily noted: "Normally, it wouldn't go to a specific airport."[47] Indeed, under congressional budget rules, Congress is supposed to decide only how much total money goes into improving airports; the Federal Aviation Administration, theoretically, is responsible for determining which airports most need the money. The other grants were also, in varying degrees, unusual; the funds had been awarded outside the normal merit-based decision-making process in a controversial Capitol Hill practice known as earmarking. Carr's freshly announced reforms did not seem to be in evidence.

Between 1992 and 1994, Carr collected a total of $86,000 on a series of trips to Florida. One Miami-area contributor, Maria Torano, who owns an environmental services consulting company, is blunt about why people in South Florida would support a congressman from Michigan: "because it serves the interests of their business, with regulations, with passage of new legislation, you name it. They have to go to the people [members of Congress] for their attention, and you have a better way to get their attention when you have contributed to their campaigns."[48]

* * *

"All funds are fungible," is Houston Mayor Bob Lanier's philosophy of municipal finance in a nutshell.[49] Running for mayor in 1991, Lanier had proposed a boldly innovative solution to the city's crime crisis: in order to pay for additional police on the streets, he would simply raid the city transportation authority's bulging treasury (half of which came from the federal government), taking millions of dollars in funds intended for buses and trains and pouring it into unrelated programs. Critics denounced the plan as illegal and fiscally foolhardy, but Lanier swore he could pull it off, and Houston voters decided to go along for the ride.

Upon taking office in 1992, Lanier promptly commenced to do as promised. The scheme was fairly simple to execute. Lanier siphoned more than $200 million out of the transportation authority to fund all manner of unrelated projects, from beefing up the police force to laying new sidewalks to building a network of bike trails. He soon became wildly popular.

While the diversion would seem unlikely to go over well in Washington, Lanier had friends there. Subcommittee chairman Carr, who had picked up $16,000 in Houston in late April of 1992 and then failed to take note of Lanier's diversion plan during a congressional hearing a week later, was presiding when Lanier and other Houston officials came before him again in March of 1993. At that time, Carr merely offered up his "endorsement of the philosophy of Houston," which was the original notion that cities needed to better manage their transportation funds, and asked two technical questions about the city's cash flow.[50] On July 11, Carr's subcommittee, in a closed door session, ordered the Federal Transit Administration to give Houston a stunning $40.5 million for a regional bus system. It was quite a coup for the city. "Compared to everybody else, this is incredible. Most cities didn't come close to getting what they asked for," said one congressional aide.[51] Eleven days after the vote, on July 22, Carr went to Houston for another fundraiser, picking up $19,000 from a group of familiar faces at a gathering hosted by a lawyer for the transit authority.[52]

By 1994, the spending spree had become an orgy. Lanier had announced plans for a new raid on the transportation authority to get an additional $25 million in order to hire still more police. One local politician even proposed to raid the authority for funds to build a new stadium. The local papers were increasingly concerned. "Hands Off Metro: Taxpayers Must Be Weaned from Transit Fund," editorialized the *Houston Post*.[53] At this point, Carr certainly would seem to have been obligated to bring up the subject at the annual appropriations hearings. Miraculously, however, there were no hearings for Houston that year; city officials merely submitted their testimony in writing on April 26, saying nothing about the diversion. A few weeks later, on May 15, Carr went back to Houston for more campaign funds, garnering $14,850. On May 26, meeting privately, Carr's subcommittee voted an additional $60 million for Houston. The day after the vote, Houston papers disclosed that the Federal Transit Administration was considering an investigation into the diversion. "We want to make sure that transit money is spent for transit purposes," an FTA official asserted.[54] Lanier's office responded that Carr's subcommittee "wouldn't be giving us the kind of money that they're giving us if anybody thought this was a problem."[55]

Frank Lautenberg was also an honored guest in Houston. A July 27, 1992, fundraiser for the senator netted $9,500, while a late March 1994 swing-through brought in $45,314. Unlike Carr, however, Lautenberg took a bite of the feeding hand in mid-July of 1994, pushing a funding bill through his subcommittee that eliminated money for Houston. The city's case had evidently been hurt by an unanticipated event: a rash of publicity about its ardent wooing of Lautenberg and Carr. Both Houston newspapers had published articles on the subject in April, and Lautenberg had also found himself caught up in controversy about the Lubalin memo. Two months later, after the controversy died down, Lautenberg agreed to a still healthy $30 million grant for the city's bus project.

On November 11, 1993, Federal Highway Administration director Rodney Slater received a rather unusual piece of mail. It was a handwritten letter from his overseer at the House Transportation Appropriations Subcommittee, chairman Bob Carr, scrawled on Carr's private stationery.

> Dear Rodney,
> I won't make it a habit to burden you with a request for a personal favor . . . but here's one that would mean a lot to me

personally—Would you, please, accept the invitation of my good friends, the Michigan Road Builders, to be in Grand Rapids, MI on Jan 14th ???? I hope you will.

Sincerely,

Bob

Slater could hardly say no—private stationery or not. He was scheduled to come before Carr two months later seeking funding for his agency. Slater assented, and the appearance was quite a coup for the congressman, who announced his candidacy for the Senate just one month later.

Road builders meant a lot to Bob Carr. In Congress, he was their staunchest ally, and warm feelings between the congressman and the industry were mutual. Road builders are generally big supporters of public works expenditures and thus natural allies of an appropriator. But they also shared with Carr a very narrow interest in one subject: asphalt.

In 1991, before Carr became subcommittee chairman, Congress had passed legislation mandating the use of shredded tires in asphalt in order to encourage tire recycling. Putting rubber in asphalt is a seemingly ingenious recycling trick, but road builders do not like it because it makes the pavement last longer. That means less work for road builders. And, in the immediate term, they are scared that the expense of shredding and adding tire crumb to asphalt will suck up some of the vast federal money spent yearly on highway construction.

When Carr became subcommittee chairman in 1993, he inserted language in that year's transportation appropriation prohibiting federal funds from being spent to pay for the recycling program, a move that had the effect of putting the program on hold.[56] And in 1994, in deference to the road builders' strong feelings on this subject, a compromise was worked out that severely weakened the rubber mandate. The amount of rubber required to be used was cut in half, and the program was revamped to be a pilot program rather than a permanent order. Carr nonetheless inserted language in his bill prohibiting funds even for that program.

He had not always been so chummy with the road builders. Bill Ballenger, a long-time observer of Michigan politics, recalled that Carr had been a "revolutionary" in his early years, before he lost his seat in 1980. Once reelected in 1982, Carr came back a different man. Appearing with Carr at a road builders' conference in Grand Rapids in the summer of 1994, "I talked to some of the lobbyists there and they confirmed what I'd always understood to be the case, and that was that they'd known Carr for years and the guy was impossible before 1982. But after that, boy the guy's totally changed, totally transformed. Of course, they thought this was great. And by the time he got to be chairman of the transportation subcommittee, they felt he was one of their greatest friends."[57]

Carr's rear-guard action against the rubber recycling law incurred the wrath of environmentalists, but he was amply rewarded. Hardly anyone knew it, but road builders were by far the biggest source of his campaign contributions. In 1993–94, the builders used bundling on four discrete occasions to direct contributions to Carr. On December 27, 1993, checks totaling $21,500 came in from contractors as far afield as Cold Springs, Minnesota, and Tarboro, North Carolina. Two weeks later, on January 12, 1994, $36,250 came in from contractors in Yazoo City, Mississippi, and Oconomowoc, Wisconsin. On April 22, $39,550 arrived from the far-flung towns of Kodiak, Alaska, and Muskogee, Oklahoma. And finally on May 20, an additional $13,250 came in from builders ranging from Fargo, North Dakota, to Pittsfield, Maine. Road builders in places as distant as Maryland, Kansas, and North Carolina said they contributed after receiving phone calls from a Michigan paver who is an officer with the National Asphalt Paving Association. On other occasions, potential contributors were encouraged to donate by their state Asphalt Paving Association or by their state Road Builders Association. On several occasions, state road building associations denied encouraging members to contribute, despite statements by members that they had. This is probably due to the potential legal problems of "bundling." If the fundraising process is proven to be completely coordinated, the Federal Election Commission could require the pavers to register as a PAC and impose limits on their activities.

The amounts Carr received from asphalt interests dwarf what could have been contributed through a PAC—indeed, they make Carr's receipts from such bountiful sources as Houston look modest. And there was the added advantage of virtual invisibility for this money. While a few of the contributors were identified in Carr's FEC filing as working for paving contractors, the vast majority could not be connected to the road-building industry by casual inspection. Only after quite a bit of investigation does one determine that the road builders, in a very organized fashion not unlike a political action committee, supplied Carr with at least $115,000 over a two-year period. Interestingly, the National Asphalt Paving Association once had a PAC but decided to disband it.[58]

There is nothing extraordinary about the Lautenberg and Carr cases. The incentives to collect campaign funds whenever and wherever possible are powerful for all legislators. Both Carr and Lautenberg have been showered with money and other rewards for strategic use of their power over the years.

Still, until 1994 the status quo had shown amazing resiliency, despite mounting public disgust with reports of such corruption. Attempts to pass campaign finance reform in the congressional terms of 1985–86, 1987–88, 1989–90, 1991–92, and 1993–94 all ultimately foundered on partisan disputes. These disputes were partly based on sincere, principled disagreements between the two parties about what constituted fair and effective reform. (Democrats, for example, believe that capping the total amount a candidate can spend is a necessary element in any reform package and are also favorably inclined toward government financing of campaigns; Republicans believe spending limits are unconstitutional and designed to benefit incumbent candidates, while they see public financing as a waste of taxpayer money.) Yet among the old guard of both parties, there was strong though rarely voiced sentiment in favor of the current order. In a recent confessional, one of the Senate aides most expert on campaign finance said members of Congress are "strongly resistant to reforming their own electoral process."

The subdivision of power into autonomous fiefdoms and the rise of the interest-group society were two of the main mechanisms of the Democratic machine. Eve Lubalin had it right. In a rich but depressing irony, Lubalin and her boss Frank Lautenberg, as well as Bob Carr, provide real-life confirmation of her doctoral thesis. The ambition to remain or advance in public office dominates the behavior of elected officials. While neither surprising nor lamentable in itself, during the era of Democratic dominance this consuming obsession translated into an unquenchable quest for financial support from those who stood to benefit economically from public policy decisions, as well as a willingness by officeholders to allow themselves routinely to be influenced by the providers of financial support. This is the stuff of which revolutions are made.

3

A Special Revolutionary Organization

The gigantic tasks thus presented to the proletariat gave rise
to an urgent necessity for a special revolutionary organization capable of quickly getting hold of the masses and getting them ready for revolutionary action.

—*Leon Trotsky*

During most of the era of Democratic dominance, few Republicans aside from Newt Gingrich grasped how steeply
the deck had been stacked against them. The vast machinery assembled by the Democrats to perpetuate themselves in power
was never visible in its entirety, even if particular elements were exposed on occasion. Moreover, many Republicans refused to believe
that this machinery could account for their party's persistently woe-
ful experiences at the ballot box. The media and other influential observers often scoffed at the notion—when they did not ignore the
Democrats' extraordinary dominance altogether.

While political scientists studied and debated the decline in competitiveness and the Democratic hegemony in Congress, the subject
came up infrequently in the larger political community (not to mention the public at large). From time to time, the media examined the
question, but, remarkably, it was rarely given prominent treatment
or sustained attention. As others have pointed out, if the presidency
remained consistently in the hands of one party for four decades, the

hand-wringing and calls for reform would have been deafening. That there was almost no comment on the situation in Congress—a coequal branch of government, after all—is indicative of the misguided executive branch bias in Washington.

In the House of Representatives, Robert H. Michel, the Republican leader for most of the 1980s, typified the party's problem. He was first elected in 1956, at the tail end of an era of robust competition at the congressional level, when parties gained and lost more than fifty House seats fairly regularly. His political consciousness having been formed in such an environment, Michel never seemed to sense that Democrats had changed the fundamental dynamics of the game. A genial man often described as "decent" by colleagues, Michel cherished the small-town camaraderie of Capitol Hill even as it evaporated around him in later years, often delivering worn homilies about the importance of cooperation as Democrats took his party to the cleaners.

Some of the more perceptive and aggressive junior Republican legislators, of whom Gingrich soon became the leader after his arrival in the House, fumed at Michel's passivity and sought the dissolution of a Democratic machine they knew to be corrupt. But in addition to the remarkably resilient tradition of comity, the instinct for self-preservation among Republican incumbents undermined them. Time and again, whether the issue was eliminating the congressional frank, reforming the campaign laws, or reducing congressional staff, Republicans who had become accustomed to or dependent upon these perquisites quietly opposed calls for their elimination. It is a rare human being who can resist the blandishments of power, because it is a rare human being who does not fear losing power. They were incumbents first, Republicans second, and thus partners in their own subjugation. Until they could develop a united front, Republican reformers could only chip away at the machinery when what was needed was a frontal assault.

Republican efforts to fight the Democratic House machine also suffered from a lack of support from Republicans in the Senate, where Democrats enjoyed more tenuous electoral advantages and the possibility that swings in the national mood would propel the Republicans to majority Senate status negated the need for new strategic thinking by the GOP. While the Senate had been dominated by Democrats for most of the post–World War II era, Republicans had occasionally won control, most recently during the Reagan administration from 1981 to 1987. As a consequence, most Republican senators were not inclined to view the party's problems as structural and were still willing to place their faith in the political pendulum.

Most Republicans outside Congress, meanwhile, fixated on the White House—the far more attainable branch for a party whose appeal lay in broad national themes such as a strong defense and federal restraint in domestic policy. Yet these partisans seemingly were oblivious to the long decline in presidential power. Since the presidency of Richard Nixon, the White House has been in some ways the weakest of the three branches, overshadowed and restrained by congressional and judicial activism: even Ronald Reagan, the most powerful and popular of the post-Nixon presidents, failed to reshape America in the Republican image. Taxes decreased only briefly, the federal government remained large and intrusive, and changes in social policy such as welfare reform and abortion prohibition remained subjects mainly for conservative policy papers. George Bush, who violated his most important campaign promise—no new taxes—at the behest of Congress, also serves as a compelling illustration of what has occurred. To mix two aphorisms, the president proposes but Congress disposes; it is the keystone of power in Washington.

The result was that lower-echelon Republicans in the House were profoundly radicalized by what appeared to them increasingly to be a dictatorship in the fullest sense of the word—a political system of unfair elections and rigged government. This radicalization, which progressed steadily through the 1980s and into the early 1990s, is not hard to understand; in political systems around the world, ossification at the top normally produces major changes in the "loyal" opposition, usually in the direction of less loyalty and more opposition. As those in power appear more and more to have abandoned the rules, those out of power, more and more, respond in kind—believing the rightness of their cause demands it. This is the genesis of some forms of terrorism.

Gingrich the Reformer

Newton Leroy Gingrich understood the political state of affairs with remarkable acuity. A believer in Mao's dictum that "politics is war without blood," he was one of the first to see vividly what the Republicans were up against, long before he was even a member of the House of Representatives.[1] Perhaps the most brilliant political tactician of his generation, Gingrich determined before anyone else that the Republicans' only hope of taking the House of Representatives was to wreck it, as he himself once famously remarked. As we have already seen, Gingrich's early campaigns show his intuitive comprehension of the rhetoric of reform, and a nearly instinctive grasp of how to translate that rhetoric into an aggressive election battle.

Looking around at the House of Representatives in the 1980s, Gingrich consolidated his natural abilities with a vital insight: in their use of the congressional frank and staff and their exploitation of the committee system to extort campaign funds, Democrats had fused themselves with the House so thoroughly as to erase most distinctions between the party and the legislative body. Only if Congress were to be destroyed in the eyes of the public would the Democrats also be destroyed, allowing the Republicans the freedom to remake America.

Gingrich rewrote the rules of modern American political combat in two critical ways. The first was to craft a modification of the old art of delegitimizing the opposition. In a twenty-year political career, Gingrich lobbed accusations of corruption at virtually everyone who stood in his way with astonishing effectiveness. While scandal-mongering is not new in American politics, Gingrich undertook the tactic in a newly aggressive and systematic manner, relentlessly attacking the Democratic party's leading members, as well as the party itself. While it is impossible to fathom with certainty what moves public opinion, Gingrich's determined efforts to delegitimize Congress coincided precisely with a drop in public esteem for Congress to historic lows, producing by 1994 the first full-scale throw-the-bums-out election since Watergate. While only time will tell for sure, Republicans may have achieved that most epochal of American political events, a realignment—"America's surrogate for revolution," in the words of Walter Dean Burnham.[2]

It would be hard to underestimate the deliberate, strategic nature of the political decisions that brought this about. It was no mere whim of the electorate that reversed the direction of American government, but the fruit of Newt Gingrich's and the Republicans' shrewd, accurate analysis of the state and direction of our political life, and of a political program designed to respond to these insights. These achievements were long in the making—their origins can literally be traced back to Gingrich's first campaign. That he had the determination and the stamina to stick with his program through countless setbacks is extraordinary, a historic feat.

Gingrich's Republicans were truly revolutionaries, albeit ones who found a way to operate more or less within the existing political system. Yet to achieve his goals, they made many compromises along the way. Most important, Gingrich adopted questionable methods of financing his revolution. That Gingrich felt compelled to do so offers an important lesson about the persistence of corruption in American politics. Ambitious people, in their quest for power—even if that quest takes the form of a moral crusade—seem inexorably driven to cross ethical, and sometimes even legal, lines. It is the rare revolutionary, indeed, who does not engage in, and justify, violating the laws and values of society.

From CHOPAC to GOPAC

Gingrich's first organizing vehicle for the coming revolution was a political action committee called Conservatives for Hope and Opportunity (CHOPAC), which he founded in 1983. It was a spectacular failure. Despite Gingrich's best efforts, the PAC struggled almost from its inception. While its donor base was wealthy, it was also small, and since federal contribution limits capped gifts at $5,000, fundraising was a struggle. Results were so poor that Democrats disingenuously accused the PAC of mail fraud in its fundraising appeals, noting that it had used its contributions mainly for overhead rather than to support Republican candidates, as it had promised prospective backers. But the explanation for CHOPAC's failure to deliver on its pledge was more simple and less sinister than fraud: the PAC was a bust. "Everything we did was clearly, without any question, within the normal pattern of American politics," declared Gingrich.[3]

This little-noticed episode in Gingrich's long drive for power is instructive. CHOPAC was an utterly orthodox means of political organizing. Many politicians set up such PACs to advance themselves and their ideas. But Gingrich's was a disaster largely because Gingrich was not well known enough—and certainly, as a junior congressman who had vowed not to seek a subcommittee empire, not nearly powerful enough—to draw the big money his vision would require. He was playing by the rules, generating positive attention for his ideas, earning a reputation as a doer, and a radical one at that. Yet this did not translate into the kind of power that could make his vision for Congress and America come true. Many politicians had come to this place before Gingrich and faced stark choices—marginalization, resignation, or accommodation. Gingrich would have to find more contributors, or find a way around the rules.

In 1986, Gingrich was offered the chairmanship of a political action committee created by former Delaware governor Pierre "Pete" DuPont, called GOPAC. CHOPAC had already begun to falter and indeed, it went dormant in 1987. It finally shut down in early 1988, having raised a mere $200,000 during its existence, closing with some $50,000 in debts that were never repaid. GOPAC, though small, was healthier and had a higher profile than CHOPAC, and was thus a promising place for Gingrich to shift his attention.

GOPAC was also like no other PAC on the national scene. It was established to aid Republican candidates seeking state legislative seats, with the idea that they would make a healthy "farm team" of future congressional candidates. As a result, it asserted that it was not required to abide by federal contribution limits and disclosure rules because it did not make direct cash contributions to candidates for national office. The only rules that bound it were those enacted by the states themselves, to regulate intrastate political activity. An added benefit of this approach was that in many states there were no contribution limits at all, and GOPAC could accept donations of any size.

Gingrich exploited these features to begin collecting money in much bigger increments than he had been able to do at CHOPAC. Kansas City construction magnate Miller Nichols was one of the early big givers, putting in $21,500 in 1986—more than four times the amount permitted under federal law. Jim Richards of Southwire kicked in $10,000, as did South Carolina textile tycoon Roger Milliken. The size of these contributions would likely have been controversial at the time they were made (since they were twice the federal limit), had they been public. But because GOPAC claimed immunity from federal regulations, it made no public filings with the Federal Election Commission and closely guarded its list of contributors.

There was a legal basis for this argument, since at the time nothing GOPAC was doing was apparently related to federal elections. Yet it was also irregular for a member of Congress to associate himself with a political committee that engaged in little or no public disclosure. It seems especially odd for a politician such as Gingrich, who had earlier in his career pledged: "I have done and will do nothing that has to be kept under lock and key. If we are to have honest, responsible government, we must begin with honest, responsible politics. It is impossible to run a closed campaign and then expect to have open government after the election."[4] The primary goal of the post-Watergate reforms, after all, had been to prevent politicians from accepting large sums of cash behind closed doors.

In 1987, Gingrich launched the defining crusade of his career, filing a series of complaints with the House Ethics Committee against Democrat Jim Wright, the Speaker of the House.[5] In a familiar tactic, Gingrich leaked information about Wright to reporters, much of it inaccurate, then cited those stories as confirmation of his charges.[6] From his perch at GOPAC, Gingrich exploited the Wright case and those of other allegedly corrupt Democrats to raise funds that he used to travel the country, preaching the need to oust the corrupt establishment in Congress. In June 1988, for example, Gingrich wrote some 19,000 potential GOPAC contributors about his ethics complaint against Wright, asking them to put up money and send postcards to the ethics committee urging it to act against the Speaker. "We need tremendous public pressure, plus major media coverage, to force the committee's Democratic majority to take action," Gingrich wrote.[7] Two additional letters thanked GOPAC contributors for helping in the campaign against Wright. This was reckless language for the leader of a PAC that depended on not participating in politics at the national level to maintain its immunity from federal disclosure regulations.

Yet Gingrich's hunch about Wright was accurate. Following a two-year investigation, the House Ethics Committee accused Wright of a slew of ethical violations (none of which had been contained in Gingrich's original complaint), and Wright was forced to resign in May 1989. Just after Wright resigned, Gingrich wrote a letter to GOPAC contributors that spoke of potential "major gains" for Republicans in the 1990 congressional elections because of the case. "Your contribution is urgently needed to help us keep the heat on the Democrats and make the gains we need this November," he wrote. Wright, Gingrich added, was "not the only corrupt Democrat."[8] After it was all over, Gingrich boasted that he had been able "to create in Jim Wright a symbol of a political machine," Gingrich told author John Barry.[9] His efforts to advance that notion were also helped along by the surprise resignation of the House's number three Democrat, Tony Coelho, just a few months after Wright in an influence-peddling scandal related to the savings and loan fiasco.

Gingrich seemed to be taking GOPAC far away from its original mission of promoting a GOP "farm team," instead converting it into a sort of national Republican attack dog, dedicated to besmirching Democrats and spreading the gospel of Newt Gingrich. This was perilously close to federal campaign activity, although it probably walked the line—which is drawn at specific efforts to elect or defeat a candidate or candidates at the polls. On the other hand, GOPAC's fundraising and propaganda were designed with a very clear campaign purpose—the ouster of the Democratic majority in Congress. Gingrich had managed to cross the line without crossing it.

Shortly before Wright's departure but long after it had become apparent that Gingrich had mortally wounded him, Gingrich's colleagues rewarded him by electing him minority whip, the number two Republican leadership position, over Edward Madigan, a far less combative, old-line Republican. It was a narrow two-vote victory; sentiment toward Gingrich remained divided among Republicans, with the more senior members still spurning his combative approach.

The Wright affair and other predominantly Democratic scandals during the 1980s greatly undermined public confidence in Congress. During the 1970s, polls regularly showed that more than 40 percent of Americans had "a great deal" or "quite a lot" of confidence in Congress, while the vast majority said they had at least "some" confidence in Congress.[10] By the time of Gingrich's election as whip, fewer than 20 percent of all Americans said they had a great deal of confidence in Congress.

By this time, Gingrich and GOPAC had a very high profile, and many people were calling on him to disclose his contributors. Gingrich, presumably well aware of the stir that revelations of such big gifts would cause, adamantly refused. The revolution required funding, even if it had to be kept "under lock and key." A look at some of the numbers reveals why GOPAC may have been defensive about its funding. A confidential internal GOPAC list of contributors shows that in 1989 one wealthy industrialist gave the PAC $25,000—five times the amount permitted under federal law.

In 1990, Gingrich grew even more ambitious. New York investor Richard Gilder ponied up $195,000, or thirty-nine times more than the federal limit. Terry Kohler, a Wisconsin businessman, put in $237,000—forty-seven times the federal limit. New York investor Tucker Anderson chipped in $60,000. Palm Beach investor Stanley Gaines threw in $30,000. Wisconsin businessman Philip Gelatt gave $40,000. Connecticut industrialist Robert Kreible gave $65,000. South Carolina textile king Roger Milliken gave $50,000. GOPAC's contributor base remained tiny—no bigger than CHOPAC's. Yet its coffers had begun to bulge thanks to the PAC's refusal to abide by conventional fundraising limits. In 1989, just seventy contributors gave a total of $874,000. That amount would have been just $350,000 had GOPAC been complying with federal rules capping individual contributions at $5,000. In 1990, a group of sixty-nine contributors put up $1.5 million—three to five times as much as would have been legal under federal rules.

Even as he assembled this machine between 1986 and 1989, Gingrich set himself up as a paragon of ethical conduct. "The one exception to my willingness to conciliate and compromise is the area of ethics and corruption," he declared in 1989.[11] "If we tolerate the growing invulnerability and growing corruption of the U.S. House, we may literally see our freedom decay and decline," he said in 1988. "The corruption grows more blatant and more destructive."[12]

His explanation for filing charges against Jim Wright was that "I'm so deeply frightened by the nature of the left-wing machine in the House that it would have been worse not to do anything."[13]

In a 1988 press release, he declared, "The price of self-government is a willingness to stand firm and insist on honesty. As long as we have ethical problems we have to deal with them."[14]

He did not let up following the resignations of Wright and Coelho in 1989: "I think the country is going to be further shocked when the news media digs deeper to discover that it doesn't stop with Coelho and Wright, that it goes on to more and more people . . . at least I think . . . another nine or ten, maybe more than that."[15]

A Visionary's Vision

The art of revolutionary leadership in its most critical moments consists nine-tenths in knowing how to sense the mood of the masses.

—*Leon Trotsky*

When Jim Wright announced his exit from the House in 1989, he colorfully denounced the "mindless cannibalism" he believed had been let loose in the body by Gingrich. But there was nothing mindless about what Gingrich was up to. His strategy was quite deliberate, more sophisticated than simply taking potshots at Democratic leaders, and directed at a more ambitious goal than electing candidates to local office. Gingrich was now using GOPAC explicitly as a vehicle for a Republican takeover of Congress. In early 1989, Gingrich put his thoughts to paper, drafting a speech for a private GOPAC-sponsored gathering of Republican activists in Washington.

The paper, "Driving Realignment from the Presidency Down to the Precincts," which we obtained from a confidential source, records Gingrich's thinking with stunning clarity.[16] Pragmatic, perceptive, and infused with an understanding of American political history, the paper lays out a precise and often prophetic scenario for a sweeping realignment of the electorate toward Republicans, revealing the method to what Democrats and political commentators perceived as Gingrich's madness.

There have been only five major realignments in U.S. history, Gingrich noted. At the turn of the eighteenth century, the Democrat-Republicans, led by Thomas Jefferson, James Madison, and Aaron Burr, ousted the Federalists, led by John Adams and Alexander Hamilton. "The 1792–1804 realignment was motivated by the Jeffersonian vision as a land of simple, self-reliant yeomen preserving republican virtue in a world of corrupt and venal monarchies," observed Gingrich. Twenty-five years later, the Democrats, led by Andrew Jackson, overwhelmed the National Republican Party led by John Q. Adams and Henry Clay. "Jackson's vision—egalitarian, democratic and strongly national—was intensely powerful and successful. The image of limitless potential and virtue of 'the West' was particularly potent."

In the run-up to the Civil War, the newly formed Republican Party, led by Abraham Lincoln, triumphed over the fractured Democrats, represented by Stephen Douglas and John Breckenbridge. " 'Free Land, Free Soil, Free Men' was the rallying cry of the 1860 Republicans. The vision of a combination of free men, in a free land, and a 'union' eternally one was one of the most powerful ever applied in American politics."

Reunification at the conclusion of the Civil War produced highly competitive elections in the Reconstruction era because it provided the minority Democrats with a cohesive voting bloc in the Southern states. While the conflict between the parties originally had centered on slavery and states' rights issues, it gradually shifted to a competition between the progressive movement (Republicans) and the populist movement (Democrats) over economic policy and, to a lesser extent, political reform. As the nineteenth century came to a close, the progressive Republicans, led by Benjamin Harrison and William McKinley, established themselves in a dominant position after the electorate soundly rejected the "free silver" economic policies of William Jennings Bryan in the election of 1896.

It was the role of political reform that Gingrich zeroed in on: "The Progressive movement not only created a powerful vision of honest, compassionate and efficient government at all levels; it also badly damaged Democratic electoral strength by reforming urban politics and removing hundreds of thousands of non-existent or illegal voters from the roll," wrote Gingrich.

Finally, in this century, there was the New Deal realignment led by Franklin D. Roosevelt starting in 1928—the longest lasting of the five. Gingrich, an admirer of FDR, had this to say of his movement: "The New Deal was positive, egalitarian, hopeful and totally inclusive. Occasional inconsistencies or downright contradictions were irrelevant. The vision was all movement, always thrusting forward, always pointing to a better tomorrow." As later events would show, Gingrich believed there were universal political lessons here.

While learned and trenchant, Gingrich's analysis was not particularly original. The theory of critical realignment elections in American politics was fathered largely by political scientists V. O. Key and Walter Dean Burnham, giants within the discipline. Key first propounded the theory in a 1955 essay, "A Theory of Critical Elections," while Burnham offered a highly developed and robust version in his 1970 classic, *Critical Elections and the Mainsprings of American Politics.*[17]

In particular, Burnham's *Critical Elections* met with wide acceptance, and it was a standard text on many college campuses in the early 1970s, around the time Gingrich was teaching at West Georgia. In *Critical Elections,* Burnham posited that tumultuous realigning elections occur with "periodicity" because of the failure of political parties to accommodate socioeconomic change. Like Gingrich, he believed that the first five realignments occurred around the years 1792, 1828, 1860, 1896, and 1928. While Burnham's was a sophisticated theory, he made the tidy observation that realigning elections occur about every three or four decades, which led him to suggest that the 1968 election of Richard Nixon might have been the start of the latest realignment, in the direction of the Republican Party. Coincidentally or not, by the time history professor Gingrich bid for Congress in 1974 as a Republican in a traditionally Democratic district, the completion of the Republican realignment prophesied by Burnham was overdue, and in the view of some, imminent.[18]

But Burnham and others, it appears, failed to anticipate either the durability of the New Deal coalition and the political machine it had produced or the forces that have recently produced dealignment among the voters, fewer and fewer of whom have a strong attachment to any political party. By 1974, moreover, the historically unique constitutional crisis of Watergate foreclosed any possibility of realignment toward Republicans—for the short term. Democrats buttressed their congressional majorities and seized the White House (in 1976) in the wake of that scandal. By the time Gingrich finally made it to Congress in 1978, there was little talk of a realignment at the congressional level.

While Gingrich's theory was not path-breaking, he was certainly one of only a handful of 1980s politicians familiar with critical elections theory (beyond having a fuzzy understanding of the now-common term "realignment"). Moreover, what Gingrich then did with this theory, as far as can be determined, was highly original. After discarding the notion of "periodicity," at least as a hard and fast temporal rule, he performed his own analysis of critical elections.[19] The distinctive feature of the major realigning elections, Gingrich concluded, is that they were by and large successful in accomplishing most or all of the following:

1. Achieving a Significant Increase in Turnout
2. Creating a Positive Organizing Vision That Arouses Support
3. Delegitimizing the Opposition
4. Creating a Civil War Within the Opposition
5. Increasing the Scale of Resources
6. Applying Cutting-Edge Technology

"These patterns of realignment provide the historical basis for constructing a strategy for completing the current, incomplete realignment from the Liberal Democrat party to the Republican party," wrote Gingrich. He then launched into a more detailed historical analysis of each item on this list. Under "Creating a Positive Organizing Vision," he noted that the Jeffersonians and Jacksonians had both successfully advanced positive and idealistic visions of America (universal agrarianism and "Manifest Destiny"). The visions of Lincoln (national unity), the Progressives (clean government), and FDR (economic security) were similarly upbeat.

Regarding turnout, Gingrich noted that each of the four realigning elections for which there are data saw major jumps in participation. Between 1824 and 1828, he noted, participation nearly doubled. Significantly, Gingrich noted that in 1936, Roosevelt won a landslide not because Republican nominee Alf Landon had received fewer votes than Herbert Hoover did in 1932 (Landon received some one million more votes than Hoover), but rather because Roosevelt increased his own total by five million. In *Critical Elections,* Burnham observed that realignments are characterized by "abnormally heavy voter participation for the time."[20]

Gingrich's observation about realigning elections "creating a civil war within the opposition" was less persuasive. As he himself acknowledged, opposition splits occurred in only three of the five realigning elections (1792, 1860, and 1896). The Republican Party was not split so much as cowed by the New Deal, a development that came after the realigning election of 1932. "It became totally reactive, never sure whether it should retain its virtue by steadfastly but hopelessly opposing the New Deal—Fair Deal juggernaut or by becoming another, but better Rooseveltian party itself," observed Gingrich. "The Democrats didn't have to divide the Republican Party; it did the job itself."[21]

Gingrich's analysis of the role of new resources in realignment elections was more perceptive and convincing. Jefferson "created the first national political organization in U.S. history," while the Jacksonians "used the spoils system to raise so much money and recruit so many workers that they may have run the most expensive per-capita campaign in U.S. history". Inevitably, Gingrich's eye also fell on Mark Hanna, whose fundraising feats in the 1890s are mentioned in chapter 5. "That money made possible the creation of an incredibly efficient and powerful national election organization that would dominate the political life of the United States for forty years," the professor observed with awe. Once again, Gingrich had plucked from the pages of history a case in which the deliberate actions of one man had profoundly affected American politics. It is interesting that Gingrich chose to focus on Hanna's organizational skills, without noting the role that money played in his era, much less the intimacy between Republicans and corporate interests that ultimately provoked a public backlash.

The New Deal coalition, Gingrich noted, was unique, "the most spectacularly successful political creation in our history."

Northern Blacks joined Southern segregationists, urban unionized workers, small town farmers and small businessmen, Catholic ethnics and Bible-belt fundamentalists, left-wing intellectuals and machine regulars—to form a combination with more combined resources than anything seen before in American politics. The ability of unions to raise and distribute political resources was increased, and the New Deal created literally millions of patronage jobs.

His analysis of the historical role of cutting-edge technology was equally incisive, though he might better have used the term "innovation." Jefferson's innovation, as noted above, was the creation of the first national political party. The Jacksonians, meanwhile, harnessed new printing technologies and socioeconomic changes to create scores of new newspapers. Using these organs, the Jacksonians "simply overwhelmed their opponents in the media war of the 1820s." But it was in his discussion of FDR's innovations that Gingrich displayed prophetic insight:

Roosevelt flew to the convention (first use of an airplane and first appearance at a convention by a candidate) to make a nationwide radio address in 1932. He and his cohorts eventually dominated completely the new techniques of communication. In particular, radio broadcasts, newsreels and Hollywood movies with political and social "content" buttressed Roosevelt's political realignment. His victory in the war of ideas was so total that for three generations the academic, artistic and intellectual establishment has been almost totally Democratic, and that establishment has continued to dominate the means of popular communication.

Of course, Gingrich himself had already mastered one new technology in the 1980s—C-Span—to great effect. And there was more to come.

"Delegitimizing the Opposition" was Gingrich's specialty, a tactic he had deployed very effectively in his own election campaigns and in the battle to unseat Jim Wright. In "Driving Realignment," Gingrich noted that President John Adams "was successfully portrayed by Jeffersonians as an aristocratic, monarchist, British-loving elitist, i.e., not 'republican' and not a normal, simple, traditional-values American 'like the rest of us.' " Five years later, in the run-up to the 1994 elections, Gingrich would describe Democrats in almost identical terms.

Similarly, noted Gingrich, Adams's son John Quincy Adams "was portrayed as a display- and luxury-loving elitist introducing European and aristocratic customs into republican America. This picture played particularly well in the western areas of the country which tended to view 'Easterners' as effete and elitist anyway." Withering as they were, Gingrich wrote, these attacks were nothing compared with the antebellum assaults by Lincoln's Republicans on the Democrats: "Few efforts at delegitimizing the opposition have been more ruthless than the Republican description of the Democrats as the party of slavery and sedition." The fin de siécle Progressives, meanwhile, "attacked Democratic legitimacy as well as electoral strength by attacking graft and corruption in urban politics." Finally, "By painting 'them' [Republicans] as the selfish, unfeeling and exclusive creators of Hoover's Depression, Roosevelt's coalition made everyone else seem like one of 'us.' Republicans were greedy, rich, uncaring members of exclusive country clubs."

Gingrich concluded by offering a "proposed vision" that the group would seek to advance between 1989 and 1992. "A caring Humanitarian Reform Republican Party can apply the principles of a governing conservatism to attract new voters, activists, and candidates by offering an agenda worth voting for," he wrote, listing his favorite contrast words:

CORRUPT		HONEST
LIBERAL	VERSUS	CONSERVATIVE
WELFARE		OPPORTUNITY
STATE		SOCIETY

Perhaps most fascinating of all, however, was Gingrich's suggestion in his "proposed vision" that Republicans lead "a movement for honest self-government." Recall that in 1973, during his first campaign for Congress, Gingrich had spoken of helping the country become "self-governing" through an "honest, really honest" campaign. There can be no mistaking what this says about Gingrich's worldview: the way to delegitimize the opposition was to make the case that American politics had become fundamentally dishonest. The re-alignment could not occur until the public perceived Democrats as the party of corruption and Republicans as the party of reform.

The GOPAC members and others in attendance endorsed Gingrich's vision with only a few changes. According to a GOPAC summary of the 1989 gathering, the members called for a broad reform movement, including "cleaning up government ethics" and "reforming election law," as well as "developing a broad 'reform doctrine' to guide candidates," and "continuing the push for Congressional reform."[22]

Of Dollars and Favors

While Gingrich and his small coterie of fellow revolutionaries plot-ted away, the national Republican Party, especially under the Wash-ington-Beltway establishment leadership of newly elected President George Bush, continued in the familiar go-along-get-along style. For the most part, Gingrich still seemed to be howling in the wilder-ness, and many of his colleagues and fellow Republicans did not take him seriously. Yet Gingrich continued on his course. GOPAC, by this time, was a wholly owned subsidiary of the minority whip. At a 1989 retreat in Crested Butte, Colorado, Gingrich and his GOPAC brain trust decided to increase even further GOPAC's role in con-gressional races. "That was probably the genesis of taking the next step beyond recruiting and training legislative candidates to begin to recruit and train congressional candidates," recalled Kay Riddle, the former GOPAC director.[23] One step they did not decide to take, however, was to register with the Federal Election Commission and thus submit themselves to public scrutiny and federal oversight.

In June of 1989, just months after Gingrich's election as minority whip, GOPAC launched a new "Campaign for Fair Elections." "As Republican Whip in the House of Representatives, I've seen first-hand how the Democrats have taken advantage of the tremendous power they've built up over the last thirty-five years as the ruling majority in Congress," Gingrich declared in a GOPAC fundraising letter.[24] "I've also seen how their abuse of that power has brought Congress to an all-time low in public esteem."

"The Democrats in Congress have set themselves up as the highest authority in the land—above the will of the American people who elected Ronald Reagan and then George Bush to be their president," he continued. "The only way to clean up the mess and restore honesty and decency to Congress is to break the Democrats' stranglehold on power by focusing public attention—and outrage—on their unethical escapades." Gingrich urged contributors to send letters to Congress complaining about the congressional frank, saying the letters would be "the first step in our two-step plan to gain a Republican majority in the House of Representatives by 1992." Promised Gingrich, "With your help, our Campaign for Fair Elections will defeat or seriously weaken a large number of Democrats in 1990."

This letter constitutes explicit involvement in campaign politics. Under federal law, a federal campaign contribution is "any gift, subscription, loan, advance, or deposit of money or anything of value made by any person for the purpose of influencing any election for federal office."[25] An expenditure, similarly, is "any purchase, payment, distribution, loan, advance, deposit or gift of money or anything of value, made by any person for the purpose of influencing any election for federal office."[26]

While any layman would perceive such a letter to be a campaign document for which money had been expended with the intention of influencing a federal election, and which sought contributions to be used for influencing a federal election, GOPAC did not deviate from its position that it was a state-based political action committee uninvolved in federal elections. It defended its propaganda by claiming it was only exercising its free speech rights and by relying on a legal concept known as "express advocacy," which holds that only campaign speech that expressly advocates the election or defeat of a clearly identified candidate—by using such phrases as "vote for Smith," "vote against Jones"—qualifies for regulation. While the concept is not universally accepted, it has been upheld by some courts. Reliance on such legalisms, however, evades the fundamental point: GOPAC, an avowedly partisan organization headed by an extremely prominent and partisan elected politician, was engaged in campaigning against other elected politicians at the federal level. As such, there can be no debate: it should have been disclosing its activities and observing the same limits as everyone else.

Inside the House, Gingrich rapidly consolidated his power

following his election as whip and developed an intensely loyal following among a majority of Republican legislators. A born pedagogue, he was constantly provoking them to think in new ways. With the guaranteed audience that a leadership position brings, he would drill his points home again and again. One of Gingrich's favorite lessons was to present his pupils with a piece of paper containing a series of nine evenly spaced dots arranged in a square. Connect all four corners of the box using three straight lines and without lifting the pencil off the page, he would challenge participants. After a few minutes of futile line-drawing, Gingrich would present the answer: by drawing lines beyond the imaginary boundaries of the square, the connections could be made. Eventually, virtually every Republican in the House became familiar with Gingrich's mind game. In conversations and speeches, he would frequently remind them to "go outside the nine dots"—to think unconventionally, to operate outside the known, or perceived, parameters.

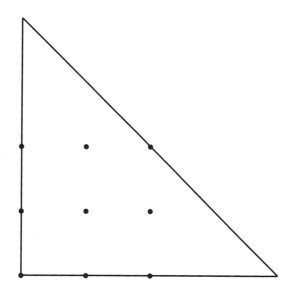

He continued to preach about the corruption issue. "After seventeen months as Republican Whip," he told an audience at the Heritage Foundation in the summer of 1990, "I have reached some very troubling conclusions about the Washington establishment and a Democratic-controlled Congress that is simply not working. Congress is a broken system. It is increasingly a system of corruption in which money politics is defeating and driving out citizen politics. Congress is a sicker and sicker institution in an imperial capital that wallows in the American people's tax money." He reminded his audience that "honesty and integrity are at the heart of a free society. Corruption, special favors, dishonesty and deception corrode the very process of freedom and alienate citizens from their country."[27]

These are, of course, some of the very points this book seeks to make. What Gingrich did not mention, however, was the extent to which he himself had become a part of this "broken system." As minority whip, Gingrich was now in a position to exercise considerable influence—and he was clearly willing to use his clout, repeatedly mixing his fundraising interests and those of his political machine with government policy making.

The intermingling of Gingrich and GOPAC's fundraising interests with policy is well illustrated by the PAC's and Gingrich's dealings with the Department of Housing and Urban Development (HUD). According to internal HUD logs, between 1989 and 1992 Gingrich and GOPAC sent Housing and Urban Development Secretary Jack Kemp at least forty-eight pieces of correspondence. Gingrich and Kemp were allies from Kemp's days in the House. Much of the correspondence concerned requests for Kemp to appear at GOPAC fundraisers and meet with GOPAC contributors. On one occasion, Gingrich, writing on GOPAC stationary, set up a meeting between Kemp and GOPAC contributor Richard Pomboy, a Connecticut businessman who headed an investment management company.[28] "I feel it would be mutually beneficial for you to meet with him," Gingrich wrote Kemp cryptically. A letter from Pomboy to Gingrich indicates Pomboy wanted to lobby Kemp on Pomboy's ideas for economic policy.[29] On September 27, 1990, Gingrich wrote to Kemp detailing the results of a GOPAC focus group on HUD issues.

Then there was the May 19, 1992, letter Gingrich sent Kemp on behalf of his long-time contributor Jan Roush of the Dorchester Corporation, which had been founded by Gingrich's long-time patron Chester Roush. The Roushes were concerned about funding for a permanent extension of the low-income housing tax credit, which was a boon to their real estate company. Roush was an early contributor to Gingrich's campaigns and had cosigned two loans to Gingrich's campaigns.[30] He also helped underwrite the 1977 book partnership that kept Gingrich afloat between campaigns for Congress (but resulted in no book). Gingrich had written to HUD on behalf of Dorchester in 1986, and Jan Roush had helped him raise funds in 1989. It was also not the first time Gingrich had helped the Roushes with the low-income housing tax credit program. In 1988 and 1989, according to the *Atlanta Business Chronicle,*[31] Gingrich backed the liberal program after requests from the Roushes.

But the coincidence of Gingrich's fundraising interests with his official work is nowhere clearer than in the case of Southwire, the Georgia cable maker with which Gingrich had been intimate for more than a decade. In his early incarnation as a moderate Republican, Gingrich had been a critic of the company, which is a notorious polluter. Like Roush (a former Southwire executive), the founders of Southwire, the Richards family, had come to Gingrich's aid in the lean period between his second and third campaigns for Congress in the 1970s. As was first recounted by the *New York Times,* the local bank, owned by the Richards family, gave Gingrich's campaign easy terms on its loans; it also proved a lenient landlord when the campaign's office in the bank fell behind on rent. Three bank officials made loans to the Gingrich campaign, and Southwire executives invested in Gingrich book deals in 1977 and 1984. Gingrich's attitude toward the company underwent a remarkable transformation and he became one of its biggest defenders.[32]

In 1989, according to one letter obtained by the authors, Gingrich asked the Department of Commerce "to pressure the Japanese to open their markets to aluminum conductor imports," a key product of Southwire.[33] In 1991, according to another letter we obtained, Gingrich sought to assist Southwire in getting a federal Economic Development Administration grant for a technology center it was constructing.[34] Also that year, Gingrich intervened with the Customs Service on behalf of Southwire in a dispute it was having with a competitor.[35] All the while, Southwire executives were pouring money into GOPAC and Gingrich's campaigns—with at least $80,000 going to GOPAC alone.

While all of this could conceivably be excused as legitimate constituent service, there was also the October 2, 1991, meeting that Gingrich helped set up between Securities and Exchange Commission Chairman Richard Breeden and Southwire executive Donald

Baker.[36] It is hard to imagine that this was a corporate constituent service, for Baker, a regular Gingrich contributor, did not seek the meeting on behalf of Southwire. Rather, the meeting was arranged on behalf of the Institute of Management Accountants (IMA), a New Jersey-based lobbying group of which Baker was serving as president. The IMA in recent years has been a loyal provider of speaking fees to Gingrich.

Was Gingrich helping Southwire because its principals were constituents, or because they had larded the coffers of his various enterprises—not to mention his own pockets early in his career? That is hard to say. What is crystal clear is that Gingrich's own constituents and the public at large never had this question put to them because they never knew about most of the money Gingrich had received from Southwire interests, nor about many of the favors he had done for the company.

Gingrich also had warm relations with textile magnate Roger Milliken, who with his brother Gerrish and other relatives had pumped some $300,000 into GOPAC and Gingrich's campaigns by 1994. An ardent protectionist, Milliken was not exactly Gingrich's intellectual soul-mate. Yet Gingrich had found occasion to deviate from his staunch free-trade ideology on several occasions, as he did in 1994 after a meeting with Milliken, who persuaded him to raise questions about GATT, the global free trade agreement. Politics cannot be carried on today without such contacts taking place. How would Gingrich's long-time supporters react if they could not secure his assistance on matters like these? But how would Gingrich's goals be affected if his political debts were widely known? Naturally, these kinds of contacts have to be kept secret.

Renewing American Civilization . . . and Newt Gingrich, Too

In late 1992 and early 1993, Gingrich began conceiving a new way to advance those political goals—a nationally broadcast college course, ambitiously titled "Renewing American Civilization," in which he would inculcate students with his Republican values. The special revolutionary organization was branching out, soon to become an entity that Gingrich's associates dubbed "Newt Inc."

Nominally an educational enterprise, internal course planning documents revealed the true nature of the course as a partisan organizing tool. The project's sophisticated partisan political rationale is spelled out in a private draft outline for the course. "The liberals have three great advantages which were developed by Franklin Roosevelt and the New Deal Democrats and which have helped them stay in power despite their failure to win the White House in five of the six elections between 1968 and 1988," the analysis states. "Despite the American people's consistent rejection of liberalism, the Republicans were unable to duplicate or overcome the advantages of a decaying but entrenched establishment." The Democrats' advantages include "a network of powerful institutions such as the big city machines, the labor unions, and the leftwing activist groups (including trial lawyers and Gays), whose collective weight dwarfs the more narrow base and resources of the competitor," and "a system for training and developing professionals whose doctrine of power and politics is simply more effective and widely understood than the opposition party." The document proposes that Gingrich's course can serve as a vehicle for developing similar advantages for the "opposition," that is, the Republican Party.[37] The documents also spoke of training 200,000 citizens "into a model for replacing the welfare state and reforming our government." In one particularly revealing letter to a group of college Republicans, Gingrich had written,

> We must ask ourselves what the future would be like if we were allowed to define it, and learn to explain that future to the American people in a way that captures first their imagination and then their votes.
>
> In that context, I am going to devote much of the next four years, starting this fall, to teaching a course entitled Renewing American Civilization.

To get the project off the ground, however, Gingrich first needed to persuade someone to host his course. Fortunately, a college dean who ran a consulting business on the side, Timothy Mescon of Kennesaw State College in western Georgia, had come to Gingrich in September of 1992 seeking favors. The development of their relationship is spelled out quite clearly in a series of letters obtained by the authors.

Chronology of a Deal

September 17, 1992. Mescon writes Gingrich seeking "a letter of introduction to the Director of the Bureau of Private Enterprise" at the U.S. Agency for International Development (USAID), where the Mescon Group is seeking consulting contracts for work in Ghana.

October 1, 1992. Gingrich writes the letter to USAID as requested by Mescon. Even though he is at best an acquaintance of Mescon, Gingrich describes the Mescon group as "a reputable organization in Atlanta," which is performing "exciting work." He tells USAID Administrator Ronald Roskens in a handwritten postscript: "Tim Mescon is very competent and well worth a meeting."

October 14, 1992. Gingrich writes Mescon to let him know he has performed as asked. "If I can help you in any way, please do not hesitate to contact me," Gingrich writes. In a handwritten postscript Gingrich adds, "I am very interested in working with you after the election." (The letter is in stark contrast to the brush-off Gingrich gave Mescon in 1991 when the professor invited him to a lecture at the college. Gingrich declined that invitation in a four-sentence letter, mailed out two days after the event took place.)

November 5, 1992. Mescon writes Gingrich to congratulate him on his reelection and thank him for intervening with USAID.

January 21, 1993. Mescon's father and business partner, Michael Mescon, who runs the Mescon Group, writes Gingrich proposing a meeting. He refers to a mid-January meeting between Gingrich and Timothy Mescon about the course project.

February 2, 1993. Timothy Mescon writes to Gingrich's legislative aide, J. Krister Holladay, about a meeting they had the previous Friday in which Mescon's business interests and the college course were discussed. Mescon says he "will submit a proposal soon regarding [Gingrich's] teaching on campus in the fall quarter." Referring to his consulting firm, Mescon adds that he "would appreciate any assistance you might be able to provide in assisting with our attempt to expand our many activities both in Ghana and domestically."

March 1, 1993. Gingrich writes Mescon a memo formalizing the college course deal.

Gingrich's college course, like all the other revolutionary activities, required funding. These fundraising efforts were conducted through nonprofit charitable foundations, namely the Progress and Freedom Foundation, the Kennesaw State College Foundation, and the West Georgia State College Foundation. The use of these foundations was a sort of revenge for Gingrich against the Democrats. Benefactors receive a tax credit for contributions to nonprofit foundations, and the nonprofits depend upon this incentive to raise funds. In effect, Gingrich's campaign to "renew American civilization" received a government subsidy.

Unfortunately, there are serious questions about the legality—not to mention the propriety—of using so-called 501(c)(3) tax-exempts for such purposes. As the Exempt Organization Tax Review dryly put it:

> Section 501(c)(3) organizations offer three enticements to politicians. First, contributions to section 501(c)(3) organizations are deductible to the contributors under section 170, while contributions to a [regular] political organization are not deductible. Being able to offer contributors, especially large contributors, a tax deduction may ease the unremitting burden of fundraising faced by all politicians. Second, contributors to section 501(c)(3) organizations are not subject to disclosure under either tax law or federal campaign finance law. Third, corporations may contribute directly to section 501(c)(3) corporations (and claim a deduction for this contribution) but federal election law prohibits direct corporate contributions to political candidates.

While the benefits of raising political capital through charitable contributions are obvious, the means of doing so are less obvious if one relies on the plain meaning of the statute. Section 501(c)(3) provides exemption only for an otherwise qualifying organization "which does not participate in, or intervene in (including the publishing or distributing of statements) any political campaign on behalf of (or in opposition to) any candidate for public office."[38]

As with the federal statute governing campaign activity, however, there is a devil in the details. The definition of intervention in a political campaign varies, depending upon which attorney or which judge or which official of the Internal Revenue Service (IRS) you ask. In any case, it is not something the IRS is quick to pursue.

In order to motivate prospective contributors, Gingrich made written promises to various companies and interest groups that he would present their viewpoints in the content of the course.

According to one memo, contributors who put up $50,000 could "work directly with the leadership of the Renewing American Civilization project in the course development process." Those who put up $25,000 would also be "invited to participate in the course development process," while those who contributed lesser amounts would also be allowed input.

Healthsouth, a conglomerate of rehabilitation centers, gave $15,000 to the course in its first year. During Gingrich's November 6, 1993, lecture on "Health and Wellness," the company was used as a shining example of quality health care. "They do a remarkable job of helping people with rehabilitation," said Gingrich. "They did it in part by emphasizing quality." He then introduced a video about the company that was entirely flattering toward Healthsouth. "Higher quality, less cost," Healthsouth CEO Richard Scrushy declared. "You know, we built our company on that premise, and we've been extremely successful."

In another instance, Washington lobbyist Richard Berman was able to get input on behalf of his client, the Employment Policy Institute. In a May 10, 1993, memo, a GOPAC official explicitly linked a contribution from the group to influence over the course. "I think there is a very real possibility here of $20,000—$25,000 if the course can incorporate some of the ideas mentioned in the Journal of Labor Research, Volume XIV, Number 3," she wrote. The scholarly papers cited advance the notion that low-level food service jobs are not necessarily "dead end."

Gingrich's financial relationship with some companies and businessmen featured in the course was never mentioned. Gingrich devoted more than twenty minutes to textile magnate Roger Milliken and his company Milliken Co. in his October 16, 1993, lecture, "Commitment to Quality," yet he never mentioned that his campaign and GOPAC together had received in excess of $300,000 from Milliken interests.

"He is an extraordinary man," Gingrich said of Milliken during the lecture. "He is personally one of the most forceful human beings I have ever dealt with." At one point, Gingrich attributed to Milliken "an act of genius," and declared that Milliken's company was "I think widely recognized as the most effective, most productive textile company in the world."

In a lecture on health, Gingrich plugged what he called "a very powerful, revolutionary" health reform proposal by Patrick Rooney, CEO of the Golden Rule Insurance company. In a video presentation Gingrich played for his students, Rooney argued for making workers pay a larger share of their own health insurance and exempting insurance companies from having to pay small claims. "You'd be a lot better off if you left insurance out entirely on small claims," Rooney asserted. The businessman and another Golden Rule executive together had contributed at least $117,000 to GOPAC during Gingrich's tenure as chairman of the political committee.

At one point in his class on entrepreneurialism, Gingrich offered his students a candid comment about his fundraising practices. "I used to hate calling for money," he said. "Now, it's a nuisance but I do it and I'm used to it. And it's a necessity in my business. If I don't close the sale, I can't raise the money for my campaign, I can't raise the money to teach the class."

Gingrich seemed to have grown more and more blatant and casual about this sort of influence-peddling during the 1990s, engaging in it almost by rote.

On June 2, 1992, Gingrich received a letter from the Republican Senatorial Inner Circle, a fundraising unit of the Republican Party.[39] The group forwarded to Gingrich a plea for assistance it had received from James Hunt, the owner of a Georgia hazardous waste disposal company. Hunt had been indicted for allegedly disposing of hazardous chemicals illegally, and he was seeking political intervention in his case.[40] The Inner Circle, noting that Hunt was a dues-paying member, asked Gingrich to "please take special consideration in this case." A prudent politician, particularly one concerned with ethics, might think twice about helping a contributor who is an accused toxic waste polluter. Gingrich showed no such concern, firing off a "Dear Bill" letter to Environmental Protection Agency administrator William Riley.[41] "I would appreciate your review of his concerns," wrote Gingrich. As it turned out, it was too late for political intervention. While Hunt had claimed he was an innocent victim of unscrupulous business partners, a jury found otherwise in July 1993, convicting him for illegally transporting and dumping seventy-six barrels of toxic waste.[42]

This willingness to blatantly mix official acts with the quest for campaign contributions was again evident in a September 1994 letter from Gingrich, on GOPAC stationery, to potential contributors.[43] "Will you help me draft the Republican legislative agenda for the 104th Congress?" he asked potential contributors. The letter instructed recipients to send in their advice about the GOP's legislative agenda, along with a contribution.

Around the same time—that is, just weeks before the 1994 Election Day "revolution"—Gingrich had received a request from a lobbyist to intervene with the Food and Drug Administration (FDA) on behalf of a company seeking approval for a home AIDS test. Gingrich did even better than that, firing off a letter to White House Chief of Staff Leon Panetta complaining about FDA delays in approving the potentially lucrative test and asking him to review the issue.[44] Shortly thereafter, the company that had designed the test, and its chief executive, made some $40,000 in contributions to a foundation backing Gingrich's college course (the foundation was run by a former executive director of GOPAC).

By mid-1994 the radicalization of the House Republicans was essentially complete; Gingrich's worldview now predominated. While he was no longer launching the kind of sustained attacks on the institution he had pioneered and perfected, a cadre of followers had taken up the standard. Nicely symbolizing the maturation and acceptance of Gingrich's anti-institutional ideology by the party establishment was "Forty Years of Single Party Control," an elaborately researched 141-page study of the corrupting effects of the Democratic hegemony released by the House Republican leadership in July of 1994.[45] Apart from a favorable notice by political columnist David Broder, the study sank without a trace. Only two reporters showed up at a press conference to introduce the document.[46] As public relations, the effort was probably doomed from the start. Gingrich's blunter blasts, such as the Campaign for Fair Elections, were probably far more effective. Yet within the House GOP, the document cemented further the new Republican worldview, as this excerpt from the report suggests:

> The Founders intended the U.S. House of Representatives to be that part of the Federal Government closest to the people. It would be the largest legislative chamber, and its members most electorally sensitive to the people and thus most representative of the citizenry. The Founders also wanted the House to be a place of open deliberation, with equality among peers in debating the issues facing the nation.
>
> The House is also the hub of a complex governmental system of separated powers and checks and balances, intended to curb the influence of special interests and limit the size of government. During much of its history, the House operated more or less as the Founders intended. High turnover ensured regular infusions of new ideas and popular impulses. Bipartisanship in committees and Floor debate restrained partisanship on most issues.
>
> But recently the House has strayed far from the Founders' intent. Controlled by only one political party for the last 40 years, the House has undergone drastic change, moving it far from the Founders' intent. The contemporary House of Representatives is neither representative nor democratic, and the government it creates and oversees knows no limits. As a result, the House of Representatives is bordering on illegitimacy in the public mind and even in the writings of prominent congressional observers.

The study drew heavily on the theories of economist Mancur Olson, whose ideas were in renaissance thanks to journalist Jonathan Rauch, who revived them in his 1994 book, *Demosclerosis: The Silent Killer of American Government*. In the view of Olson, and Rauch, increasing "hyperpluralism"—the rise of the interest group state—makes society ungovernable. Entrenched power centers resist change and constantly seek to reapportion the economic pie, rather than expand it.[47]

While such a complex theoretical discussion was probably not of interest to most Americans, the GOP message was, one way or another, getting through: only 18 percent of Americans now said they had a great deal of confidence in Congress.[48] This mood had been building for some time, largely on the strength of forces no political party can control, such as the economy. Yet it is also clear that politicians had been massaging public opinion quite skillfully. While the conclusion of Gingrich and his followers—that incumbent politicians had stacked the deck overwhelmingly in their own favor—was accurate and fundamentally nonpartisan, they were successful in directing public anger toward the Democrats. As we have seen, not even Gingrich was able to resist the blandishments of power. Perhaps more important, during the period when Gingrich was remaking his party's political strategy, parallel, interlocking developments were taking place elsewhere in the electorate that would ultimately result in the 1994 landslide.

4

The Lord's Work

The growth and use . . . by one special interest group of political power which has no effective check is not the fault of
those who achieve power, for it is their right to try. Rather,
the fault is principally on the part of those who, by their in-
activity and silence, allowed it to happen.
                    —*Christian Coalition Leadership Manual*

In June of 1978, at the Virginia Democratic Party's convention in
Colonial Williamsburg, religious broadcaster Marion Gordon
"Pat" Robertson made his first major public foray into politics
since his father's unsuccessful 1966 U.S. Senate reelection campaign,
giving the nominating speech for evangelical car dealer G. Conoly
Phillips, a candidate for the Senate. The Senate contest was of particular interest to Robertson for reasons not of religion or gover-
nance, but blood: the seat for which Phillips sought the Democratic
nomination had been held for two decades by Absalom Willis
Robertson (Pat Robertson's father). Phillips, who said he was moved
to run for the position when God spoke to him one morning, was an
old friend of Robertson's and benefited mightily from the minister's
phenomenal organizing abilities. At the convention, Phillips received an impressive 327 votes on the first ballot, nearly half the
number needed to win. But Phillips's bid for the nomination was
doomed: his evangelical supporters, while fervent and numerous,
were newcomers to politics and not particularly welcome in a
mainly liberal party.[1] His support was rock-hard but it could not be
expanded. Seemingly resigned to Phillips's fate, Robertson warned

the Democrats that the nation's fifty million evangelicals were a "great sleeping giant" of politics that would soon awaken. As society grew increasingly secular and liberal, their alienation would transform into activism. A year later he elaborated on his prediction in a magazine interview: "We have enough votes to run the country. And when the people say, 'We've had enough,' we are going to run the country."[2]

It was increasingly obvious, however, that the Democratic Party was not the vehicle for such a takeover. By 1978, the Virginia Democratic Party was no longer the party Willis Robertson had represented in the Senate from 1946 to 1966. Scripture-quoting segregationists such as the senior Robertson and Bible-thumping conservatives such as his son were now alien to the party's constituency groups. Many evangelicals already knew this themselves; but for the candidacy of Phillips, they would have been more likely to show up at the Republican convention. Indeed, a survey of Phillips delegates at the Democratic convention found that two of five identified themselves as strong Republicans or Republican leaders.[3] Pat Robertson's first foray into politics was also his last major attempt to influence Democratic Party politics.

Robertson's experience with the Virginia Democratic Party was similar to evangelicals' experience with President Jimmy Carter at the national level. The first president to profess to having been "born again," Carter attracted massive evangelical support in 1976. But once in office, Carter followed policies that, in the view of many evangelicals, were not indicative of an evangelical worldview. On the social issues important to evangelicals—abortion, homosexual rights, and the Equal Rights Amendment—Carter was on the wrong side. Nonetheless, Democrats continued to hold on to much of the evangelical vote, in part because many African-Americans were Christian evangelicals. One 1980 poll showed that nearly half of all evangelicals described themselves as Democrats, while only a quarter called themselves Republicans. Nearly a third were not even registered to vote.[4]

In a sense, the political strand of the evangelical movement, such as it then was, found itself in the same position Newt Gingrich was in during the mid- to late-1970s—aware of their potential but thwarted in finding a way to make it manifest. In the end, the movement would avail itself of many of the same techniques and tactics pioneered by the labor unions—techniques that might not always pass muster at the pearly gates.

Pat Robertson's Long and Winding Road

For a long time after his defeat in Williamsburg, Pat Robertson merely dabbled in politics, concentrating most of his energies on his burgeoning broadcast empire. Starting from a tiny UHF station in Portsmouth, Virginia, in 1960, Robertson had been building a nationwide following with his religious talk show, the 700 Club. In 1981, Robertson's Christian Broadcasting Network (CBN) founded the Family Channel, which went on to huge success in the new cable television industry. CBN was a nonprofit entity, registered with the Internal Revenue Service as a strictly religious endeavor and thus exempt from income taxes. Robertson built a for-profit empire around CBN that would eventually make him a very rich man, providing an object lesson in the blessings of exemption from taxation.[5]

While Robertson pursued the business of the Lord, declaring "active partisan politics" to be off-limits, another Virginia minister, Jerry Falwell of Lynchburg, became the dominant political force in the evangelical movement.[6] He was the founder and leader of the newly formed Moral Majority, which by 1980 had more than 400,000 members.[7] Falwell believed that "we need more Christians in politics," and in addition to the lobbying and other activities to which he devoted the Moral Majority, he also aligned himself unabashedly with the presidential campaign of Republican Ronald Reagan in 1980.[8] Falwell and other evangelicals also became involved in congressional races. One group, Christian Voice, devised a "morality rating" of legislators to help it determine whom to support and oppose. It was a technique borrowed from secular ideological organizations such as Americans for Democratic Action: compose a list of litmus votes or positions, then apply the criteria consistently to every candidate. Among the many virtues of this issue-based method for screening candidates was that it neatly sidestepped partisanship, an important facet of many religious political activities, since evidence of partisanship was cause for getting one's tax exemption revoked. Yet the groups walked a fine line; nominally nonpartisan, they openly expressed their preference for conservative Republican candidates and forged alliances with conservative Republican activists such as Paul Weyrich, founder of the Committee for the Survival of a Free Congress.

It was a coy, semantic game. While never literally making endorsements, the groups associated themselves with those politicians they liked, praising them warmly. At a summer 1980 meeting of the Religious Roundtable, an influential nonprofit steering committee of religious conservatives the only presidential candidate to appear was Reagan. "I know you can't endorse me," said Reagan. "I want you to know that I endorse you."[9]

Reagan's election in 1980 and the defeat of numerous liberal Democratic legislators opposed by evangelical groups seemed to signal the coming of age of the movement. But Weyrich and other veteran conservative activists such as Howard Phillips knew better. "Anybody who thinks this group is going to contribute to a political revolution this election is going to be disappointed," Weyrich told *Newsweek*. "The basic problem, only now being overcome, is to get people involved," said Phillips. The movement was just beginning to get organized. As later elections would show, the sleeping giant was still groggy.

While Gingrich laid siege to the Democratic congressional empire, Robertson was emerging from the shadows after undergoing a political revival. He had watched during the early 1980s as Falwell's power and that of the evangelical movement had multiplied. In 1984, Reagan received four-fifths of the evangelical vote, a remarkable shift since the 1976 election, when Republican Gerald Ford pulled only 43 percent of evangelical votes.[10] The Republican Party had assiduously courted evangelicals in 1984, by both conventional and unconventional means. Most unconventionally, Republican National Committee finance chairman Joe Rodgers funneled more than $2 million to evangelical groups through a nonprofit organization he had set up, Americans for Responsible Government.[11] Taking a page from the labor unions' political organizing book, the group used the money to register nonvoters, an ostensibly nonpartisan activity easily manipulated for partisan ends.

Liberals and the media reacted harshly to this strange and often arrogant new force, laying siege to the movement and mocking its pretensions. "The Moral Majority is neither," a popular bumper sticker read. During the Reagan presidency, Falwell seemed to lurch from one controversy to another, defending himself for controversial statements and helping bail out the corrupt empire of his colleague Jim Bakker in 1987. In addition to his public relations problems, Falwell was neither a born politician nor a born organizer. Falwell's empire was in a state of perpetual fiscal crisis, and he proved unable to mobilize his followers into a cohesive political force.

Robertson's media empire, on the other hand, was going great guns with more than $200 million in annual revenues. A Yale-educated lawyer born to a "public" Virginia family, he was much more of a political natural than Falwell. In 1981, he had set up the Freedom Council, a tax-exempt lobbying group dedicated to fighting abortion, pornography, and secular education. The organization had remained largely dormant until 1985, when Robertson decided to use it to get back into politics with a vengeance, gearing up for a run at the presidency. The Freedom Council—despite the dependence of its charitable status on abstaining from political involvement—began developing precinct-level organizations nationwide, frequently involving itself in Republican party and electoral politics. The group was particularly active in a 1986 precinct-delegate election in Michigan created as a proving-ground of sorts for 1988 GOP presidential candidates. Of the council's fourteen staff members, nine were recruiting precinct delegate candidates.[12] At one rally organized by the Freedom Council, Robertson declared, "Michigan will become the first state in America in 1986 to be saying who the Republican candidate for president should be. . . . Christians in Michigan can say we stand for values, we stand for family, we stand for God and country, we stand for liberty and freedom."[13] If there is a distinction between such a statement and the sort of political involvement expressly forbidden to a charitable group by federal law, we are hard put to find it. The analogies with Newt Gingrich's use of GOPAC are striking. Once again, when political power is at stake, the laws designed to prevent abuses do not seem to be sufficient.

Robertson's shading of the laws did not end there. He also

brazenly mingled the activities of his PAC and his nonprofit. At one 1986 fundraiser covered by the *Washington Post,* big contributors were asked to pony up $25,000 each. The money was then split up, with $5,000—the legal limit—going into the PAC and $20,000 going to the Freedom Council.[14] The money going to the Freedom Council, Robertson swore, "is not political money, that is educational money."[15] Another source of funds for the Freedom Council was Robertson's own CBN, which at one point was transferring some $250,000 a month into the group.[16] Media reports alleging political activity by the Freedom Council caused problems with the Internal Revenue Service, which began to hedge on formally approving the council's tax-exempt status. The IRS finally approved the exemption after the council submitted articles of incorporation that stated, "The Freedom Council shall not participate in or intervene in any political campaign on behalf of any candidate for public office."[17] Notwithstanding his promise to the IRS, Robertson continued to use the Freedom Council as his primary organizing vehicle in Michigan and demonstrated sufficient strength to be considered a serious presidential contender by winning roughly half of all the Michigan delegates. A month after the Michigan delegate elections, however, the Freedom Council announced it was disbanding, citing criticism about its involvement in politics as the reason. A month after that, just as an IRS audit of the group was getting started, the *New York Times* disclosed that filings with the IRS by three Robertson tax-exempt operations, including CBN and the Freedom Council, were replete with "incomplete and false information."[18]

In the fall of 1987, as the presidential campaign Robertson intended to run in was heating up, reporters began asking new questions about his use of tax-exempts. The *Washington Post* presented detailed evidence showing that the tax-exempt CBN's mailing list had apparently found its way into the hands of Robertson's presidential campaign, a seemingly illegal use of nonprofit assets.[19] The *Post* also uncovered a questionable financial transaction in which the Robertson campaign, desperate for cash, sold its computer system for $337,000 to a shell company headed by a Robertson campaign official.[20]

The *Post* put it succinctly: "Robertson's blurring of the lines between his charitable activities and his political ambitions has given him a major advantage over other candidates, who did not control the tax-exempt assets of a major corporation."[21] Despite all this negative publicity, Robertson carried on, taking second place in the Iowa caucus. On April 5, however, three former aides flatly accused Robertson of having used the Freedom Council to advance his presidential campaign in an investigative report by NBC News, reigniting the controversy. A few days later, the Robertson campaign was forced to turn over its records to the Internal Revenue Service, and on May 11, Robertson dropped out of the presidential race, announcing that his campaign would be converted into a new political action committee. The controversy over his campaign financing activities quickly subsided. As of the writing of this book—more than seven years after the events in question took place—there has been no known resolution of the IRS inquiry.

The Resurrection . . . and Ralph Reed

I want to be invisible. I do guerilla warfare. I paint my face and travel at night. You don't know it's over until you're in a body bag. You don't know until election night.
—*Ralph Reed, November 9, 1991*

The collapse of the Robertson presidential campaign in 1988 seemed to augur poorly for the minister's political ambitions and those of the religious right at large. Despite nearly a decade of organizing and their important role in the three presidential elections, evangelicals remained a relatively marginal force, unable to expand their influence and support beyond their most committed followers. And while Republican George Bush went on to win the presidential election in part by paying lip service to evangelical issues, his Eastern blueblood roots caused many doubts. Then there was Congress: even if Bush had been willing to push the evangelical agenda, Democrats had retained control of Capitol Hill. Furthermore, by late 1988 rumors abounded in conservative circles that Falwell was planning to fold the Moral Majority, which he did in early 1989.

But a fateful encounter occurred at the Bush inaugural in 1989.

Ralph Reed, a bright young conservative activist who had undergone a religious conversion several years earlier in a Capitol Hill bar, struck up a conversation with Pat Robertson, whose base of operations was near Reed's hometown of Portsmouth, Virginia. Reed was a die-hard Republican activist with extensive campaign experience. In college he had won election to the chairmanship of the College Republican National Committee, helped register voters for Republican Senator Jesse Helms of North Carolina in 1984 and had also worked on the successful Senate campaign of Georgia Republican Mack Mattingly, coming to Washington for a summer to intern in his office. He had helped found Students for America in 1984, a political training group for young conservatives, and had come to believe that "there is a Christian revival going on and that this is changing the American political landscape."[22] He had been able to bridge the often gaping chasm between social and economic conservatives: in 1988, he had worked on the presidential campaign of Jack Kemp, known more for his economic than social conservatism.

Reed asked Robertson what he planned to do now that the campaign was over and the Moral Majority was folding, and Robertson replied that he had received some offers of financial support for a new organization. Reed thought the idea had potential, but he could not resist pointing out to the minister what he thought were some of the mistakes committed by Robertson in his presidential campaign:

> The thing that I specifically raised with him was the fact that his people in Georgia putting together the [Robertson] delegation had bounced one of the leading conservatives because he wasn't a Christian. And I told him that that was rather silly, and in fact counterproductive, and what it had done was make it difficult for his people to build bridges within the party. And he agreed, and did not know that had gone on, and to make a long story short, at the end of the dinner, he pulled me out into the hall and said: "I'm going to start this new organization, it's going to change America; would you like to come work for me?"[23]

While Reed initially declined because he was still working on his doctorate at Emory University, he later reversed himself and thus was present at the birth of the Christian Coalition. Reed brought new thinking to the evangelical movement. His mind-set can also be seen in the name given to Robertson's new group, a striking contrast to Falwell's. Whereas "moral," implies righteousness, Christian is simply suggestive of faith. Whereas "majority" implies dominance, "coalition" implies cooperation.

The Christian Coalition started out with materials from Robertson's presidential campaign, which sold the new group its mailing list and office equipment. The Republican National Committee was an early contributor, putting up some $67,000 in seed money. Despite these clearly political ties and Ralph Reed's professional background, the new group did not organize itself under federal law as a campaign committee. Continuing in the tradition of the Freedom Council, the Christian Coalition was set up under the internal revenue code as a tax-exempt "social welfare organization." Under the tax laws, "social welfare" organizations are those concerned with the "common good and general welfare" of society as well as "civic betterments and improvements."[24]

In its articles of incorporation, the Christian Coalition stated that its principal purpose was "to encourage active citizenship among people professing the Christian faith.

> Other purposes are to support and uphold values and moral principles that accord with the Holy Bible; to defend religious freedom; to enunciate an interpretation of the United States Constitution which is in accordance with the original intention of the framers of the United States Constitution; and to promulgate and teach concern for the sanctity of life, traditional family values, an economic system which fosters individual self-reliance, opposition to tyranny, and faith in God.

The group intended to achieve its goals by means of "education, the publication and distribution of literature, citizenship mobilization, the advocacy of public policy, and representation before public bodies." Other than the oblique reference made to "citizenship mobilization," the articles, which were submitted to the Internal Revenue Service for approval, made no mention of any plans by the group to become involved in political campaigns. That made some sense, since most social welfare organizations do not get involved in elections. They may lobby—in fact, many social welfare organizations lobby extensively—and they may go so far as to tell their membership which politicians they like and which ones they do not like. But social welfare organizations are restricted from directly or indirectly intervening in elections, and involvement in campaigns generally must not be their "primary" purpose. Not only does the IRS prohibit such activity, but the Federal Election Campaign Act requires those that intervene directly in elections to register as political committees.

Notwithstanding these restrictions and the broader IRS guidelines on social welfare organizations being engaged primarily in activities concerning "the common good and general welfare" of society at large, Reed immediately began organizing a nationwide organization that had all the appearances of a campaign group. One of his first steps was to begin bringing recruits to Robertson's headquarters in Chesapeake, Virginia, to learn about politics.

"During the next two days you will participate in one of the most intensive and comprehensive reviews of grassroots political technology in the nation," Reed promised his disciples.[25] "The departure of Ronald Reagan means that Christians can no longer look to the White House to set their agenda or rally their forces," he explained. In addition, "The folding of the Moral Majority has left a vacuum at the grassroots and created the impression that Christian political-involvement is waning." And finally, "The Robertson presidential campaign laid the foundation for a new political movement. It was the beginning, not the end of a new wave of Christian involvement in public policy and politics."[26]

Reed laid out his overarching strategy:

National Christian political organizations have often developed a bad reputation among local leadership because of their propensity to draw financial resources from the grassroots and spend them unwisely or inefficiently at the national level. The results of many such organizations are not impressive, especially in light of their expensive national staffs and large mailing lists.

How can Christian Coalition transcend previous efforts and truly mobilize Christians at the grassroots as citizens, activists, and candidates?

The answer lies in a strategy that is directed at serving the local community. The most effective way to influence public policy in the United States is to organize a strong grassroots company of committed Christians who know and understand how public policy affects them and the world in which they live and work. Mobilizing a trained force of Christian activists at the local levels of government will make it possible for Christians to accomplish results that will astound those who are on the sidelines watching. What Christian Coalition plans to do through grassroots political action by committed, trained and motivated Christians has never been done. It has never been done because it has never been tried at the magnitude that Christian Coalition plans to do it.[27]

He listed seven main objectives for the early 1990s:

1. Chartered affiliates in 48 states
2. Chapters in 2,000 counties
3. Membership of 250,000
4. Precinct captains in 10,000 precincts
5. 2,500 graduates from Leadership Schools
6. Annual budget of $5 million
7. Media program reaching ten million people

The group's structure would closely resemble that of a political party, with regional subdivisions, state affiliates, congressional district chairmen, county chapters, and precinct captains. In a hint of what was to come, the manual noted that structuring state affiliates according to a state's congressional districts "will work very well for the purposes of the Christian Coalition."[28] The training schools were also reminiscent of a political party, as were the Christian Coalition's plans to hold an annual national convention. Affiliates would be established in every state. "Some states are more prepared to be organized as a result of the 1988 presidential campaign of Pat Robertson," the manual noted.[29] But wait. Wasn't the Robertson campaign a registered political committee, and the Christian coalition a tax-exempt "social welfare" organization?

Reed has said the connections between the Robertson campaign and the Christian Coalition were minimal. The Christian Coalition "emerged from that campaign in the sense that some of the lists from that campaign were utilized. But I think it is fair to say that it is a clean break and that it was a new phenomenon undertaken."[30] Reed acknowledges that the Christian Coalition received funds from the GOP but minimized the significance. "We would have accepted a contribution from the DNC if they had offered it," he said.[31] Had the Democrats, not the Republicans, provided the money, it still seems clear that the Christian Coalition's first steps were taking it in the direction of political involvements that should probably have invalidated its tax exemption and made it subject to the full range of federal disclosure laws. In the event, the result was to unleash a powerful, secretly partisan, unregulated fundraising machine on the political stage. Few could see it at the time, but five years hence, its influence would be decisive in the 1994 elections.

Reed also set about composing a "leadership manual" for his new recruits. A handbook for political action, the manual was a remarkable document, a sophisticated how-to guide for winning elections. It would have made the National Education Association or the AFL-CIO proud, though it did not do much to bolster the coalition's claims to be involved strictly in voter education and policy advocacy. For example, Dick Weinhold, finance director for Robertson's presidential campaign and the founder of the Christian Coalition's first state affiliate (Texas) in 1990, contributed a detailed sixty-nine-page chapter on fundraising, including a sample minute-by-minute schedule for fundraising events ("7:34, invocation; 7:35, Pledge of Allegiance; 7:36, National Anthem; 7:38, Begin dinner"); suggested songs for such events; and provided a list of twenty-three "Tips for the Dinner Chairman." A chapter on political speech-making was adapted from a paper published by the National Republican Congressional Committee. William Fisher, a University of Texas economist and former corporate lobbyist, composed most of the original chapters on political organizing.

While the manual made occasional references to participation in the Democratic Party, it also urged recruits to "contact politically active lay leaders in area churches, Christians active in the local Republican Party, friends in your church or bible study, veterans of the Robertson presidential campaign, former and present Christian candidates and officeholders, and leaders of other pro-family organizations."[32] The manual did not suggest contacting Christians active in the local Democratic Party, or the veterans of any Democratic presidential campaigns.

The coalition's intentions came through in other ways as well. For example, the manual reminded activists of Abraham Lincoln's four rules for winning elections: (1) obtain a complete list of voters, (2) determine how they will vote, (3) contact the favorable voters, and (4) get your voters to the polls. "Lincoln's four campaign laws are the foundation of modern grassroots politics," the manual observed.[33] It instructed activists to assemble canvassing questionnaires designed "to weed out unfavorable voters without wasting a great deal of time." In addition to issue-based questions, a suggested questionnaire contained two obviously partisan queries, "Bush or Dukakis support in 1988?" and "Republican or Democrat?"[34]

Why would such information be of interest to a nonpartisan group? "The only reason why we wanted to know party affiliation was because we would always like to know what percentage of our members are Republicans and Democrats," asserted Reed. "It is for purely internal informational purposes only." Yet the manual makes no reference to using such information for internal information purposes. Indeed, the manual said quite explicitly that with the canvassing information "you will know those who are your allies and those who are not."[35] (At some point in the second half of 1994, long after most of his disciples were trained, and possibly after the election, Reed removed the partisan questions from the suggested questionnaire.)[36]

A similar mind-set marked the manual's discussion of targeting voters, "Saints, Sinners and Savables: Targeting Your Votes." It explained the importance of understanding where one's own candidate is strongest and weakest:

> In the jargon of political campaigns, these areas of strength and weakness are given religious names: Saints, Sinners and Savables. The saints are your supporters, the sinners are supporting the other candidate and the savables are somewhere between. The district should be studied precinct by precinct to identify voting patterns in past elections. Once this is done, each precinct is prioritized. The ones that have consistently

supported candidates in your party in the last three elections by as much as 60% are saints. The precinct that delivered the highest vote for your party will be the first precinct on the priority list and will receive first claim on the campaign's resources.

Those precincts that went for the other party by 60% or better are sinners. Leave them alone! Do not waste your resources on them.[37]

Tellingly, after first using the words "your candidate," the manual began substituting "your party." The message then became even clearer: "A precinct that has traditionally voted for the Democrat seventy percent of the time is not likely to suddenly change and vote Republican," the book warned, "even if the Republican candidate spends all of his or her time campaigning in that precinct.[38]

While there is a single section in the book on lobbying, it is at base a training manual for campaign operatives:

Once you have identified your precinct priorities, you will have the beginning of your plan of attack. Always remember that the purpose of the election campaign is to get more votes than the other side and win the election so your candidate can serve in office and accomplish what he or she had campaigned to do. This should be obvious, but after watching how some candidates approach their campaigns, it must not be as obvious as it seems. Keep your focus on your purpose![39]

Leaving aside the issue of partisanship, all of this is very sound political advice. Indeed, the manual is chock full of good advice—about how to win elections.

Between 1989 and 1994, using the manual and the classes, Reed developed the Christian Coalition into a training school for evangelical campaign operatives. In that sense it was strikingly similar to GOPAC, which during this period also put a heavy emphasis on teaching conservatives how to wage campaigns. GOPAC had a manual as well, "Flying Upside Down" (the title is a metaphor for unconventionality), through which it dispensed similar advice on fundraising and other such topics. And one of the most distinctive aspects of GOPAC was the training tapes it produced featuring advice on campaign tactics from Gingrich and his chief lieutenant, political consultant Joseph Gaylord.

Practiced on such a broad scale, this was a new development for the conservative movement. In years past, Republicans had tended to rely mainly on money to wage their campaigns. Grassroots organizing and training were tactics of the left, particularly of labor.

5

Insurrection

Being historically conditioned by a certain stage in the
growth of a revolution, a mass insurrection is never purely
spontaneous.

—*Leon Trotsky,* Russian Revolution

W hile the Christian Coalition was interplanting its grassroots network with the one that GOPAC and the Republican Party had been developing under Newt
Gingrich's direction, the GOP began to survey the electoral landscape for 1994 and found considerable cause for optimism.

In June of 1994, Haley Barbour went to see Newt Gingrich and
Senate minority leader Robert Dole to discuss some of these auspicious events. Republicans had just won upset victories in two special
House elections for seats that had long been held by Democrats. The
three men also reviewed the GOP's prospects for the upcoming
midterm election, noting with amazement that their consultants
were estimating 180 "competitive" House races—an unusually high
number.

"This isn't just going to be a good year," Barbour told Dole and
Gingrich, "This could be a tidal wave."

"The problem is," replied Dole, "our opportunities exceed our resources."[1] They concluded they were on the verge of a big victory,
and decided to use that perception to gather massive resources for
the autumn campaigns. The finance laws, which both parties already viewed as mere obstacles to be evaded in pursuit of power, are
never easier to twist, stretch or break than when victory is in one's
grasp.

Barbour proposed to increase the Republican National Committee (RNC) budget by $12 million, committing $10 million of that to direct spending on campaigns. He pledged to seek authorization from the members of the committee to borrow $5 million from banks, on the condition that Dole and Gingrich commit to helping him raise extra funds. The three musketeers of GOP fundraising then set out to fulfill their pact.

Dole and Gingrich became more aggressive in their fundraising pitches. Gingrich, in particular, came on strong, meeting regularly with political action committee directors for all the major corporations and trade associations. In late September, as things continued to look good for the Republicans, he began warning them to give more money to Republicans. "For anybody that's not on board now, it's going to be the two coldest years in Washington," he threatened.[2] At another meeting, he warned business executives of the folly of supporting Democrats, echoing his own remarks to GOPAC six years earlier, saying they would be portrayed as "the enemy of normal Americans."[3]

The Road Show

As part of their newly aggressive fundraising campaign, ten weeks before the election, Gingrich, Barbour, and Senate minority leader Robert Dole embarked on a low-profile, high-stakes fundraising "road show" around the country—luncheons in New York and Dallas, a dinner in Los Angeles, two events in Minneapolis-St. Paul, Phoenix, and Denver—hitting up wealthy executives for a massive last-minute infusion of cash. Barbour told us that "even though we largely fund our operation on small contributions, we knew that if we were going to get this last $10 million, it had to be in big chunks at a time."

Barbour's slide presentation detailed the party's special election victories and described the party's prospects as indicated by polling data: a plurality of voters were saying they planned to vote Republican; Barbour interpreted this as a sign that the party was headed for a House takeover. Dole and Gingrich would then get up and tell the businessmen how much better life would be for them under a GOP Congress. The Republicans solicited huge donations from those in attendance, and many came through, giving $25,000, $50,000, $100,000, and more. Often the money came straight out of the treasuries of the companies they ran. Donations this large are usually difficult to sneak past the Federal Election Commission. While individuals can give up to $25,000 per election to a political party, most give just a few hundred or a few thousand. But in this case, the donations were primarily solicited as soft money, which the FEC is largely powerless to regulate since the funds are supposedly not used to influence federal elections.[4] Theoretically, soft money which can comprise up to 40 percent of the RNC's operating expenses, is not to be used for direct campaign expenditures. But money is fungible, and as Barbour readily admits, these contributions subsidized campaign spending. Until 1994, hard money still dwarfed soft money, but Barbour managed to equalize the ratio. "Typically we would not even be close to paying for 40 percent of our operational expenditures in non-FEC dollars," he observed. But this time, Republicans actually came close to bumping up against the limit. In the end, the RNC put $20.2 million into campaigns—more than doubling its previous record of $9 million.

It is a big country. "One of the things I learned, particularly when we went out to Minnesota, is that if you work hard in a state you can find a whole lot of people who will give you either ten, fifteen, or one hundred thousand dollars that you never knew were there," said Barbour. The Minnesota events pulled in some $750,000, an unprecedented success. Barbour's account of this fundraising drive is modest. Taking their cue from Gingrich's extortionate appeals in Washington, the three Republican leaders informed contributors that their party was likely to take over Congress and implied dire consequences for those who did not chip in. Former Republican Senator David Durenberger, who attended two of the mid-October meetings in Minnesota, described the pitch as "pretty blatant." Many contributors, Durenberger said, are sincerely motivated by ideology and partisan loyalty. But others, he added, "just buy influence so blatantly [that] it's hard to believe. Most of the people I work with are pretty careful. The real good corporations are very very responsible and careful about how they spend their money. But the ones that are dominated by an individual or are privately held . . . hell, they'll do anything. You just tell them it's legal and they aren't going to get in trouble and they'll give you half a million dollars without batting an eye."[5]

Actually, sometimes they will give you $2.5 million. That is how much Barbour extracted from the Amway Corporation after he made his presentation at the company headquarters in Ada, Michigan.[6] The funds went to a critical project of Barbour's—a new television studio that the RNC had begun building in 1993. The studio had enabled the RNC to begin airing a weekly television program on cable television as well as to provide Republican candidates with state-of-the-art production facilities for their advertisements. It was all part of Barbour's larger effort to have the RNC take advantage of a range of new communications technologies; another was "broadcast" faxing, in which a mass mailing is sent via the phone lines to hundreds or even thousands of affiliates simultaneously. This helped Republicans run "a strong message campaign," part of Barbour's strategy of "rebuilding the party from the bottom up." As part of the strategy, Barbour's staff developed a list of 800 "opinion leaders" that was dubbed "the Echo Chamber." Each received briefing papers and talking points on an almost daily basis—sometimes several times in a day. Later the list was expanded to include some 350 to 400 conservative talk radio hosts, an increasingly powerful political force. (House Republicans, at the direction of Gingrich and Dick Armey, also set up a fax pipeline to sympathetic talk radio hosts.)

Amway is a privately held direct marketing conglomerate founded and controlled by Richard DeVos, with revenues of $5 billion a year from its door-to-door sales of household cleaning items, vitamins, and dietary supplements and other products commonly sold by retailers. The company, which has far-flung global operations, has a great deal of business in Washington. It has fought with both the Federal Trade Commission and the Food and Drug Administration over its selling practices and is perennially concerned with various arcane—but high-dollar—tax law matters.

Shortly after Republicans assumed control of Congress in 1995, Amway began cashing in. The company, which is part owner of a telecommunications concern, helped persuade Senate majority leader Dole to support a series of amendments to telecommunications industry deregulation legislation that benefited the company's interests.[7] Meanwhile, Gingrich's tax-exempt foundation (to which Amway also contributed) launched a blistering attack on the Food and Drug Administration, calling for its abolition.[8]

GOPAC Fundraising: Newt Gingrich, Inc.

GOPAC's much-vaunted candidate training tapes were not the only service it provided to Republican candidates. Behind the scenes, GOPAC was steering tens of thousands of dollars to Republicans challenging incumbent Democrats, and in so doing, skirting the edge of legal permissibility and violating the spirit of disclosure rules. For the first time in years, Republicans were contesting virtually every potentially vulnerable Democratic candidate in 1994. Former GOPAC director Kay Riddle believes the group's role in helping produce this bumper crop of candidates cannot be overestimated. In the 1980s, Riddle said, "there were only two people who believed we could take over Congress, and they were Bo Calloway and Newt Gingrich. And between the two of them, they began a process of convincing people that with the right candidates and the right philosophical base, we could in fact do that."[9]

Recall that GOPAC was founded to support state legislative candidates, not aspirants to the U.S. House of Representatives or the U.S. Senate. But in the 1994 campaign, GOPAC widened its mandate considerably. While most Republican candidates for the U.S. House either denied they had received financial help from GOPAC or would not talk about the subject, a few, including Brian Bilbray of California and Kevin Vigilante of Rhode Island, acknowledge that GOPAC funneled money to them indirectly though they were unsure of how much support they had really received.[10]

GOPAC, it turns out, engaged in a "bundling" operation similar to the one the asphalt lobby assembled to help Bob Carr. Many of the contributions can be reconstructed by computer analysis of the publicly reported giving patterns of GOPAC backers, whose identities we learned from a confidential internal GOPAC roster. Under an extremely conservative interpretation of the pattern that emerges, GOPAC used this method to funnel at least $200,000 to GOP House candidates around the country (see Table 1). A less strict accounting would boost that figure by $100,000 or more.

Table 1. GOPAC's Targeted Individual Giving Program

GOP House candidate	State/district	Total amount contributed (dollars)	Status of contest
Kevin Vigilante	R.I.-1	30,000	Challenger, lost
Ron Freeman	Mo.-5	22,000	Open, lost
George Nethercutt	Wash.-5	20,000	Challenger, won
Mark Neumann '94	Wis.-1	19,000	Challenger, won
Mark Neumann '93	Wis.-1	16,000	Special open seat, lost
Frank Lucas	Okla.-6	16,000	Special open scat, won
Jim Nalepa	Ill.-3	15,000	Challenger, lost
David McIntosh	Ind.-2	11,000	Challenger, won
Don Devine	Md.-5	11,000	Challenger, lost
Frederick Levering	Pa.-5	10,000	Challenger, lost
Bob Barr	Ga.-7	9,000	Challenger, won
Steve Gill	Tenn.-6	7,000	Challenger, lost
Ed Munster	Conn.-2	7,000	Challenger, lost
Steve LaTourette	Ohio-19	6,000	Challenger, won
Jon Christensen	Nebr.-2	6,000	Challenger, won
Total		205,000	
Win–Loss	7–8		

Note: Candidates with less than $6,000 in receipts from GOPAC members were not listed.

The records show that GOPAC backers made at least $20,000 in contributions to George Nethercutt, the Republican who defeated House Speaker Thomas Foley; at least $20,000 to Mark Neumann of Wisconsin, who upset a Democratic incumbent to win a House seat on his second try in 1994; and so on. While this fundraising program is of questionable legality, its intent is indisputably contrary to the intent of the law. When a PAC raises money for candidates, it is required to disclose its expenses publicly even if none of the funds pass through the PAC's bank account. Yet right beneath the noses of the press and the Federal Election Commission, GOPAC was operating a covert fundraising scheme, whereby the group channeled money from individuals to Republican House contenders without disclosing GOPAC's role. That scheme—which involved contacting sympathetic individuals and encouraging them to give directly to favored candidates—undermines GOPAC's claim to regulatory exemption. "Yes, [GOPAC officials] will call occasionally and say,

'We need a little help here,' or send a note and tell you, 'If you could possibly help this one,' " said one GOPAC contributor, Claudine Cox.[11] She told us that the letters would say, "There is a very fine person running for Congress, and if you could possibly see a way to help with a donation, and of course that would go directly to the candidate, because your GOPAC money goes directly to the states, for state offices." No one could argue in good faith that this strategy is not a direct attempt to influence a federal election.

Newt Gingrich and GOPAC were not alone in their cavalier attitude toward the campaign finance laws. His allies on the Senate side included Phil Gramm of Texas. In the 1994 election's final days, Gramm, the ambitious chairman of the National Republican Senatorial Committee (NRSC), had already contributed the legal limit to each candidate. But Gramm wanted to do more.

On October 31, 1994, the NRSC made a $50,000 "soft money" contribution to the National Right to Life Committee's political action committee. The next day, it gave the group another $50,000, then $60,000 more on November 3, and a final $15,000 on November 5. In a letter accompanying the donations, the NRSC's general counsel stated that the contribution was to be used "for good government activities that are consistent with your organization's not-for-profit character." In addition, the lawyer warned, "utilizing any of this money in any way to influence a federal election is strictly prohibited."

Some of the money went to pay for push-polls on behalf of pro-life Senate candidates in Tennessee, Michigan, Minnesota, and Pennsylvania. As we will examine fully in chapter 9, push-polls aim to discredit a political candidate by disseminating damaging information about him or her under the guise of a legitimate survey of voter opinion. Over 100,000 of the calls were made in a three-day period. In at least two of the states where many of the calls were made, Minnesota and Pennsylvania, the Republican Senate candidate won by a narrow margin. (This incident is discussed in greater detail in chapter 9.)

After the election, Gramm was meeting with reporters and editors of the *Washington Post* to talk about his presidential candidacy. While they were not aware of the push-poll, the *Post* reporters asked about the Right to Life donations. "I made a decision," Gramm blurted out, "to provide some money to help activate pro-life voters in key states where they would be pivotal to the election." He later called the *Post* to retract his comments, asserting that he had misspoken.[12]

That does not appear to be the case, as the push-poll came to light when an employee of the telemarketing company that placed the calls spoke to reporters. Presented with the findings of our investigation, a high-level source close to Gramm with firsthand knowledge confirmed the entire transaction, acknowledging that the NRSC deliberately violated the law and calling the move "stupid." But like many a Washington operative, the source's primary objection to the move was not that it evaded the campaign laws, but that it had the potential to be detected. The source suggested it would have been far safer to do the following: "Go call five guys you know, who really want to help but are up to their [contribution] limits, and say, 'Hey, you want to help? Why don't you go give X-thousand dollars to the National Right to Life and they don't report it.' "

Of course, this is exactly the strategy GOPAC followed, and it makes a mockery of the central tenet of American election law. The issue is not whether the Republicans deserved to win back a congressional majority, or whether the outcome of the elections might have been different without such massive infusions of cash. The point is that the American voter is deprived of information crucial to making decisions in the voting booth when disclosure laws are violated. Many have also argued persuasively that the influence of money in politics can dilute the power of the ideas that are supposed to underlie partisan differences, and this is never truer than when money is spent secretly. It was their lock on special-interest money and the leveraging of the frank that enabled the Democratic Party to maintain hegemony in the House of Representatives for forty years. But if, in 1994, the Republican Party defeated the Democrats at their own game by adopting its own illegitimate fundraising tactics, it would cast a measure of doubt on the much-touted ideological basis of their victory.

God Takes Sides

The Christian Coalition did not rely solely on spiritual vigor in the 1994 elections, either. Its last-minute efforts set the stage for the moment when the now well-trained Republican revolutionary forces and the public mood would converge to produce an electoral explosion. In September 1994, it convened a "Road to Victory" conference at the Hilton hotel in downtown Washington, D.C., site of many a political soirée, to help plan for the election and build momentum. While nominally a nonpartisan affair, those in attendance frequently dropped the pretense, notably Pat Robertson himself.

"They call me a radical," Pat Robertson complained of the Democrats in the opening speech. "Well, just because I used to be a Democrat is no reason for them to call me by their name. You know, for most of my life I was a Democrat. I grew up in the party of Harry Truman, when that party still stood for what was good and decent in this country, when, like Harry Truman, it represented mainstream America and mainstream values. But starting back in the 1960s, the Democrats began their leftward march into the liberal fever swamps, and I, like millions of Americans, just couldn't follow. As Ronald Reagan used to say, I didn't leave the Democratic Party, the Democratic Party left me."[13]

While the major public events were devoted to political speechmaking, Ralph Reed and other coalition operatives got down to the real business of the weekend in smaller presentations, instructing their followers in the do's and don'ts of political activism and laying out their campaign strategy. "Our objective is to get out thirty million non-partisan voter guides in the churches in November," said Reed at one such meeting. "We won't be advocating the election or defeat of any candidate. We won't be endorsing any candidate. They are purely informational and non-partisan."

Yet Reed's associates did not seem to hear him. "There's a lot of election opportunities this year," voter guide coordinator and long-time political activist Charles "Chuck" Cunningham told the group. Normally a taciturn man, Cunningham's excitement was palpable. "Congressman Newt Gingrich of Georgia, who is the House Republican Whip, stated that 'if we Republicans gain the numbers of House seats under Clinton that we gained under Carter, we will elect a Republican House Speaker.' However, absolute control may not be necessary for real policy change. Congressman Steny Hoyer and the Democratic House leadership admitted that 'if we Democrats lose 20 seats in the House in this midterm election, the effective ability to pass programs will be jeopardized.'"

While voter registration efforts and other programs were important, Cunningham felt the voter guides would be the most important project of the year. Pat Garland, head of the Georgia chapter of the coalition, endorsed Cunningham's view, calling the voter guides "the heartbeat of the Christian Coalition. Bottom line, what this guy's doing . . . that's our life story, that's our life blood."

As we noted earlier in this volume, voter guides have a long tradition in American politics, and groups across the political spectrum issue them. They are perfectly legal as long as they are nonpartisan, as the coalition's guides claimed to be. Traditionally, however, voter guides are rather complicated documents listing how a legislator voted on numerous issues, sometimes dozens. Oftentimes, the information is presented in a complicated graph or grid form, in very small print, and the guides have been targeted at sophisticated voters who are willing to take the time to figure them out. As the coalition's Cunningham has pointed out, this greatly limits their effectiveness. The Christian Coalition's guides were different. Distributed in handbill form, they were a simple table, in large print, listing no more than ten issues and sometimes as few as four. The issues were stated simply: "Balanced Budget Amendment," "Term Limits for Congress," "Homosexuals in the Military." The tables were printed on single-page handbills or postcards. Taken as a whole, the effect was to make the guides seem like campaign fliers. Simple as it sounds, these were major innovations in the long tradition of voter guides.

"The beauty of voter guides is the efficient and effective means by which they allow us to communicate with the electorate, educate voters, and bypass an expensive and biased media," continued Cunningham. "Now some pastors may be concerned about the legal liability in distributing this type of election material. These voter guides are non-partisan. They do not advocate the election of any one candidate. There is absolutely zero legal problem in distributing this information in a church." Later, however, Cunningham let slip that the coalition was "constantly under attack from the FEC and the IRS."

Cunningham urged the activists to target only the competitive races. "Just because there's an election doesn't mean that you have to produce and distribute a voter guide," he said. However, he warned them not to be too selective, since "that's sort of a grey area in legal matters." Cunningham made another important observation: "The voter guide does no good if you have candidates who are identical on issues, because there's no distinction."

Another part of the strategy was to wait until just a few days before the election to spring the voter guides on "the opposition." Explained Cunningham, "It's in their interest to attack the credibility of the voter guide and that's why you don't want to release it weeks before, even though it will be shipped weeks before the election. You want to hold it until that last Sunday because if they start raising doubts about the voter guide, you're going to have a real skittish pastor that's just going to pull them. You've distributed them. You had a commitment that they were going to be distributed and he reads in the paper that candidate so and so says that this misrepresents his position on the issues and then it becomes a public relations problem and he pulls them."

More important than GOPAC, more vital to Republican victory than Senator Gramm's dealings, on a par with the political party itself in many areas was the Christian Coalition. It is no exaggeration to assert that the GOP would still be Congress's minority party without the group. And it is equally true that the coalition's tactics were characterized neither by Christian charity nor by adherence to the spirit of the law.

October 30, 1994, was Ralph Reed's D-Day, which in this case meant "drop day." More than twenty million voter guides, which had arrived in churches across America two weeks before but had remained under lock and key, were unleashed on the electorate. In some critical areas, in addition to distributing them at churches, the group mailed voter guides to its members in postcard form and urged them to run off photocopies for distribution at polling places. "Those two together, the mail combined with the church distribution, were really critical," Reed said. The effect was dramatic, amounting to a multimillion dollar advertising campaign for some candidates and against others. Typically, the beneficiaries were Republicans while the victims were Democrats.

In interviews, Republicans and Democrats alike indicated the voter guides were important factors in the campaigns. The case of former Democratic Representative Don Johnson of Georgia is a powerful example of what the guides could do. "When we did some polling in 1992, I had a pretty high support level among the people who consider themselves to be evangelical or fundamentalist Christians," said Johnson, a conservative Democrat who is a Baptist deacon.[14] "I think that's because the Christian Coalition hadn't really worked on them." Though the group did distribute a voter guide on Johnson in 1992, it was only done on a modest scale. Two years later, after the coalition blanketed his district with a voter guide accusing him of taking all manner of liberal positions, Johnson found that religious voters were almost uniformly against him.

One incident in particular during Johnson's 1994 campaign showed the power of the voting guides. After a frustrating final week of campaigning in which he had attempted to rebut the charges made against him in the guides, Johnson was doing some last-minute campaigning near a polling place on Election Day when he saw a woman carrying a coalition guide. He approached the woman as she entered the polling booth and unsuccessfully sought to give her a pamphlet stating his positions. Pointing to the coalition voter guide the woman was carrying, he implored, "Don't believe everything that's on that card." But the woman merely turned and walked away. "When she came back out, she made it a point to come up to me, and said 'Listen, these people are Christians. They don't lie.' "[15]

Many Democrats complained bitterly that the voter guides distorted their positions. Arizona's Sam Coppersmith, a Democratic congressman running for the U.S. Senate, said the guide wrongly claimed he opposed the balanced budget constitutional amendment. Coppersmith said he tried to point out the distortions in the voter guide to the press, but "reporters, being relatively work averse, basically let it go as a piece of paper."[16]

"Not only were they [the coalition] slanted against me, but they misinformed about my votes," said another defeated Arizona Democrat, Karan English. "They just outright lied about what I did."[17]

"It's interesting that they said I was against the balanced budget amendment, when I was a co-sponsor of the balanced budget amendment," said ousted Virginia Democrat Leslie Byrne, "that I had voted for obscene art when there was a specific amendment in the [National Endowment for the Arts act] to take out obscene art.

It was purely political in terms of what they chose to put in that brochure and how they misrepresented positions."[18]

"It never even occurred to me in any shape or form that this was an objective organization that was interested in distributing information," said Eric Fingerhut, former Democratic congressman from Ohio, who was ousted by Republican Steve LaTourette. "This was a private coalition of people trying to defeat me."[19] This is not what one would expect from a group that exists ostensibly to generate support for a broad, national "social welfare" agenda.

Fingerhut accused the Christian Coalition of seeking to exploit a state controversy over so-called outcome-based education (OBE). "There was a category that said LaTourette opposed outcome-based education, and Fingerhut voted for outcome-based education," he recalled.

> Well you know, I had a number of conversations with the Christian Coalition people about education issues. First of all, outcome-based education was a state controversy, it wasn't even a federal controversy. If you pressed them, they were opposed to the [Federal] Goals 2000 bill because some of these fluff-type education requirements were embodied in there. But the problem is that I voted against Goals 2000, somewhat uncharacteristically for me, but I did, mostly because I thought ultimately it was a bunch of bureaucratic gobbledygook and there wasn't really any money going to education. When I asked them about that, the only thing they could come back with was H.R. 6, which was the Elementary and Secondary Education Act, which you really have to stretch to possibly find anything that could be called OBE. But accuse them of misleading literature . . . and they point to a 1,500 page document and they'll find some line in there somewhere that justifies their position.[20]

Interestingly, the coalition rated only Ohio candidates on the OBE issue, despite the group's ostensible focus on national issues. Reed acknowledged that the coalition tried to emphasize local issues. "We did an awful lot of polling, not necessarily state by state, but nationally and regionally, to determine what the issues were that were on people's minds, and tried to skew the voter guides in the direction of what was on peoples' minds as we moved through the country."[21]

Another defeated Ohio Democrat, former U.S. Representative Ted Strickland, told a similar story. The voter guide issued by the coalition for his race

> consisted of some truths, some partial truths and some outright lies or falsehoods. For example, it indicated that I supported public funding of abortions. Now that's something that in a political sense I wouldn't want spread around to all the churches, but it was accurate. I never criticized them for that because it was an accurate assessment of my performance as a member of Congress. But then other accusations were real stretches. For example, I don't remember the exact words they used, but they accused me of voting to establish a national school board—Goals 2000. That was a real stretch. Because I voted against an amendment which would have cut the funding for the National Endowment for the Arts by 40 percent, they interpreted that as that I supported funding obscene art. . . . So in those kinds of ways they really crossed the line.[22]

Christian Coalition officials blamed such complaints on sour grapes and, less subjectively, the refusal of many Democratic candidates to respond to the group's questionnaires. "They've really got nobody to blame but themselves, because they refused to even respond to the questionnaire, and that left us no choice but to rely upon their voting record," said Reed.[23] Many of the ousted incumbent Democrats admitted they had not responded to the coalition's requests for their stands on the issues. "I figured that they were just going to do it anyway, that they were just locked in," said Kentucky Democrat Tom Barlow.[24] "I think that it's fairly pointless in terms of how they approach Democratic candidates," said Byrne.[25] Johnson said there were "value judgments built into the questions."[26]

Indeed, Johnson's experience suggests answering the questionnaire may not have mattered. In 1992, he refused to answer the questionnaire and partly blamed himself when the Christian Coalition issued its own interpretations of his positions. Johnson concluded that he had given the group an opening by failing to tell them where he stood: "What they did was they picked out things that were not in my favor, at least with their group, they put 'opposed' or 'favored'—whatever the opposite was that their group wanted— and then when it came down to a question where I was consistent to what their group wanted, they put 'no response.'"

In 1994, he decided it would be smarter to cooperate and fill out the group's questionnaire. One of the questions, he recalled, asked his position on requiring parental notification when minors seek to obtain abortions. "I had consistently voted for that," he said. "Well, they put that I was opposed to it. My answer on the [questionnaire] response was that I was in favor of parental notification [but] still they put the answers that they wanted to put in there. And they didn't have any no-responses this time, because I did respond to them. But they took different answers and put their own interpretive spin on it." Reed denied this: "If and when they responded to the questionnaire they were sent by us, we listed the answers they sent us, even if we didn't agree with them."

Another complaint was that the coalition appeared to be targeting races. Coalition officials freely acknowledged that they were selective about which races they profiled. Reed said that the coalition sent extra voter guides to its members in "between 75 and 100 of the highest-profile districts."[27]

"In some cases, you have a challenger to a seat that never even appeared on radar, as far as polling data," said Jeff Barren, executive director of the New York state chapter. "We might have chosen for the sake of space not to even include a race like that. We looked at every race and tried to see what the significance of each race was, if they were considered important to our particular constituency in that given district or area, and made our determinations from there."[28] While the law does not require interest groups to rate every candidate in every race, it does require groups to rate candidates in any reasonably competitive contest. But Democrats complained that the coalition seemed to be targeting critical "swing" districts. At one point, Byrne said, some congressional Democrats serving swing districts discussed exploring a class action lawsuit over the practice. (No such suit has yet been filed.)

There are also indications that Christian Coalition members co-

ordinated their activities with Republican campaigns and sometimes even actually worked in those campaigns. Fingerhut cites
local news accounts repeating vows by Christian Coalition officials
to defeat him. "They were explicit about it. Of course they had
meetings on a regular basis. They had my opponent . . . he spoke at
the meeting a number of times and people spoke up about the campaign a number of times. I was never invited or even considered as
someone who ought to come to speak and address issues."[29] Kevin
Bishop, press secretary to Steve Stockman, the Republican who defeated Judiciary Committee chairman Jack Brooks, recalled that the
campaign was given stacks of voter guides by the Christian Coalition, which campaign volunteers then distributed.[30] In Oklahoma,
Republican Senate nominee James Inhofe was caught on tape telling
a Baptist minister, "Be sure to go down to the headquarters and pick
up the Christian Coalition voting thing."[31]

An incident similar to the Stockman case was accidentally uncovered in the hotly contested race between Republican Ron Freeman
and Democrat Karen McCarthy for an open Missouri seat in the
House. A liberal Presbyterian minister had ordered 100 copies of the
guide in the summer, out of curiosity. One afternoon shortly before
the election, a Freeman campaign worker appeared with a stack of
guides. "He said, 'I'm with the Freeman campaign and here are the
voter guides that you ordered,' " the pastor told the *Kansas City
Star*.[32] The aide also had a copy of the pastor's original order form.
"This is what blows my mind," said the pastor; "he had the order
form I sent to Chesapeake, Va." A Freeman campaign official told
the paper that Freeman's workers had distributed the guides to
some two dozen churches. "When we're asked to help distribute literature that will be helpful to us, we're glad to comply," he explained. Such coordination between an interest group and political
campaigns is distinctly illegal under federal campaign law. Said
Reed: "We do not want campaigns distributing those voter guides.
And if they do, to the best of my knowledge, it would be without our
knowledge or authorization."

While reporters sometimes covered Democratic claims of impropriety by the Christian Coalition, the coverage tended to be
very superficial. Our review of media reports on the voter guides
reveals that while Democratic charges about the guides were

quoted often, reporters rarely went to any lengths to verify or refute statements that the Christian Coalition was making about where the candidates stood on the issues. That lack of in-depth reporting is regrettable, because the evidence regarding the Christian Coalition's partisan orientation is more than anecdotal. Democrats who lost their reelection campaigns naturally and quite emotionally believe they were victims of a partisan hit, and a closer look at the voter guides confirms many of their charges. Rather than simply seeking to inform voters of where candidates stood on the issues, the guides give every appearance of having been designed with the explicit intention of influencing voting decisions in favor of Republicans.[33] Why, in the absence of a pure ideological divergence between the parties, would the coalition do this? The answers, in our opinion, are two. First, officials made the not unreasonable judgment that they could accomplish more of their agenda with the Republicans in power. Second, it is indisputable that the leaders of the Christian Coalition are themselves partisan Republicans.

Guiding Manipulation

This manipulation occurred on several levels. To begin with, Republicans and Democrats were portrayed in the voter guides as agreeing on very little. Indeed, in 74 percent of House race voter guides and 73 percent of Senate race guides we studied, the nominees from the two parties were shown to agree on nothing. When the two candidates did agree, it was usually just on one issue out of five or ten. That is unusual, because, despite representing different political parties, in most states and congressional districts, both candidates generally reflect the ideology and economic concerns of their prospective constituents, agreeing on far more than they disagree. The reason candidates were portrayed as being in almost total conflict was that the coalition manipulated the content of the guides, changing the issues from race to race. If the two candidates in district A agreed on abortion, for instance, that issue was dropped from the guide; in its place was something they disagreed on, gays in the military, perhaps. If the two candidates in district B agreed on gays in the military but not on abortion, abortion would be used and gays in the military would be dropped.

Manipulation of ratings content to show contrast—particularly on a massive scale—is unorthodox. For if the Christian Coalition's or any other group's goals and concerns regarding national policy are as constant as they claim, there is seemingly no need to vary content much from race to race. For example, its articles of incorporation list as one of its primary goals the protection of "the sanctity of life." Yet candidates were rated on the "abortion on demand" issue in just 62 of the 219 voter guides we studied. Most voter guides published by other interests rate every candidate on the same ten, fifteen, or twenty issues. The desire to show contrast, while it sounds benign, is difficult to defend for a nonpartisan, issues-based interest group. (Unlike much of what follows, this fact about the voter guides was easily discoverable by the media, and the press should have pointed this out prominently and frequently.)

However, this is the least of the voter guide curiosities. Another interesting factor was the placement of the issues in the scorecards. In virtually every contest, the first issue the coalition listed was "Raising Federal Income Taxes," while the last was frequently term limits. Taxes and term limits, of course, were two of the hottest issues in 1994, though they appear to fall outside the coalition's main areas of interest. Republicans, however, were almost monolithically opposed to raising income taxes and almost monolithically in support of term limits, and many candidates made these issues the centerpiece of their campaigns. A longstanding dictum of marketing science holds that in printed messages, the first thing and the last thing in a list are the ones best remembered. Thus, if they remembered nothing else about the Christian Coalition guides, voters could be expected to remember a candidate's position—or purported position—on taxes and term limits.

Of the 193 voter guides we examined concerning House of Representatives elections, 112 rated candidates on the "Raising Federal Income Taxes" question. In 92 percent of these cases, the Democrat was listed as supporting increases in federal income taxes or not taking a position. Even more telling, only five Republicans were listed as unclear or not responding to this question, while not once was a Republican listed as supporting increases in federal income taxes. It is certainly true that Democrats are generally more inclined to support raising taxes than Republicans. Yet it is impossible to make blanket characterizations: a fair number of Republican moderates vote for tax increases, while conservative Democrats vote against them. Often it depends on whose taxes are being raised (the budget passed by congressional Democrats in 1993 raised taxes primarily on the wealthy, but there was no such qualifier in the coalition's voter guides), but some Democrats even vote against raising taxes on the rich. Republicans in the House did uniformly oppose President Clinton's 1993 budget (which raised taxes on the wealthy), but some Democrats opposed the legislation as well.

While taxes are a perennial concern of voters, term limits are a relatively new issue. But intraparty divisions on taxes are mild compared with intraparty divisions on term limits. A sizable minority of Democrats support some form of term limits, while an equally large minority of Republicans oppose them. The coalition's voter guides did not reflect this reality. In the ninety-eight House races where candidates were rated on term limits, only five Democrats were listed as term limits supporters, less than 5 percent. Equally remarkable, only two Republicans were described as term limits opponents, while another three were described as having failed to respond or giving an unclear answer. All the rest—some 95 percent of the Republicans rated—were listed as term limits boosters. There were no votes in Congress on term limits in the 1993–94 session, but the 1995 House vote on this issue similarly suggests the voter guides are at variance with reality: nearly a fourth of Republicans in the House voted against term limits, while nearly a quarter of Democrats voted for them.[34]

What is going on here? One explanation is that the Christian Coalition, despite its best efforts, failed accurately to discern where candidates stood on these issues. That is not inconceivable: politicians have been known to obfuscate and prevaricate. Further investigation, however, shows this explanation to be charitable at best.

Consider term limits. As now former Speaker of the House Thomas Foley learned, opposing term limits could be fatal, even if your record on bringing home pork barrel projects and your reputation as an effective representative were otherwise good. As noted above, this was a potentially big problem for the many Republicans who oppose term limits. But somehow these Republicans managed to avoid being fingered by the coalition as term limits opponents.

Take the example of Kentucky, where there were six House races. In four races, the coalition rated both the Democratic and Republican candidate for their stance on term limits. In each of those cases, the Democrat was listed as either opposing term limits or refusing to respond to the survey, while the Republican candidate was listed, in all four cases, as a term limits supporter—nothing untoward here. In the other two Kentucky House contests, however, the term limits rating was mysteriously missing from the scorecard, replaced by another issue. Curiously, in each of those two races, the Republican candidate was a well-documented opponent of term limits.

There is another possible explanation for the coalition's decision to remove term limits from these two races: Ralph Reed's stated desire to show "contrast" between candidates. That explanation is valid if the Democrat was also an opponent of term limits, in which case there would be little reason to list the issue under the "contrast" standard. But that was not the case in one of the races, a hard-fought contest in the fifth district of Kentucky. In that race, fourteen-year incumbent Republican Harold Rogers opposed term limits, while Democratic challenger Sally Skaggs supported them.

Another big issue in 1994 was the proposed amendment to the U.S. Constitution requiring a balanced federal budget, a measure for which polls consistently show there is overwhelming public support. Out of 143 Democrats whom it rated on the issue, the coalition credited only 19 with supporting the balanced budget amendment—a mere 13 percent of all Democrats. Yet when the House voted on the balanced budget amendment in 1994, 99 Democrats—nearly 40 percent of the party's members—voted for the proposal. How could this be? The answer is that when the coalition rated Democrats who voted for the balanced budget amendment, it put tiny asterisks next to the box labeling them opponents of the amendment. Down at the bottom of the flier, in even smaller type, were corresponding asterisks, followed by this notation: "Position is based on Roll Call Vote 62 in the U.S. House of Representatives on March 17, 1994." While it is unlikely than most voters would stop by the library to look up this roll call, an examination of the Congressional Record for that day reveals roll call vote number 62 was not a vote on the balanced budget amendment. Rather, vote 62 was on a measure, offered by a Republican, requiring a three-fifths vote of the House in order to raise taxes. That is a very different beast from a balanced budget amendment, which simply states that the budget must be balanced, saying nothing at all about how that feat should be achieved.

"If two people were in favor of the Balanced Budget Amendment, but one favored a tax limitation procedure and the other didn't, we would go to the tax limitation version," explained Reed. "Because the voter guides are really designed to give voters a full picture of the differences between candidates and not the similarities."[35] Yet the coalition failed to explain this in its voter guides, describing the tax limitation vote as a vote on the balanced budget amendment.

It might seem difficult to imagine a more misleading distortion than this, but there was one. In nineteen key races, the coalition accused Democrats—including Representative Dan Rostenkowski of Illinois, who chaired the Ways and Means Committee and whose defeat was a priority for Republicans—of support for "Promoting Homosexuality to Schoolchildren." Undoubtedly, the allegation was very damaging to Rostenkowski, who represented a heavily Catholic district in Chicago. In tiny print at the bottom of the guide, the coalition said it based this highly dubious claim—a smear, to be blunt—on House of Representatives roll call vote number 91. Once again, an examination of the legislation finds no support for the Christian Coalition's characterization. Vote 91 was on an amendment *prohibiting* the dissemination of obscene material on school grounds and *barring* the use of federal funds for any educational program set up to promote homosexuality. The Democrats accused by the Christian Coalition of supporting homosexuality education actually voted for this proposal. The amendment can be characterized as pro-gay only insofar as it was less stringent than a competing proposal, which would have barred federal funding for any educational program which teaches about homosexuality. (The House never voted on that amendment.)

Admittedly, reasonable people can (and do) disagree about the meaning of congressional votes. But we think there can be no confusion in this case, since nothing in the amendment could be construed as even remotely supporting pro-homosexuality instruction in public schools. To accuse a public official of supporting the promotion of homosexuality on the basis of these facts is a lie. Moreover, in voting for the amendment, Dan Rostenkowski put himself in the company of such other well-known promoters of homosexuality as Republicans Jon Kyl (now a senator) and Dana Rohrabacher (a virulent critic of homoerotic art), who also cast their ballots in support of the measure. Yet the coalition, in its voter guides for these Republicans, did not mention their supposed support for teaching homosexuality to children.

The possible effect of the Christian Coalition's manipulations, distortions, and outright falsehoods was clear on Election Day. A number of underdog Republican candidates with seemingly dismal prospects and tiny campaign treasuries pulled off major upsets. Among these were Michael Patrick Flanagan, who ousted Rostenkowski (who was also tainted by financial scandal) despite being outspent 20 to 1, and Steve Stockman, outspent by Brooks 11 to 1. If their campaign reports were to be believed, between the two of them Stockman and Flanagan had received only $217,000, which does not buy much in politics these days. But the campaign reports failed to reflect the untold sums spent on their behalf by the Christian Coalition, which had plastered their districts with flattering handbills. By systematically rigging the content of its voter guides to help Republican candidates like Stockman, Flanagan, and more than a hundred others, the group had essentially donated hundreds of thousands of dollars (perhaps millions) in free advertising to the Republican Party. The point is not that the incumbents should necessarily have remained in office, nor that they would have won had the coalition not been active. But the fact remains that they were unseated in part through ethically questionable manipulations.

Reed, even as he stoutly maintained the Christian Coalition's nonpartisanship, did not shy away from taking credit for the Republican victory. Shortly after the election, he issued a statement saying the Christian Coalition was responsible for turning twenty-five Democratic House seats over to the Republicans. This is probably not far from the truth, given the narrowness of many GOP wins and the massive pro-GOP voter guide program.

In an interview with us, Reed noted that exit polls show the public favored Republicans over Democrats by 53 percent to 47 percent, "and we contributed 9 to 10 percent of the total vote, and our vote broke 70–30 their way. What does that tell you? It tells you that it was probably the margin. Your standard off-year pickup of 15 to 20 House seats and 3 Senate seats is what you would have expected. Instead they got 8 Senate seats, and 53 House seats. So I think that [the Christian Coalition] was a huge contributing factor."[36]

Asked whether his organization was, in effect, a crypto-political party, Reed replied,

> I see the Christian Coalition as more of an analog to the labor unions or the National Education Association. We have state affiliates, we have local chapters, which is kind of the equivalent of a local in a union, and we have precinct and neighborhood coordinators and church coordinators. And I think that it's more of a civic league or lobby group than a political party. We do not, as political parties do, elect officers or have annual conventions to choose leadership, and we do not engage in the kinds of activities that political parties engage in, that is to say, recruiting candidates, fielding candidates, and funding candidates, which is, after all, one of the central functions of a political party.

On this last point, we disagree. The Christian Coalition is indeed funding candidates through backdoor channels. Nonetheless, Reed's point is well taken. The coalition has not supplanted the GOP, nor is it fairly called a chartered subsidiary of the party. But its interests and those of the party are obviously entwined, and the evidence is fairly conclusive that the coalition engaged in pro-Republican electioneering. When it was suggested to Reed that the Christian Coalition is to the Republican Party what organized labor is to the Democratic Party, Reed at first clarified, "what organized labor *was* to the Democratic Party," and then later argued that "there are some similarities [but] even more differences," pointing out that the coalition "will not issue any endorsement of any Republican candidate for president in 1996 in sharp contrast to the labor union strategy in 1984 of anointing Walter Mondale in advance."[37]

In his travels around the country setting up the Christian Coalition, however, Reed said he often encountered organizers for the National Education Association, "and that's when I really began to understand that they were doing what we were doing, only they were mobilizing the base liberal vote." Comparisons to the unions are instructive on more than one level. Like unions, the Christian Coalition abuses its nominally independent status to engage in covert unregulated campaign activity and thus defeats the central purpose of the campaign finance statutes—public disclosure.

But more than election laws are implicated by the coalition's apparent rigging of its voter guides. It is unclear whether the coalition is violating its own tax status by circulating partisan endorsements, since the group is registered with the IRS not as a religious charity but rather as a social welfare organization and is thus not enjoined from all partisan activity. But the same cannot be said for the thousands of churches that serve as the Christian Coalition's conduits for the leaflets. As 501(c)(3) organizations, churches are strictly prohibited from engaging in any partisan campaign activities.[38] Obviously, if the voter guides are partisan, churches cannot distribute them without breaking the law.

For the Love of Loopholes

GOPAC and the Christian Coalition were not the only Republican allies operating in the shadows and testing the limits of the law. Two other important members of the Republican "coalition," Americans for Limited Terms and the National Rifle Association (NRA), together poured some $3 million in questionable expenditures into the 1994 elections.[39]

Much has been written and said in recent years about the NRA's controversial campaign tactics, but at least on the surface, the group would appear to be in compliance with both the letter and the spirit of the law. The NRA has a well-funded PAC, which files regularly with the FEC, and the veracity of its filings has largely gone unquestioned. Many of the NRA's critics have questioned the propriety of the large "independent expenditures" the NRA makes on behalf of candidates (the NRA's PAC spent $4.2 million on contributions and independent expenditures in 1993–94), but absent evidence that this spending is not really "independent," the practice is specifically permitted under the campaign laws (and indeed, according to the Supreme Court, constitutionally protected).

However, there are a few limits on independent expenditures that can hamper their effectiveness. The law says independent expenditures can be financed only with contributions that are fully disclosed to the FEC and regulated under the standard PAC rules. Thus the amount of independent expenditures a PAC can make is limited by the number and generosity of one's PAC contributors.

There is another way for interest groups to get their message out, an obscure area of campaign financing known as "communications costs." Communications costs were actually pioneered by organized labor, and unions remain among the biggest communications spenders. This spending is explicitly permitted under federal law, basically under one condition: the money must be spent for communicating with a group's members, not the general public. That is a severe limitation, of course, but as long as that one rule is met, the remaining restrictions are few indeed. Unlike independent expenditures, communications costs can be funded with money that comes straight out of the corporate (or union) treasury. There is no need to engage in the painstaking, expensive fundraising practices of a PAC; you just dip into the company till. Such expenditures do, however, have to be reported to the Federal Election Commission.

In 1993–94, the National Rifle Association's Institute for Legislative Action (ILA), a nonprofit corporation funded in part by gun manufacturers, spent $1.9 million on communications costs, making it the biggest spender by far of such funds.[40] That is a staggering amount of money for a group that claims some 2.5 million members; the AFL-CIO, which claims a membership of 13 million, spent just $573,000 on communications costs. The NRA money went to influence some 260 House and Senate contests and was spent on behalf of the Republican candidate about 75 percent of the time.

In some races, the NRA-ILA spent very substantial sums, including $232,000 on behalf of the successful Republican candidate for Senate in Pennsylvania, Rick Santorum; $67,000 on behalf of the winning Republican candidate for Senate in Minnesota, Rod Grams; and $81,000 on behalf of Texas Republican candidate (now

Senator) Kay Bailey Hutchison. Among House candidates, the biggest beneficiary was Republican George Nethercutt, Democratic House Speaker Thomas Foley's triumphant opponent, who received more than $12,000 worth of help. None of this spending is ever reported in the press, in part because many reporters are unaware of its existence, while others do not think it matters much since they think it is money that is supposed to be spent within the organization.[41]

The latter notion, as it turns out, is untrue. Less than two weeks before the 1994 election, NRA members in northern North Carolina received a letter from Tanya Metaksa, executive director of the Institute for Legislative Action, urging them to "throw out of office those politicians who have tried to kill our firearms freedoms."[42] Democratic incumbent Martin Lancaster, Metaksa warned, "has a very disappointing record on firearms, consistently voting for the 'Brady Bill.' " Republican challenger Walter Jones Jr., on the other hand, "will give North Carolina gun owners better representation in Congress." These sorts of communications are the type envisioned under the communications costs section of the campaign laws. But that was not all the letter contained. Also enclosed was a bumper sticker that read, "Protect Freedom: Elect Jones." "Put the enclosed bumper sticker on your car or truck," Metaksa urged. Thus did funds intended for internal communications wind up paying for campaign advertising to the general public.

The Jones-Lancaster race was not an isolated case. In the Oklahoma Senate race, Republican James Inhofe benefited from a similar line: "Protect Freedom, Elect Inhofe." In a Georgia race, the NRA supplied a sticker reading, "Protect the 2nd–Barr–Congress." In House races alone, the NRA appears to have mailed out some 2.4 million bumper stickers.[43]

Distributing free bumper stickers, even if it is done on a massive scale, sounds almost trivial in the ever-lengthening pantheon of abuses in American campaigns. But bumper stickers, which have played an important role in American politics for decades, constitute an extremely effective form of political advertising. When thousands of people are driving around with the same message on their cars, the advertiser has achieved marketing nirvana—repetition. Moreover, the message is conveyed in an environment attractive to advertisers—one where the audience is basically captive. (If you are driving down the road and want to avoid crashing your car, you keep your eyes on the rear end of the car in front of you.) Bumper stickers also spread messages in a credible, grassroots fashion. When people read a bumper sticker they interpret it as a message from their fellow driver, not the NRA (particularly when the message is not identifiable as coming from the NRA, as in the case of "Protect Freedom: Elect Jones"). In the southern states, people seem to have a special affection for bumper stickers, and they are significantly more prevalent there than elsewhere in the country: according to one poll, more than a fifth of the population say they have bumper stickers on their vehicles.[44] The NRA's bumper sticker program appears never to have been legally challenged, but according to attorney Kenneth Gross, a former FEC enforcement attorney, it was in all probability a violation.[45]

Americans for Limited Terms (ALT), founded just months before the election, felt no need to keep up appearances for the FEC. Funded by several of the same wealthy conservatives backing GOPAC,[46] ALT declined to register with the agency, asserting that its activities were nonpartisan and issue-based and thus could be conducted unfettered under the First Amendment to the Constitution.

On November 2, only days before the election, ALT launched a $1.3 million mail and media campaign against congressional term limit opponents. ALT focused mainly on Democrats, despite the fact that many Republicans running were term limit opponents.[47] It would be difficult to construe ALT's activities as anything other than direct campaign expenditures. Consider this radio script, which was aired in Oklahoma in the closing days of the race between U.S. Representatives James Inhofe (Republican) and Dave McCurdy (Democrat) for a U.S. Senate seat:

> Less than two months ago Oklahomans voted overwhelmingly for term limits for members of Congress.
>
> So naturally, you'd expect both candidates now running for U.S. Senate in Oklahoma to support the people's wishes and support term limits.
>
> Well, you'd be only half right.

Jim Inhofe sides with the people of Oklahoma in favor of a citizen legislature. Inhofe has pledged to support term limits in the U.S. Congress and supported the people's initiative for term limits in Oklahoma.

But Dave McCurdy opposed the people's initiative for term limits and despite a direct vote by the people of Oklahoma for term limits, he thinks he knows better.

Ask Dave McCurdy to change his mind. Ask him to join you in supporting term limits for career politicians.[48]

While the ad refrained from directly advocating a vote for Inhofe, the eventual winner, the language was a code even the dullest-witted voter could crack. Inhofe "sides with the people of Oklahoma," while McCurdy "opposed the peoples' initiative for term limits." How much more explicit does one need to be? Similar ads ran all over the country:

- "Patrick Kennedy, who wants to be your congressman, opposes term limits. He thinks he knows better than the people of Rhode Island and America." (Rhode Island, 2nd District; Kennedy won anyway.)
- "Neal Smith. He's been in Congress for 36 years—since 1958! Smith, despite the clear desire of the people for term limits, opposes them. In fact, Smith has even voted to spend your tax dollars to fight term limits in the courts. The other candidate in the fourth district, Greg Ganske, not only supports term limits, he has signed a formal pledge to vote for term limits in the U.S. Congress. Smith and Congress think they know better than the people of Iowa and America on term limits. What do you think?" (Iowa, 4th district; Ganske defeated Smith.)

The ATL defended its tactics as legitimate issue-based political speech on which there were no restrictions. But as long-time Common Cause president Fred Wertheimer put it, "When a group is running TV ads in the closing days of a campaign that deals with a candidate for Congress, the presumption has to be that these are election activities, not advocacy."[49] Indeed, the Federal Election Commission has enacted rules that say almost precisely that. This presumption is even stronger in light of the fact that Congress was no longer in session when the advertisements were aired, and thus the ads could not possibly be construed as an effort to lobby a member of Congress on an issue on which he or she would soon have to vote.

It is fair to say that the tactics of the NRA and ATL played a role in a number of Democratic defeats. Clearly, the NRA's corporate spending made a difference in some few races, especially in predominantly rural areas of the country. Yet its claims to have played a decisive role in the Republican takeover are less persuasive than those of the Christian Coalition. Other groups such as the term limit advocates, who were active in only a limited number of races, should be put in a different league altogether.

As one Republican operative noted, "The Christian Coalition is the most effective because they have the broadest reach and the strongest management . . . [and] can touch the most people. The NRA is second because it has a wide reach—not as big as the Christian Coalition—and spends a lot of money." However, the operative noted, the NRA was less partisan than the Christian Coalition. The number of Democrats it helped were a minority to be sure, but a significant one. "The NRA does incite some people to vote, [but] the people it gets to vote are not as likely to agree with us on the wide spectrum of issues as those touched by the Christian Coalition." The Republican said that while there were any number of groups allied with the GOP that were seeking to influence the elections, it was these two that made the difference for Republicans, with ALT perhaps third on the list. "Once you get down past them, there is a pretty large drop off."

In retrospect, many Democrats see these new methods of campaigning as a signal advantage for Republicans. "There's clearly a covert communications engine which is huge in the Republican Party that absolutely does not exist in the Democratic Party," one Democratic consultant who has managed campaigns in the South for more than a decade told us. He acknowledged that organized labor has long engaged in similar tactics, but ridiculed its efforts in 1994. "So what if labor sends out leaflets? They no longer have their membership doing anything. And their appeals are tired, they feel so out of step."

The consultant, who has managed the campaigns of a veteran conservative Democratic congressman, sketched out the changes that have occurred just in the evangelical electorate. "In 1982 in the general election we got a large number of those folks. The Christian folks were still mobile enough. Faced with two people who were sort of saying the same thing about abortion, they were equally likely to vote for a Democrat as a Republican. In 1994, we didn't get a vote. And I think now a right-to-life Democrat in the South wouldn't get anything. Like labor unions, all these people are completely captive. Except unlike labor unions, they deliver their votes."

The consultant said that frequently the charges made against Democrats in these "covert" communications are either distorted or flatly untrue, "but the press has no enforcement ability and it doesn't really care. So in an era where the press basically has no effective role as an umpire, the covert communication program absorbs a lot of money. . . . There's a whole level of communications strategy that these folks do that I just do not think Democrats do."

In the first 100 days of the new Congress, House Republicans (though not the Senate) passed much of the agenda that Gingrich had been pushing for years. They approved bills to rein in federal spending, cut taxes, and give citizens more control over their own lives. Yet not all the Democrats' rules were rewritten. Curiously absent from the package was the centerpiece of the agenda Gingrich had been pushing for two decades: political reform.

Since his ascension to the Speakership, Gingrich has repeatedly seemed reluctant to deny himself and his corevolutionaries the luxuries most enjoyed by the "dictatorship" he had replaced, such as access to a bountiful supply of campaign contributions from those who eagerly pay tribute to rulers. Gingrich is undeniably a historic figure whose accomplishments and insights deserve recognition and admiration. Yet his hypocrisy, his legal corner-cutting, and his refusal to live up to his pledges of openness are dangerous flaws that cannot be overlooked. As this was being written, it remained to be seen whether Gingrich and the Republican Party would come to recognize the peril they faced in failing to tame the force he had used so effectively in his long march to power—America's populist fury at self-serving leaders and the erosion of integrity in the conduct of public affairs. Gingrich seemed likely to neglect the lesson of political boss Mark Hanna, who built a Republican political money empire in the 1890s that was so great public opinion could not abide it.

The beginnings of the new world were not auspicious. On January 12, 1995, just one week after the new Republican Congress took the oath of office, Charles Mack, president of the influential Business-Industry Political Action Committee, sent an unusually blunt letter to the heads of Washington's major corporate and trade association lobbying offices:

> In meetings with the new leadership, I am being told that they are scrutinizing to whom companies and business associations are currently giving—that they take a very dim view indeed of access contributions to lawmakers who have tended to vote against business. You heard this before, during the campaign. The purpose of this memo is to tell you that I believe they mean it. What I am told is this:
>
> • Legislative interests of those who help the congressional enemies of business, and don't support our friends, could be affected negatively. Some committee chairmen are reportedly denying access to lobbyists who support the other side.
>
> • Campaign finance legislation will be taken up after 100 days, and the treatment of political action committees will be heavily influenced by PAC behavior in the next few months.
>
> • There is little private objection to support for members of the minority party with strong pro-business voting records. It is the contributions to lawmakers with weak or non-existent business support histories that create the problem. Lobbyists who are hedging their bets with an eye toward reversal of last November's outcome in 1996 will find the next two years rather lean ones, I'm informed.[50]

Subsequent events only reinforced the warnings Mack had received. Republican Party leaders issued a series of blunt threats to political contributors contemplating assistance to Democrats. The threats had their desired effect, proving once again that the permanent interests care far less about who is in power than they do about their ability to influence them. An epochal shift in the political money river occurred, like the mighty Mississippi jumping its banks to carve out a new streambed. Republicans quickly shattered all previous fundraising records, reaping gargantuan sums from special interests. In just the first four months of 1995, the National Republican Campaign Committee raised in excess of $10 million—more than the committee raised in all of 1994.[51] The GOP's extortionate tactics were understandable, and they are no worse than the strong-arm practices employed by former Democratic House Whip Tony Coelho and his successors over the years to keep the Republicans down. It was Democrats, after all, who first drove competition out of congressional elections—the original sin.

It was also Democrats who pioneered the tactics adopted so successfully by the Christian Coalition—the use of nominally nonpartisan mass membership organizations to run covert partisan campaigns. There is also a degree of hypocrisy to Democratic criticism of the Christian Coalition, because their critique advances the notion that there is something alarming about the involvement of religious organizations in politics. When Father Robert Drinan was a congressman in the 1970s and the religious left joined the grand coalition for civil rights and against the war in Vietnam in the 1960s, not a peep was heard from Democrats about dangerous encroachments on the Constitutional separation of church and state. When Democrats petition ministers to permit them inside their churches for speeches, or reimburse ministers for the expenses involved in getting their parishioners to the polls, they have not been known to express qualms about the sacred separation of church and state. Religious organizations should be involved in public life; indeed, any enlargement in the body politic can only be positive. What is unhealthy, and unethical for an avowedly moral organization, is the eager evasion of high standards of political conduct. Like so many of its predecessors on the right and left, the Christian Coalition has been delighted merely to rely on loose, convenient definitions of the law carved out by high-priced lawyers, all the while trampling the law's spirit. It is easier, quicker, and more effective than taking the high road—and no real justification to say that what the coalition does is simply a more sophisticated and effective version of what the Democrats have long done. Similarly, GOPAC and other groups' willingness to bypass the post-Watergate reforms calls their own legitimacy into question.

After years of complaining loudly and accurately about the corruption in the Democrats' system, the Republicans could not resist the temptation to tilt the table in their own direction rather than set it level—a kind of perverted poetic justice and testimony to the blandishments of corruption. They have started down the path to becoming that which they so insightfully decried.

PART II

"Everybody's Doin' It": Bipartisan Corruption

★ ★ ★

The modern-day corruption of American elections is bigger than partisan politics because many corrupt techniques recognize no partisan boundaries. The Democrats created an institutional machine, paid for through the courtesy of special interests and the taxpayers, to ensure a four-decade stranglehold on the U.S. House of Representatives. In order to break that stranglehold, the Republicans assembled an extra-institutional revolutionary machine, fueled by their own coalition of moneyed interests and questionable manipulation of the tax laws. And the similarities do not end there.

To one degree or another, *both* major parties have employed additional distasteful techniques. These bipartisan practices are doubly foul. Not only do they continue to degrade politics and all those connected to it, but they give justification to an already cynical citizenry's belief that "everybody does it." This attitude increases the prevalent "plague-on-both-their-houses" view of America's two political parties. In truth, both parties are deserving of opprobrium for some of the means they have chosen to achieve victory. So are the ubiquitous political consultants who sell and supervise the sad campaign techniques we will sketch shortly.

Thanks in good measure to these campaign strategists, the health of virtually all the contemporary mechanisms of politics across the United States is in decline. Many of the television and radio advertisements aired by candidates are exceptionally negative and nasty, the campaign direct mail has become ever more vicious, and so on. Yet these unsavory techniques are not necessarily corrupt practices (at least according to our original definition). But five other areas of politics do truly qualify as sources of corruption—several of them little investigated before now.

We turn first to the renaissance of political dirty tricks, which most Americans may think are a relic of a bygone era. Then we examine "street money," the all-too-traditional provision of money to political organizers in exchange for votes supposedly produced on Election Day. We look next at the abuse of the perks of elective office by the incumbent members of both parties, and some of the reasons neither party is especially anxious to eliminate them.

We also examine an exceptionally sleazy new form of telephone polling, termed the push-poll, which is all the rage in many regions of the nation. Finally, voter fraud goes on the chopping block, and our dissection reveals surprisingly extensive abuses.

Corrupt practices flourish in the shadows. Where the press and public raise few objections or demonstrate little outrage, the decline of campaign standards inevitably accelerates. And when cheating is deemed necessary to win, even ethical, well-intentioned people will justify their use; no one, they say, should be forced to disarm unilaterally, and we must play by the rules of the game until the rules are changed. Reform is the good fight, and it is always just around the corner. But the United States will never turn that corner until the people demand it.

6

Dirty Tricks Redux

Power can be a narcotic as potent as heroin, and most of those who are hooked will do whatever they must to keep the supply flowing. Only if a tried-and-true technique for supplying votes becomes counterproductive—that is, politically costly—will it be abandoned. Therefore, *standards matter:* standards about what is permissible and impermissible in campaigns, as enforced by the press and the public. Following the abuses of Watergate, those enforcers were correctly and refreshingly intolerant of campaign spying, invasion of candidates' legitimate personal privacy rights, and dirty tricks in all their malevolent variety. As a result, to avoid punishing criticism and possible defeat at the polls, politicians and their agents ran remarkably clean campaigns, for the most part, in the immediate wake of Watergate. But the darker side of political human nature is reasserting itself. Standards have fallen, and in stark contrast to bedroom politics, this particular aspect of backroom politics has come under less scrutiny. Our investigation of dirty tricks leads to the sad conclusion that some political professionals—many of whom fancy themselves the product of a ménage à trois among Svengali, Sam Spade, and Lucrezia Borgia—are once again pushing the edge of the ethical envelope.

With remarkably little fanfare, skulduggery appears to have made a revival during the past few election cycles, and there has been an upsurge in all manner of dirty tricks, including the gathering of information about the opposition through illegal or deceptive means. Joseph Cerrell, a respected veteran campaign consultant and past president of the American Association of Political Consultants, correctly notes that American politics has always had a sizable share of mudslinging and underhanded trickery, but there has recently been a rise in the incidence of dirty tricks "because the consultants, the candidates, campaign staffs, and contributors increasingly think that the way to get ahead is to knock down the other guy."[1] Perhaps the most famous political consultant of all, James Carville, the mastermind of Bill Clinton's 1992 presidential victory, gives another convincing explanation: "I don't know how much dirtier campaigns are than before, but they're a hell of a lot longer—the campaign never stops anymore—and there are more opportunities" for hanky-panky.[2] Whatever the reasons, not only are the private eyes and spies back; they now come armed with keyboards and modems. For the most part, the political establishment does not seem concerned and is even amused when the public learns about these scandalous undercurrents. Most citizens appear disgusted but not surprised. As for the press, newspapers and magazines have not ignored these developments altogether. Many regional papers have published feature articles about the return to pre-Watergate politics, and at the national level, for example, Michael Isikoff has reported extensively on the trend in *Newsweek* magazine and the *Washington Post*. But in the main the media have failed to conduct searching examinations.

Information for Sale

I look at (my job) this way. The tabloid newspapers sell many millions of copies every week in this country. So people are interested in reading dirt about other people. . . . Look at your magazine tabloid shows today on TV. And I think the same holds true in elections. If someone can find something on their opponent that they feel will give them an advantage, be it fair or unfair, they want it.

—*Bob Sherman, a Florida information broker and opposition researcher*[3]

Digging up and combing through the details of an opponent's professional and personal past is not a recent phenomenon. While tawdry tales have surfaced with some regularity in the history of American campaigns (the apocryphal allegations about Thomas Jefferson's illicit affair with a slave are an early example), until recently most candidates lacked the money and technology necessary to conduct a systematic examination of their opponent's life. From time to time, private investigators or moonlighting reporters were hired, but they proved too expensive for most campaigns and a poor financial gamble in the absence of preexisting indications that the opposition had something to hide. (They were also difficult to justify to voters if caught.) A more popular choice, relying on inexperienced campaign staff, rarely produced the quality of information desired. So most campaigns caged embarrassing details on the opposition haphazardly, relying on "people who held grudges against the candidate, or who had run against him before, or ex-wives—a great source," commented Democratic consultant Gary Nordlinger.[4]

During the early 1990s, however, an emerging field of political consulting began giving politicians what they wanted. Taking advantage of the efficiencies of the information age, such as cheap access to computer databases, the "opposition research" field (known as "oppo" or "op research," for short) blossomed into a multimillion-dollar industry. Offering useful products at affordable prices, opposition researchers "to a large degree, are private investigators," observed one consultant familiar with the field. "They might not be licensed by the police and carry badges, but they are specialists in going around and digging into the opponent's background." With fees rarely exceeding $20,000 for a basic report, even modestly funded campaigns found they could play the game, and the number of firms selling such services grew by 200 percent between 1990 and 1994.[5] At least forty-four firms advertised such services by 1995.[6]

The keys to the growth of the opposition research field are first, the advances in computer technology that permit it to flourish; second, the increasing meanness of American politics that feeds the market for damaging information on candidates; and third, the flood of money into politics that encourages candidates to buy every campaign toy. As long-time Republican strategist Eddie Mahe observed, "The intensity of the opposition research done today is much greater than it used to be because the technology allows for it [and] campaigns have become a lot tougher. I mean, the types of attacks that we launched twenty years ago would be laughed off the TV screen now."[7] Veteran Democratic campaign consultant Doc Sweitzer agreed, pointing out that opposition researchers "do such a good job of finding information on people that they enable you to [transfer] the old rumor mill into fact, to shift from innuendo and speculation into reality."[8] And of course, there is relatively easy money to be made in the business. With many thousands of state, local, and national candidates potentially in the market for opposition each election cycle, the scrupulous and unscrupulous alike are attracted to offer their wares. One prominent consultant told us that he has been approached by opposition researchers and essentially blackmailed: "They said, 'Either pay us or we are going to release damaging information about a client-candidate.' "

Blackmail aside, there is nothing about opposition research that is objectionable per se. The sustenance of democracy is information, and theoretically at least, the more legitimate information that is in the public domain, the better. Unfortunately, information today frequently works against enlightenment rather than for it, powering smears or meaningless diversions rather than robust debate. Equally troubling is the invasive psychology that often is produced by the practice. As Nixon's plumbers unit showed, once you decide to begin investigating your enemies, it is hard to know when to stop. A perfectly acceptable scouring of the public record can easily veer off into dangerous territory. And there are many more occasions for sin today compared with Nixon's time. "People are constantly coming forward with something for sale about your opponent," reported Republican operative Sal Russo.[9] "It's more prevalent and extensive than it used to be, and the sophistication has improved."

Opposition researchers bluntly say their main goal is to get the skinny on a client's opponents and, if all goes well, expose them as hypocrites, liars, thieves, or just plain unsavory characters. They market their skills proudly because they claim to operate aboveboard and use only publicly available information. The information that is available publicly, though, suggests why political dialogue in this country is at curb level—and how privacy has become endangered in the United States—and not just in political campaigns. While the rapidly increasing availability of government records, lists of campaign contributions, and newspaper files is undeniably a good thing, there is cause for ambivalence about other data that are coming on-line. A computer user with basic skills and a modem can now access a startling quantity of information on even completely private citizens that most people would regard as personal. Never moving from their desks, thousands of authorized and unauthorized investigators can at will uncover intimate details about any person's financial situation, property tax history, and voter registration background, and they can find out if someone has ever been sued, arrested, or divorced. In the words of Jane Churchill, a former opposition researcher from Texas, "You find out who their friends are. You look to see if there are any lawsuits against them, outstanding judgments, unhappy wives, nasty children. You know, did they kill the neighbor's cat? And those are all *public* records."[10]

Most opposition researchers claim to pay attention mostly to legislative votes and floor statements to see if their opponent's words jibe with his or her record. Without question, many do abide strictly by this unwritten code. Yet many of their brethren also examine highly personal information, with the result that issues often surface that are only marginally related, or even completely unrelated, to the office being contested. In these situations negative one-upsmanship prevails, as each side's consultant tries to outmaneuver the other on a high-tech search-and-destroy mission.

Thus the most obvious products of the investigatory mind-set are contests marked by a debate over irrelevancies. In 1994 in California alone, opposition researchers unearthed mounds of trivial personal information about candidates that could do nothing but sour the political climate. For instance, researchers found that incumbent governor Pete Wilson failed the bar exam three times before passing it, while his Democratic opponent, Kathleen Brown, forged her parents' signatures on a college application when she was a teenager. Both of the candidates for U.S. Senate, Republican Michael Huffington and Democrat Dianne Feinstein, were found to own homes with deeds containing so-called racial covenants (provisions prohibiting the sale of property to non-whites)—an obscure vestige of another time. Neither politician knew the covenants existed before the opponent discovered it. (Such ignorance is understandable since covenants are usually unearthed only after exhaustive legal searches of all past deeds associated with the property.) Searches of other candidates' histories revealed assorted traffic violations and one instance of a candidate's wife being ticketed for not renewing a dog license.[11] The major issues at stake in California in 1994 were crime, taxes, and immigration, but the campaigns could not resist unleashing these factoids upon the public. Of course, the point was not to influence debate on the issues, but to reflect on the character of the contestants, which is certainly a relevant issue. Yet it is hard to see how decades-old misdemeanor transgressions or mistakes of the most minor variety speak meaningfully about someone's character.

Often, though, the personal information has a far more serious impact. In 1994, Republican millionaire Bruce Benson's bid for the Colorado governor's chair took a nosedive after a court ordered the opening of a divorce settlement. Several nasty personal details were revealed, including an affair in which he had spent lavishly on his paramour while still married to his first wife. Although the record was sealed, the news came out when a Colorado judge, citing public interest over the family's private life, ordered it opened six weeks before the election. (In most states, divorce records are public unless a judge seals them.)[12] Voters were then treated to soap-opera-style revelations about Benson's love life. It did not seem to matter that Benson was estranged from his wife at the time he had the affair, or that he immediately married the woman with whom he had taken up after the divorce from his first wife was finalized. Benson's own opposition researcher, Gary Maloney, blamed "opposition types" from Benson's Democratic opponent, Governor Roy Romer, for helping bring the sealed divorce settlement to the attention of a local television station, which then sued for access.[13] Another Republican activist who did not wish to be named made the same charge, which Romer denied.

But the most damaging allegation contained in the records was that Benson had threatened to kill his then-wife. Benson said the comment was not serious, and given that Benson's wife never reported him to the police—only raising the issue in the context of the divorce—there is reason for skepticism about the charge. After all, some $50 million was at stake. As Maloney put it,

> Remember, in divorces people [often claim] wife beating. . . .
> You have lawyers for both sides trying to paint the other side in
> the most obscenely negative light possible. So those emotion-

ally charged accounts are released and portrayed as fact by the media, and you can't win on that one. You may not have laid a finger on somebody but the most horrible things come out. And I saw that being used in '94 to an unprecedented degree.[14]

The *Rocky Mountain News* concurred: "In hindsight, that [threat] claim appears to be a hard-ball legal tactic by Nancy Benson's attorney, who himself insists there had been no abuse at any time during [a] long marriage."[15]

The Benson campaign was not above conducting some serious opposition research itself. Hired-gun Maloney is considered one of the best in the business and also among the most adventurous. Perhaps his most famous exploit was an attempt in the closing weeks of the 1992 presidential election, on behalf of the George Bush campaign, to locate in England a twenty-year-old picture allegedly showing Bill Clinton burning an American flag at an anti-Vietnam war rally. Maloney never found it, and to the best of anyone's knowledge no such picture ever existed. A few days before the 1994 Colorado election, Benson produced documents showing that Romer had made eleven phone calls from airplanes to a woman who had previously served as his deputy chief of staff. The woman, claimed a Denver alternative newspaper four years earlier, had allegedly had an affair with Romer. (Romer said the calls were about official business.) The Benson campaign also produced allegations that Romer misused his security staff as personal servants.

But perhaps the most sensational event of all occurred one day when Romer was traveling between campaign stops on a rural interstate. The governor's driver noticed that their car was being followed, and he attempted to elude the pursuers, eventually reaching a speed of 110 miles per hour. While the press treated the incident as a bizarre potential threat to Romer's safety, insiders claimed to know what Romer's pursuers were up to. While the report could not be confirmed, a Republican opposition researcher with long involvement in Colorado politics suggested that Romer's determined "tails" were not hitmen but private investigators who were mindful of the extramarital rumors and who apparently believed the governor was on his way to an illicit liaison. Most likely, no one will ever know what the chase was about, but this account is certainly more plausible than an attempted hit on Romer. There is no indication that the car sought to overtake Romer's vehicle. In fact, while referred to as a "chase" in news accounts, a transcript of radio calls made by Romer's driver shows that he merely indicated they were being followed by a suspicious vehicle. At one point the driver said the vehicle was "three cars back."

In any case, the result of all these shenanigans was a campaign mainly devoid of substantive debate. The same pattern emerged in races all around the country. Opposition researcher Bob Sherman told us how information gained from searches of publicly available databases can spin out of control:

> Deep down in their minds, they have these suspicions about their opponent. Maybe he's a sex degenerate. Maybe he got a nasty divorce. Or maybe he flip-flopped on a stand or something. Each opponent has his own ideas about what he's looking for. And they will send you off spinning wheels on these types of things. Another time, I had a candidate who wanted names and addresses of neighbors where his opponent lived, so he could solicit them on the phone and maybe find out that the guy threw wild parties or something. Or he always ran around in a drunken stupor.[16]

Sherman also reported that another client wanted proof that the son of his opponent was living with a woman he was not married to: "I mean, the kid wasn't going to be running for office, and he didn't live at home. I told [the client] he was barking up the wrong tree, but he insisted on the information, and I gave it to him. And what he ever did with it, I have no idea."[17]

Opposition researchers themselves pin a number of sins on their profession. Many told us that picking apart an opponent's record often enables a politician to distort, not clarify, an opponent's stances. For example, veteran Republican opposition researcher Kevin Spillane, of the California-based Stonecreek Group, said he cooked up a creative gimmick to help his 1994 U.S. House client, southern California Republican (and now Representative) Sonny Bono, whose own life would be fodder for a thick dossier. To obscure Bono's weak attendance record at city council sessions while mayor of Palm Springs, Spillane said he examined Democratic opponent Steve Clute's attendance record during his lengthy career in the California Assembly. While overall, Clute had an excellent attendance record, Spillane said he found that the Democrat had missed a small percentage of votes during his last four years in the legislature:

> In California, they pass over 4,000 laws a year, so there are literally thousands of votes every legislative session. And just by combining the two most recent sessions for the Democrat (the '89–90 session and the '91–92 session) if you averaged it out, he missed about 7 or 8 percent of the votes. For Congress that's a large amount, but for supervisors or state legislators, it's not that atrocious. But when we added it up, he had a couple thousand votes that he had missed. So, in a radio debate, Clute went after Sonny on his attendance. And Sonny was able to come back with the fact that Clute had missed, you know, 1,800 votes as a member of the state legislature. Well, Clute absolutely lost it. He was infuriated because apparently he had always prided himself on his attendance. It completely changed the dynamics of that issue, and put him on the defensive and took away that issue against Sonny. And then we never heard about that issue for the rest of the campaign.[18]

In the same race, Spillane also exploited California's xenophobic mood. Although Clute had rarely voted on immigration issues (he left the assembly in 1992, just before most such bills hit the legislature), Bono attacked him as having a pro-immigrant record, which, Spillane said, consisted of a "couple" of votes on "small resolutions."[19]

These tactics should perhaps come as no surprise: modern opposition research truly came into its own in 1988, when Senator Albert Gore of Tennessee, running for the Democratic presidential nomination, came across the notorious Willie Horton case through a scan of newspaper articles while trying to dig up dirt on Michael Dukakis.[20] (Horton was a convicted murderer who was paroled in Massachusetts while Dukakis was governor and who then committed a brutal rape.) The attack failed to work for Gore, but Republican presidential nominee George Bush and some supporters revived the incident and used it prominently, claiming it was representative of Dukakis's alleged coddling of violent criminals. Taking a page from the Bush playbook, a Washington-based opposition researcher boasted that he used a computer database to look up "really grotesque criminals" in a client's district. By doing so, he hoped to give his client, who supported the death penalty, something to use against his opponent, who did not, and stir outrage in local voters. "I'm able to now come up with murder cases for a campaign I'm working on in Washington state," he said. "It's just wonderful."[21]

While the use of opposition research to launch unfair, scurrilous, or irrelevant allegations is deplorable, snooping gets a lot more hair-raising the deeper the digging goes. In an extraordinary incident in 1992, through a string of coincidences, the raw work product of one opposition researcher fell into the wrong hands. In early October, about six weeks before the election, a paralegal in an Atlanta courthouse was cleaning up at the end of the day and noticed a yellow legal pad.[22] Hoping to be helpful, she flipped through it looking for the name of the owner. The first seven pages contained a wealth of data about a Robert Goodlatte and a Maryellen Goodlatte, including their social security numbers. Assuming the pad had something to do with politics, the paralegal turned it over to a friend active in the local Republican Party, who in turn gave it to her husband, the Republican candidate for sheriff, who in turn gave it to the local party chairman. The chairman's wife, it so happened, was from Roanoke, Virginia, and recognized Goodlatte as the Republican candidate for Congress from the Roanoke area. Soon Goodlatte had a copy of his own dossier—the product of an extensive fishing expedition into his and his wife's past.

While the coincidences by which Goodlatte found out he was under investigation by his opponent are remarkable, what was really notable was the level of detail of the investigation. Every aspect of the Goodlattes' life from age eighteen onward had apparently been subjected to microscopic examination, in the hope that something—anything—untoward would be uncovered. The sleuth, who was never identified by name (he worked for the San Francisco–based Research Group), had actually gone to the trouble of visiting the college Goodlatte had attended twenty years earlier, perusing the yearbook and interviewing the dean of students.[23]

There was even a hand-drawn diagram of Washington and Lee University law school, where Goodlatte had met his wife. "Maryellen, especially, was incredibly stunned, because she had her whole life pass before her eyes," said Goodlatte. "All this detail . . . I mean, this was a thorough job." While Goodlatte said he took the incident in stride (and used it effectively against his opponent), he does not like the implications: "My impression is they wanted to find anything they could. . . . They can embarrass you in some way if some family member did something." Perhaps in part because there was nothing embarrassing in his record, Goodlatte won the election easily.

It is perhaps understandable that Gary Maloney would go a long distance to look at the college yearbook of a presidential candidate. After all, the stakes are very high. But to order up a protoscopic examination of a candidate for the House?

The extensiveness, sophistication, and explosive growth of this kind of opposition research has given pause even to some campaign professionals. Democratic media consultant Dan Payne expressed misgivings that reflected those of many of his colleagues:

> Firms doing opposition research are much more capable of ferreting out every vote, every utterance of a candidate over a lifetime. I've seen oppo information books that are three and four tomes large on candidates. And it raises the bar for potential candidates knowing that every remark, every activity, every contemplation is going to be investigated, catalogued, and possibly used against that person if he or she should decide to run. While I certainly don't begrudge the [oppo] business the right to make a living, I do wonder whether what they're doing is good for the democratic system. Are we systematically screening out people who realize that there has been an embarrassing personal event such as a messy divorce in their past that they really would rather not have dragged up if they run? And I think the degree to which that knowledge helps voters understand what a candidate is like is very dubious.[24]

Of course, many political professionals were quick to note that campaigns depend upon the news media to publish and air the fruits of opposition research. Journalists certainly discard a great deal of the critical information they are given, and it would be unfair to blame them for the ills of "oppo." After all, candidates and their staffs often bypass the media and air "oppo" findings in TV and radio advertisements. Yet many consultants choose to point the finger at people they regard as co-conspirators. We heard many remarks similar to (though less colorful than) this comment of James Carville's: "I have an old saying. If it's too scummy and slimy for a political consultant, give it to a reporter. There's no depths to which they won't go!"[25]

Spy vs. Spy

The purpose of the second Watergate break-in was to find out what O'Brien had of a derogatory nature about us, not for us to get something on him or the Democrats.
—*G. Gordon Liddy,* Will: The Autobiography of G. Gordon Liddy[26]

At its worst, opposition research can be a gateway to acts that are not just offensive but duplicitous and sometimes illegal. Frequently these cases involve the hiring of private investigators, who by definition have little regard for privacy. Many opposition researchers say they would not hire an investigator or otherwise snoop around. For example, veteran researcher Michael Segal from Cambridge, Massachusetts, insisted: "I actually stipulate [to clients] I'm not a private investigator. I don't do that kind of shit. I'm not photographing anybody. I'm not trying to get anything that's not publicly available. And I'm not going to tell them about any sexual or drug-related matters."[27] Segal, though, has less faith in the scruples of his colleagues. When told that many opposition researchers claimed to have little contact with private investigators, the veteran Democratic researcher said, "I think most of them are lying to you."[28]

Whether through an opposition researcher or on their own, candidates increasingly appear to be turning to private investigators and other information brokers to verify rumors and dig a little deeper for information not readily available through public databases or in county courthouses. To some extent, these moves may be spurred by a political arms race in which one side feels it must devote resources to accumulating factoids on an opponent, for fear that the other side already has committed resources against it. Given this atmosphere of growing mutual suspicion, it is not surprising that candidates are being lured to malevolent practices. For example, Democratic strategist Bill Carrick, a veteran of many dozen campaigns, reported he "had no experience with private eyes until 1994," when he consulted for U.S. Senator Dianne Feinstein (Democrat of California) in her close and expensive race with Republican Michael Huffington. "It was revealed that Huffington had an unregistered [illegal alien] employee working for him at his residence. So in the wake of that, Huffington was desperately trying to dig up the same sort of thing on Feinstein. . . . There were private detectives all over the place, and they were literally harassing people," claimed Carrick.[29]

Another 1994 case of private detective work took place in Massachusetts. Democrat Edward M. Kennedy, one of the Senate's most powerful veterans who has a checkered personal life, appeared to have a serious reelection problem. Although only about 13 percent of Massachusetts voters are registered Republicans, Kennedy seemed in danger of defeat after thirty-two years in office. Just two years before, voters had elected a Republican as governor and Kennedy's nagging personal problems and the rightward drift of the state were imperiling the man who embodied old-time Democratic, government-can-do liberalism. It was well known to insiders that the Republican National Committee already had put together a 460-page report on Kennedy, and Kennedy opponent Mitt Romney had launched his own opposition research efforts, which included one aide who did nothing all day but research Kennedy.[30]

Adding to Kennedy's problems, Romney was a successful businessman but a political unknown. While in years past inexperience may have been a political strike, today it often works in a candidate's favor as the absence of a record gives opponents fewer positions to muddle and distort and less ammunition for attack. Kennedy needed information fast. He turned to the Washington office of a large, elite private investigative agency called Investigative Group Inc. (IGI), which is headed by former Senate Watergate Committee deputy counsel Terry Lenzner, to dig up information about Romney by examining his company, a venture capital firm called Bain Capital. Because Romney had no real public record, any incriminating information likely would be found in his business dealings. Detectives soon were on the case, trying to find evidence linking Romney's company with a 1980s-style insider trading scandal, or even better, linking Romney's business partners with right-wing death squads in El Salvador.[31] (They failed.)

The Kennedy campaign appears to have sought to keep the investigation a secret, with the senator claiming at one point, "I have not spent a great deal of time in terms of assessing opposition or opposition candidates."[32] There was no evidence in Kennedy's campaign finance reports of any money going from the campaign to IGI, and former associates of Romney who received calls from IGI investigators said the probers denied that they were working for Kennedy. (IGI denied any deceptions.) When confronted by the *Boston Globe,* however, the Kennedy campaign admitted using IGI, saying it had to even out the playing field because of Kennedy's long public record. The curious lack of any reported payments to IGI from Kennedy's campaign reports to the Federal Election Commission was explained by a $7,000 disbursement to a Washington attorney, James Flug. The campaign said Flug was coordinating Kennedy's opposition research efforts and that the deal with IGI was a subcontract of that work.[33] A less delicate explanation would be that Kennedy was trying to hide his use of a detective agency. (Having the name Investigative Group Inc. in an FEC report would tip off even the most dull-witted reporter.)

While the revelation was damaging, Kennedy got the last laugh. His in-house "oppo" unit came across an incident in which Romney's firm bought a company and then laid off many of its workers, allowing Kennedy to paint Romney—quite damagingly—as a heartless capitalist. On Election Day the liberal icon won handily.

The use of the Investigative Group Inc. for political discovery also became a hot issue in the 1994 gubernatorial race in Tennessee, with the circumstances closely paralleling those of the Kennedy affair. Three associates of Democratic candidate and Nashville mayor Phil Bredesen said they were contacted by IGI investigators, who asked questions about Bredesen's business and political past, particularly his relationship with his former company, Coventry Corp. In all three cases, the people contacted said they refused to give the callers information because the probers would not identify their employer. "They wanted to know how his mayoral reign had gone, if I thought there were conflicts of interest between his appointments and his positions," said one colleague.[34]

Bredesen accused his Republican opponent, now Governor Don Sundquist, of orchestrating the search, a charge the Sundquist camp denied. Bredensen's campaign manager filed a complaint against Investigative Group Inc. with Tennessee's Department of Commerce and Insurance, which found that the firm did not have a license to operate in the state and issued an order to stop the investigation. According to a state official, the firm applied for a company license and six individual licenses to perform investigative work in Tennessee on September 30, just days before its inquiry began.[35] However, the state had not yet granted them. As with many previous incidents cited in this volume, it would appear that disclosure laws were violated. If someone were investigating Bredesen in relation to the gubernatorial election, that person was spending money to influence an election and was therefore required to disclose the act.

There is a major precedent for such evasions. In 1992, the campaign of presidential candidate Bill Clinton retained the services of San Francisco gumshoe Jack Palladino to stop "bimbo eruptions," a term used by Clinton's own campaign team, before they occurred. Clinton, of course, had been the subject of numerous charges of marital infidelity since the campaign's early days, when former nightclub singer Gennifer Flowers claimed she had a long-term affair with the future president. At the time, the campaign said these eruptions resulted not from substantiated fact, but from tabloid news organizations and other private detectives offering big money for stories. The detective firm, Palladino & Sutherland, was supposed to discover (apparently with some success) when additional claims would come and from where, thereby allowing the campaign to discredit them once they emerged or, even better, prevent them from emerging at all.

The Clinton team, like Kennedy's, apparently decided that disguising the hire would be a better strategy than disclosure, despite Federal Election Commission rules that require making such payments part of the public record. During a one-month FEC reporting period in 1994, the Clinton campaign funneled about $28,000 to Palladino & Sutherland through a Denver law firm that was performing Clinton campaign legal work.[36] A firm attorney, Jim Lyons, also chaired a pro-Clinton lawyer's group. Betsey Wright, a Clinton aide who headed up the "bimbo eruption" suppression effort, justified the transfer, saying the money given to Palladino could be called "legal expenses." Wright claimed Palladino "has the skills as an attorney to interview witnesses that I don't have."[37] This is not how the FEC usually interprets its own regulation. "The bottom line is, you're not supposed to pay someone else in order to cover up your campaign expenditures," said an FEC spokesman.[38] "Otherwise, what good would disclosure be?"

Even up-front reports to the FEC, however, can prove a challenge to reporters trying to follow the money trail in a campaign. Many investigative firms, including opposition research groups, purposely choose innocuous, generic-sounding names to mask their firm's business. "Most people think we're a bunch of developers," said Kevin Spillane of the obliquely named Stonecreek Group. "We didn't want to say 'Dirt Digging R-Us.' "[39]

In a sense, the effort to hide snooping activities is a good sign: apparently some people still have a sense of shame about engaging in such conduct, or at least a fear of what the public will think. On the other hand, the amount of opprobrium placed on candidates who get caught hiring detectives is usually minimal. An incident involving Gary Maloney is depressingly instructive. In 1990, while working for the House GOP's campaign arm, Maloney was caught doing some free-lance snooping into the personal life of Texas gubernatorial candidate Clayton Williams, including a late-night call to the ex-wife of a Williams business partner to ask about Williams's drinking habits and use of profanity.[40] Maloney was widely condemned for his actions, but apparently his employer did not think ill of him: a few weeks later he was promoted.[41]

Perhaps the best-known recent snooping cases involve the campaign of independent candidate H. Ross Perot. Even as Perot was forming his political team in early 1992, his presidential petition committee hired the San Francisco–based Callahan and Gibbons Group to check up on Perot's own volunteers. The campaign later admitted that Callahan and Gibbons had been paid more than

$78,000 to perform background checks of state coordinators. (In his campaign finance report, Perot listed most of those payments as "legal fees.") The campaign claimed the checks were justified because it received information that some volunteers were crooks and con men and they needed to be weeded out.[42] After learning of the investigations, several volunteers resigned and even formed an anti-Perot movement called Disenchanted United People for Equality and Democracy (DUPED). The case was afforded a huge amount of publicity, which, in retrospect, was a bit unfair to Perot in one way. As the above examples show, the diminutive billionaire was well within contemporary norms.

Hiring private eyes is no longer just the province of billionaire candidates for president or well-financed campaigns for high office. The practice is also becoming part of campaigns for local positions. Democratic consultant Dan Payne provided one example from a 1993 contest for a Pennsylvania Commonwealth Court judgeship between Sandra Schultz Newman (the eventual winner) and Democrat Joseph Mistick:

> My candidate [Mistick] had been married twice before, and Newman hired a private eye to call up his ex-wives to ask: "Did he ever abuse you, did he ever get drunk, what can you tell me that might be embarrassing?" And of course the wives immediately called Joe and said, in a spirit of friendship if not forgiveness, "you should know that there is a creep out there who's been calling around." . . . Newman never actually used any of the information [the investigator gathered]. . . . She's a divorce attorney, so she may be used to employing private eyes like this all the time.[43]

In this Pennsylvania case, the detective work had no public effect on the campaign, but in a recent Democratic Party primary race for county prosecutor in an urban area on the West Coast, a private investigator actually changed the outcome of an election. One candidate decided to play vicious hardball politics, and with help from her cronies, she had her opponent's photograph placed in the rogues' line-up for a well-publicized child-molestation case involving multiple children. Even though the targeted candidate apparently had nothing to do with the pederasty, about a tenth of the young children pointed to his picture when asked to identify their molesters. The victim-candidate was then privately and bluntly told by his opponent to withdraw or face public humiliation. At first, he decided to drop out to spare his family, but his campaign consultant asked for forty-eight hours and hired a detective. The p.i. hit pay dirt: early in her career, the other candidate had been a Las Vegas showgirl and, on the side, a $1,000-a-night prostitute. The two candidates quickly reached an accommodation and kept their nuclear weapons in permanent storage. Incidentally, in a modest victory for justice, the contender who was blackmailed first went on to win the election and still serves in public office.[44]

Recognizing that private eyes are a part of the contemporary political landscape, some candidates have actually decided to scrutinize themselves before their opponents have the chance. Republican consultant David Keene cited an incident with one of his own clients during a recent period when the press began focusing hard on certain private life behaviors such as womanizing:

> I have used a private investigator to look at my own candidate before the client made the decision to run. . . . I said that the client should undergo a cursory examination by a private investigator, because, if there is anything he can find out on you, your opponents can find it out, too. Then you can evaluate whether or not you want to run and deal with all that possibly being made public.[45]

This instance is worth recalling whenever we wonder why many talented citizens refuse to run for public office.

Lend Me an Ear

While many campaigns skirt the margins of propriety seeking intelligence about the other side, some plunge headlong into outright illegality.

In 1992, veteran North Carolina Democrat Jim Hunt was seeking to return to his old roost in the governor's mansion. While polls indicated he was favored to do so, the Hunt campaign had an extra edge: campaign officials had discovered that they could listen in on cellular phone calls made by the campaign of Republican nominee Jim Gardner by tuning into a certain channel on a scanner. The eavesdropping continued from spring until late October and included calls made by state Republican chairman Jack Hawke, as well as Gardner himself. The aides went so far as to tape-record some calls and write out the contents in notes. Unfortunately for the snoopers, these provided excellent evidence when prosecutors caught wind of the eavesdropping. Eventually, two of Hunt's former law partners and one campaign worker accepted pleas in the case and received sentences of six months' probation, sixty hours of community service, and fines ranging from $1,000 for the campaign worker to $5,000 for the lawyers. Despite his close relationship with the snoopers, Hunt said he had no knowledge of the wrongdoing and insisted that he had not tried to cover up the matter.[46]

At first glance, his crime may not seem so egregious. In some important details, it differed significantly from the Watergate scandal, in which a group of men broke into the headquarters of the Democratic National Committee in an attempt to repair previously planted telephone bugs. In the North Carolina case, there was no break-in, no premeditated effort to install taps. Lawyer Phil Carlton, one of the defendants and a former state Supreme Court justice, nonchalantly claimed the phone conversations were almost waiting for someone to pick them out of the air. "Accidents happen," he said just after his sentencing, employing a rationalization for his crime that is especially jarring coming from a former judge. "What we thought was a very casual thing, sort of like in the old days when you'd pick up the telephone and hear the neighbors talking on a party line, grew into something more than that."[47]

In truth, little difference exists between eavesdropping on a telephone conversation through a wiretap or through the air. The only difference is technology. In 1972, E. Howard Hunt and G. Gordon Liddy and the rest of the Watergate plumbers had no choice but to break in and physically set up tapping devices if they wanted to listen to the phone conversations of Richard Nixon's political opponents. Twenty years later, a revolution in telecommunications technology has reduced the need for, but not the seriousness of, hands-on snooping.

While the Hunt campaign's eavesdropping is only the second

major instance of politically motivated cellular eavesdropping reported in this country, there is ample indication that the practice goes on quite a bit.[48] Republican consultant Mike Murphy said he has been warned by phone companies that some scanner buffs make a living selling tapes of surreptitiously recorded cell calls by public officials and other well-known people. Adds Murphy: "I've never met such people and I have never been contacted by them and I plan never to be. But the technology is so easy it makes some sense to me." Murphy said he sometimes shows his clients how easily his own scanner picks up conversations. "It is my little way to teach them never to talk on the cell phone."

While no consultant will admit to engaging in these illegal acts, many say such conduct goes on. "I have had people approach me in past campaigns offering those kind of services," said John Roberts, a veteran Republican consultant. Normally the idea was broached not by opposition researchers but by high-tech security firms, he said. "A lot of them will come in and talk to you about countermeasures. 'We should sweep your phones, we want to make sure your offices are secure, and all that.' What they're doing is they're using that as an entree to get in there and offer you other kinds of services. . . . Usually they start with countermeasures, but you're not a very far walk at that point over to the other side of the street."[49]

In 1994, a contest for a Salt Lake City–area House seat was wracked with allegations of illegal break-ins and wiretapping. The two opponents, Republican Enid Greene Waldholtz and incumbent Democrat Karen Shepherd, were old political rivals, having run against each other in the more mild-mannered election of 1992. As the 1994 campaign wound down in October, the Shepherd camp discovered that Waldholtz had hired a private detective earlier in the year. As part of his investigation, California private eye Malcolm Shannon had reviewed contributor records from Shepherd's campaign, as well as those of independent candidate Merrill Cook. That review turned up no leads.[50]

Waldholtz claimed she hired Shannon because of repeated death threats against her since her unsuccessful run for the seat in 1992. The threats, she said, had accelerated as the 1994 race neared. She merely sought to find out who could be behind the threats and wanted to ensure the safety of her family and her campaign staff.

For his part, investigator Shannon said he discovered "very definite indications" of attempted break-ins at Waldholtz's campaign headquarters and her Salt Lake City home, and indications of telephone monitoring and alarm tampering.[51]

Shepherd refrained from making public her own allegations against Waldholtz, but in a post-election interview she claimed to have received information that her home, office, and person may have been compromised. She also said she took counterespionage moves. "[Sources] said that I was followed, that members of my family were followed, that our office in D.C. was broken into, that our phones were tapped. Now, we had both our home phones, here and in D.C., and both our district and our D.C. offices, swept. But when you sweep, all you can tell is if there is a bug on that day."[52] The sweep yielded nothing.

An unhealthy symptom of the proliferation of opposition researchers and private detectives is the sense of paranoia now pervading many campaigns. One of the first acts by 1994 Democratic U.S. Senate candidate Alan Wheat of Missouri, upon moving into a new headquarters across the street from the base of his Republican rival, John Ashcroft, was to hire a private detective, Allied Intelligence of St. Louis. Allied Intelligence proceeded to "debug" the place, even though the Wheat campaign had no evidence of tampering. "We wanted to make sure that the phones were secure, that the fax was secure, that phone lines weren't crossed, that we had privacy," explained Wheat spokesman Tony Lakavage. "This is standard operating procedure in modern campaigns."[53] A political consultant with decades of experience agreed: "In the bigger campaigns we hire security firms to come in and electronically sweep our offices every few weeks. We know that someone might be going through our trash, so we make sure there is nothing there for them to read. You must be vigilant today; it's damage control."

Roberts, himself an expert in communications technology, said there is reason for paranoia. "In order today to be really secure, you need equipment that's extremely sophisticated to pick up some of the bugs. It's no longer a crude tap on a phone line. If somebody's really serious, they can pick up your conversation through vibrating panes of glass in a window. And it's not that expensive anymore to do that."[54]

Murphy recalls one case in which he exploited the opposition's paranoia for his side's gain. Someone working for his opponent, apparently disgruntled, had been anonymously sending Murphy the campaign's internal polling. The material was largely useless as intelligence, Murphy said, but it had another value. "We found out that our opponent was a security obsessed neurotic. So what we would always do was, we would stick one of our bumper stickers on top and send the poll back to him at his home address. So he would know one of his staff had sent it to us, and he would kill everybody. Shoot them all and have lie detectors and stuff."

But Murphy's lighthearted tale of paranoia is outweighed by the numerous reports of serious, illegal security breaches we received from his fellow consultants of both parties. Far too many campaign operatives had had an experience like Republican Sal Russo's:

> We had a break-in in our [California] campaign offices a few years ago. It was politically motivated because the [only] files that were missing involved accusations that [the] opponent may have been involved in drugs. . . . [The opponent's] troops did not want us to have the information. The break-in happened shortly before the election, and afterwards we hired security guards to stay in the offices all night long for the duration of the campaign.[55]

Extra Credit

As disturbing as it may be to get tailed or tapped, or have one's divorce or college days scrutinized, there are other tricks of the political espionage trade that are still more invasive. Ever miss a credit card payment? Use your Visa at an X-rated bookstore? You might want to think twice about a bid for public office, as you could well find your credit records on the front page of the local paper. Clear violations of the federal Fair Credit Reporting Act, which allows personal credit checks only if the targeted individual is requesting credit, are increasingly common.[56]

In the autumn of 1994, Shirley Miller, wife of Georgia governor Zell Miller (Democrat), discovered that someone with access to the secret code of a business in suburban Seattle had twice (in July 1994) perused her credit file on the database of Equifax, a major Atlanta-based credit data clearinghouse. Since she had never heard of the Seattle company, Miller and her husband suspected something untoward. In an interview with us, Governor Miller's campaign consultant, Paul Begala, claimed the effort had Republican fingerprints on it, and he charged Miller's GOP opponent, Guy Millner. "It was Millner's oppo research," said Begala. "The person digging into Shirley Miller's credit record did so under the guise of checking for a mortgage [application]. Now when you live in the governor's mansion, you don't need a mortgage, and the Millers had never applied for one."[57]

Word got out among Georgia Democrats, and local politicians began requesting their credit reports from Equifax to see whether anyone unusual had been looking at them (Equifax set up a toll-free number for this purpose). Two Democratic candidates for the state legislature soon found that someone with the Equifax secret code for a local repossession firm, Georgia Recovery Inc., had been recorded as accessing their files. While Republicans quickly denied any involvement (as did Georgia Recovery), the snooping was traced to Ted Viator, a veteran GOP investigator. Among other clients, Viator did work for Reverend Ron Crews, a Republican who was running for reelection to the state legislature against Democrat Curt Thompson II, whose credit record had been searched along with that of state Representative Jim Martin (Democrat of Atlanta). Crews, a Presbyterian minister running on a pro-family, conservative Christian platform, admitted paying Viator $450 for research on Thompson because he wanted to see if Thompson met a residency requirement for running. He said Viator, as part of the research, offered to run a credit check on Thompson, but that he told Viator not to do it.[58] Crews and Viator later had a falling out, with Viator at first denying that he worked for Crews at all, then denying he was a private investigator. When Crews admitted he hired him, Viator said he lied to protect the identity of his client. Crews also said that Viator misrepresented himself to Crews as a licensed investigator.[59] It was also revealed that Viator had a long history with the Georgia GOP. He had worked on several campaigns in the late 1980s and early 1990s, and in August 1994 he had helped the state party investigate a political scandal involving a home health care company in Augusta, Georgia. State GOP chairman Billy Lovett said the investigation linked Republican legislator Robin Williams to the scandal (denied by Williams). Coincidentally, Williams was the only Republican to report a breach of his credit record.[60] And, like Crews, another state GOP lawmaker, Daniel Lakly, said Viator also had contacted him, telling him he could get confidential credit reports.[61]

Viator's denials turned out to be lies. On June 15, 1995, he admitted in open court that he had illegally accessed Thompson's credit file on behalf of Crews.[62]

While somewhat spectacular, certain aspects of the Viator case are now common. Credit reports, supposedly private and limited to people who are authorized to approve or issue credit, are ridiculously easy to access, according to privacy experts. "You can go to any private investigator and a private investigator is going to be able to get it," remarked Barry Fraser of the Privacy Rights Clearinghouse, a consumer privacy complaints bureau at the University of San Diego.[63] Another suggestion: "Just work for a car dealership or any employer that has access to a credit report and get a credit report," said Evan Hendricks, publisher of *Privacy Times* magazine.[64] Other privacy experts said credit records are routinely, illegally received because a private investigator has a contact at a company authorized to perform credit checks. If that does not work, merely set up an account yourself, said a New York computer security expert. "You can also run a credit report if you're a business. You can run a credit report on really anybody you want. You can—quote—be an authorized subscriber to TRW or Equifax or any of those credit reporting services."[65]

"There is always somebody who is a donor who owns a greeting card or appliance store who does a credit check on your opponent," said political consultant Mike Murphy. "And they bring in the stuff on your opponent and you find out that they had nine Master Cards pulled back for forgery or something. But it's illegal to do a phony credit search, so you have to go back and tell the brother-in-law to take the crap out of there."[66] It is probably safe to assume that not everyone is as scrupulous as Murphy says he is.[67]

Indeed, the 1992 Perot campaign illegally obtained credit reports for some of its own volunteers. One such worker claimed a New York–based private investigator had requested a report on him and others in Perot's Ohio operation.[68] Equifax later said that as many as seventeen credit files of Perot volunteers may have been illegally searched during April and May of 1992. Former volunteers claimed workers for Perot had broken into the credit files, a charge denied by the Perot camp. A New Jersey company, Orix Consumer Leasing, which has an account with Equifax to check the credit of its customers, said some reports were obtained using its security code. Because Orix had never requested the reports on the Perot volunteers, it appeared the code was stolen. An FBI probe ensued but was dropped after the U.S. attorney's office in Dallas refused to prosecute the case.[69]

Some political consultants understand the dangers of using materials such as credit files. Veteran Republican consultant Jim Innocenzi put it bluntly:

> Anytime somebody has approached me with it I tell them to get the fuck out of my face because I don't want to know about it, it has nothing to do with the public discourse in this country. Those people are scumbags. And any campaigns that have somehow gotten their hands on material like this, I tell them to don't even touch it. You're toast if you use it. I have had a couple of campaigns that have come up with it and they've tried to use it, and I say throw the fucking shit away, pretend like you never knew it existed. It backfires more than it helps, it blows up in people's faces.

This is good advice, which is clearly not universally taken. Many of the consultants we interviewed verified that campaigns are discreetly but increasingly using the wares of information brokers. "Oh yeah, that happens all the time," said one, in a response we frequently heard. Had this consultant employed the tactic on behalf of his candidates? He begged off: "I can't give you specifics." Since it "happens all the time," someone's certainly doing it.

An Unhealthy Tactic

After you've been through banking, bedroom, and business secrets, what dirt could possibly be left to scrounge for? There is always the doctor's office. In 1972, New York Democrat Nydia Velazquez had a host of potential enemies in her Brooklyn-based district, having just survived a bitter primary in her redrawn, majority-Hispanic district for an open congressional seat. She had turned her attention to the general election when she became the victim of one of the most egregious invasions of privacy in U.S. political history.

A year before the election, she was in personal crisis. Following a fight with her boyfriend in September 1991, Velazquez attempted to commit suicide by swallowing a large quantity of sleeping pills and vodka. She was rushed to St. Clare's Hospital and Health Center, where she recovered. Until October 1992, her medical records were sealed and private, as dictated by law. Then someone, still unknown, somehow got copies of the records and faxed them to a local Spanish-language radio station and to the *New York Post*. The station refused to broadcast the news, but the *Post*, with typical editorial restraint, prominently featured the story.[70] "The records were leaked for one purpose only: to destroy my candidacy for the U.S. House of Representatives by discrediting me in the eyes of my constituents," Velazquez said.[71]

A privacy expert in southern California believes that medical records violations are becoming even more widespread than violations of credit privacy. "Investigators have their ways where they can obtain all kinds of medical records," said Barry Fraser of the Privacy Rights Clearinghouse at the University of San Diego. "There are private investigators who basically specialize in certain hospitals and have their inside contacts and either through payouts or some type of relationship, they get the insiders to access information whenever it's needed."[72] Velazquez, who was nonetheless elected by a large margin in the heavily Democratic district, later sued the New York hospital for $10 million for failing to protect her privacy and testified before Congress about violations of medical privacy.[73]

Another incident of an illegal distribution of medical records occurred in the 1994 mayoral election in New Orleans, when the records of a 1986 emergency room visit by candidate Marc Morial were provided to the *New Orleans Times-Picayune* two days before the election by a confidential source. The records indicated that Morial had been treated for a cocaine overdose. To its credit, the *Times-*

Picayune waited until it received confirmation from a nurse who had been present at the time before publishing the story (a few weeks after Morial won the election).

Republican Barbara Cubin of Wyoming, who won a House seat in 1994, recalled opening the newspaper one day during the heat of a bitter campaign to find an article naming her biological father. "Apparently someone was able to get into my adoption records— my sealed adoption records," she said. "I don't know how else they could find out my biological father's name."[74]

Moles

While technology has wrought vast changes in political intelligence-gathering, experts say the most popular way of snooping remains the old-fashioned mole planting. Says one prominent political consultant: "Some campaigns are obsessed with 'We're gonna spy,' so what they always try to do is stick a ringer in the phone bank, a ringer volunteer, that kind of stuff. . . . Your average campaign has five hundred volunteers walking around, and it's very easy to get in and wander around."

According to the many consultants we interviewed, sometimes the mole is a disgruntled campaign staffer who will call at regular intervals to spill the beans; or a fired employee of the candidate who takes revenge; or a member of a candidate's finance committee who likes to impress business associates at the club by being "in the know" ("Rich people don't keep their mouths shut," noted one consultant); or a TV station salesperson who, for a few bucks on the side, informs the opposition camp everytime a new political advertisement arrives, scheduled for a future airing. Media consultants are especially aware of the latter, and several we contacted noted that the problem is significant. "There have been some uncanny coincidences between the time we've delivered a new spot to the TV stations and the time the opposition is up [on the air] with a counter-spot that included part of our initial message," observed GOP media consultant Adam Goodman.[75] A Democratic counterpart, Dan Payne, was blunter: "Now when we send a spot to the stations my assumption is that [a station employee] will see it and tell the other campaign. So I advise my candidates not to send the station anything they don't want their opponents to see quickly."[76]

Even the girlfriend or boyfriend of a campaign staffer who is ideologically at odds with their mate's choice of politicians can turn out to be a culprit. Long-time Republican strategist David Keene gave us a marvelous personal example of this honey trap:

> Years ago I ran for office and my opponents placed a young lady in my campaign who got close, as they put it in those days, to my press secretary, and they got some information that they used at a crucial point. After the campaign was over and I had lost, they held a congratulatory dinner, at which she was called to the head table and given a state job by the majority leader of the state senate in the state I had run in. Now, I don't think that would happen today; you would have to reward her some other way.[77]

Other kinds of traps are also set, but the lesson is the same: loose lips can sink campaign ships. Democratic campaign professional Mark Mellman recounted one example from a campaign he consulted for: "Several years ago our opponent's consultant happened to be sitting at a well-known Washington watering hole and he described to someone sitting at their table everything they were going to do against our client. A friend of our client happened to be sitting at the next booth hearing every word, and he wrote it down."[78] Sometimes the transcampaign communication is less coincidental. While Democratic consultant Doc Sweitzer was working for the reelection of a member of Congress, "the manager of the opposition campaign would go to a bar every night and lay out his plans. But the bartender was friendly with us, so we'd feed him questions, he'd ask them and then we'd learn what [the other side] was up to."[79]

The wise campaigner today can trust no one—not the neighborhood bartender, or even the person sitting in the next seat on an airplane, as a Texas politician's spouse discovered recently. By 1994 Democrats were losing their grip on Texas, one of their former southern strongholds. Two years earlier, Texas voters, almost unfailingly loyal to the Democratic Party for more than 100 years, had elected a Republican, Kay Bailey Hutchison, to fill out the Senate term of Lloyd Bentsen, who had taken a cabinet job with the Clinton administration. Now she was running for a full, six-year term and the Democrats were pressing hard to regain the seat. One of the issues they used was espionage: they said the Hutchison campaign had planted a mole in the campaign of her Democratic opponent, Richard Fisher.

The story is rather bizarre and its lesson probably is covered in day one of the spy school syllabus: do not talk (or brag) in public about your business. On a crowded Southwest Airlines flight between Dallas and Austin, Fisher's campaign manager, Robin Rorapaugh, said she serendipitously sat down next to Hutchison's husband, Ray, and Texas GOP chairman Tom Pauken. Not aware of each other's identity, she said she listened while Ray Hutchison told Pauken about a spy they had planted in the Fisher campaign. "We know what's going on from East Dallas stretching all the way to Tyler," Hutchison allegedly boasted to Pauken.[80]

After that conversation ended, Rorapaugh said Hutchison, being friendly, turned to her and asked her what she did for a living. Rorapaugh then identified herself, prompting Hutchison to reportedly respond, "Well, that's just great!" After the alleged incident, Fisher filed a complaint with the FEC alleging that Hutchison had planted the mole. Under FEC regulations, employees of one campaign cannot misrepresent themselves as working for another.

The Hutchison campaign denied that there was a spy in the Fisher campaign, and Pauken said that he never heard the term spy used in the conversation. Nonetheless, the campaign accused Rorapaugh of eavesdropping. "The only spy I hear in this story is someone eavesdropping on someone else's conversations," said David Beckwith, Hutchison's spokesman.[81]

According to some members of Congress, planting moles has become virtual standard operating procedure in congressional campaigns. Several members reported that one-time volunteers for their campaign mysteriously ended up in the opponent's camp by the end of the election. "I think this happens in all campaigns," said former northern Virginia Representative Leslie Byrne, another of the Democrats elected in 1992 who went down to defeat two years later. She continued: "We've had volunteers come in, and they're usually college students, who will, on the pretense of wanting to help, look around, scurry around, look at scheduling and that sort of thing. The other thing that we started doing is shredding garbage. Any sensitive material would be shredded because we are convinced that people were going through the garbage."[82]

Some contend this technique never produces much. Mike Murphy, for one, says it is rarely worth the effort: "All a ringer volunteer finds out is that the coffee machine broke and that a hundred voters were called and twenty-eight are coming to the picnic. Most campaigns have a really tight inner circle who hold the real information and that stuff is kept under lock and key." Still, the occasional "Deep Throat" can be devastating, as Richard Nixon would certainly agree.

Garbage Politics and "Pranks"

Garbage searching, the traditional low-tech espionage that Byrne was guarding against, is known as "dumpster diving" and is probably common. One national party official recalled a recent incident that circumstantial evidence suggests could only have come from a dumpster dive. The official had been considering a fundraising operation that never got off the ground but generated some internal notes. The jottings somehow ended up in the hands of a reporter. "These were hand-written notes that were still in someone's desk. The only other set—a Xerox—was thrown away," recalled the party official. "Either I gave it to the reporter, or it was gotten out of our garbage." When a second reporter from another news organization called to say he had obtained the notes also, the official concluded that he had been the subject of opposition espionage. "There was no question in our mind then that somebody had this and was shopping it around. We swept our phones and they were clean—we do it periodically. We went through files, and everything was where it was supposed to be. The only unaccountable thing was that I had made a photocopy of these notes for a meeting and thrown it away. So that is when we upgraded our shredding information and our security."

"There is always a perky person in a campaign that gets the idea to go search the garbage," observes a campaign veteran. Shredders, he adds, are standard equipment in many modern campaigns. The warning flags are up, and knowledgeable political consultants reveal the likely current practices by the countermeasures they regularly take.

Sometimes the skulduggery leads to so-called pranks, some harmless and others vile. Campaigns can bring out the worst in otherwise intelligent professionals, from the cruel (sending dead flowers to a losing campaign) to the merely childish (ordering C.O.D. pizzas for the opposition camp). One must concede that some such efforts are playful or shrewd. Democrat Joe Trippi gives an example of each from his days with the 1984 presidential campaign of former vice president Walter F. Mondale:

> I was running Pennsylvania for Mondale in the 1984 primary against Gary Hart. We had this huge Mondale for President dinner, with four or five thousand people there. Then, after dessert, I see out of the corner of my eye that all the waiters are bringing out plates of fortune cookies, and it hits me about ten minutes later that I never ordered any cookies. To my shock and horror Mondale gets up to give his speech, grabs a cookie, opens it, and it reads, as they all did, "Hart wins Pennsylvania." Mondale got this horrid, pale look on his face. But we won Pennsylvania by 14 points anyway!

> We were trying to compete in the 1984 Iowa Democratic straw poll, where each campaign buys a ton of tickets and tries to get their people there so that every news network in the country will say that they won the damn thing. Well Alan Cranston [California U.S. senator] had bought a zillion tickets; he had literally bought the whole hall out, which left Mondale, who had more support in the state, out in the cold. So what the Mondale campaign did was we recruited people from little towns and picked them up with Mondale buses. And about five miles outside of the straw poll site, the buses stopped and we took all the Mondale buttons and posters off and dressed our people in Cranston colors and put a Cranston for President sign on the buses. When we got to their straw poll we pulled

the Mondale buses up to the Cranston tent. There was a bunch of excited Cranston supporters out front ushering people in, yelling "Cranston, Cranston." So we were shouting for Cranston as we got off the bus, we got our tickets from their tent, and we went into the hall and pulled out our Mondale gear and won the convention.[83]

But campaign pranks seem to have taken a nasty turn since the good-humored days of 1984. For instance, Karan English, a former Democratic representative from Arizona, recalled that in 1992 her office was burglarized and her schedule stolen. Someone, apparently the thief, then called up and canceled all her meetings, attempting to wreak havoc on her campaign.[84]

Central Florida saw a rash of similar "pranks" in 1992. Among the stunts: phony fliers alleging one candidate had AIDS and anonymous letters alleging child abuse by another candidate.[85] Democratic political consultant Vic Kamber recalled an incident involving phony letters being sent out under a campaign's name and another in which a candidate's television advertising "time buys" were canceled by someone purporting to represent the campaign. And many campaign veterans commented on the wave of destructive vandalism they have noticed in recent years: an upturn in slashed tires, headquarters damaged, signs torn down in the middle of the night.

A case in point was cited by well-known Democratic consultant Paul Begala, who recalled the vitriolic nastiness of the 1994 U.S. Senate contest in Pennsylvania.[86] He mentioned the experience of one young woman, Olivia Morgan, who worked for Begala's candidate, Senator Harris Wofford. Morgan's chief duty was to videotape the public speeches and press conferences of Wofford's GOP challenger, now Senator Rick Santorum. Recording the opponent's public utterances is a common practice engaged in by both parties; it obviously comes in handy for TV and radio advertisements when a candidate commits a gaffe or contradicts himself. Normally, the professionals on both sides tolerate this activity and permit their rivals to go about their business unimpeded. As Begala noted, "The kids with this assignment always introduce themselves and they're taught to be very polite." But with Morgan, according to Begala, "They roughed her up and slammed her around pretty good. She's not a big person, but they'd make a point of bumping into her." Morgan reported to us that her treatment worsened as the race got closer in October: the air was let out of her tires, her car was blocked on a one-way street so she could not drive away, and on occasion Santorum himself would point her out in public and egg his supporters on in their behavior toward her.[87]

Sadly, this example is not exceptional. As the fictional Mr. Dooley remarked, "Politics ain't beanbag," and emotions have always run high among partisans. Yet there has usually existed a degree of professional comity and courtesy that, like many of society's genteel standards, seems to be breaking down. Even political consultants who denied to us that dirty tricks were on the increase admitted that viciousness on the campaign trail has become a virus grown epidemic.

The list of such incidents grows longer every year. And if 1995 is any indication, 1996 promises to be a banner year. In late June 1995, someone called a Chicago hotel where freshman Republican Representative Michael Patrick Flanagan was planning a fundraiser and informed the management that the event had been canceled owing to the death of Flanagan's mother.[88] One happy note: the joke backfired, with the hotel charging Flanagan $4,000 less on account of the confusion, thereby increasing the net profits for the congressman's war chest.[89]

Like many other such incidents, the Flanagan case was treated as humorous in media reports, including an item on Cable News Network.[90] "Nowadays journalists have a tendency to say, 'Both sides do it, so what the hell,'" noted James Carville.[91] Our times, and our press, are more cynical than in the early 1970s. Similar "pranks" by aides to the 1972 reelection campaign of President Richard Nixon, once disclosed in 1973 and 1974, met with considerable media condemnation. Among the many stunts pulled by legendary Nixon trickster Donald Segretti: planting "moles" in Democratic campaigns, forging damaging letters, pilfering documents, and disrupting Democratic campaign events by phoning in cancellations to hotels.[92] Sound familiar?

Segretti was eventually convicted of distributing campaign literature illegally and spent four and a half months in prison. His tricks were treated gravely in part because it was obvious at that time where they had eventually led: to acts both illegal and profoundly corrupt.

We are not going to argue that there is *never* any cause for hiring a private investigator or otherwise digging into an opponent's personal life, or that some pranks are not relatively harmless. As for opposition research that is confined to a politician's record in conducting public business, the problem is not the digging so much as what is done with the dirt. The common feature of all these practices is the slippery slope on which they place candidates and campaigns. Such tactics frequently go too far, becoming acts that either constitute or lead to "significant impairment in the conduct of public affairs"—our definition of corruption.

One of the little-known aspects of Watergate is the role of Democratic operative Richard Tuck, a famous dirty trickster, who began harassing Republicans in the 1940s. Tuck started tormenting Richard Nixon long before Nixon set up the Committee to Re-elect the President. In 1960, during a controversy over Nixon's brother's acceptance of a large loan from Howard Hughes, Tuck arranged to have Nixon photographed during a visit to San Francisco's Chinatown meeting a group of children holding a sign printed in Chinese. Informed by a Chinese supporter that the sign read "What about the Hughes Loan?" Nixon threw a widely publicized tantrum. On another occasion, Nixon was on a whistle-stop tour and had just begun addressing a campaign rally from the back of a train when Tuck, disguised as a trainman, instructed the conductor to pull away from the station.

For the 1972 race, Nixon's operatives vowed that they would have a "Dick Tuck capability." And that, by some accounts, was one origin of a constitutional crisis. During the Senate Watergate hearings, Nixon's chief of staff, H. R. Haldeman, muttered to Tuck: "You S.O.B., you started this."[93]

The decision to wage a dirty war against one's opponent tends to spiral downward into unethical conduct so easily that, for the vast majority of campaigns, it would be wiser not to take that first step. The public, certainly, would be much better off. And as we will argue in chapter 11, it is the press that must elevate this hidden side of politics—so that, as in the wake of Watergate, the costs of doing dirty business will once again exceed the benefits.

7

Street Money: Minority Votes for Sale or Rent?

> There's not a lot of money that any individual is going to get and put in his pocket, and just make a killing on election day. That's not what it's all about. That's not the kind of money that flows into the black community.
>
> —*A black political organizer in Arkansas*

The Democrats' best-known external resources—and the ones that most pain Republicans—are organized labor and minority groups. As noted earlier, organized labor has for decades provided Democrats with an army of volunteers and huge amounts of untraceable financial support, even as their rank-and-file membership has defected to the Republicans in increasing numbers. Minorities, meanwhile, have been the single most loyal Democratic voting bloc—in raw vote terms even more indispensable to the Democrats than labor. The problem for Democrats has been getting their minority base to the polls. The sordid truth about Democratic methods in minority communities is yet another prime example of the power of money in politics: the dollar, not common interest or belief, is the most prominent element linking American politics from top to bottom.

As our investigation has uncovered, a great deal of money is going right into the pockets of some African-American community leaders in various states. Some do make "a killing," often to the chagrin of the Democratic officials who pay them. And we have also found

87

evidence of small payments in exchange for the votes of average citizens in minority areas.

Not surprisingly, senior Democrats have been unwilling to criticize these practices publicly because (1) the minority vote has been vital to Democratic electoral success since the 1960s, and (2) increasingly, money has become a key to securing the party's minority base. More surprisingly, perhaps, journalists have been very reluctant to look into this apparently taboo subject, even when serious complaints and irregularities have surfaced over the years. Political correctness in the newsrooms of America may permit full-fledged investigation of alleged *suppression* of the minority vote but squash journalistic inquiry into potential *corruption* of the same vote.

Granted, candidates have given inducements and enticements to voters for as long as the American Republic has existed.[1] While running for the Virginia House of Burgesses in 1758, George Washington provided 160 gallons of rum, beer, and cider at the polls for just 391 voters and their friends.[2] (The continued swilling at the polls moved one newspaper in 1792 to remark that the "Voice of the People" was really the "Voice of Grog.")[3] Later on, big-city bosses handed out jobs, housing, and education to immigrants in exchange for their loyalty on election day. In the early decades of the twentieth century, campaign finance scholars such as Louise Overacker were already noting "occasions when money paid to 'organizers' or field workers smacks unpleasantly of bribery." The same accusations have been made against modern-day politicians, mainly in the Democratic Party, who give "street money" or "walking-around money" to influential activists in certain communities. The money is usually described as remuneration to the recipients for their efforts in boosting voter turnout, not as a payment for votes per se.

Often the activists taking the money are African-American. Sometimes the money is spread around the community, to hire "flushers" and "haulers"— those who, respectively, find potential voters on election day and then take them to the polls. Cash is also paid to precinct workers, those who man the polls all day. But, frankly, many inside the election world know that the payment is simply a payoff, pocketed by the recipients and considered a fee for a vote or an endorsement.

Perhaps because of the racial dimension, as suggested above, street money has rarely been the focus of much news coverage, pundit commentary, or academic research. But the controversy has been brewing privately in the Democratic camp, especially in the South, fed by the resentments of some candidates and consultants who are forced to budget the item.

The Democrats and the Black Vote

While street money is used today mainly by Democrats in minority communities, the technique was refined in the nineteenth century extensively by Republicans and almost exclusively on white voters in most states. For example, in the presidential election of 1888, Republican nominee Benjamin Harrison ousted incumbent Democratic President Grover Cleveland in good part with purchased votes.[4] The price per "independent" vote, even in Harrison's native Indiana, was either three of the new $5 gold pieces or a crisp $20 bill. Much of the street money planning was orchestrated by the corrupt chairman of the Republican National Committee, Matthew S. Quay of Pennsylvania (appropriately enough, a former state treasurer). After the election, a naive President-elect Harrison, who was shielded from much of the skulduggery, remarked to Quay, "Providence has given us the victory!" Later Quay retorted to associates, "Providence hadn't a damned thing to do with it!"[5]

In recent years, no one—Democrat or Republican—has had Quay's gall or has employed methods as blatant as his. But some Democrats have come close on occasion, and the root cause is the vital importance of the minority vote to the Democratic Party.

It is no exaggeration to say that the Democrats would almost never win a presidential election, and only occasionally win major elections in many states, without minority Americans (especially African-Americans and Hispanics, whose support is vital in the South and large cities nationwide). In 1992, for example, George Bush maintained a slight edge among whites on Election Day, but Bill Clinton's enormous margins among blacks and Hispanics delivered the White House to the Democrats.[6] Similarly, in the only other recent presidential victory for the Democrats, Jimmy Carter's in 1976, blacks and Hispanics provided far more than Carter's 1.7

million vote national margin over President Ford. Not incidentally, both our Democratic and Republican interviewees credited Southern Governors Clinton and Carter with especially effective use of street money. "Carter taught the Democratic Party a lot about walking around money in the South," RNC chairman Haley Barbour remarked. "There was a quantum leap for the Democrats in the '76 campaign." Particularly in the South, Democrats usually rely on 80 to 90 percent (or more) of the African-American votes to overcome solid white majorities for many GOP candidates for president, U.S. Senate, House, and governor; when Democrats win, African-Americans can often take the credit. In Virginia, where the Democrats have a particularly aggressive minority turnout operation, Democrats fared far better in 1994 than they did elsewhere in the South. "We spent all of our energy at the grassroots level, just knowing that the numbers were there if we could get them to the polls," said Jean Jensen, executive director of the Virginia Democratic Party.[7]

White support for Democrats has been declining to some degree in every section of the country. But it is in the South that the Democratic proportion of the white vote has fallen most dramatically. Consequently, the Democratic Party has become increasingly dependent upon its ability to turn out a large minority vote. Over time, the sophistication of these turnout operations has grown and the resources poured into minority areas have multiplied.

How does the system work? In the black community, ministers, officeholders, and "voter league" leaders are critical to Democratic organizing efforts, and they are explicitly targeted. But the means necessary to secure their endorsements and cooperation vary from the wholly legitimate (pledges by the candidate to back certain policies and programs) to the seedy (transfers of large amounts of money to key individuals). In return, black ministers typically endorse their chosen candidates from the pulpit on the Sunday prior to election day, and they provide church membership lists to campaigns. Minority officeholders can lend their political operatives and personal networks of backers. And black voter leagues each distribute their trademark "sample ballots" at the polls, with their chosen candidates highlighted. (One such league in a Southern state has passed out sample ballots on yellow paper each year, and voters have learned to look for the so-called goldenrod ballot at the polls.) These efforts add up.

Much of the Democratic Party's traditional efforts are concentrated in a massive election-day get-out-the-vote (GOTV) drive, which requires the participation or forbearance of the minority leadership. In Virginia, for example, a statewide Democratic campaign will budget at least $250,000–300,000 for a minority GOTV effort, and it can be much higher. In 1989, Douglas Wilder's successful campaign to become the nation's first elected African-American state governor dedicated approximately one million dollars to get out the vote in black communities.

Even in a less ambitious effort, hundreds of flushers are hired; they are frequently black high school students organized by a Democratic teacher, or college students who have the scheduling flexibility to spend all of Election Day prowling minority neighborhoods for potential voters. The flushing activity becomes frenzied late in the day as poll closing time approaches. In the tight 1994 Virginia U.S. Senate race between Democrat Charles Robb and Republican Oliver North, for instance, "some [black] neighborhoods in Richmond were flushed five or six times between four o'clock in the afternoon and seven o'clock at night," reported Jean Jensen. Each flusher is typically paid $20 to $50. Fleets of cars, buses, and other vehicles are also at the ready to ferry voters to and from the polls, with the drivers paid expenses plus the flusher's fee. For every two dozen flushers or drivers there is a coordinating supervisor, paid up to $100 for the day's work. Supervisors are often loyal party workers, but the cooperating ministers and community leaders normally get to designate a fair share of these vote captains. Some are also checking the rolls at the polls, to see which predesignated black voters have not yet cast a ballot and need to be found and transported. "The Democrats have got it down to a science," commented one admiring GOP operative. "They use tons of money; in a typical campaign it is a significant part of a Democrat's budget."

SUPPRESSION VERSUS TURNOUT

On paper, this scheme seems innocuous enough, as well as effective. In practice, hidden abuses are rampant. The national and state political consultants who organize these campaign extravaganzas are well aware of the mischief. *Campaigns and Elections* magazine publisher Ron Faucheux surveyed a bipartisan group of 202 consultants and party officials on the subject, and three-quarters said "using illegal, unreported street money to get out their vote" was a practice that happened often (24 percent) or sometimes (51 percent).[8] Interestingly, just 19 percent said "using illegal, unreported street money to help suppress opposition voter turnout" occurred often (1 percent) or sometimes (18 percent).[9] Yet when GOP consultant Ed Rollins, a key decision maker in now-Governor Christine Todd Whitman's 1993 campaign in New Jersey, bragged to a post-election gathering of reporters that he had financed a half-million-dollar voter suppression operation to bribe black ministers not to endorse Democratic Governor James Florio for reelection, it was banner-headline news for days. (Apparently, Rollins fabricated the claim; no credible evidence of any such scheme ever surfaced, even with two grand jury investigations—one federal and the other state sponsored, and Rollins himself apologized profusely and admitted that he had essentially made it all up to impress the scribes.)[10] Contrast the mega-coverage given the Rollins dust-up about unproven voter suppression with the dearth of reporting on the ample flow of turnout money, even though consultants freely acknowledge that dubious cash flows abundantly into minority areas. In that controversial New Jersey 1993 gubernatorial election, for example, the Democrats spent over $540,000 in street money, compared with the Republicans' paltry $43,000.[11]

ON THE STREET: DEMOCRATS REASSESS AN OLD TECHNIQUE

"Street money has become a way of life in lots of areas, and the cash goes beyond turning out the vote," charges one veteran Republican official. Perhaps surprisingly, quite a number of senior Democrats confirmed the allegation, and even went further. In our discussions with almost two dozen veteran Democratic political consultants, party operatives, and officeholders—including some of the most experienced and high-level campaigners in the country—we discovered two general facts: (1) no Democrat was willing to be quoted by name on this hypersensitive subject, lest the vitally important black leadership be alienated; but (2) despite a belief that street money in small increments (to flushers and the like) is defensible and harmless, many Democrats have become critical and resentful of street money's excesses, in which they feel forced to participate. Some are irritated that, as one congressman put it, "Unlike in white neighborhoods, in black precincts you have to pay every single poll worker. Almost no one does anything for free."[12] But mainly, they are angry about the mercenary practices of some leading members of the black leadership, and they have wised up to the games being played by a substantial number of minority organizers, whose goal is primarily personal gain.

One high-ranking and well known liberal Southern Democrat, who "cut my teeth on street money back in the '60s," called the contemporary practice of street money "a scam" for some people. He described a deterioration in leadership standards in Southern minority communities that has occurred over many years. While at one time political involvement was a high and urgent calling for the best and brightest, now politics is often a refuge for fast-buck scoundrels:

> Three decades ago we had very substantial people of integrity who were managing the process—people who are now judges and members of Congress and church bishops who did [election work] out of an urgent sense of moral, ethical, and political necessity. They're now mainly retired, dead, or unavailable, and many of the ones who've replaced them are out for themselves.
>
> It is a terrible waste of money today [in some locales]. In the black community, you can do more with phone banks, direct mail, and other media than you can with street money . . . primarily because you cannot recruit the necessary operatives who are effective and trustworthy in administering the process.

From time to time, hints of street money scandals have surfaced. News that Whitewater special prosecutor Kenneth Starr was investigating Bill Clinton's 1990 Arkansas gubernatorial campaign for its cash distribution in black areas brought additional attention to the subject in early 1995.[13] (At least $33,000 in the Democratic primary and $50,000 in the general election fueled Clinton's street money program in his seventh and last campaign for governor.) And in every election cycle there are occasional, scattered reports of massive street money expenditures in high-profile races. For example, in August 1994 intraparty warfare broke out among South Carolina Democrats during a close gubernatorial runoff between Lieutenant Governor Nick Theodore and Charleston Mayor Joseph Riley. After Theodore placed ahead of Riley in the summer primary, Riley charged that Theodore's campaign had paid $7,500 to a county elections commissioner who steered minority votes to Theodore, in part by circling Theodore's name on the sample ballots passed out at the polls.[14]

But far more often than not, the controversies, and the facts, do not break out into the open, and street money abuse remains in the shadowy world of backroom politics. Yet when those who are knowledgeable about it tell what they know, even hardened observers can be amazed by the extent of the sleaze, and also the chutzpah of some who extort cash from vulnerable candidates. Consider these examples from past campaigns cited to us by our interviewees; the tales are a representative sampling of the stories we were told:

"TRIBUTE" TO BLACK MINISTERS. Churches have always played a special role in the African-American community, and they are often the center of its politics, too. That sometimes makes black ministers of large churches into political powerhouses who can command a candidate's attention—and wallet. Many of these men of God appear to have substantial worldly needs. The more subtle among them request "gifts"—usually in the thousands of dollars— to the church "building fund," which may be personally controlled by the minister (and possibly some associates). What onerous work does the minister do in exchange for this sizable gift? "Usually he hands over the church membership list, makes a few phone calls, lets us use the building for meetings, and permits the sample [endorsement] ballot to be handed out the Sunday before the election," reported one long-time Democratic organizer, who noted that these demands on the minister's time were certainly not taxing.

Other ministers are bolder still. Another Democratic consultant who has worked in the black community in over forty campaigns at the state and local levels explained that in most urban areas, "the ministers have a price, which they call an 'honorarium.' I rely on their political aide or contact to tell me what the price actually is to get their support." In one major city in his Southern state, the going rate is $3,000 apiece. A third Democratic campaign veteran said the usual price for a significant minister in his state is about $5,000, although it varies a bit by pecking order: "We basically go in and pay our dues; we give the appropriate tribute to the appropriate minister."

A Southern member of the U.S. House of Representatives described a strange form of honorarium—the reverse speaking fee. "When I speak from the pulpit of certain black churches I have to pay $400 or so for the privilege." The congressman called it "a shakedown, pure and simple."

ENTREPRENEURS AT WORK. Several Democratic activists in one state cited a clever scheme developed over the years by a minister-entrepreneur who had a substantial financial stake in a radio station. Candidates are "encouraged" to buy "a lot of radio time [on the station]," revealed one frequent campaign manager with firsthand experience. The "smart" candidate would start radio ads on the station early, with a large purchase, said the manager, "and I know that some candidates have ended up buying the air time at premium rates instead of the lowest unit rate." (Candidates are supposed to be offered preelection air time at a discounted rate rather than the regular price for commercial advertisers.)[15]

The Democrats we contacted also had stories galore of street money activists who once may have been motivated by issues but now operated strictly for cash:

> Lucy was somebody who used to do it for the cause and the good of the community, and then she started doing it for the good of Lucy.

> Chuck was paid $15,000 to get his fellow black officials and poll workers to the polls, but when you went to the polling stations, there was no one there.

> Carolyn was paid $6,000 to turn out voters for the [Democratic] mass meeting, and she turned out exactly three people.

> We got a call from the aide to [a particular black officeholder] to tell us that [the official's] endorsement would cost $6,000 this year.

Even when some of these individuals ascend to high party office, the price does not change. One powerful black community official in a Southern rural area was promoted to the chairmanship of the Democratic congressional district committee. When the local congressman, also a Democrat, ran for reelection in 1994, he had hoped to save the substantial sum he had regularly paid the official in past campaigns, under the assumption that political organizing is one of the duties of a district chair. The congressman was quickly disabused of the notion, according to a senior aide: "[The district chair] said he was highly insulted, and that he fully expected to get paid the same amount he was paid in the past. But it really is ridiculous, because he was not doing anything he shouldn't do as the chair of the party's district committee."

The Democratic gravy train gives a ride to lower-level entrepreneurs as well. After a special state legislative election in the mid-1980s, the Virginia Democratic Party headquarters was the designated site for the payment of $20 to each poll worker and driver. But according to one of the party staffers, "The word got out in the black community that all you had to do to get $20 was to say you did some work, and before we knew it, the line of petitioners wound all through our building and out the door. We ran through $10,000 in two hours, and had to lock ourselves into the office and hope people would drift away."

THE BIDDING WAR. Press reports about street money are not only sparse, they also focus mainly on general elections. Yet it is in Democratic nominating primaries and caucuses that street money has far more impact, and it is "where the dirty stuff really goes on," as one highly experienced Democratic consultant phrased it. There are two reasons for this. First, in many states the African-American vote is very substantial—a quarter to a third or more of the total ballots cast. Second, in a general election black leaders, overwhelmingly Democrats, have less maneuverability once the party nominee is chosen. But prior to the primary or convention, many black leaders and organizers (and some white activists, too) are up for bid to Democrats competing for the nomination.

Among the many examples cited by sources was one that occurred in a recent Democratic primary contest for governor in a Southern state. A key black leader was highly sought after by both of the major gubernatorial candidates, and "the bidding for him was hilarious," recalled the campaign manager for one of the contenders: "My opposite number [in the other campaign] bought him, then I bought him, then the other guy outbid me. And I only found out he had deserted me when he showed up at a big Democratic dinner wearing a sticker for [the other candidate.] To top it off, he had come [to the dinner] at *my* expense, so I had to be restrained from hitting him. He and I had solidified a deal—it was a done deal—but the other side had obviously offered him enough so that it was worth going back on his word to me." The exact price was never determined, but "it had to be in the thousands of dollars," in view of the original deal, the outbid manager guessed.

Some activists claim to have their own mini-organizations to sell, according to Democratic political consultants, and they sometimes auction them off in intraparty contests. Conveniently, a favored arrangement doubles their money and lets them rest on election day, as described by a Democratic campaign professional: "Many times people go to both sides and say, 'This campaign has given us money to have doughnuts for the volunteers and we're going to work hard for them. Now, if *you* give us money for doughnuts, our people will be too busy eating doughnuts to go out and work.'" This was confirmed by yet another Democratic consultant, nationally known but with special expertise in certain Southern states. According to him, "Some people kinda knew they could pick up some easy money . . . I gave a few of 'em $200 to go and *be* for the other guy, so long as they never came back in my headquarters again!"

AFFIRMATIVE ACTION PLUS. Democratic experts on street money complain as much about some of the minority organizations they work with as about the individual entrepreneurs out to make a fast buck. These groups—such as state and local chapters of the National Association for the Advancement of Colored People (NAACP) and "Crusade for Voters" committees—not only frequently request large payments but also designate the companies and agents through which the party is supposed to operate in their communities. This special political form of minority contracting is the opposite of competitive bidding, judging by the hefty fees the Democrats are often charged. One state party officer remembered a particularly egregious example involving the NAACP in a governor's race:

> We were specifically told to hire three African-Americans by the [state] NAACP's executive director. They had formed a company, and every month we had to send them a check for around $4,000, plus whatever expenses they had incurred. And it's happened in other campaigns, too. We have to take on people we don't know, or who have bad reputations, or who don't know what the hell they're doing. And there's not a damn thing we can do about it.

Another party official recalled the terms of agreement with one small city's black "Crusade for Voters": "We went ahead and gave them a $6,000 lump-sum payment, made out to the organization. Of course, the officers get to spend it anyway they like, and there's little or no accountability. Then they also kept telling us who our printer's going to be, who's going to cater the luncheons, what restaurant we have to go to. . . . The final nerve was when they submitted a list to us of all the poll workers we had to hire: [the officers] had every one of their names on there to get just one more payment." Some black ministers also make similar demands. "There are always a few people who are a minister's leg men or whatever, and you know that in order to get the endorsement you've really got to hire those people," explained a long-time Democratic field worker.

This system can be oddly reminiscent of government, where a new agency is created to accomplish a task that an established part of the bureaucracy should be doing but for idiosyncratic reasons is resisting. The result, as a veteran campaign manager knows, is as redundant and wasteful in politics as it is in government:

> I've learned that in the minority areas you've got to pay the "right" person, even if it makes no sense. If you find someone

better qualified or more energetic, you still need to pay the veteran, [lest] he get pissed off. So you pay multiple people just to appease them even if they don't really do anything, so that they won't get mad and go out and badmouth the campaign and cause trouble. It's wasted money used for damage control, and over time there's more of it and it's becoming a headache and a half.

Despite the best efforts of national and state Democratic leaders who clearly recognize the drain on their limited resources, the street money problem is spreading like a malignant cancer in some areas. While long a part of the culture in urban minority communities, the expectation that one will be paid for political work has now taken root in many rural locales—sometimes through stupidity. In Virginia's hot 1994 U.S. Senate campaign, incumbent Democrat Charles Robb, desperate to generate the African-American turnout, sent an out-of-state consultant into rural central and southside counties that had no history of street money payments. This individual had no familiarity with the area's norms but was obviously experienced with street money, as he immediately went about setting up a system to pay poll workers, flushers, and telephoners. Senior Democrats in the region were furious, bemoaning the sad precedent that had irretrievably been established. Said one: "From now on Democrats are going to have to pay people to do things they typically did before for free because they thought it was the right thing to do."

SHELL ORGANIZATIONS. In most places Democrats simply accept reality, however grudgingly, and they set about finding ways to achieve their minority goals without attracting undue attention from the press or the opposition. One method is to pour street money into "shell" organizations established for that sole purpose. This technique allows party organizations to evade election law reporting rules, which require campaign committees to itemize all significant expenditures. Instead of reporting dozens of payments to various community leaders, the party committees disclose a few large payments to vaguely named organizations that never publicly account for where the money goes.

A few weeks before the 1994 gubernatorial election in Georgia, for example, state Democrats sent $30,000 to a firm with no offices that was owned by a black political consultant, Munson Steed. The state party chair denied the payment was "street money," but he could cite no instance of Steed's work other than the printing of T-shirts.[16]

The same year in Tennessee, during the week of the election the state Democratic Party paid out more than $110,000 to several groups whose actual existence can not be established. These include a company called American Business Planning ($23,500), the North Memphis Voters League ($3,000), the Ninth District Democratic Voters Drive ($93,000), and the West Tennessee Voter Council ($20,925). Even allowing for the transient nature of campaign organizations, we were surprised at our inability to track down these groups, which are not listed in telephone directories and are not registered with the state of Tennessee as businesses or campaign organizations. The finance director of the Tennessee Democratic Party, Mark Henshaw, steadfastly refused to give us any information about who ran the groups or where we could reach anyone associated with them. "That's something that's kind of fairly confidential," he said. "I doubt there's any way I could provide you with that information because it's confidential, campaign related."[17] A written request to the chairman of the Tennessee Democratic Party seeking even the most general information about the groups was also spurned.

However, it is not a complete secret where the money goes. U.S. Representative Harold Ford, the African American-Democrat who represents the Memphis area's Ninth Congressional District, acknowledges that much of the money flows into his political organization. He insists, however, that the money is used for legitimate purposes.[18] There is no available documentation of this, but news reports do indicate that Ford conducted a major turnout operation. One white Democratic operative who has managed statewide campaigns in Tennessee said he does not believe most of the money is pocketed outright:

> What it is—don't quote me—is it's three weeks' worth of employment for a lot of people. Does anybody make out like a bandit? I don't know. I don't think so. What happens is, a lot of state senators get to hire 22 people for three weeks. Not an

outrageous wage but it's a job, and they feel great about being able to hire [them], and all those people run around and put up signs. . . . Now is there padding in that? Probably. But it's not like somebody sits there and rakes in a huge amount of money.

Yet Republicans—who also will not discuss this subject for the record—firmly believe that large amounts of this money *are* pocketed. The truth is elusive in cases like this, simply because Democrats appear to be deliberately obscuring how they spend their money and thereby frustrating one of the essential purposes of the campaign finance disclosure laws. As the reader has already seen in earlier chapters and will see again throughout this volume, deliberate obscurantism is a foul, bipartisan practice increasingly exercised across the campaign landscape.

ALASKA'S GAS-GATE. So far the focus in this chapter has been on street money poured into the African-American community. But other areas with concentrations of non-black minorities have witnessed similar schemes. One creative, and possibly decisive, example is found in Alaska's close 1994 gubernatorial contest, which Democrat Tony Knowles won over Republican Jim Campbell by just 583 votes out of 213,354 cast.

The state's North Slope Borough, which includes the town of Barrow and is located near the oil-rich Prudhoe Bay, is home to a heavy concentration of Native Americans. The population is overwhelmingly Democratic, and the borough's mayor had endorsed Democratic nominee Knowles. During 1994 the borough had requested and received an informal opinion from the Criminal Division of the U.S. Justice Department about its plans to assist voters with their transportation to the polls by providing free gasoline. The Justice Department made clear that this help would run afoul of the law unless it was narrowly targeted to isolated Native Alaskans in need and the provision of gas did not exceed the amount required for the actual trip.[19] However, borough leaders had a more expansive "Gas for Votes" plan in mind in order to produce a good turnout of voters for their favored ticket. On Election Day, the borough set up tables within thirty feet of the polls and made available a government voucher good for ten gallons of gasoline for any voter who asked. (Enough vouchers had been prepared to cover every one of the borough's 3,500 voters.)[20] The offer was well publicized in advance, and after the election it was credited in news accounts with generating a high turnout of Democratic voters.

Incidentally, the vast majority of borough voters lived within a few miles of their polling stations, and ten gallons of gas (worth $27 at local rates) was no minor gift in a place where refined fuel is expensive. There is clear evidence that borough officials knew exactly what they were doing and which candidate they were boosting with their unique tundra twist on the "street money" gambit.[21] One high-ranking borough officeholder openly bragged that "without the Gas for Votes [program], Tony Knowles would not have been elected governor."[22]

REPUBLICAN COUNTERSTRATEGIES

Whenever Republicans try to win a substantive portion of the minority vote or compete in areas where street money is an honored tradition, they can play the game as aggressively as the Democrats. GOP pollster Frank Luntz, while still a student at the University of Pennsylvania, participated in a mayoral campaign in Philadelphia that served as his eye-opening initiation to the world of street money. While in headquarters one day,

> they brought in a briefcase full of money—well over $20,000. I don't think I've ever seen so much cash in one place at one time. And people came in and got their stacks of dough. . . . There was a list of names, and an amount after each name, and people came in one after the other. Supposedly this was to go to pay precinct-workers. Who knows where the money went.
>
> I said, "I can't believe that you're doing this. This is not democracy, this is not what this country is supposed to be about." They basically told me to grow up, that this is the way it's done. I got so upset that I was sent out of the office because [they said] I was making people nervous.[23]

In most elections, however, the GOP makes little serious attempt to win a sizable segment of the minority vote, but the party does

sometimes employ counterstrategies to minimize black turnout—
and these techniques can be unsavory. The Ed Rollins episode of
vote suppression has been generally discounted, but a handful of
Democratic operatives insisted to us that they have witnessed such
efforts on occasion. Democratic pollster Keith Frederick recalled
that one of his clients, Congressman John Breaux of Louisiana, was
the target of a national Republican Party program of "ballot suppression" in minority precincts when he ran for the U.S. Senate in
1986.[24] A memorandum outlining GOP plans to discourage the voting participation of African-Americans became public, however,
and the resulting backlash in the black community apparently increased minority turnout and enabled Breaux to defeat his Republican opponent, Congressman Henson Moore.[25] Frederick claims that
the GOP still undertakes similar efforts in California, particularly
targeting Mexican-Americans in Democratic precincts.[26] A high-
ranking Democratic Party official also recounted an instance in his
Southern state in a 1986 gubernatorial contest where the GOP
"hired a number of black people to neutralize the effort [in the black
community] that had been made on our side, just to keep the vote
down. The Republicans paid some blacks to go around and discourage voting [on election day] through 'persuasion'—I won't say
bribery, but there was a monetary inducement." Democratic consultant Karl Struble also told us: "I know of a number of occasions
where Republicans have used street money to pay people to intimidate others so they don't vote. I've seen it firsthand in some Southern states. . . . The Republicans can get away with it particularly in
rural areas because the press mainly covers the big cities."[27]

While we did not secure a confession of such hijinks from Republicans in that state or any other, we were able to coax admissions
of some other unsavory GOP practices in the black community.
Naturally, all mea culpas (or boasting in some cases) were given on
background, without precise attribution permitted.

A few examples involving big money are already on record. In
October 1994, the Georgia Republican Party attempted to woo
African-American voters by paying $52,000 to a firm owned by a
black Atlanta Democrat, state Representative Tyrone Brooks, who
was to undertake various political organizing activities.[28] As his
windfall was publicly disclosed, Brooks crossed party lines and en-

dorsed GOP gubernatorial nominee Guy Millner (who eventually lost narrowly to Democratic Governor Zell Miller). Also in 1994, the South Carolina Republican Party hired a black organizer, Wilma Neal, for the general election.[29] Neal had worked for Democrat Joseph Riley, who lost the party gubernatorial nomination to Lieutenant Governor Nick Theodore. After Riley's defeat, Neal unsuccessfully "lobbied Democrats to run a detailed get-out-the-vote effort" in black precincts for $400,000, according to John Moylan, Theodore's campaign manager. She then defected to the campaign of Republican nominee (and now governor) David Beasley. Neal denied being on the Beasley campaign payroll, but later took a $56,000-a-year executive job with his administration.[30] A year earlier, in the 1993 New York City mayoral election, Republican nominee Rudolph Giuliani spent almost $200,000 in street money in an attempt, his campaign asserted, to beat the Democrats at their own game. But controversy developed over a $40,000 effort by the state GOP to operate a "ballot security program." Blacks, including residents of a homeless shelter, were hired as "poll watchers" for $60 to $75 on Election Day.[31] Democrats charged that this was somehow a systematic plan to harass and intimidate minority voters at their polling stations.[32]

As is frequently true, though, the cleverest techniques never see the light of the TV cameras. A favorite GOP sport in minority communities is, in the words of an experienced political consultant, "to drive up the cost of doing business for the Democrats":

> We'll offer certain black activists a large sum of money, so they can go back to the Democrats and ask for more, thereby costing the Democrats more cash to operate. We also like to advertise in black newspapers and on black radio. Invariably, even though the Democrats know they've got over 90 percent of the black vote, they panic. Then they waste money nailing down their base and it keeps them from doing other things that would be more advantageous for them.

Even more devilish are two successful counterstrategies executed in recent years in South Carolina. When Democrats controlled state government, they would reportedly put taxpayer-owned vehicles (such as vans assigned to antipoverty agencies) to work hauling black voters to the polls on Election Day. But when the Republicans took over the executive branch in the latter 1980s, according to a state GOP political adviser, "we started a special 'inspection program' for all federally funded vehicles, and we picked election day for the inspection and, you know, all those vans were no longer available for [get-out-the-vote activities]. The first year the Democrats really hollered." Besides the vans, Democrats in some areas of South Carolina would depend on the commercial taxi companies to supply transportation, but according to the same GOP activist, "We'd tie them up by using our phone banks. We'd keep calling taxicabs on the phone and get them to go to bogus addresses."

Realpolitik is seldom pretty, particularly in the field of street money.

STREET MONEY LESSONS

Is there anything worse about street money than George Washington's largesse with liquid refreshment? If it is just a nominal "honorarium" for work performed (manning the vehicles or telephones, for instance), street money is nothing much out of the ordinary, and it can be abided. Ideally, volunteers would handle the necessary chores, but practically, the level of political participation is not high enough in most locales to generate sufficient volunteer labor.

But what about the money (often in larger amounts) that is transferred to the bank accounts of community leaders as a reward for their endorsement? Charging for an endorsement, or for an opportunity to mount the pulpit in a church, is an outrageous practice, but it now happens with frequency. Equally disturbing are the less common GOP attempts to suppress minority turnout by buying off some community leaders, who then sit at home on Election Day rather than working the polls. But while paying to suppress turnout is clearly wrong, paying large sums to a select few to *gin up* turnout is not really morally superior. The vote, which tens of thousands gave their blood and sweat to secure, is not a commodity that ought to be crassly traded for cash in the political marketplace.

Besides reemphasizing the power of cash and the decline of ethical standards in today's politics, our saga of street money is yet another example of how the American system is corrupting. Many good, ethical candidates are forced to play the street money game if they are to have any chance of election; a contender who questions this system or its unethical rules is inviting a split in his ranks and therefore flirting with defeat. Even worse, secrecy is again a problem, with efforts to inform the public hampered by inadequate disclosure of street cash. The entrenched interests and hidden nature of street money corruption guarantee that change will only come with great difficulty—but we will offer some remedies to speed reform in the concluding chapter.

8

Perks

> It is the abuse of certain privileges, which all governments accord to a portion of its officers, which leads to fraud, crime, and corruption.
>
> —*Writer Henry Reeves, 1870*

In 1994 in Paramus, New Jersey, a comfortable suburb of New York city, a controversy was raging over the cloverleaf at the junction of Routes 4 and 17. Leading the charge to relieve traffic congestion at the intersection, which had been troublesome for years, was the *Bergen Record*. The newspaper was applying heavy pressure on New Jersey Senator Frank Lautenberg, chairman of the Senate Appropriations Subcommittee on Transportation, to come up with $15 million in federal funds to fix the intersection.

In tough editorials, the paper that spring called on Lautenberg "to show how much muscle he really has" and "show he can come through in the clutch."[1] Lautenberg's reaction was statesmanlike but took account of the realities of the funding process. He said he would do what he could but that his ability to deal with the problem was constrained by federal budget rules, which give state governments discretion over how to spend federal transportation funds. "We're going to get as much money as we can, and then the decision will be the state's as to priorities," he told the paper. State officials already had enough money to fix the project, "if they wanted," he tried to explain.

The explanation failed to satisfy the *Record*, which was not shy about noting that the senator faced a tough reelection campaign. "It was disturbing when Mr. Lautenberg, who heads the transportation subcommittee of the Senate Appropriations committee, tried this week to shift responsibility to state officials," the paper opined. "Mr. Lautenberg should stop trying to pass the buck."[2]

Lautenberg was obviously greatly concerned that the paper might withhold its endorsement. He arranged a meeting with the paper's editors, bringing the head of the Federal Highway Administration, Rodney Slater, up from Washington to back him up. It is not often that the head of a federal agency accompanies a senator to an editorial board meeting back home. The two sought to explain that under federal law, it was the North Jersey Planning Authority (NJPA), not Frank Lautenberg, that was in charge of deciding how to spend federal grants for local road work—and the NJPA had decided the cloverleaf was not a priority. The *Record*, however, remained unconvinced.

Behind the scenes in Lautenberg's office, his chief of staff, Eve Lubalin, was apparently growing desperate. "She was convinced that if we didn't get the money for 4 and 17, then the Bergen *Record* wasn't going to endorse Frank Lautenberg and therefore we were going to lose," said one Lautenberg aide. At a meeting on the problem, "Eve walked in and said, 'We have to get the money, we just have to,'" recounted another source who was present. "And the transportation staff was saying, 'You just can't do it. You can't.'"

Nevertheless, the staff was ordered to find a way, which it ultimately did, slipping the $15 million into a list of special projects.[3] "Sen. Frank Lautenberg, facing a tough re-election bid, has finally seen the light," the *Record* crowed.[4] Two months later, the paper endorsed Lautenberg for reelection.

The episode is a poignant example of the codependent relationship that has developed in recent decades between legislator and legislatee. It is based upon an ethic of service that is relatively new in American politics. While their only constitutional duty is to legislate, members of Congress have increasingly become the Mr. Fixits of American politics, voluntarily taking on an extraconstitutional assignment as official ombudsman for their constituents.

The editors of the Bergen *Record* were convinced that Frank Lautenberg had the power to rustle up the money to fix the interchange because Frank Lautenberg, like his colleagues, was in the habit of advertising his ability to minister to such parochial concerns. People like special attention, and it is something to which they quickly become accustomed once they get a taste. Politicians also quickly become accustomed to the political rewards of giving special attention. Rarely do the people, or the politicians, acknowledge that much of what they hate about modern politics arises from the special attention they now take for granted.

Most people seem to think that the government is much too big, and that far too much is spent on personnel and perquisites. Yet these features endure because on an individual basis, people have come to expect them. Polls consistently show, for example, that most people like, indeed expect, to get regular mail from their congressman. Yet in the abstract, people hate the idea of congressmen having free mailing privileges. Similarly, everyone seems convinced that the government—particularly the legislature—is bloated with staff. Yet when the Social Security check does not arrive on time, we call the staff of our friendly local congressman.

It is hard to blame the average congressman, desperate to win reelection, for exploiting for political gain our fondness for special attention. Indeed, of all the corruption in American politics today, the abuse and waste resulting from our politicians' obsessive service ethic is the one that can be most directly blamed not on the politicians but on the public itself.

The growth of the service ethic, as we shall see, has led to a profound deformation in our politics. When politicians are equipped to be Mr. Fixits, it seems, they invariably use the equipment to serve not just the public but themselves. Staff become campaign workers, and mail becomes campaign advertising.

Staff Infection

It is a poorly held secret inside the Washington Beltway that legions of congressional staff now actively promote and participate in incumbent reelection campaigns. Indeed, the practice is similar to some of the other abuses discussed in this book: institutionalized over the decades but never discussed openly, a scandal many are aware of but whose dimensions and consequences few actually ap-

preciate. The congressmen themselves, of course, do not call attention to the active political support they receive from their large taxpayer-funded staffs. The media typically prefer to dwell on other
issues.[5] For their part, staff members, who in the courtlike atmosphere of the congressional office feel fealty only to the congressman,
quietly carry out tasks that have no legislative implications because
they know the congressman must retain his job in order for them to
retain theirs.

Political scientists often point to the campaign-related advantages
presented by large staffs to explain the lack of competitiveness in
many congressional elections, but how congressmen actually use
their staff to aid their reelection campaigns has never been bared in
detail. Studies of this question that do exist have focused on the im-
plicit political benefits of having a large staff (that is, lots of people to
do casework and send out mail), rather than on explicit evidence
that members of Congress use staff in an abusive and politically self-
serving manner. "Congressmen, after all, do not keep public records
of the time they spend in various activities," wrote one accomplished
scholar who has pondered this issue.[6] But in fact, there *are* records
that provide considerable information about how congressmen and
their staffs spend their time. For decades, the House has published
quarterly reports—available to anyone who asks for them—that describe in considerable detail the spending practices of each House
member's office. These data may indicate that the problem is worse
than thought.

Power in Numbers

As usual, Congress has given itself all the tools necessary to carry out
an abuse while still being able to claim a legislative imperative. The
first tool needed for this purpose is bodies.

For much of the history of the Republic, Congress functioned
with hardly any staff. Around 1900, House offices were virtual one-
man shops, while senators operated with just a few dozen assistants
for the whole body. Committee staffing was similarly sparse.[7]

Growth remained relatively benign until just after World War II,
when hiring on Capitol Hill began to take off. At the dawn of the

war, representatives averaged about two staff members, while senators averaged four. But in the ensuing half-century of the Democratic hegemony of Congress, personal staffs exploded. The greatest increases occurred during the reformist 1970s. In 1967, House members had a total of about 4,000 personal staff and senators about 1,700. Ten years later, the number was 7,000 for the House offices and 3,300 for the Senate, increases of 75 percent and 94 percent, respectively. And by 1989, there were nearly 18 employees for each House representative and 38 for each senator.[8]

Why did congressmen serving in the postwar period, particularly during the 1970s and 1980s, need a small army of workers, when previous generations of congressmen saw little use for large offices? Undoubtedly, part of the reason was the explosive growth of the executive branch beginning with the New Deal and continuing up until the Great Society of the 1960s. Yet committee staffs—where oversight of the executive branch takes place—leveled off in the early 1970s, while personal staff continued to grow. Something else about the government had changed, something more subtle: although their only constitutional duty is to legislate, members of Congress have increasingly become political nannies. This tedious activity has come to consume the lion's share of congressional staff time; legions of Hill staffers do nothing all day but write letters and make phone calls to federal bureaucrats on behalf of constituents who have problems with federal agencies ranging from a lost benefit check to a dispute with the Internal Revenue Service.

It is now fashionable for congressmen to complain that their constituent responsibilities leave them little time for their legislative responsibilities. Of course, they are partly to blame. In their obsessive quest for reelection, our legislators have come to believe they must respond to every letter, phone call, and request for a favor, even the most outrageous. When five senators were accused of beating up on federal savings and loan regulators on behalf of Charles Keating, each claimed the controversial businessman was their constituent— despite the fact that one senator was from Michigan, another was from Ohio, two were from Arizona, and the fifth was from California. They seemed to be suggesting that it mattered not whether Keating's case against the regulators had merit or whether the senators had been inappropriately rough on the regulators, so long as

Keating was a constituent. The Keating affair prompted a small boomlet in criticism of the constituent service ethic, but this was quickly brushed aside. A committee appointed by the Senate to study the question actually erected a noble-sounding justification for the practice, which the chamber then enshrined in a unanimously passed resolution. "Whereas the First Amendment of the Constitution guarantees the 'right of the people . . . to petition the Government for a redress of grievances,' the Senate recognizes that responding to petitions for assistance is an appropriate exercise of the representative function of each Member."[9] The logic here takes a great leap. Because the Constitution allows citizens to appeal to their government, the thinking apparently goes, part of the job of a member of Congress is to help advance such petitions on a case-by-case basis.

Such a notion would seem to greatly cheapen both the Constitution and the Congress (formerly known as a deliberative body), but it has infected Congress thoroughly. In the mid-1970s, approximately three-quarters of House and Senate personal staff were based in Washington. This made sense if congressmen believed their chief duty was to legislate or to keep an eye out for misuse of power by the executive branch (the duties to which the Constitution explicitly appoints them). For the next two decades, though, more and more staff positions were transferred from Washington to district and state offices. By 1990, nearly 42 percent of House staff and 35 percent of Senate staff worked outside of Washington. Little, if any, legislative or oversight work is carried on outside the Beltway. District offices are dedicated nearly 100 percent to constituent services, that is, to solving the problems of individual people. Is this really any way to run a government? Would we not all be better off if every member of Congress were forbidden from solving individual problems, and thus every member of Congress would demand that the bureaucracy get its act together? Perhaps the constituent service ethic has corrupted *us*.

Rules of Rubber

That the best justification the U.S. Senate could come up with for the constituent service ethic should be so flimsy suggests members of

Congress perform constituent service because they think it gets them reelected. No doubt, some of them are under the misperception that it also is (and always has been) a part of their job definition, which is just further evidence that the line between governing and campaigning has become even more blurred than it already was.

The staff are similarly confused. While keeping constituents happy is many a staffer's priority, it often is only part of keeping the boss in office. Many members of Congress ask their staffs to participate in overtly political activities, including their own reelection campaigns. In October of every election year, many Capitol Hill offices empty out, the staff packed off to the district. For their part, the staff already based in the district take to their automobiles, fanning out in search of votes for their congressman. This type of activity may seem illegal on its face, for the staff members in question are government employees whose regular salaries are paid with tax dollars, not campaign contributions. Yet Congress construes much of this activity as perfectly legal.

According to the House *Ethics Manual,* congressional staff can participate in political activities for their congressman in their "free time" after they have finished their "official," taxpayer-financed duties. This includes time taken off "while on annual leave" or "leave-without-pay."[10] They can legally receive compensation from the campaign, as long as the time they spend is not during the hours they work for the government. This language leaves congressmen enormous leeway to use official staff for their own political purposes, while still paying them their government salary. If questioned, a staffer can simply say he performed only "volunteer" work at night from his house or during his vacation, à la the peripatetic Eve Lubalin. Proving otherwise is nearly impossible. Conveniently, Congress has long exempted itself from the Hatch Act, a controversial law that restricted all other federal workers from most forms of political participation until it was effectively repealed for executive branch employees in 1994.

These rules make staff members virtual pawns in their congressmen's reelection gambits. Each congressional office is like a self-contained duchy, with the staff obligated to the needs and promotion of one individual, the congressman. Suggestions and requests, especially when they come from the top, are followed as a matter of course. Therefore, staff members tend to "volunteer" when they are asked to "volunteer" and retreat to the district when they are asked to retreat, even though campaigning has never been included in their job descriptions. Some congressmen even draft staff members from congressional committees they serve on to campaign for them.

The result is a bizarre flurry of personnel moves and salaries that would puzzle even the best human resources manager. For any given fiscal quarter, a staffer may suddenly disappear from the official payroll and appear on the campaign payroll. Then, the next quarter, he may be back on the official rolls. Often he appears on both. Sometimes his official salary is reduced, sometimes it is not. Often, his official salary spikes upward dramatically in one quarter for no traceable reason, other than a possible connection to the fact that he was on the campaign payroll the previous quarter at a very low salary. Sometimes, his title changes. Or he may have two or more official titles for a given quarter, drawing a salary for each. Occasionally, a staffer receives a committee salary, a congressional office salary, and a campaign salary, all in the course of three months. More frequently, a staffer flies to the district at taxpayer expense, then bills hundreds of dollars in expenses to the campaign.

In 1994, for example, Representative Joe Skeen, a New Mexico Republican who had served quietly in the House for fourteen years, found himself in unusual political peril. The long-time incumbent had coasted to reelection for years, but in 1992 he had been reelected with a modest 56 percent of the vote after redistricting brought a flood of new Democratic-leaning Hispanic voters into his district. For 1994 he was facing a well-known Hispanic as his opponent, former judge Ben Chavez.

Despite this jeopardy, Skeen neglected to assemble the large campaign staff that seemingly would be required to meet the challenge. Through the spring and summer, when most congressional campaigns are getting revved up, Skeen had only two aides on his campaign payroll, both of them part-time. The two aides, Dorothy Thomas and Mary Gayle Wood, later became Skeen's only full-time campaign employees, according to campaign payroll records. By comparison, most moderately well-funded campaigns (Skeen spent $384,000 in 1984) have at least half a dozen full-time paid staff members.

Instead, Skeen relied on Thomas and Wood, as well as a few part-timers at the very end of the campaign. Aides Bruce Donisthorpe and Sherry Kiesling were paid a modest $595 for their services, while Quin Dodd and John Ryan received just $300 each. Senior staffer Suzanne Eisold made $1,085. All told, the Skeen campaign's entire budget for staff salaries during the whole campaign year totaled only $26,000—an amount approximately equivalent to half the going rate for the services of a single, full-time campaign manager for the duration of the campaign. So how did Skeen manage to win the election with 62 percent of the vote?

Skeen's campaign payroll records suggest that his campaign was run by a skeleton crew. Other records tell a very different story. Skeen's campaign aides, House of Representatives documents show, were also on Skeen's congressional payroll in 1994. Kiesling was Skeen's Washington-based press secretary. Eisold was his Washington-based chief of staff. Dodd was a Washington-based legislative assistant handling budget, taxes, education, and health issues. Ryan was a Washington-based legislative assistant handling agriculture, environment, and energy issues, and Donisthorpe handled defense issues.

While Wood and Thomas left the official payroll for the fall, the other five Skeen aides received their full taxpayer-funded salaries during the campaign—despite the fact that they weren't even in Washington, where they usually work. In fact, Donisthorpe and Ryan were actually only part-time Skeen employees to begin with, drawing most of their salaries from the House Committee on Appropriations and only a small portion from Skeen's office payroll. Donisthorpe, the defense specialist, was in Skeen's district from October 12 through November 1, then again right around Election Day, from November 7 through the 11th. Despite the three weeks he spent in Skeen's district just before the election, he received his full official salary of $19,000 for the fiscal quarter while getting just $595 from the campaign. Ryan, meanwhile, was in the district from October 20 to November 9, earning his full $14,212 quarterly salary all the while, not to mention the $300 from the campaign.

How did the Washington-based staff get to New Mexico to campaign for Skeen? The answer is not to be found in Skeen's campaign report. House of Representatives records show that six of Skeen's legislative staffers flew from Washington to New Mexico a week before the November 8 election. Altogether, they ran up about $11,000 in "official" bills for airfare, hotels, food, rental cars, taxis, and gasoline—all billed to the public tab (one aide, Chief of Staff Eisold, even spent $190 for a first-class upgrade). Curiously, they all returned to their jobs in Washington in the days immediately following the election.

Another oddity is the compensation of Thomas and Wood. House payroll records show that the two earned higher salaries in the fourth quarter of the year than in previous quarters. The fourth quarter includes the five weeks leading up to the election, when the two were apparently working as campaign staffers and receiving several thousand dollars each in campaign salary.

A similar pattern can be seen in the office operations of California Republican Ken Calvert, one incumbent who found himself in deep trouble following the revelation of his dalliance with a prostitute. Calvert apparently deputized four of his major staffers into campaign workers during the crucial last six weeks of his reelection effort. From October through mid-November 1994, Calvert reduced their "official" salaries slightly and gave the four a total of $54,654 in campaign-related compensation.

Calvert's administrative assistant, Ed Slevin, alone received about $30,000 from the campaign from October 1 to November 11. In addition, Slevin earned $13,529 in official salary for the quarter, bringing his princely take to more than $43,000 during the fourth fiscal quarter, or $470 an hour—if it is assumed Slevin worked forty-four weeks.[11] There's another way of looking at it: perhaps Slevin was just working for the campaign at night and the congressional office during the day. If the campaign paid him at the $28-an-hour rate he was receiving from the congressional office, Slevin put in 1,071 hours on the campaign and 200 hours on the congressional office during the five weeks when he was on both payrolls, for a total of 1,271 hours of work. Unfortunately, there are only 840 hours in five weeks.

Like Skeen's people, several of Calvert's full-time congressional staffers in Washington had a sudden urge to fly west during October of 1994. Press Secretary C. Lee Raudonis and Legislative Assistant Mark Foehr flew out on October 14, while Appointments Secretary Linda Ulrich made the trip to Ontario, California, on the

Table 2. Washington-Based Trips to District by Staff of Selected
Members of Congress, Charged as Official Travel,
Fall 1993 and Fall 1994

| | *Trips* | | | |
Representative	*1993*	*1994*	*Increase*	*Change (%)*
Jim Bacchus (D-Fla.)	2	7	+5	250
Sonny Callahan (R-Ala.)	0	9	+9	900
Randy Cunningham (R-Calif.)	1	8	+7	700
Ken Calvert (R-Calif.)	0	3	+3	300
Anna Eshoo (D-Calif.)	1	4	+3	300
Jane Harman (D-Calif.)	0	4	+4	400
James Inhofe (R-Okla.)[a]	0	4	+4	400
John Kyl (R-Ariz.)[a]	0	4	+4	400
John Lewis (D-Ga.)	0	4	+4	400
Martin Meehan (D-Mass.)	1	6	+5	500
Bill Sarpalius (D-Tex.)	1	9	+8	800
Joe Skeen (R-N. Mex.)	3	9	+6	200
Don Young (R-Alaska)	3	7	+4	130
Curt Weldon (R-Pa.)	2	19	+17	950

Note: The members of Congress listed here were selected to make our point, and thus their practices are not representative of the average legislator. Indeed, most of these members, like most of the members who abuse the frank, were in unusual electoral jeopardy. The 1993 numbers are for the five-week period immediately after the House recessed on November 22. The 1994 figures correspond to the same period in the congressional calendar, that is, the five weeks.
a. Candidates for Senate in 1994.
Source: House of Representatives quarterly office reports, 1993–94.

21st. Never leaving the official payroll, they all returned to Washington the day after the election, sticking taxpayers with a bill of about $6,000 for their out-of-town travel, half of which went for lodging. No such expedition from Washington was deemed necessary during the same quarter of 1993, a noncampaign year, when no Washington-based Calvert staff flew to the district (see Table 2 above).

Texas Democrat Bill Sarpalius was also in grave need of all the help he could get as Election Day approached in 1994. Like Calvert, Sarpalius had been caught up in a scandal. Whereas Calvert's involved sex, the one surrounding Sarpalius had to do with taking favors from a moving firm. Sarpalius had quite a bit of manpower working with him as he frantically crisscrossed his district in the final days before the election, official records show. Seven of his ten Washington-based legislative and administrative staffers flew to his district in the weeks leading up to the election, all on taxpayer money, racking up a bill of about $8,100 for airfare, hotel, rental cars, taxis, and the like. Several stayed for about a month. On Election Day, fifteen of Sarpalius's eighteen congressional staffers (including those based in the district) were with him in Texas.

While most of these aides "volunteered" to help out the boss, Sarpalius placed two of his official staffers on his campaign staff, giving them campaign salaries. However, that seemed to have little detrimental effect on their official salaries, which actually increased once the two got involved with the campaign. Legislative assistant Andrew Dodson and district representative Lisa Hunsaker were each earning a paltry $1,500 a month in early 1994, but their official salaries soon escalated. Dodson earned $5,666 in the third fiscal quarter and $8,083 in the final quarter, periods in which he also earned substantial money from the campaign. Hunsaker's official salary also increased, despite her campaign work.

But even a federal subsidy could not save Sarpalius, whom the voters gave mandatory retirement. The day after the November 8 election, four of Sarpalius's staff flew back to Washington, while one returned on November 12, and two others touched down on November 13.

Another case in point is that of Representative Carroll Hubbard, a Kentucky Democrat who ordered his personal staff and his staff on the House Banking Committee to perform a series of common campaign chores for his wife (who wanted to join her husband in Congress), such as sending out fundraising invitations and preparing campaign records. Hubbard would almost certainly have gotten away with this misuse of his staff but for the eruption in 1992 of the House Bank scandal, which made him a subject of interest to a special prosecution task force on the bank. Hubbard's personal financial affairs, it turned out, were intimately connected to his campaign activities (he was stealing from his own campaign), and prosecutors soon learned about how he was using his staff. In 1994, Hubbard pleaded guilty to theft of government property, that is, the taxpayer-funded labor of his staff. In court, federal prosecutor Thomas

Eicher said the scheme initially succeeded because Hubbard's employees feared for their jobs if they refused to help him. In addition, Eicher said, Hubbard ordered the staff to claim they were on vacation if anyone questioned their campaign work.[12] Hubbard is currently serving a five-year term in federal prison.[13]

Stranding Washington staff in the district for a month before Election Day and billing the public for it is a well-worn biannual routine for Congress (see Table 2). While most do not go to the extremes of Calvert, Skeen, and Sarpalius, few are immune from the practice. Florida Republican Dan Miller transformed just one staff member, Press Secretary Kevin Borland, into a campaigner for his successful reelection bid in 1994, according to his campaign finance records. However, two other legislative aides—health care assistant Marty Reiser and legislative director and budget aide Matthew Kibbe—flew out of Washington in early October, stayed a month in the district, and returned just after the election wrapped up on November 8. During this time, they drew their full official salaries. Kibbe's actually increased substantially for the quarter. In the July-to-September quarter, Miller's office paid Kibbe just $1,250, while he worked full-time at his $60,000-a-year job as a staffer for the House Budget Committee. During the next quarter, which included the month he spent in Florida, Kibbe earned $2,500 from Miller's office, while still drawing his full salary from the Budget Committee. As in the case of the two Skeen staffers, it is difficult to understand how a House committee staffer can earn a full committee salary while a large chunk of his or her time is spent in a congressman's district, far from committee offices in Washington.

Because of Congress's liberal staffing practices, it can be nearly impossible for an outsider to discern what official staffers did for a campaign. For instance, according to his campaign finance reports, Montana's sole representative, Democrat Pat Williams (yet another incumbent in trouble), paid nearly his entire legislative staff—fifteen government employees—a campaign salary. One Williams aide, J. Fred Sargeson, is a permanent employee of both the campaign and the legislative office, simultaneously serving as congressional field representative and as Williams's assistant campaign treasurer. Three other staffers worked nearly full-time for the campaign in its waning days, earning thousands of dollars apiece. A dozen others were paid exactly $250 on November 18, ten days after Williams was narrowly reelected. The line item states the Washington, D.C., and district staff performed "services" for Williams's campaign, although the types of services undertaken that would yield the very same salaries for twelve people are unspecified. These economies apparently were crucial to Williams, who won reelection with just 48 percent of the vote in a three-way race. All told, more than two-thirds of Williams's legislative staff worked for his campaign.

A similar mystery surrounds the staff of Connecticut Democrat Sam Gejdenson, regarded in 1994 as New England's most vulnerable incumbent. Like numerous other legislators whose records we examined, Gejdenson's official and campaign staffs are so intermingled that it is difficult to tell where one begins and the other ends.

During the course of the election year, Gejdenson used six legislative workers to aid his campaign. One staffer, "congressional aide" Donald Mazeau, was also Gejdenson's assistant campaign treasurer. He drew a meager monthly stipend of $134.70 from the campaign. For most of the year, his campaign duties were limited mostly to keeping financial records and filling out occasional Federal Election Commission reports. Six weeks before the 1994 election, however, Mazeau's campaign-related activity suddenly picked up. On October 2, he put in for $81.40 of mileage reimbursement and on November 1 requested another $162.70 for mileage. In addition, he recorded personal reimbursements from "petty cash" of exactly $100 on October 14, 19, 20, 21, and 26, then again on November 4, 5, and 7. Despite his extensive travel for the campaign and about $800 in other campaign-related spending, Mazeau received no campaign salary other than the $134.70. Nevertheless, his official, taxpayer-provided salary increased handsomely. Mazeau earned $9,175 for the January-to-March quarter of 1994, $11,075 for the July-to-September quarter, and $13,075 for the October-to-December quarter—the same quarter he also asked to be reimbursed for more than $1,000 in campaign expenses but received no additional campaign salary.

An even more implausible situation surrounds a staffer for Representative Don Young, Alaska's at-large Republican. On October 31, Press Secretary Steven Hansen had the campaign reimburse him for

$702 in per diem meals. The request could have been understand-able, for most campaigns give their workers $20 or $25 a day to defer the cost of eating when on the road. Therefore, $702 would repre-sent quite a few days of out-of-the-office work for the campaign. This request, though, is puzzling, since Young's campaign records show no entry for Hansen receiving a campaign salary. Instead, he received his full official salary of $12,340 for the final quarter of 1994, compared with $11,108 for the third quarter and $11,340 for the first. The question arises again: how did this aide fulfill his offi-cial, full-time office duties while driving around Alaska on behalf of the campaign, racking up travel reimbursements from the cam-paign? More "vacationing," apparently.

In addition to Hansen, Young drafted much of the rest of his Washington office staff to the district just before the election, creat-ing a small army of campaign workers. Taxpayers dished out about $15,000 to fly and feed four staffers in the month before the election, according to official House expense reports. Administrative assis-tant Lloyd Jones alone accounted for about $11,500 of the amount, making three round trips in four weeks, at $2,650, $2,650, and $3,335 a trip, respectively. While in Alaska, they all did work for the campaign, as evidenced by the fact they racked up a number of cam-paign expenditures (albeit, totaling a relatively paltry $1,100). Nonetheless, none of the four (Jones, administrative assistants John Ralston and Levon Boyagian, and congressional office worker Jean Davin) took campaign salaries, and their official salaries either stayed the same or increased during the October-to-December quarter.[14] Ralston returned home to Washington on November 7, Boyagian and Davin on November 10, and Jones, for the third and final time, on November 12. Congressional staff, unlike the rest of us, apparently like to spend their vacations working.

Perhaps Young's strangest personnel move was to take office worker Davin along for the campaign ride. As already discussed, Congress's staffing shell game is a curious and puzzling business. One week a worker may be a committee staffer, the next a member of some congressman's personal staff, and the next a partisan hack manning a campaign phone bank. Usually, though, there is a certain pecking order. For instance, a member's district staff, comprised mostly of taxpayer-compensated constituent service personnel, is most likely to become completely absorbed in a congressman's campaign. The administrative assistants and other legislative aides from Washington usually just come in as reinforcements during the final weeks. Davin fit neither of these two categories. She was, during all of 1994, the office receptionist. Somehow, though, Young deputized her, sent her to Alaska on October 29, where she remained until November 10. Along the way, she spent about $1,200 in official funds and $436 in campaign funds, including $139.39 in per diem meals for the campaign. While members of Congress often try to claim their Washington-based legislative staff are somehow needed in a far-off district two weeks before an election, there can be little excuse (even a transparent one) for flying a receptionist four thousand miles from Washington to Anchorage, then bringing her back two days after the election.

We Deliver for You

Following the Iraqi invasion of Kuwait in 1990, when the state of Israel seemed greatly imperiled by threatened attacks from dictator Saddam Hussein, it received a visit from Senator Alfonse D'Amato, the master New York politician with a knack for headline-grabbing political stunts. Shortly after the trip, D'Amato dipped into the U.S. treasury to finance a mass mailing of letters to thousands of his constituents detailing his perilous journey. But the citizens of New York State did not all get the same letter. Two versions were sent out with identical typeface and dates.

"I am writing to you on an airplane returning from the Middle East," D'Amato wrote some of his constituents.

"I am writing you on an El Al flight from Israel," D'Amato wrote others.

The second letter was for Jews, and the other was for everybody else.

In the "Middle East" letter, D'Amato made numerous references to "our brave troops" in Saudi Arabia and to "the courage they show in defending our nation and our values." In the "El Al" letter (El Al is the Israeli national airline), American troops were bit players, other than in the context of their job manning batteries of Patriot missiles "in Israel's defense."

"As a United States Senator from New York, my going *to the Middle East to visit out troops* would send a clear message of commitment, compassion, and concern," he wrote in one letter (emphasis added).

"As a United States Senator from New York, my going *to Tel Aviv and Jerusalem* would send a clear message of commitment, compassion, and concern," he wrote in the other letter.

Notwithstanding their similar wording and appearance, the text of the first letter mentioned Saudi Arabia once and Israel four times, while the text of the second letter referred to Israel twelve times and made no mention of Saudi Arabia at all.

D'Amato added different postscripts to each letter as well. "Our troops asked me to let you know how much your support and prayers mean to them," D'Amato wrote in the letter to non-Jewish constituents. "The government of Israel has asked me to deliver a confidential message to President Bush, which I will do," D'Amato said in the other letter's postscript.[15]

Two years later, D'Amato won an upset reelection battle with a victory margin of only 1 percent. Among the critical reasons for his win was his amazing success with Jewish voters. Despite the fact that his opponent was Robert Abrams, an observant Jew and prominent figure in the state's Jewish community, D'Amato managed to pull in 41 percent of the Jewish vote, a 6 percent increase from his last campaign.

One of the enduring images of the modern Congress, painted by its members and its chroniclers, is of a body ravaged by incoming mail, with legislators in each of 535 offices receiving thousands of pieces each day.[16] Included in the deluge may be a retiree's insistence that a congressman investigate the status of his government pension or a plea from a school group in Nebraska for fifteen minutes of a senator's time during an Easter break visit to Washington. Naturally, congressmen must answer their mail, thereby performing what may be the most basic act of constituent service. Hence they have the "franking" privilege, the right to send mail at government expense.

The rationale for the frank is plainly legitimate. Citizens expect and deserve to hear back from their representatives in Congress when they write. Yet as every congressman and every staff member knows (and some will even admit), the franking privilege is routinely and systematically abused. Instead of simply answering questions, congressmen bombard their districts with self-serving propaganda. Millions of taxpayer dollars are gobbled up each year by this congressional mail monster.

In a sense, this is a story as old as the Republic. (The frank itself is, in fact, slightly older than the Republic; the right to frank was one of the first points of business resolved by the Continental Congress on November 8, 1775, despite the heavy load of seemingly more pressing matters such as the impending war with England. The U.S. Congress reaffirmed the right in 1789.)[17] Periodic spates of reform have tried to do away with or curtail the abuse of the frank. Yet, like so much of corruption, none of the attempts have ever truly been successful. It often seems that reform has been the mother of invention, spurring innovations in the use of the frank. Indeed, what may have changed most over the years is the way in which the frank is abused. What was originally a perk Congress exploited primarily for personal convenience, or at worst a barnacle on the body politic, has mutated into one of the most potent tools incumbents have at their disposal to maintain their grip on power. The frank is not merely about free postage. The cost of producing the mail itself is also met by the taxpayers through general office budgets. Sophisticated direct mail is an expensive proposition, and not having to pay for it relieves a candidate of a major drain on resources.

Whereas candidates once devoted most of their energies toward contacting as many voters as possible in person, by the 1970s most voter contact was through television, radio, and direct mail. On a cost-per-voter basis, direct mail is by far the most expensive, yet it is also believed to be among the most effective. The financial advantages of a direct mail subsidy are thus tremendous.

The advantage in exposure is beyond what incumbents might expect simply from their prominence as officeholders. In one 1990 study, House challengers and incumbents were almost at parity in their contacts with voters via television. Fifty-nine percent of voters surveyed said they had seen the incumbent on television ads, while 57 percent said they had seen the challenger. However, 76 percent of voters said they had received mail from the incumbent candidate, while only 40 percent said they had received mail from the challenger.[18] The difference is not accounted for by incumbent fundraising advantages: incumbents outspend challengers on television ads in the same proportion that they outspend challengers for campaign-financed direct mail.[19]

Rampant political use of the frank appears to have begun around the middle of the century, when at least one observer called it "a corollary of being reelected."[20] It was about that time that major mass circulation magazines such as *Time* began developing mailed subscription solicitations into a sophisticated marketing tool.[21] Slowly this new mass-marketing technique, direct mail—which came to resemble science with its reliance on strict, elaborately tested formulae—was adopted by politicians and their consultants.[22] By the mid-1970s, members of Congress were routinely combining direct mail techniques with the frank, often using official funds to hire direct mail consultants.

As a result, Congress was forced to revise its franking rules twice in the mid-1970s to ban blatantly political messages. The reforms sought to eliminate the worst abuses, such as letters soliciting votes or campaign donations or those sent for obviously "unofficial" purposes, such as Christmas cards. They also encouraged legislators to reduce the number of times their likeness or name appeared on a piece of franked mass mail. Showing just how little faith could be placed in its members to use the frank with discretion, the House went so far as to place a limit on the number of times the pronouns "I" or "me" could be used on each page. In addition, it prohibited mass franked mailings from being sent twenty-eight days before an election (a period later extended to two months) in an effort to combat the congressional tradition of sending franked mailings just before election time.[23]

In 1973, the consumer lobby, Common Cause, decided the reforms did not go far enough and launched a suit claiming the frank violated the Constitution because its usefulness as a reelection tool denied challengers equal protection under the law.[24] For more than a decade, the litigants were involved in the process of discovery, until finally in 1982 the U.S. District Court of Appeals for the District of Columbia ruled that franked mail serves a legitimate informational purpose and that Common Cause had not provided evidence of the political use of the frank sufficient to justify the interference of the courts. The Supreme Court later affirmed the district court's decision.[25]

Claiming to further tighten loopholes, Congress had already

passed more franking reforms in 1981. But the reforms were actually a few relatively limp restrictions wrapped up in a series of expanded privileges. For instance, congressmen lost the right to frank letters for condolences, birthdays, and other "personal" distinctions, a minuscule portion of franked mail. But they were explicitly permitted to send personal messages in letters that otherwise were regarded as business and frankable, including regards to the recipient's spouse and family, and also retained the right to send franked congratulations for "public" distinctions, such as winning an award.[26] Meanwhile, the "reforms" permitted senators to make mass mailings to every address in their state, a privilege previously denied them.

The new rules also expanded and strengthened the role of a body called the House Congressional Commission on Mailing Standards, known colloquially on Capitol Hill as the franking commission. The commission, though, still had little authority to police mailings that fell beneath the 500-piece threshold that Congress said constituted a mass mailing. Members of Congress suddenly felt the itch to frank their mail in bundles of 490 pieces or so. These mailings frequently violated the spirit, and sometimes the letter, of the franking rules. Cynically, the press and even congressional staffers soon dubbed these "499-mailings."

All the while, the cost to the taxpayer of sending franked mail continued to balloon. In 1972, just before the first series of franking reforms, the House and Senate sent out approximately $23 million worth of franked mail. That figure rose to nearly $62 million in 1980, then skyrocketed to $100 million in 1982, far outstripping hikes in postal rates. More telling, throughout the 1970s and 1980s Congress consistently spent far more franking dollars in election years than in the preceding off-years, sometimes upping the election-year total by as much as 100 percent.[27] By this measure alone, as much as 50 percent of franked mail is election related.

Mailings were permitted if they "directly or indirectly pertain to the legislative process or to any congressional representative functions generally."[28] But this regulation is rather difficult to construe strictly. Although mail "unrelated to the official business, activities, and duties of members" is prohibited, as is "mail matter which specifically solicits political support for the sender or any other person or any political party, or a vote or financial assistance for any candidate for any political office," it is not difficult to violate these guidelines while observing the first one.[29] In any case, the chance of getting caught (much less sanctioned) has been slight. From 1984 to 1994, Congress sent out approximately six billion pieces of franked mail, with only about a dozen findings of wrongdoing.[30] These statistics are suspicious on their face and are clearly ludicrous in practice. Finding abusive mailings in the endless river of franked mail is like casting into a salmon hatchery.

Loaded Surveys and Letter Bombs

So what are incumbents doing with their direct mail privilege? During the past twenty years, letter content has become increasingly creative, as legislators go on testing the limits of the rules. The questionnaire has become extremely popular, with legislators claiming they need to survey their constituents to know what is on their minds. In reality, these questionnaires are an excuse to get the congressman's name out to his constituents, reinforce his image in their minds as their representative, and manipulate public opinion in their favor.

The questions in these highly unscientific surveys are highly suspect. Unlike legitimate polling, the queries are grossly skewed to elicit a response in the reader that supports the stance a legislator has already taken, and they are worded to give the impression that the only correct stance is the congressman's. The following loaded question was contained in a "survey" conducted by Indiana Congressman Dan Burton, a Republican, in 1994: "The President's [health care] plan includes a $165 billion tax increase to pay for health insurance for the uninsured. If these taxes are included in a final bill, would you support or oppose the bill?"[31]

Burton had neglected to mention that most people would not have to pay the new tax: a $1 per pack levy on cigarettes. Not surprisingly, then, 95 percent of those constituents who responded agreed with the congressman that they did not desire health care reform if the price was a $165 billion tax increase to pay for the benefits of people without insurance.[32]

227

"Illegal aliens cost California taxpayers at least $3 billion every year in state and local services," said a 1994 survey question by Congressman Elton Gallegly, a California Republican. "Do you believe illegal immigration must be reduced?"[33]

Many newsletters still take the form of the legislative update, a tried-and-true method dating back 150 years in which a congressman informs his constituents of action she has taken on their behalf. Sometimes these updates are sincere efforts to fill in the citizenry. Just as often, they are propaganda posing as news. Many such newsletters contain texts of speeches a legislator made in Congress—without informing constituents that, in all probability, no meaningful legislative action ever ensued from the speech and it likely was delivered to a half-empty or even completely empty chamber. And despite the putative limits placed on self-promotion, such newsletters still contain copious photographs of members, usually standing amidst a circle of Boy Scouts, senior citizens, or war veterans who have just received an award of some sort from the member. (Sometimes, the member has received an award from them.) Members' names and the pronouns "I" and "me" are sprinkled across the pages of these newsletters, often far exceeding Congress's own rule of eight personal references per mailing. In 1990 mailings, Illinois Republican Congressman Dennis Hastert referred to himself forty-eight times, while Georgia Republican Newt Gingrich jammed fifty-four personal mentions into a few pages.[34]

The mailings also frequently leave the reader with the mistaken impression that the sender, no matter how obscure in reality, plays a starring role in Congress. Maryland Congresswoman Helen Delich Bentley, a Republican, sent out three taxpayer-funded postal patron newsletters in 1994 even as she campaigned for the governorship of Maryland, including one that reported: "The House Appropriations Subcommittee on Labor, Health and Human Services and Education has increased funding for Family Resource and Support Centers, In-Home Services for the Frail Elderly, State Independent Living Grants for the Disabled, Healthy Start Infant Mortality Prevention and 'Meals-on-Wheels,' all programs requested by Representative Bentley."[35]

The claim was not flatly dishonest—Bentley did request the programs. But so did numerous other legislators, and the implication that Bentley, a Republican in a Democratic Congress, was the initiator or driving force behind any of them was disingenuous. Similarly, Chicago-area Congressman Luis Gutierrez, early in his first term in 1993, sent his constituents a franked newsletter containing the banner headline, "Gutierrez Bill to Aid Persian Gulf Veterans Becomes Law." The article was accompanied by a picture of the congressman surrounded by smiling veterans. Gutierrez, a first-term Democrat, was actually a minor player at best in passage of the legislation; as the small text revealed, he had merely signed onto the popular and uncontroversial bill (like dozens of other House members), not authored it. Not very admirable behavior, but nothing especially scandalous, either. But over the last ten years, far more malign techniques have been perfected.

Targeting Constituents—With Their Money

You've got to get his name out seven times in a two-year period, so that they'll remember [him] at the polls. I sometimes go in and do a training session and say, "Hey, you guys are in the advertising business. You guys got to get your member's name out over and over."

—*A Capitol Hill computer vendor on his advice to congressional staffers*[36]

In 1990, the franking budget outlay actually declined slightly from the year before, an unprecedented feat made all the more surprising by the fact that 1990 was an election year for Congress. These developments were accompanied by much harrumphing by Democrats about their reformist achievements, though in truth the reductions came only after public anger forced Congress to change its habits. The declining franking budgets in succeeding years seemed to show that the reforms were working, and franking has grown less controversial. Yet it is now apparent that the members found they could do just as fine a job of advertising themselves to their constituents for far less cost by simply adopting cutting-edge direct mail methods tied to sophisticated computer programs.

When members of Congress send out targeted mailings, they

want to let constituents know they care about the district's concerns and are doing something about them. They often paint themselves as waging a virtual jihad against the evils of Washington and, inevitably, list their accomplishments and crusades. Unlike a mass mailing, however, the targeted mailing can tell a particular group of people exactly what they want to hear. Franking critic David Keating describes how this often works:

> Let's say you're a congressman and you're pro-choice, but you've got a big pro-life constituency. Well, you might decide you're against fetal tissue research or some such thing. So, you co-sponsor a bill banning that, and you write, "Knowing of your concern for the sanctity of life, I thought you'd like to know my position on fetal tissue research." Or another fine point could be, "I've come out against Medicaid funding of abortions." And then, to the pro-choice people, you could write another letter, saying, "I've sponsored the Right to Choose Act," or, "I fully support the *Roe v. Wade* decision," or, "I'm going to scrutinize presidential appointees to the [Supreme] Court." Those people would probably never share those letters with each other, and so would never know that some congressman's practically talking out of both sides of his mouth.[37]

A few months before the 1994 elections, Indiana Congressman Dan Burton posted franked letters to numerous targeted constituencies, sending a batch to "target.business.july.1994," another [to "ag.target.summer.1994," and a third to "lab.target.july.94."[38] These were not actual addresses. Rather, they were computer coding used by Burton's staff to divide mail into list categories. Before the letters were sent out, the coding was replaced by names of people he had identified as having business interests, agricultural ("ag") interests and labor ("lab") interests, respectively, getting their own "personal" letters from him. The letters specifically addressed issues they would be concerned about and, of course, boasted of things their congressman was doing just for them. Similar letters found their way into mailboxes of veterans (target.va11) and social security recipients (soc.target.mail). Suddenly, veterans in Burton's district knew he sponsored H.R. 4386, which would aid "Persian

Gulf war veterans who are suffering from chronic disabilities resulting from undiagnosed diseases." Farmers knew Burton sponsored H.R. 1490, the Private Property Rights Act, and the elderly realized he cosponsored H.R. 300, the Older Americans Freedom to Work Act.[39]

Undoubtedly, more than one person has received mail from her congressman, then scratched her head wondering how the member knew her name, much less knew that she is interested in issues affecting the elderly or students or veterans or the future of health care. Then, perhaps, this person has talked to her neighbor, who also is interested in issues affecting the elderly or students or veterans or the future of health care. The neighbor, though, did not receive a letter. Why?

Since the early 1970s, the market in mailing lists has probably grown even faster than the frank. Many local governments sell electronic lists of homeowners, car owners, and registered voters, while the Social Security Administration provides members of Congress with lists of social security recipients in their district, and the Veterans Administration does the same with veterans. Meanwhile, commercial firms offer zip code lists, lists based on census data, and just about any other conceivable list. At the same time, database programs and the computers that run them have become capable of handling and manipulating huge quantities of ever more detailed data. Today a person may receive congressional mail because he is on a particular list of registered voters, or homeowners, or car owners, while his neighbor is not. He might also get a letter only because he is all three: a homeowner, a car owner, and a registered voter. From various private and public sources, a congressional staffer can learn a great deal about a constituent, so tailoring a message to specific groups of voters becomes a relatively simple task.[40]

John Aristotle Phillips is one of Washington's better-known political database salesmen. A minor American character, Phillips enjoyed a Warholian run of national notoriety in the late 1970s as a Princeton undergraduate when he published a paper on how to build an atomic bomb and was dubbed the "A-Bomb Kid" by the media. He later launched two unsuccessful bids for a seat in Congress.

After leaving Princeton, Phillips founded a company—Aristotle

Industries—which became one of Congress's chief database suppliers during the 1980s. Phillips and his growing staff scoured the country for voter registration lists and made this information available to members of Congress for a few cents per voter. These data proved invaluable to members who wanted to use their frank to target their constituencies, but had little idea of who lived in their districts. By purchasing the Aristotle product, members could find out a wealth of information about their constituents and could target according to age, sex, zip code, neighborhood . . . you name it. While Congress allegedly protects these data from being abused for political purposes by forbidding members to obtain a person's party affiliation, this is yet another toothless restriction: sophisticated voter targeting does not require knowing a subject's party affiliation. (Members, moreover, still had access to party identification information, for the full database product could be sold to their campaign organizations. Members simply pledged that they would not use those database disks for their legislative work.)

Phillips's relationship with Congress had gone smoothly for years when it hit an unexpected snag in 1991 after the House Administration Committee (the only committee on which Newt Gingrich served), which oversees the internal operations of the House, granted Aristotle a $250,000 development loan to transfer its database lists onto CD-ROM format.[41] Until then, Aristotle sold most database lists on computer disk or tape, which then had to be loaded into a member's computer. While still valuable, information stored on disks and tapes has many limitations. Among other hindrances, disks and tapes have limited storage capacity, requiring the member to purchase dozens, even hundreds, of diskettes or tapes to have a meaningful constituent database. Those data, then, have to be loaded, disk by disk or tape by tape, into a member's computer; this takes an enormous amount of time, not to mention huge storage space and memory.

On the other hand, a CD-ROM disk—an acronym for compact disk, read-only memory—can store as many as two million constituent entries, according to Kari Grant, Aristotle Industries political director. With the right software, it also lets members manipulate data without having to store the data inside a computer permanently:

It allows you to say, "O.K., I want to know everybody in my universe," [that universe] being maybe the 12th congressional District of Michigan, who has been ethnically coded "black," who is in a certain age group, the head of the household, or something like that. Whatever it is. You can manipulate the data, massage the data, so that you can accurately depict exactly how many people represent that target audience.[42]

As with its earlier spending sprees for franked mail, the House came under criticism after word of the highly unusual loan to Aristotle leaked out. Congress had not previously been in the business of using taxpayer money as developmental capital for political consultants. One Republican congressman expressed concern about "the ethics involved in having voter lists in members' offices."[43] The press by and large ignored the controversy, however, and an effort by a few Republicans to scotch the deal failed. By the end of 1991, about ninety lawmakers had spent $127,000 in taxpayer funds on mailing lists. By the following summer, fifty-six legislators had bought Aristotle CD-ROM disks for the total sum of $250,000—curiously enough, almost the exact amount of Aristotle's loan from the House.[44] It was innovative financing for an innovative project. Subsequent attempts by reformers to get Congress to outlaw purchase of voter registration lists with official funds have failed.[45]

Aristotle is not the only businessman trying to tap this lucrative market. Former House Administration Committee Chairman Charlie Rose has also pushed an even more sophisticated computer product—Monarch Constituent Management, a computer system from Monarch Constituent Services, a North Hollywood, California, computer software firm. Technically, the Monarch product is a "constituent mail manager," meaning that it contains software that helps staffers answer constituent mail, a theoretically legitimate use of both a computer software product and the frank. Yet the system's similarities to a campaign direct mail system are striking. In fact, the company markets an almost identical product to campaigns. As Monarch chief financial officer Jeff Shulem boasts, the right computer system can offer a comfortable degree of incumbency protection:

> We've always felt that, [with] running a good constituent office on the legislative side you'll never use the campaign system.
>
> If you do your homework on the off-years and know your constituency, you won't have to really run a full-blown campaign. With our members who use our software, no one can ever say that they are not in touch with their constituents.[46]

The Monarch system stores and retrieves a variety of form letters, which make up a large part of a member's outgoing mail since constituents tend to write Congress about the same issues over and over. It also contains mailing lists and other data, enabling legislators to operate a highly sophisticated direct mail operation.

While offering perhaps the most sophisticated program, Monarch was not the first company on Capitol Hill to offer such a product. Many staffers cut their teeth in the mid-1980s on a product called Quorum, which has been continually upgraded and now offers features similar to Monarch. In addition, Texas-based Electronic Data Systems recently received Hill approval to market a constituent mail product. Interestingly, these systems are not paid for out of the congressional franking budget. Rather, the expense—which can be as much as $60,000—comes from a general office account. (Often, an additional annual expenditure, also from the general office account, is needed for yearly database updates.)[47]

These systems do far more than just help answer letters. They all allow legislators to construct their own detailed databases of their constituents over and above what is available commercially. For instance, a new congressman can purchase a voter registration database from Aristotle or some other list broker, then input the names into his new computer system. Along the way, he can code the names so that in the future he can simply enter a specific sequence, and all the names and addresses of constituents of a certain age, gender, locale, or race pop up. By keeping track of constituents' contacts with his office, the detail and usefulness of the files grow.

One of the preferred means of collecting such data is the constituent questionnaire. As noted earlier, some questionnaires are propaganda masquerading as polls. Other questionnaires are data prospecting devices masquerading as polls. Typically advertised as an attempt by the legislator to take the pulse of the district, such mailings are actually designed to accumulate more data on their constituents for future persuasive mailings. When the completed questionnaires are returned, one congressional staff member who has run a mail operation said, "You pick out four or five issues that fit into your political agenda and you send them a response based on their opinion." The aide noted that the "surveys" go out to thousands of households at a time, and all responses are painstakingly tabulated. Were the practice truly survey research, a sample of a few hundred would be statistically sufficient for a reliable reading. "This is blanketly abused by both sides," the aide said of prospecting through questionnaires. "It is a crass re-election tool." The practice has lately become even more sophisticated. Some legislators now conduct random telephone "polling" in their district, a function assisted by computer systems that include telemarketing software and tracking forms.

In 1995, Michigan's Vernon Ehlers was testing the new Quick Response system from Electronic Data Systems, which, like the Monarch system, can code constituents according to issues. "You can code them by topic, by the groups they belong to, you know, whatever it is that is key to you," said Debbie Marshall, senior legislative assistant, who explained how the office sent out one targeted mailing:

> A lot of "home schoolers" wrote my boss because he was home-schooled when he was younger, so he was like the unofficial champion of their cause when [home schooling legislation] was going through. So, we had a lot of calls from them, and he did a very nice floor speech. And we looked those people up again and we sent a copy of the floor speech to them to say, "Thank you for calling, and, you know, we did follow up and this is what we said, in case you didn't see it."[48]

Chicago's Luis Gutierrez purchased a Monarch system shortly after taking office and during his first term was able to supplement the large database already in the system with more than 12,000 additional names, mostly from phone calls and incoming mail, which were then coded according to issue. "One thing we did in the 102nd [Congress] is that we wrote to everyone who had previously written to us about NAFTA, after the vote," said Gutierrez aide Juan Rodriguez. "We wrote before the vote, when they initially wrote us, and then we wrote them again after the vote explaining to them why he voted no. We were able to target and isolate those people."[49]

The Monarch system also enables legislators to target mail on all sides of an issue, thereby giving constituents the impression their congressman agrees with them, no matter their stance:

> On the targeting side, one thing that we have that no one else has, for example, is the ability to swap paragraphs within a letter. So, you can do just one targeted mailing and you can get hundreds of different combinations of a letter coming out. And you swap paragraphs based on if they're pro or anti. And you might have a middle-of-the-road paragraph if they're anti and the member's pro.[50]

These systems also provide "personal touches," such as digitized signatures that make it appear the congressman actually signed the letter. The Monarch system even notifies staffers if they are sending correspondence to someone with a birthday coming up, so a birthday greeting can be included. "Our goal is to have politicians have the appearance of being very personal, even though we know and you know that this is done on computer," Monarch's Shulem said. "If someone could get a letter, especially if they're a senior citizen, who gets a letter from his congressman, and it looks very personalized, they're going to put it up on their refrigerator. That's going to mean a lot to them. And they don't know it was a digitized signature, for example. And maybe the person will now go out and vote."[51]

A constituent might find it unnerving that so much of his personal information may be hidden in the computer of his congressman. However, he probably should not write or call to complain about it, for this will only lengthen his entry in the computer. Congressional offices routinely log every piece of constituent mail and every constituent phone call received into their computer databases, accumulating vast archives of personal and sometimes private information.

The Great Franking Fraud

One of the strongest arguments made on behalf of the frank is that Congress needs it to keep up with the huge volume of incoming mail.

For years, House officials claimed that legislators were under virtual siege. "In the last decade the amount of mail pouring into the House of Representatives has jumped 277%, from 47.7 million pieces in 1977 to an eye-glazing 180 million in 1986," reported the *Los Angeles Times* in 1988, citing statistics supplied by House officials.[52] There have been dozens of other similarly wide-eyed stories in other media. During the 1980s, House officials, particularly House Postmaster Robert Rota, a patronage appointee, frequently lamented the mail "blizzard," tossing off estimates placing the amount of incoming mail at 250 million to 500 million pieces annually—one or two pieces of mail for every man, woman, and child in the United States.

The figures were at odds with Postal Service data, which consistently put the incoming mail rate in the far more modest range of 30 million to 50 million pieces annually—a fraction of the amount claimed by the House. But Rota insisted that the Postal Service's method of counting was inaccurate. The huge figures for incoming mail put forth by Rota were extremely important politically, since they allowed incumbents to claim at least a semblance of parity between incoming correspondence and the 500-million-plus annual outgoing letters. But after a drug and patronage scandal struck the House Post Office in 1992, public pressure forced the House to hire a professional postmaster, Postal Service executive Michael Shinay, to work alongside Rota. Shinay says he soon discovered major discrepancies in Rota's numbers for incoming mail. "Some of the stuff Rota was throwing around was just unbelievable. He just made the numbers up," Shinay says. "Honest to God, he put an extra zero on the end. He made a hundred thousand into a million." Under Rota's numbers, Shinay said, the average congressman would be receiving thousands of pieces of mail per day. "They don't have enough people to open that much mail, let alone answer it."[53] In truth, Shinay says, each House office receives about 250 letters a day on average, while sending out thousands.[54]

The other primary defense of the frank was that it was abused by a small minority of congressmen, and the body's entire membership (not to mention their constituents) should not suffer for the abuses of a few. This argument may carry some weight if the criticism of the frank is simply about waste of taxpayer funds. But the issue also is the integrity of the political system, and on this score, the defense of the frank crumbles.

A wealth of new data indicates that franking affects a particularly sensitive point in the electoral system—the relatively small number of congressional districts that are not firmly in the hands of either political party, the ones that hold the balance of partisan power when it comes to organizing the House. Of the 435 seats in the House, fewer than one-fourth are usually "in play" in any given election year. In other words, at least 75 percent of the 435 House seats are very likely not to change partisan hands regardless of the national political mood. (The 1994 election was exceptional, as we have already pointed out.) Partisan control of the House thus comes down to a relatively small number of seats, and an uneven playing field in these few races can therefore have a huge impact.

Under new reforms in 1990, each House member was required for the first time to begin disclosing how much he or she had spent on franked mail. The numbers reveal that the ranks of the big spenders are consistently dominated by congressmen facing rough reelection fights.[55] This is critical factual evidence for an inquiry into political competition in congressional elections and a deconstruction of the House the Democrats built.

In the first six months of 1994, the period when most preelection mailing activity is believed to have taken place, 62 of the top 100 mailers were facing competitive reelection fights. By contrast, fewer than a fourth of seats in the entire House were competitive (see Table 3). But these numbers fail to capture just how motley a crew the top 100 were. The sixth-ranked franker, California Republican Jay Kim, was battling widely publicized allegations of sizable illegal campaign funding activity during his 1992 race. Thirtieth-ranked Ken Calvert, another California Republican, had been caught with a prostitute. Still another Republican, Martin Hoke of Ohio, had been caught on tape making tasteless observations about a woman newscaster's breasts. Many of the Democrats on the list, meanwhile, were scandal-free but nonetheless in abysmal political shape. Ten had received less than 51 percent of the vote in their 1992 campaigns; they were people like Democratic Representative Collin Peterson of Minnesota, whose victory margin was just 3,490 votes.

Table 3. Top 100 House Frankers, January to June 30, 1994

Representative	Competitive or noncompetitive race?	Representative	Competitive or noncompetitive race?
1. Peter King (R-N.Y.)	C	39. Don Young (R-Alaska)	C
2. Richard Gephardt (D-Mo.)	C	40. Nydia Velazquez (D-N.Y.)	NC
3. David Levy (R-N.Y.)	C	41. Don Sundquist (R-Tenn.)	C
4. Eliot Engel (D-N.Y.)	C	42. John LaFalce (D-N.Y.)	C
5. Esteban Torres (D-Calif.)	NC	43. Collin Peterson (D-Minn.)	C
6. Jay Kim (R-Calif.)	C	44. James Sensenbrenner (R-Wis.)	NC
7. Charles Rangel (D-N.Y.)	C	45. Ed Towns (D-N.Y.)	NC
8. Jerry Nadler (D-N.Y.)	C	46. Bill Baker (R-Calif.)	C
9. Peter Deutsch (D-Fla.)	C	47. Bill Goodling (R-Pa.)	C
10. Tom Foglietta (D-Pa.)	NC	48. Billy Tauzin (D-La.)	NC
11. Steve Schiff (R-N.M.)	NC	49. Bob Livingston (R-La.)	NC
12. Ileana Ros-Lehtinen (R-Fla.)	NC	50. Sander Levin (D-Mich.)	C
13. Jim Slattery (D-Kans.)	C	51. Rick Boucher (D-Va.)	C
14. John Tanner (D-Tenn.)	NC	52. Wally Herger (D-Calif.)	NC
15. Leslie Byrne (D-Va.)	C	53. Pete Stark (D-Calif.)	NC
16. Toby Roth (R-Wis.)	NC	54. Maurice Hinchey (D-N.Y.)	C
17. Bill Richardson (D-N.M.)	NC	55. Carolyn Maloney (D-N.Y.)	C
18. Jimmy Duncan (R-Tenn.)	NC	56. Frank Wolf (R-Va.)	NC
19. Helen Bentley (R-Md.)	C	57. Bruce Vento (D-Minn.)	C
20. Floyd Flake (D-N.Y.)	NC	58. Bob Filner (D-Calif.)	C
21. Tom Lantos (D-Calif.)	NC	59. Alcee Hastings (D-Fla.)	NC
22. Rosa DeLauro (D-Conn.)	NC	60. Bob Carr (D-Mich.)	C
23. Bart Stupak (D-Mich.)	C	61. Roscoe Bartlett (R-Md.)	C
24. Mike Synar (D-Okla.)	C	62. Charles Taylor (R-N.C.)	C
25. Barbara Rose Collins (D-Mich.)	NC	63. Thomas Petri (R-Wisc.)	C
26. John Bryant (D-Tex.)	C	64. Bill Paxon (R-N.Y.)	NC
27. Rod Grams (R-Minn.)	C	65. John Olver (D-Mass.)	C
28. John Conyers (D-Mich.)	C	66. Lincoln Diaz-Ballart (R-Fla.)	NC
29. Karen Shepherd (D-Utah)	C	67. Martin Sabo (D-Minn.)	NC
30. Ken Calvert (R-Calif.)	C	68. Doug Bereuter (R-Nebr.)	C
31. Bart Gordon (D-Tenn.)	C	69. Chris Shays (R-Conn.)	NC
32. Gary Ackerman (D-N.Y.)	C	70. Martin Hoke (R-Ohio)	C
33. Jack Quinn (R-N.Y.)	C	71. Martin Lancaster (D-N.C.)	C
34. Pat Williams (D-Mont.)	C	72. Frank Pallone (D-N.J.)	C
35. Lucille Roybal-Allard (D-Calif.)	NC	73. Marge Roukema (R-N.J.)	NC
36. Anthony Beilenson (D-Calif.)	C	74. David Skaggs (D-Colo.)	C
37. Mike Kreidler (D-Wash.)	C	75. Xavier Becerra (D-Calif.)	C
38. Matt Martinez (D-Calif.)	C	76. Peter Barca (D-Wis.)	C

77. Phil Crane (R-Ill.)	C	89. Dan Burton (R-Ind.)	NC
78. Richard Lehman (D-Calif.)	C	90. Richard Baker (R-La.)	C
79. Martin Frost (D-Tex.)	C	91. Major Owens (D-N.Y.)	NC
80. Susan Molinari (R-N.Y.)	NC	92. Sanford Bishop (D-Ga.)	NC
81. James Clyburn (D-S.C.)	NC	93. John Mica (R-Fla.)	C
82. Chris Smith (R-N.J.)	NC	94. Herb Bateman (R-Va.)	C
83. Sam Gejdenson (D-Conn.)	C	95. Gene Green (D-Tex.)	C
84. George Sangmeister (D-Ill.)	C	96. Ben Gilman (R-N.Y.)	NC
85. Bill McCollum (R-Fla.)	NC	97. Charles Wilson (D-Tex.)	C
86. Jim Bunning (R-Ky.)	NC	98. David Minge (D-Minn.)	C
87. Eric Fingerhut (D-Ohio)	C	99. Nancy Johnson (R-Conn.)	NC
88. Gary Franks (R-Conn.)	C	100. Harry Johnston (D-Fla.)	NC

Source: The rankings in this chart are drawn from a Freedom of Information Act request filed by the National Taxpayers Union with the Postal Service. Their rankings of members of the House are derived by dividing the amount each member spends by the number of addresses in the legislator's district. The description of each member's status as competitive or noncompetitive is our own and is based on our analysis of various factors. The most important determinant was the percentage of the vote each incumbent received in the 1992 and 1994 elections. If the incumbent received less than 60 percent in both elections, he or she was automatically classed competitive. Several additional incumbents were classed competitive on the basis of less tangible factors. As a top House leader, for example, Representative Richard Gephardt is perennially a major target of the Republican Party and also hails from a district where party affiliation is split relatively evenly. He is thus classified competitive even though he received 64 percent of the vote in 1992 and 58 percent in 1994. We also classed as "competitive" those incumbents in the top 100 who were seeking other office. There are five such candidates in this table. Tellingly, far less than 5 percent of the entire House sought other office in 1992.
*Top frankers are defined as those who use the largest amount of funds in proportion to the number of addresses in their congressional district. This has been proven to be a reliable and fair means of measuring the extent to which legislators avail themselves of the franking privilege.

Even charting the big spenders fails to fully show how the franking privilege is abused by desperate incumbents. Another egregious tactic is the so-called "499-mailing". Under House rules, congressmen are prohibited from sending out "mass mail" less than sixty days before an election. As always in Washington, however, there is a devil in the details: a "mass mailing" is defined as consisting of 500 letters or more that are substantially similar. Many incumbents who are in weak shape with the voters save their franking dollars until just before election time, then send out huge amounts of mail in small batches. Sometimes the letters are tailored to small subsets of the constituency, whereas other times a large mass of correspondence is broken up into a number of separate mailings, with the content in each batch altered just enough so legislators can claim each bundle

Table 4. House Members Who Used the 499 Rule in 1994

Representative	Percent of the vote In 1992	In 1994	Average	Competitive status of congressional district
Bill Baker (R-La.)	52	59	55	C
Tom Barlow (D-Ky.)	60	49	55	C
Ken Calvert (R-Calif.)	47	55	51	C
Jim Chapman (D-Tex.)	100	55	77	C
Anna Eshoo (D-La.)	57	61	59	C
Harris Fawell (R-Ill.)	68	73	70	C
Vic Fazio (D-La.)	51	49	50	C
Bob Franks (R-N.J.)	53	59	56	C
Bart Gordon (D-Tenn.)	57	51	54	C
Rod Grams (R-Minn.)	44	NA[a]	44	C
Lee Hamilton (D-Ind.)	70	52	61	C
G. Hochbrueckner (D-N.Y.)	52	48	50	C
Tim Holden (D-Pa.)	52	57	55	C
Mike Kreidler (D-Wash.)	52	49	51	C
Blanche Lambert (D-Ark.)	70	54	62	C
Larry Larocco (D-Ind.)	58	45	52	C
Richard Lehman (D-N.M.)	47	39	43	C
Jerry Lewis (R-Calif.)	63	70	67	NC
Nita Lowey (D-N.Y.)	56	67	62	C
Carolyn Maloney (D-N.Y.)	50	63	57	C
Richard Pombo (R-Calif.)	48	62	55	C
Bill Richardson (D-N.M.)	67	64	66	C
Lynn Schenk (D-Calif.)	61	46	49	C
Karen Shepherd (D-Utah)	50	36	43	C
Louis Stokes (D-Ohio)	69	77	73	NC
Charles Taylor (R-N.C.)	55	60	58	C
Jolene Unsoeld (D-Wash.)	56	45	51	C
Average	58	54	57	93% C

a. Grams ran for the Senate in 1994.
Source: This table is based on data supplied by the National Taxpayers Union (NTU) and our own analysis. The NTU defines an "abuser"—and we strongly concur—as an incumbent who mailed at least six "499-mailings" in the two months before the elections.

contains a different letter. The trick is effortless with a decent computer.

As Table 4 documents, of the twenty-seven incumbents whose

abuse of the rule in 1994 was the most blatant, twenty-five were facing competitive elections. The abuses may well have been even worse than Table 4 suggests. The 1995 audit of House operations found that controls over franking operations were virtually nonexistent, and in many cases the 499 rule may have been violated without anyone knowing.[56]

Political scientists have yet to devise a method for proving with absolute scientific certainty that things like the franking privilege change the outcome of elections. Indeed, many of the heaviest frankers go on to lose their reelection bids. What we cannot know is whether even more members of Congress would lose their elections without having access to the frank. Given the mass of circumstantial evidence that now exists, however, it is difficult to conclude otherwise. Certainly, the numbers show beyond doubt that incumbent politicians *believe* the frank makes a difference, and they are perhaps the best analysts of their own races.

The frank—which has shown such remarkable longevity and adaptability over the last two centuries—may have reached its zenith under the Democrats in the last two decades. As this book was being written, the reformist Republican Congress was debating some of the most severe restrictions on the franking privilege in more than a hundred years. Skeptics, though, have seen this before. Historically, the frank has come under pressure whenever a reformist Congress has stormed into office. Yet it has always survived and been restored to full potency after a relatively short interval. "Without a big enough franking allowance, I cannot possible serve and inform my constituents—I can't do it," freshman Republican Wes Cooley of Oregon said in early 1995, commenting on calls to slash franking budgets in half.[57]

Political power is something that no one who possesses it relinquishes lightly. Any practice or procedure that confers an advantage in holding power is going to be discovered sooner or later, and as soon as it is curtailed, the drive that no longer finds expression through it will seek a new outlet. The frank is no different.

As the use and misuse of congressional staff and the frank clearly illustrate, for members of Congress the line between official duties and campaign work has become so blurry as to not exist. It is little wonder that congressional staff rarely complain publicly about their involvement in campaign activities of dubious propriety, given their socialization in an environment where even "official duties" like constituent service have an obvious electoral purpose. Inevitably, then, government funds end up illegally subsidizing campaign activities. The real issue is not legality, but the distortions these developments have helped produce in our electoral system. Sadly, the abuse has gotten so out of hand that one can now argue the United States should not necessarily hold claim to the world's fairest elections. American correspondents and election observers in developing countries such as Mexico often go to great lengths to point out how the governing party has stacked the deck in its own favor, often with an air of contempt and condescension. Yet such issues have often received short shrift in this country. In many developing countries, the government puts the squeeze on the media around election time by threatening to hold up the supply of newsprint. How different is it for our government officials to establish a taxpayer-funded propaganda machine?

9

Reach Out and Slime Someone: The Age of Telephone Sleaze

Oh, the telephone is now a very evil technique.
—*Republican pollster Frank Luntz, November 1994*

The one thing I see repeatedly is the total abuse of the phone. It's really running rampant and getting worse.
—*Democratic consultant Joe Trippi, August 1995*

P erks, and the abuse of them, are both as old as Congress, although the nature of the abuse has evolved considerably. But both major political parties make use of new technology, too, and not just in developing sophisticated direct-mail operations. Computerized telephone banks, made available to the candidates by the professional beneficiaries of big-money politics—the for-hire campaign consultants—have begun to make their mark. While consultants have a separate profit motive, they share with candidates a steely determination to do whatever it takes to win.

During every campaign season, a great deal of attention is properly devoted to condemning misleading television advertisements and nasty direct-mail letters. But "push-polling" has largely been ignored, even though it has become the rage in American campaigns, to the detriment of both civility and the truth. It was a factor most recently in Iowa during the 1996 Republican Caucus, when candidate Steve Forbes accused the Bob Dole campaign of tactics akin to those discussed in this chaper. Unless aggressive action is taken, this difficult-to-catch form of political sleaze threatens to drag our already debased electioneering even lower.

The push-poll operates under the guise of legitimate survey research to spread lies, rumors, and innuendo about candidates. Hundreds of thousands, probably millions, of voters were telephoned and push-polled during the 1994 elections. This effort dramatically increased the degree of negativity in American politics. Many voters and observers were disgusted and enraged by the tactic, but sleaze telephoning can work efficiently and effectively—and so, unless exposed and checked, it is bound to become standard ammunition in campaign arsenals across the United States.

What Is Push-Polling?

A push-poll is a survey instrument containing questions which attempt to change the opinion of contacted voters, generally by divulging negative information about the opponent which is designed to *push* the voter away from him or her and *pull* the voter toward the candidate paying for the polling.[1] In other words, push-polling is *campaigning under the guise of research.* This operational definition parallels the push-poll used by businesses, "sugging"—*s*elling *u*nder the guise of a telephone research poll products or publications. But the push-poll is actually several forms of public opinion surveying and targeted voter contact, some legitimate and others dismaying.

The most common and defensible type is an adjunct to "opposition research," a campaigner's effort to learn about the opponents' record and discover what might reduce public support for them. Commonly, a pollster working for a candidate will pre-test positive and negative campaign themes in a random-sample public opinion survey by telephone early in the campaign season. Voters will be asked for their reactions to the virtues and the vices of the major-party candidates, including some blemishes that may not yet be publicly known. For instance, in a standard research push-poll, a respondent (that is, a citizen called by the pollster) is often read a relatively fair, paragraph-long biographical description of each candidate and asked which contender he or she supports. Then additional information is added, question by question, to test the voter's commitment, and to assess what issues might "push" a voter away from his or her initial choice. For example,

> If you learned that [Candidate A] has voted for six tax increases in the state legislature, would this make you more or less likely to support her?

> If you learned that [Candidate B] opposes a woman's right to choose an abortion, would this make you more or less likely to support him?

Some push-polls give voters several choices for answers: "Would this make you a great deal *more* likely to support him, somewhat *more* likely, somewhat *less* likely, a great deal *less* likely, or would it not make any difference to you?" In this way, a campaign can prepare itself by determining which assaults actually move opinion. Naturally, the candidate wants to know what will work or whether his ammunition is mostly blanks. One well-known national political pollster, Frederick/Schneiders, Inc. (FSI), even advertises its "extensive use" of this type of push-poll in a promotional brochure given to prospective clients: "Every poll is a mini campaign. Respondents are exposed to candidate information during a poll the same way they will during the campaign. By testing which set of information 'stimuli' best produces a maximum vote for the client, FSI polls provide a clear picture of where a race is going and how to get there, not just where it stands today."[2]

The information contained in research-oriented push-polls is fact-based and essentially true (even if presented in a blunt and exaggerated partisan style). The primary goal of this type of push-poll is to obtain the unbiased views of voters, not necessarily to turn the respondents off to the opponent. The respondents are "pushed" to determine what the campaign may need to do to change the image of the opponent, and the negative issues being tested in the survey will probably be ones easily transferable to public, on-the-record attacks made during the campaign (using television advertising, direct mail, or simple stump speeches). Box 1 (see p. 248) shows a research-oriented push-poll from a 1994 U.S. House race. Taken almost a year in advance of the election, it is obvious that the sponsoring candidate is testing themes for positive and negative advertising, as well as probing her own vulnerabilities.

But even this "legitimate" manifestation of push-polling can be troubling. Such a survey may reach 400 to 1,500 respondents in a relatively small geographic area (say, a compact congressional district), and negative personal information about a freely discussed candidate with this many people can quickly become fodder for a districtwide gossip mill. Professional pollsters may object to this characterization. If a survey asks questions about issues or character that portray both candidates in a negative light, they reason that the research poll does no harm. However, they evaluate questions on the basis of their professional perspective—here, the goal is questionnaire balance and unbiased survey results. The trouble is that even balanced surveys yielding unbiased responses will disseminate negative information. This adversely affects the tenor and character of the campaign, and adds to the rampant negativism of modern politics.

Such information is still more worrisome if it is exaggerated or outright false, as is frequently the case with a second type of push-poll, the so-called agenda-driven survey, also known as deliberative polling. Here the pollster is still conducting a random-sample telephone survey with a representative group of voters, but the goal has changed. The agenda is to produce a favorable horse race result for the client-candidate, so that potential contributors and the press can be apprised of the candidate's "impending victory." The technique does not always work, but donors want to give hard-earned dollars to a likely winner, and the news media love to publish and air horse race polls. With a little luck, such a poll could create a bandwagon effect for the leading candidate. A good example of this "agenda-driven" push-poll can be found in Missouri's Fifth Congressional District race in 1994. A loaded survey taken in September by Republican pollster Frank Luntz for GOP nominee Ron Freeman produced an eight percentage point lead for Freeman over Democratic nominee Karen McCarthy for an open seat. Yet on election day McCarthy won easily (56.6 percent to 43.4 percent), despite the overall GOP tide.[3] There may actually be little or no real "bandwagon effect," but politicians and consultants *believe* there is such a thing and strive to create it by looking like a winner.[4]

They do so by providing the respondents with loads of derogatory background on the opponent. Before respondents are asked how they will vote, they may be read biographical sketches heavily biased against the opponent. The client may be portrayed as Mother Teresa and the opponent painted as one step away from the sheriff's manacles. Sometimes the poll asks a series of questions incorporating damaging assertions about the opponent. Often the worst is saved for last, culminating in the classic horse race question, "If the election were held today, would you vote for [Candidate A] or [Candidate B]?"[5] Not surprisingly, at this point a sizable plurality tends to favor the unsullied client.[6] The "good news" numbers are triumphantly released, with no mention of the poll format or non–horse race questions. And gullible contributors open their wallets; undiscerning journalists, usually the more inexperienced press persons, write the desired headlines; and the hundreds of voter-respondents may talk to family and friends about the shocking (though perhaps false) information they have learned about a prominent politician.[7] Thus, the ripple effects can be far-reaching. The agenda-driven poll is sometimes merged with the less egregious "research" form, which can include a horse race question carefully inserted after negative facts about the opponent are presented. The biased results can then be disseminated in the same manner as the second type of push-poll.

Box 1
The "Research" Push-Poll: An Example

The following poll questions are excerpted from a draft survey questionnaire produced in January 1994 for freshman U.S. Representative Leslie Byrne (Democrat of Virginia). It was already clear by January that her Republican opponent would be Thomas M. "Tom" Davis III, chairman of the Fairfax County Board of Supervisors. Both candidates were exceptionally well-funded, and it would be a close, hard-fought race to the wire. (Davis ousted Byrne in the end.) The questionnaire was written by the Democratic firm of Cooper & Secrest, although interviewers were instructed to say they were calling "from Virginia Public Opinion, the national public opinion research firm"—presumably, one would guess, to make the poll's sponsorship hard for a respondent to trace. After running through twenty-four other questions (many of them standard polling fare and some of them multipart), the interviewer turns to the "research" push–poll sections of the survey, as reproduced below. Note that both the positive and negative attributes of Byrne are tested, whereas only Davis's negatives are explored. The interviewer then gathers fourteen pieces of demographic data and background information (race, sex, income, religion, party affiliation, and the like) and signs off.

Q25. Next I'm going to read you several arguments some people have made as to why Leslie Byrne *should not* be reelected as Congress-woman. That is, these are arguments some people are making *against* Leslie Byrne. For each one I read, please tell me how persuasive you think it is as a reason *not* to reelect Leslie Byrne, a *very persuasive reason not* to reelect her, an *only somewhat persuasive reason not to reelect her*, or a *not at all persuasive reason.*

	Very Persuasive Reason	Only Somewhat Persuasive Reason	Not At All Persuasive Reason	Not Sure
a. Leslie Byrne voted in favor of the Clinton budget plan, which includes $241 billion in new taxes.	___ 1	___ 2	___ 3	___ 4
b. Leslie Byrne failed to prevent the closing of the NASA space station headquarters in Reston, resulting in the loss of hundreds of area jobs.	___ 1	___ 2	___ 3	___ 4
c. Although she campaigned against government waste, Leslie Byrne refused to kill several unnecessary congressional subcommittees.	___ 1	___ 2	___ 3	___ 4
d. Leslie Byrne voted against the North American Free Trade Agreement, a treaty which would reduce tariffs and other trade barriers with other North American countries.	___ 1	___ 2	___ 3	___ 4
e. After the budget vote, Leslie Byrne tried to strip House committee chairmen who voted against the President of their chairmanships, and yet Byrne opposed the President on the NAFTA agreement.	___ 1	___ 2	___ 3	___ 4
f. Leslie Byrne voted to raise the ceiling on the national debt by $225 billion.	___ 1	___ 2	___ 3	___ 4

g. In her first year, Leslie Byrne
supported President Clinton
76% of the time. ____ 1 ____ 2 ____ 3 ____ 4

h. Leslie Byrne supports allowing
public funding for abortions in
Washington, D.C. ____ 1 ____ 2 ____ 3 ____ 4

i. Leslie Byrne supports allowing
homosexuals in the military. ____ 1 ____ 2 ____ 3 ____ 4

j. Even though the government
runs a $400 billion deficit,
Leslie Byrne supported using
taxpayer money for artists,
including some artists who
produce art many
consider obscene. ____ 1 ____ 2 ____ 3 ____ 4

k. Leslie Byrne voted for a
campaign finance bill which
would have allowed taxpayer
money to subsidize
congressional campaigns. ____ 1 ____ 2 ____ 3 ____ 4

l. At a time of worldwide unrest,
Leslie Byrne has fought
continuously to cut military
spending and has voted to
eliminate registration for the
draft. ____ 1 ____ 2 ____ 3 ____ 4

m. Leslie Byrne voted against a
measure which would have
forced testimony in the House
Post Office scandal to be placed
into the public record. ____ 1 ____ 2 ____ 3 ____ 4

n. Leslie Byrne supports
government funding for
abortions for poor women. ____ 1 ____ 2 ____ 3 ____ 4

Q26. Now I'm going to read you several arguments some people have
made as to why Leslie Byrne *should* be reelected as Congresswoman.
That is, these are arguments some people are making for Leslie Byrne.
For each one I read, please tell me how persuasive you think it is as
a reason to reelect Leslie Byrne, a *very persuasive reason* to reelect
her, an *only somewhat persuasive reason* to reelect her, or a *not at
all persuasive reason.*

	Very Persuasive Reason	Only Somewhat Persuasive Reason	Not At All Persuasive Reason	Not Sure
a. Leslie Byrne voted for the 5-day waiting period for the purchase of handguns and cosponsored a bill to eliminate the sale and possession of assault rifles.	____ 1	____ 2	____ 3	____ 4

b. To protect Northern Virginia taxpayers, Leslie Byrne has fought against D.C. statehood.   ___ 1   ___ 2   ___ 3   ___ 4

c. Leslie Byrne successfully fought to kill the multi-billion dollar super collider science project in Texas that many consider unnecessary and too expensive.   ___ 1   ___ 2   ___ 3   ___ 4

d. Leslie Byrne voted to reduce our overseas military bases and force countries like Germany and Japan to pay more for their own defense.   ___ 1   ___ 2   ___ 3   ___ 4

e. Leslie Byrne co-sponsored a bill which would have forced Congress to operate under the same civil rights and work protection laws everyone else must work under.   ___ 1   ___ 2   ___ 3   ___ 4

f. Leslie Byrne has more legislation she sponsored pending than any other freshman member of Congress.   ___ 1   ___ 2   ___ 3   ___ 4

g. In order to control spending, Leslie Byrne voted in favor of the line-item veto for presidents or a measure to allow the president to kill individual spending bills he or she considers.   ___ 1   ___ 2   ___ 3   ___ 4

h. Leslie Byrne has cosponsored and helped pass a bill which would allow federal employees to participate fully in the political process by removing Hatch Act restrictions.   ___ 1   ___ 2   ___ 3   ___ 4

i. Leslie Byrne has fought for a bill to prevent foreign companies from "dumping" products in the American market, a process which helps foreign companies drive out competition.   ___ 1   ___ 2   ___ 3   ___ 4

j. Leslie Byrne has sponsored legislation which allows penalty-free withdrawals from individual retirement accounts for taxpayers who want to buy their first home or send their child to college.   ___ 1   ___ 2   ___ 3   ___ 4

Q27. And now I'm going to read you several arguments some people have made as to why Tom Davis *should not* be elected to Congress. That is, these are arguments some people are making *against* Tom Davis. For each one I read, please tell me how persuasive you think it is as a reason *not* to elect Tom Davis, a *very persuasive reason not* to elect him, an *only somewhat persuasive reason not* to elect him, or a *not at all persuasive reason.*

	Very Persuasive Reason	Only Somewhat Persuasive Reason	Not At All Persuasive Reason	Not Sure
a. Less than a week after being sworn in as Chairman of the Board of Supervisors, Tom Davis proposed three separate tax increases and since then has supported or proposed at least eight tax or fee increases in Fairfax County.	___ 1	___ 2	___ 3	___ 4
b. Fairfax voters now pay more in real estate taxes than when Tom Davis took over as Chairman of the Board of Supervisors.	___ 1	___ 2	___ 3	___ 4
c. As a member of the Fairfax Board of Supervisors, Tom Davis fought against efforts to control the rate of growth in Fairfax County after accepting thousands of dollars in campaign contributions from area developers.	___ 1	___ 2	___ 3	___ 4
d. After accepting thousands of dollars in campaign contributions from millionaire Herbert Haft, Tom Davis orchestrated a meeting between Haft and zoning officials to help Haft get around the usual local zoning application process.	___ 1	___ 2	___ 3	___ 4
e. Tom Davis supports reverse restrictions on a woman's right to choose to have an abortion.	___ 1	___ 2	___ 3	___ 4
f. When he ran for Chairman of the Board of Supervisors, Tom Davis promised to quit a job he held with a defense contractor, although he has yet to quit this second job.	___ 1	___ 2	___ 3	___ 4

g. As a member of the Board of
   Supervisors, Tom Davis
   supported the building of the
   Fairfax Government Center, the
   so-called Taj Mahal which has
   cost the County millions of
   dollars in waste and cost
   overruns.   ___ 1   ___ 2   ___ 3   ___ 4

The first two types of push-polls seem almost harmless when compared with the third form, called "negative persuasive" or "advocacy phoning." This push-poll is not really a poll at all, but a form of targeted voter contact and canvassing, since no random sample of the population is selected.[8] Instead, the emphasis is on volume: as many voters in a target population as possible (union members, gun owners, conservative Christians, or whatever) are contacted with a highly negative message that is short—even a minute or less—and asks no demographical background information on the respondents. First, respondents are asked which candidate they favor. If the client-candidate is chosen, the respondent is thanked and placed on the get-out-the-vote (GOTV) list for election day. But if the respondent picks the opponent or says she is undecided, then a torrent of negativity is unleashed: "Would you still support this if you learned that he [is a tax-evader, a baby-killer, or shoots newborn puppies for sport]?" As one frank push-pollster put it on background, "What you're trying to do is mobilize voters *against* a candidate. . . . You're taking a specific audience and literally telling them why they shouldn't be voting for somebody."

The target audience can be voters in swing districts, or even voters in the opponent's areas of greatest strength. In both cases, push-pollsters are attempting to persuade voters that the opponent is not worthy of their backing and thereby *suppressing* his turnout. This "suppression phoning" is the reverse of a form of GOTV called "positive persuasive phoning," which delivers favorable information about the candidate-client to any respondent who is undecided. Obviously, this positive phoning is far preferable ethically to the negative variety, but this once-dominant kind of GOTV is being supplanted in many areas by attack push-polling. But like GOTV, it is done largely in the final weeks or days of a campaign—when the rush of events makes it least likely to be detected or exposed by the

253

opposition or the press. Naturally, the harshest and most untruthful messages are saved for election eve or the weekend prior to Election Day, according to several telephone-bank consultants we interviewed. And, of course, the beauty of this ugly technique is stealth. Unless, by some wild circumstance, a respondent has his phone fitted with a recording device and has the presence of mind to turn on the tape as the interview begins, or someone on the inside talks, there is no way to find fingerprints and fix blame.

The Rise of Telephone Sleaze

The scale and telephone technology of push-polling are new; the concept itself, and the depths to which it can descend, are unfortunately not. It will surprise few to learn that Richard Nixon, whose lack of an ethical compass eventually resulted in his presidency's destruction, was one of push-polling's pioneers. In his very first campaign, a successful 1946 run for the U.S. House against Democratic incumbent Jerry Voorhis, Democratic voters throughout his district reported receiving telephone calls that began, "This is a friend of yours, but I can't tell you who I am. Did you know that Jerry Voorhis is a Communist?" at which point the caller hung up.[9] While no firsthand evidence was produced to link the Nixon campaign directly with the calls, at least one individual has come forward admitting that she worked for Nixon at $9 a day, in a telephone-bank room where the attack calls were made.[10] The technique, according to distinguished Nixon biographer Stephen E. Ambrose, was well-suited to the "vicious, snarling . . . dirty" Nixon campaign, which "was full of half-truths, full lies, and innuendoes, hurled at such a pace that Voorhis could never catch up with them."[11]

Nixon was not alone in his use of gutter tactics, of course, but for decades this kind of negativity was regularly and roundly condemned by the press and most political professionals. It may be a commentary on our times that this is no longer so. In fact, candidates, parties, and consultants sometimes brag openly about their excursions into sleaze, once the campaign is over. In 1986, for example, the Democrats and their allies in the labor unions undertook massive negative persuasive phoning just before the midterm congressional elections that saw a Democratic majority in the U.S. Senate restored after six years of GOP rule.[12] The telephone message centered upon the Reagan administration's supposed plans to undermine and reduce funding for social security—a highly suspect allegation that nonetheless appeared to do the trick, according to strategists for both parties. This episode has been repeatedly cited by Democrats as a clever tactic to employ in the years since.[13] Perhaps not incidentally, the social security push-poll against Republicans has continued to be a mainstay of Democratic "outreach" to senior citizens until the present day. Many of the 1994 Republican congressional candidates we interviewed complained about it.[14]

Over a hundred political consulting firms specializing in persuasive phoning have sprung up over the past two decades.[15] For example, 154 telephone firms offering political "direct contact" services were listed by *Campaigns and Elections* magazine, a well-known trade journal for consultants and aspiring officeholders, in a publication released in February 1995. The new technology of computer-aided telephoning and target selection has made the process of political and commercial marketing by phone vastly easier and more efficient. A single operator can make 80 to 100 *completed* calls with a short message *each evening hour,* at a cost (depending on message length and company) of $0.45 to $1.30 per call.[16] In other words, a quarter million targeted calls can be made for $112,000 to $325,000—arguably a solid investment for a multimillion-dollar statewide campaign that is probably spending many times that on diffuse television advertising.

Dial N for Negative

The proliferation of telephone marketing technology and the firms that sell it not only fills a campaign need but creates one. The firms' aggressive entrepreneurs—another variety of the ubiquitous political consultants that specialize in attack politics—advertise the technology's availability, and also ignite the latent fear in every campaign manager that the other side may be employing the technique already.[17] (This same psychology once fueled the superpowers' arms race.)

Take Mac Hansbrough, the pleasant and forthcoming president of Washington, D.C.–based National Telecommunications Services, whose clients have included the Democratic National Committee, abortion-rights groups, and various Democratic candidates. Hansbrough wrote a remarkably candid 1992 article, "Dial N for Negative," in *Campaigns and Elections*.[18] Calling negative phoning "the single most important and cost-effective communications tool a campaign can employ" and predicting its widespread use in the 1990s, Hansbrough correctly suggested that the technique would "take its place beside negative television, radio, and direct mail as a necessary tool in the . . . consultant's arsenal." And he cited the "lack of spill-over" as one vital reason why:

> One can deliver different messages to multiple groups of voters with little chance that one group will receive the other's message or that the larger constituency of uncalled voters will receive any of the messages. This is a major advantage when controversial issues are being discussed, and it is an advantage that TV and radio cannot offer. . . .
>
> Negative phoning leaves few footprints. TV and radio ads can be heard by anyone and are often reported in the newspaper. Direct mail is available to find its way into anyone's hands and has the lasting effect that goes with all printed matter. Phone calls, of course, are verbal. Scripts are tightly controlled and rarely get out to the press, general public, or opponents. Phone calls are the true communications stealth technology of the future.

In follow-up interviews, Hansbrough told us that in his experience, negative phoning was most likely to occur in a close campaign, where a desperate candidate is hard-pressed and increasingly willing to do whatever it takes to win: "You use a negative approach only when you have to, and in my opinion, you only have to when you are very sure or reasonably sure that you may be losing the election."[19] Even in these cases, though, candidates—fearing a backlash or a damaging news story—usually desire a buffer between their campaigns and the telephoning. So the sponsorship is passed to the national or state party committee, or a friendly allied group (say, a labor union for a Democratic nominee or a conservative organization for a Republican nominee). In some cases, a separate front vehicle is actually invented, such as "Citizens for Tax Fairness" or a neutral-sounding polling research company. (See the negative persuasion phoning scripts in Box 2, which have been used in a recent campaign by Hansbrough clients.) However, Hansbrough stressed that whatever the sponsorship, the campaign controls the message, and the final scripting normally is approved by it. Hansbrough freely admits that most of the calling occurs at the election's last minute, and that there is much hand-wringing about the practice in many campaigns. But if the race is tight enough, the doubts are usually resolved *in favor* of negative phoning. Adds Hansbrough: "There's another good reason for doing it late: . . . negative campaigning is controversial [so] don't stir it up until you have to," or until it is likely the press will not pick up on the tactic until the election is over.

Two examples of these negative persuasion phoning scripts are reproduced below. These scripts were used by the campaign of

---

Negative Persuasion Phoning: Two Examples

Script 1

Hello, this is [interviewer's name] calling on behalf of the Florida Association of Senior Citizens.
We are calling to let you know that [Republican nominee for governor] Jeb Bush is no friend of seniors.
Bush's running mate has advocated the abolition of Social Security and called Medicare a welfare program that should be cut.
We just can't trust Jeb Bush and [lieutenant governor nominee] Tom Feeney.
Thank you and have a good day/evening.

Script 2

Hello, my name is [interviewer's name] calling from the Citizens for Tax Fairness.
I am calling to remind you that unlike thousands of your fellow citizens, Jeb Bush failed to pay local and state taxes and he has profited at the taxpayers' expense from business deals involving failed savings and loan properties. Mr. Bush doesn't play by the same rules like the rest of

us and we want to make sure you are aware of this before you cast your vote on Tuesday.
Thank you and have a good day/evening.

Source: Scripts were provided by Mac Hansbrough. The campaigns using them were not identified by Hansbrough. But a year after the November 1994 election, these scripts became the center of controversy in Florida, where Republicans claimed they unfairly attacked Jeb Bush and helped to reelect Democratic Governor Lawton Chiles.

Florida Democratic Governor Lawton Chiles, a Hansbrough client, in his successful 1994 reelection bid against Republican Jeb Bush, son of former President George Bush. After the election, Republicans claimed that Chiles's narrow victory (65,000 votes out of 4.2 million cast) was due to these negative telephone scripts, read to tens of thousands of Floridians shortly before the election.[20]

Negative phoning is just the latest, and perhaps nastiest, extension of the harsh tone of modern American politics. The technique "is effective because voters are much more prepared today to believe negative things about candidates than they once were. Negative TV ads, radio, direct mail, and news coverage have really paved the way" for negative phoning, asserts Hansbrough. Sleaze and cynicism do indeed feast at each other's table, as push-polling is proving anew.

The Sleaze of '94

As the campaigns of 1994 proved, Mac Hansbrough was a prophet when he predicted in 1992 that "negative phoning will probably be used quite heavily in the next decade."[21] Of the forty-five 1994 candidates for Congress we interviewed for this book, fully thirty-four [almost 80 percent] *claimed* that push-polling was used against them. Only one, freshman Republican U.S. Representative Bob Ehrlich of Maryland, was honest enough to admit doing it himself: "I think all the pollsters are doing that now. I mean, ours did."[22] Bob Ehrlich's Democratic opponent, Gerry Brewster, also used a research push-poll, admitted Brewster consultant David Heller of Politics, Inc.: "We tested different arguments against Ehrlich. [One question asked was,] 'If you knew that Bob Ehrlich supported a bill to give family leave to convicted murders and allowed them to go back into their communities, [would you be less likely to support him?]'" Agreeing that the statement was a strong one, Heller insisted that

"Bob Ehrlich had more baggage than Samsonite."[23] Further, using additional press reports on other races, we have been able to identify another three dozen cases of *alleged* push-polling that occurred during the 1994 election year. Given the iceberg nature of push-polling—one-eighth above the surface and seven-eighths below—the actual number of push-poll incidents was likely far higher than our data indicated. And those who have been around politics and in the trenches for a long time claim there was an explosion of push-polling in 1994. "It's existed for years, but I'm telling you it was heavy duty this cycle," said one veteran operative.

As some of the following examples suggest, however, it is difficult to know what kind of push-poll was employed in most cases: was it a legitimate research survey or dastardly negative phoning? Moreover, in most cases it is next to impossible to trace the source of the calls. Because so much of push-polling occurs under the radar screen, it is rarely covered or investigated by the news media.[24] Nonetheless, these examples—drawn mainly from campaigns in the 1990s, most in 1994, clearly document how widespread push-polling has become.

THE PRO-LIFE PUSH-POLLS IN 1994

Just a few days before the November 8, 1994 elections, Joshua Harris reported as usual for work to his telemarketing company in Austin, Texas, known as the Southern Education Council. "It's a fundraising company, and we work with a lot of charities like the Texas Department of Public Safety Officers Association, the firefighters and fire marshals associations in Texas, and so forth," Harris said.[25] But on this particular night, a very different kind of script, prompted by a new rush order, popped up on the computer terminal for the calls Harris was supposed to make. As he described it:

> We had to say, "Hello, Mr. So and So, we're calling from the state pro-life federation. There are over 4,000 abortions performed every day in our state. Candidate A supports abortion on demand and using your tax dollars to pay for it. Candidate B does not support abortion on demand and opposes using your tax dollars to pay for it." And then we mentioned something to the pro-life candidate's benefit, one of their accomplish-

259

ments or whatever, and then we got off the phone. They're info-blitzes. We never interacted with the customer. We were on the phone for no more than ten to twenty seconds, and it worked. You got about 40 people [each] making about 100 calls an hour. It went on Friday night, then all day Saturday, from nine in the morning to nine at night, all day Sunday, nine to nine, and Monday nine to nine. And then on election day it went on nine to five. Easily 100,000 calls were made, maybe more.

The calls went out to Pennsylvania, to help Republican Rick Santorum in his race against Democratic U.S. Senator Harris Wofford; to Michigan, on behalf of the GOP's Spencer Abraham, running for an open U.S. Senate seat; to Tennessee, for various Republican nominees; and to Minnesota, where Republican Rod Grams was locked in a tight contest for an open U.S. Senate berth with Democrat Ann Wynia.[26]

It was all too much for Harris, a twenty-four-year-old African-American and Democratic party activist who also worked as a paid staffer for the Austin-area Democrats. He alerted the Wynia campaign on November 5; the campaign tipped off Dennis J. McGrath, a reporter for the *Minneapolis Star-Tribune,* and on November 7, a brief mention of the calls was made in his story about the frantic efforts of both sides at the eleventh hour.[27] No more notice was taken of the telephone operation in Minnesota or in any of the other states—except that someone in Minnesota who saw the *Star-Tribune* article called the Southern Education Council's parent company in New Jersey to complain about Harris's leak. And soon Harris was temporarily suspended from his council job as a penalty for his pangs of conscience. "I was really pissed off," said Harris. And the calls? "They were sleazy," noted Harris, but "sleazy and *effective*—that's the bad part." All the candidates whom the phoning was designed to help won their races.

The phoning's sponsor has not heretofore been publicly known. Chris Georgacas, chair of the Minnesota GOP, speculated that it was financed by the National Right to Life Committee or the Christian Coalition.[28] The Southern Education Council refused to identify its client to us. A thorough check of all relevant Federal Election Commission records revealed nothing, meaning no group disclosed payments to the council or its parent company even though the expenditure was clearly made, federal elections were directly affected, and therefore disclosure of the money spent was required under the Federal Election Campaign Act. But as we suggested in chapter 5, it appears that the original source of funding for the telephoning was the National Republican Senatorial Committee.[29]

A number of Democratic U.S. House candidates also reported distorted push calls about their abortion records to us. For instance, former Representative Ted Strickland of Ohio attributes his very close defeat for reelection in 1994 in part to blunt negative persuasion calls that flooded his district in the last week of the campaign.[30] "Basically, the message was this: 'Do you know that Congressman Strickland supports abortion on demand through the ninth month [of pregnancy]? And that he wants to use public tax dollars to pay for it?'" remembers Strickland. "Now it's true I support public funding, but I have never supported abortion on demand through the ninth month [of pregnancy], and would never, obviously." Strickland is convinced that the phoning came from outside his district because "on the one message left on a recording device that I heard, the [interviewer] mispronounced the name of my opponent. So the people making the calls were not familiar enough with him to pronounce his name correctly."

For the record, pro-choice groups also did push-polling in 1994. For example, Republican U.S. House candidate Matt Salmon of Arizona (who is pro-life and eventually won his race) reported to us that his pro-choice Democratic opponent sponsored persuasion calls throughout the district.[31] The interviewer would first ask, "Are you pro-choice or pro-life?" If the answer was pro-life, the interviewer would say thank you and hang up, because "they didn't want to alienate people who were pro-life," suggested Salmon. But if the respondent said "pro-choice," the interviewer would interject, "Did you know Matt Salmon is anti-choice?" "Obviously, it wasn't a poll," despite being presented as one, Salmon noted. "It was real deceptive."

PUSH-POLL SPONSORSHIP: PSEUDO-INDEPENDENT, SEMI-INDEPENDENT, OR TRULY INDEPENDENT?

Earlier we mentioned the formation of phony shell groups or nonexistent polling firms to hide sponsorship of push-polling. According to most of the telephone bank consultants we contacted, this is far and away the most common phoning technique. In addition, there are apparently cases in which outside interest groups and *even the political parties* choose to conduct negative persuasion phoning *without* the specific approval of, or script review by, individual campaigns.

Such a situation occurred in Maine, in a hard-fought U.S. House contest in 1994. Republican nominee Rick Bennett denounced a late-campaign push-poll that asked respondents if their opinion of Bennett would be changed if they knew that he had "defaulted" on $10,000 worth of student loans, yet loaned the same amount to his campaign.[32] Bennett actually had $7,000 remaining on his student loans, but had consistently met his required monthly payments and abided by all the terms of the loan agreement. "There's nothing illegal or improper about owing money on your student loans; just about everybody does," asserted Bennett. Incidentally, Bennett learned of the push-polling from an outraged citizen, insurance salesman Scott Landry of Wilton, Maine. Landry, a registered Democrat, had planned to vote for Democratic nominee John Baldacci (the eventual winner of the seat), but was so enraged by what he called the poll's "libel" of Bennett that he contacted Bennett's campaign.[33]

Landry challenged the interviewer about the nature of the "poll," and was told the results would go to "the Democratic Party." In the heat of the campaign, though, the chairwoman of the Maine Democratic Party flatly denied that the party was engaging in any push-polling.[34] But one of Baldacci's campaign consultants, David Heller of Politics, Inc., now confirms the Democratic Party's role:

> The [Maine] Democratic Party hired a big D.C. polling firm, Lauer, Lalley & Associates to do push-polling against Bennett that was paid for by the unions. . . . I think it was an independent expenditure, done by labor at the behest of the Democratic Party. . . . They asked [the student loan question and also] "If you knew Bennett sponsored a bill in the Maine Legislature that would have cut the state attorney general's budget down to virtually nothing and allowed murderers to go back out on the streets, would you support him?"

According to Heller, this was one occasion when a campaign did not desire the push-polling assistance:[35]

> John Baldacci had promised not to run a negative campaign. We went out of our way to portray John as somebody who's not a politician, somebody different, somebody who's not going to throw mud. John looked great in comparison to all the other nasty races going on in Maine. And then, people start reading in the paper that the Baldacci camp is going negative and they say, "we knew he was just like everybody else." We tried to say, "We don't know about this, we don't know what it is." But it was very damaging to us. [Baldacci won a closer-than-expected race.]
>
> This is one of my biggest frustrations. The Democratic party decided they could run the race better than the candidate and his campaign. They tried to browbeat us into going negative and we wouldn't do it. Then they ran a negative poll to say, "look, it works." Because they know everything, we don't know anything. In their minds, John Baldacci is some hick from rural Maine.

As for the defeated Rick Bennett, he does not care much at this point who sponsored the push-poll. He believes his candidacy was severely damaged by the student loan allegation, even though he attempted to refute it in a press conference held shortly before election day: "There's really no way to effectively combat this kind of under-handed campaigning. You come out at a press conference and announce, 'They're saying I defaulted, and it's not true.' So you publicize the charge and people start wondering if you did it or not. You can't win, and there's no good way to respond. This push-polling is terrible, just completely reprehensible."[36]

THE HOMOSEXUAL HOT BUTTON

Since negative persuasion phoning tries to cause the respondent's adrenaline to pump with outrage toward the opponent after just a brief encounter, it must search for hot-button issues that can be communicated in shorthand soundbites. Abortion, gun control, and taxes all do the trick with the appropriate target audiences, but one of the most reliable—and apparently, relied upon—topics is gay rights. The homosexual hot button turned up in push-polls all across America in 1994.

Most common was simply a focus on various Democratic congressmen's alleged support for President Clinton's initial attempt to let homosexuals serve openly in the U.S. military (later compromised into the current "don't ask, don't tell" policy). "The areas around a military base in my district were targeted," reported former U.S. Representative Tom Barlow (Democrat of Kentucky), who was defeated for reelection."[37] "People got calls asking 'Do you know that Mr. Barlow is for gay rights?' "

The gay-baiting went further in Alaska's extremely close gubernatorial contest between Democrat Tony Knowles and Republican Jim Campbell.[38] An interviewer for Campbell's push-pollster had the misfortune to telephone Bob King, the communications director for the Knowles campaign. According to King, the interviewer asserted that "Tony Knowles supports gay rights, including gay marriages and adoptions. Knowing this, does this make you more or less likely to vote for Tony Knowles?" King was incensed at this fabrication; while his candidate was opposed to discrimination on the basis of sexual preference, he had never endorsed gay marriage and adoption.

Knowles quickly challenged Campbell on the point, and the Republican admitted that the poll was being taken. But Campbell defended the question, claiming that Knowles had never *explicitly* ruled out gay marriage and adoption. Furthermore, Knowles had voted for an Anchorage ordinance in the 1970s that protected gays from housing and job discrimination. Campbell's argument collapsed, however, when reporters discovered that as a member of the local governing body, Campbell had voted for precisely the same ordinance. The embarrassment appeared to hurt Campbell at first, and he fell precipitously in the public opinion polls in October. But the issue may have quietly helped Campbell on Election Day, when he surprised pollsters by finishing just a few hundred votes behind Knowles (who still became governor).

The ultimate in anti-gay push-polling though, came in a number of U.S. House and Senate contests around the country, where heterosexual Democratic candidates were "revealed" as gay or les-

bian in last-minute negative persuasion calls. These phony "out-
ings" were true smear polls and may well have proved costly to their
victims. According to Beth Bernard, campaign manager for Minnesota Democratic U.S. Senate nominee Ann Wynia, the "lesbian
calls" came on election eve: "Would it make a difference if you knew
that Ann Wynia was a lesbian?"[39] Bernard thought the calls originated with the Republican Party, and indeed, the NRSC did conduct push-polling against Wynia in her state.[40] Ohio Democratic
U.S. Representative Eric Fingerhut received much the same treatment: "I'm single, and I kept getting reports about the push-polling
calls that would ask anyone who said they were for me, 'Would you
still vote for him if you knew he was gay?' Of course, that would be
the end of the phone call. It happens not to be true and my friends
laughed about it. But it was a catch-22. What do you do? Do you
hold a press conference and say, 'I'm not gay!'?"[41] Fingerhut did not
hold the press conference. He also did not get reelected.

SLEAZE POLLING'S NEW FEDERALISM

If, as former U.S. House Speaker Thomas P. "Tip" O'Neill once
said, all politics is local, it was inevitable that push-polling would be
used in local election contests. And indeed it has been employed,
with no holds barred.

For example, more than a dozen 1993 state legislative races in Virginia featured "lies, rumors, half-truths, smears, and gross distortions"
in push-polls, according to an enterprising state politics reporter who
obtained actual copies of the suspect questions and who staked out the
pollster's phone bank headquarters.[42] Bob Gibson of the *Charlottesville
Daily Progress* determined that Cooper & Secrest Associates, one of the
nation's largest Democratic polling firms, directed 400 to 500 calls to
registered voters in each targeted House of Delegates district, and these
calls in many districts contained highly misleading push-poll "research" questions about Republican candidates, such as the following:[43]

• Listing reasons "some people have given us as to why" Delegate
Robert D. Orrock should not be reelected, the interviewers
claimed "although his mother-in-law runs a private day-care center, Bobby Orrock voted against legislation that would have led to

increased state oversight and regulation of private day-care centers."[44] In fact, Orrock's mother-in-law is a retired bank teller who has never run any day-care center or even baby-sat for children on a regular basis, and the bills referred to in the question were killed by Orrock's committee at the request of the sponsor.

• Voters were asked their opinion of the seriousness of Delegate Riley Ingram's "dozens of misdemeanor violations" for "the properties he rents." Ingram has never been taken to court, much less been convicted, of violations on any of his properties. (Ingram's sister was called by the pollster, and tipped off her brother.)

• Respondents in Delegate Robert Marshall's district were told that he had a lien against his house, implying that the legislator was a tax delinquent. Actually, the lien was placed by mutual agreement with Marshall's homeowners' association; Marshall did not want to pay dues to retain swimming privileges at the subdivision's pond, but the lien allowed future owners of Marshall's house to pick up the swimming option if they so chose.

• Other voters were asked their opinion of Republican H. Morgan Griffith's defense "in court [of] a swim coach who had been accused of [sexual] misconduct with two children he was coaching." A judge had appointed Griffith to represent the man.

• Another Cooper & Secrest push-poll asked respondents whether they would be inclined to support Republican Terry Kilgore if they knew he had taken $4,000 from a client. Kilgore, a lawyer, had received the money as a completely legitimate legal fee for services he had performed.

Cooper & Secrest's polling techniques were apparently not restricted to the Old Dominion. In a 1992 congressional race in Ohio, the pollster's interviewers engaged in religious bigotry while informing respondents that the Republican, Martin Hoke, had "switched religions three times in the last few years and in the past was part of a religious cult where he wore a turban, a beard, and had an assumed name." In truth, Hoke had joined the Sikh religion two decades earlier while a student at Amherst College. But the Sikhs—a respected religious entity—are certainly not a "cult," even though male members wear a turban and grow their hair long. In any event, Hoke had since returned to the Presbyterian Church as an active participant.

Republicans were the targets in these Virginia and Ohio examples, but both parties' local candidates around the country have
suffered as a result of attack calls.[45] To cite but two examples, Democratic state legislative nominees in Pennsylvania were the victims
of an apparently orchestrated effort similar to Virginia's (in partisan
reverse) in 1992, as was a contender for Florida state representative
in a 1994 Democratic *primary*. [46]

INOCULATION PUSH-POLLING

Not all push-polling is irredeemably nasty. As noted earlier, in the
research type of push-poll, respondents are often tested to see
whether positive arguments and facts about a candidate move them
toward him or her. And in a remarkably innovative twist, one national party committee used a positive push-poll to inoculate its candidates against a suspected, forthcoming negative push-poll in the
general election of 1994.

Republican National Committee chair Haley Barbour remembered Democratic and labor union efforts in 1982, 1986, and subsequent years to tar GOP nominees as anti–social security, using
telephone-bank scripts.[47] In 1990, the RNC had an "early-warning"
system whereby its pollster asked respondents in key states whether
they had been called (by the Democrats) about social security, so the
GOP would know where to try to neutralize the attacks. By 1994
Barbour assumed (correctly) that similar efforts would be made, and
so he decided to strike first: "I said, 'What the hell, we know they're
going to do it, they've shown their hand, so let's go on out there and
take remedial action before they go after us.' " It was Barbour who
originated the idea of calling senior citizens in swing districts in October with the following message: "Republicans are for the Balanced
Budget Amendment, and you are going to get called and told that
Republicans will cut Social Security to balance the budget. But Republicans won't touch Social Security. So when you get called, I
hope you will tell whoever calls that you know it's not true."[48]

The RNC telephoned about 25,000 seniors in fifty key areas, principally in the Midwest, at a total cost of $800,000, estimated Barbour.
"We figured if the Democrats didn't reach [the contacted senior cit-
izens], we hadn't lost anything. But if the Democrats did do it, then
we felt some of those who might have been swayed would instead be

insulted." As Barbour noted, inoculation push-polling is "just the logical next step if you already know what someone else is going to do." There is precedent for it. Since the mid-1980s some political consultants have been airing inoculation TV ads, in which candidates attempt to counteract their opponents' expected attacks before they are made. Inoculation push-polling is obviously based on the same principle.

A PUSH-POLLING ROUNDUP

Positive persuasion aside, negative push-polling's methods and madness are limited only by the ingenuity—and devilishness—of the technique's practitioners. In our search for political telephoning's excesses, we came across dozens of examples, each unique in at least one aspect. Following is a mere sampler of these variations on a sinister theme.

LIES, DAMN LIES, AND RENT CONTROL. In a heavily Democratic district like U.S. Representative Carolyn Maloney's in New York City, a Republican's only real hope is to depress Democratic turnout. In 1994, this was the approach taken against Maloney. First, according to Maloney, registered Democrats in high-turnout precincts received calls saying she wasn't "a good Democrat."[49] Then voters residing in rent-controlled apartments got telephoned messages claiming, falsely, that Maloney was against rent control and stabilization—a highly popular concept in New York City, particularly among those living in such domiciles. The calls were "anonymous," occurred "in the waning days of the campaign," and were designed "to confuse voters and lower possible Democratic turnout," asserts Maloney.

FROM LEFT TO RIGHT. Push-polling is truly an equal-opportunity basher, as archliberal Edward M. Kennedy (Democrat of Massachusetts) and archconservative Oliver North (Republican of Virginia), both push-poll targets, demonstrated in their Senate contests in 1994. Kennedy's camp was infuriated by a telephone effort sponsored by GOP Senate nominee Mitt Romney.[50] Callers identifying themselves as being from "Advanced Research" asked pro-Kennedy respondents whether they would still support their senator if they knew he supposedly (1) opposed drug-testing for welfare recipients; (2) had voted against making able-bodied welfare recipients work for benefits; and (3) had supported letting convicted drug addicts live in housing projects.

Meanwhile, Virginia Democrats were operating a persuasive phone bank (run out of Kentucky) that plied African-American voters with a message linking Oliver North to Louisiana racist David Duke.[51] (A Republican Party official who lived in a predominantly black Richmond neighborhood received one of the calls and tipped off reporters, who then obtained the script.) Whatever North's other sins, he could not fairly be linked to Duke. In 1990, North had campaigned against Duke in the bayou state when Duke was himself seeking a U.S. Senate seat.

ONE CANDIDATE'S FLAT LEARNING CURVE. Republican gubernatorial candidate Bruce Benson of Colorado proved to be a persistent and consistent politician in 1994, repeatedly using push-polling despite recurrent public controversy, which eventually helped to sink his election chances—demonstrating that push-polling *can* backfire.

Benson first used push-polling against his two GOP rivals in the party primary.[52] In surveys of likely Republican voters, Benson's campaign (pretending to be the nonexistent "Colorado Pulse" poll firm) first asked the respondent's preferences. If it was Benson, he or she was told to call the county clerk to arrange to vote early by absentee ballot. But if either of the other two candidates were selected, the respondent was treated to a recitation of the contender's shortcomings (mainly, the alleged tendency to raise taxes). Benson won the primary, but at some cost to party unity.

In the general election, Benson quickly proved he was not chastened and followed the same game plan against incumbent Democratic Governor Roy Romer.[53] Ignoring the determining role of the judicial system in administering capital punishment, Benson's persuasion phoning alerted respondents to the fact that "there have been nearly 1,300 murders in Colorado since Romer was elected and not one murderer has been put to death." Romer hotly protested and made Benson's tactics a major theme of his campaign in the closing weeks. In a bad year for Democrats, Romer won a third term by nearly seventeen percentage points.

MISSION: MISREPRESENTATION. In many cases, as we have seen, a push-polling question will contain a grain of truth, but it is planted in toxic topsoil. The resulting mutation is a grotesque exaggeration or a gross distortion of a candidate's actual platform.

Sometimes only in the perspective of history can we judge just how unfair an attack was. Democrat Douglas Wilder won the governorship of Virginia in 1989, but not before weathering a withering phone-bank assault. The "National Research Center," later connected to his Republican opponent, Marshall Coleman, made many thousands of calls in the last few weeks of the campaign in order to pose this question: "Did you know Doug Wilder has said that he would probably sign a tax increase into law and that it was irresponsible to cap real estate taxes?"[54] Wilder did once say a real estate tax cap was irresponsible, and he later indicated he could consider it under the right set of circumstances. But Wilder was consistently emphatic that he would not raise taxes if elected. And indeed, once he was very narrowly elevated to the governorship, he became the first Virginia governor since the early 1960s not to ask for or approve any general tax increase (on income, sales, or gasoline).

BILL CLINTON'S REPUBLICAN BUDDY. In any 1994 Republican primary, Bill Clinton was certain to be nearly unanimously unpopular among the activists who voted in those contests. Consequently, few GOP contenders had anything good to say about the president; most vied with one another to utter the most vituperative denunciation. So conservative Republican Mark Sanford, no fan of Clinton's, was surprised to discover the push-poll tactic being used against him by his GOP opponent for the U.S. House, former party chairman Vann Hipp, in a South Carolina party primary. As Sanford recalled it for us:[55]

> In the last week of the election we got calls from volunteers telling us about the "poll." [The interviewer would ask:] "If you learned Mark Sanford is really a liberal Democrat and a friend of Bill Clinton, would you still vote for him?" So I went over to my opponent's house at midnight and woke him up, and he said, "I don't know anything about it." But we ended up getting it pinned down; one of the folks in his campaign confessed it to us later on.

Sanford makes it clear he was and is unhappy about the incident, as well as the ploy of push-polling: "Politicians can, excuse the expression, piss on each other, and it's [supposedly] normal. But it's outrageous. It's unethical. It's wrong. I have a real problem with that kind of stuff going on, because it's so misleading."

DIRTY TRICKS BY PHONE. At least as reported by some of the candidates who were the targets, many of the push-polls of 1994 were awfully rough—contradicting the record, making outrageous charges, fanning the flames of prejudice. To be fair, it is entirely possible that some of these reports are inaccurate or exaggerated, because none of the polling was tape-recorded. But the legislators listed here are recounting what random citizens and supporters told them or their staff after push-polling. The wordings often ring true or sound familiar. Of course, whether the questions could have been part of a research push-poll rather than advocacy phoning is much more difficult to determine, and accounts from the opposing camps often directly conflict. For example, we tried to trace the negative questions used in 1992 against U.S. Representative Tom Petri (Republican of Wisconsin). Petri's chief of staff, Joseph Flader, told us in an interview on April 10, 1995, that a woman employed by the Garin-Hart Democratic polling firm called the Petri campaign because she was disgusted by the negative tone of the anti-Petri poll she was conducting. The short push-poll asked leading questions about Petri. For example, Petri was accused of "taking thousands of dollars from Japanese auto companies." The implication was bribery, but the money actually came in the form of legal PAC contributions. Petri was also associated with savings and loan crook Charles Keating, but Petri's staff says there was no linkage. Some of the same issues were used in Democratic literature about Petri.

When we contacted pollster Geoff Garin, he categorically denied that his firm had ever conducted a smear-poll against Petri.[56] Garin did admit to arranging a "research poll" that contained negative information about both Petri and the Democratic candidate, a survey that might well fit our research definition of push-polling.

Flader of the Petri staff believes it is possible that a group somewhat independent of the Democrat's campaign (such as a prominent education union association in Wisconsin) conducted the push-polling. But there is no way to know for sure at this late date. Similar ambiguity marked many of the cases we investigated, and we can only relate the many allegations made by various candidates who report they were victimized via telephone. Former U.S. Representative Karan English (Democrat of Arizona), who was unseated, claimed a push-poll in her district alleged she had voted against the 1993 family and medical leave bill, when she had not only voted for it but championed it when it passed through one of her committees.[57] Moderate Republican Congressman Steve Horn, though reelected, was the victim of a push-poll that claimed he was "against a woman's right to choose," even though he is pro-choice on abortion; in 1992 a push-poll claimed that Horn was in favor of street gangs' right to "buy Uzis and other assault weapons."[58] Defeated U.S. Representative David Price (Democrat of North Carolina) was allegedly taken to task via push-poll for supposedly voting "for federal funding for the education of convicted murderers."[59] Republican candidate, now Congressman, Steve Chabot of Ohio said calls into predominantly black areas in his district claimed he was "a racist."[60] Former U.S. Representative Herb Klein of New Jersey, another 1994 Democratic loser, was disgusted by push-polls "making very, very ugly charges . . . that I had supported giving benefits to illegal aliens."[61] Finally, few candidates have been the target of more special interests at once—from the National Rifle Association to the tobacco industry—than Mike Synar, the Oklahoma Democratic congressman who lost his seat in a party runoff primary in 1994. Synar told us that some of his opponents sponsored a computerized push-poll in which a respondent's choice of Synar (when asked voting intentions) produced an unusual retort from a computer-automated interviewer: "Mike Synar? I can't believe you'd vote for him! He's a jerk!"[62]

Another telephone-bank dirty trick was played on Synar. According to his campaign manager Amy Tobe, "Voters were getting calls from people with foreign accents, basically talking gibberish, claiming to be from our campaign. It was bizarre, and very annoying to voters," and thus harmful to the Synar campaign. A somewhat related dirty trick occurred in the Orlando, Florida, area in 1992 just before the state's September primary election, when residents were awakened by after midnight calls urging support for a particular candidate.[63] The angry recipients of these unwelcome calls were certainly less likely to back the "sponsoring" candidate—

exactly the intent of the callers. The Synar and Orlando cases are examples of the "reverse phone bank," yet another exploding cigar in the apparently growing bag of telephoned dirty tricks.

Push-Polling in Retrospect

And so it goes in the dastardly and depraved world of push-polling, especially negative persuasion phoning. While there is a place for accurate, relevant negative information about a candidate to be made available to voters, phoning is a highly suspect means of accomplishing this. By its very nature, the telephone is a private instrument that is difficult to check, and attacks by phone are hard to pinpoint and refute. This makes the telephone irresistible to sleaze-mongers.

Anyone who has studied the field of political consulting and campaign technologies understands that now the push-polling genie is outside the bottle, it will not easily be recorked. To the contrary, the genie will probably turn up almost everywhere, and his shiny electronic marvels will soon be parked in the driveway of every campaign headquarters—just to keep up with the Joneses, you understand.

Only a sharp, sustained rebuke from the press, and an informed public bent on punishing the perpetrators, can stop the swift spread of this clearly sleazy campaign cancer. The practice is so fundamentally unethical and blatantly demeaning that, once it is exposed, one would hope for a spontaneous uprising against it—although, given the numbing torment of political shenanigans over the last three decades, this may be too much to expect. More realistically, we propose in the concluding chapter a few remedies for this latest twisted innovation in campaign technology.

10

Vote Fraud: Back to the Future

Well, everybody knows that election officials never cheat, and after all, nobody can prove they cheat. The only thing that we know is that they're all from the same political party. And nobody would ever think that they would dare violate their oaths of office. And if I sound cynical about it, I am.

—*Attorney Albert Jordan*

Push-polling, like street money, gives an unsavory taint to the already maligned field of politics. But if there is any corruption that goes straight to the foundations of American democracy, it is vote fraud—a catchall term that includes ballot-box stuffing, phony voter registrations, and the manufacture of absentee ballot submissions. Nothing else in this book so convincingly proves that a free system such as ours, with its bias toward minimal control of the electoral process, keeps generating the same kinds of corruptions every few decades. This study of current vote fraud will remind us that we can never declare victory over, and we must be ever-vigilant about, corruption—particularly those practices that tempt politicians with the promise of power while operating in the shadows and on the hidden periphery of politics.

The idea of progress is fundamental to understanding the American character. As a people, we have always wanted to believe that the future is destined to be better than the past by dint of our unceasing efforts at improvement, which we have usually managed to bring about. Unsavory practices such as election fraud belong in the dustbin of our discarded and long outgrown history. Surely, the ballot boxes in Texas are no longer stuffed! Votes are not stolen or manufactured anymore in Alabama! Elections in Philadelphia and California are certainly clean now! The press does not look for what it does not expect to find, and the public ignores the occasional muffled sounds emanating from ballot boxes hither and yon.

But the press and the public are in for a rude shock. Voting fraud is back, is becoming more serious with each passing election cycle, and soon—because of recent changes in the law—is destined to become even worse.[1] For our purposes here, we define voting fraud as any serious violation of election laws controlling the registration of voters or the casting of absentee, mail-in, or polling-site ballots. Many of the examples in this chapter are derived from local elections, but the corrupt practices certainly extend to elections for district, state, and national offices. After all, generally the same group of political party organizers, consultants, and precinct workers are employed at all levels. Christmas past and Christmas future are merging for those who profit from such perfidy. And it is past time for the press and public to receive a loud wake-up call, lest the ultimate corruption in a democratic system—the stealing of elections—becomes widespread, corroding trust in the essential process of democracy itself.

In this chapter, we focus on four U.S. locales—Philadelphia, Alabama, Texas, and California—to illustrate the current slide back to the bad old days of election fraud. Our interviews and other research have convinced us that we could just as easily have selected at least a dozen other states or many dozens of sizable cities to prove our thesis. The quartet we have chosen demonstrate the problem dramatically—maybe fulsomely. The scale of fraud may sometimes be small compared with the anything-goes days of a century ago, but several kinds of fraud are clearly ingrained and resurgent, and this trend ought to be of immediate and pressing concern to all people who care about the integrity of the American political system.

America's Sordid History of Voting Fraud

Our nation has a long and depressing history as a happy haven for the vote thief. For much of the last century and a good part of this one, elections in many states and localities became contests of the voting fraud capacities of various factions and parties. The chief question on Election Day sometimes was: who could manufacture the requisite number of votes most easily and shrewdly, giving the other side insufficient time to make necessary adjustments to its tallies and insufficient evidence to cry foul convincingly.

Sometimes no specific evidence of fraud was required to know it had taken place. For the 1844 election, New York City had a reasonably large voter pool of 41,000, but the turnout on Election Day was far more spectacular: *55,000,* or 135 percent of the entire pool of voters! As one observer put it, "the dead filled in for the sick," and the city's dogs and cats must have been imbued with irresistible civic spirit, too.[2]

The nation as a whole got a taste of this kind of election snake oil in the 1876 presidential election, arguably the most corrupt in America's history before or since. On Election Day, Democrat Samuel J. Tilden of New York garnered about a quarter million more popular votes than Republican Rutherford B. Hayes of Ohio, and Tilden was the undisputed leader in states with 184 electoral votes (with 185 required for victory).[3] However, twenty electoral votes in Florida, Louisiana, South Carolina, and Oregon were in dispute. Tilden had actually carried the first three of these states, but GOP-controlled election boards disqualified enough Democratic votes, for dubious reasons, to potentially tip the states to Hayes. Congress established a fifteen-member electoral commission, supposedly nonpartisan, to arbitrate the disputes, but the commission's partisan breakdown turned out to be eight Republicans to seven Democrats. As a result, every single controversial electoral vote was awarded to Hayes by a vote of eight-to-seven, and Hayes took office in 1877—and was called "His Fraudulency" by Democrats throughout his one term.

Historians and political scientists faithfully cataloged the abominable arts that were practiced at America's polls throughout the centuries. Not long after the Hayes–Tilden election, for example, the "use of direct bribery in the United States" became "widespread."[4] Most states and large localities began formally registering voters in this period, and it thus became more difficult to simply stuff the ballot box or hire so-called floaters or repeaters to vote twice or thrice.[5] Resourceful political organizers changed tactics and began to buy votes on a large scale. One study in 1892 concluded that almost 16 percent of all voters in Connecticut were "purchasable."[6] In 1910, a judge in Adams County, Ohio, convicted 1,679 persons of selling their votes—more than a quarter of all the electors; further, his inquiries showed that fully 85 percent of the county's voters had engaged in buying or selling their votes at some time in their lives![7]

Ballot-box stuffing was not abandoned everywhere, of course, as suggested by the exceedingly close 1960 presidential election, which Democrat John F. Kennedy won over Republican Richard M. Nixon by only 118,574 votes.[8] Strong suspicions exist that the Illinois electoral votes were stolen for Kennedy by Mayor Richard J. Daley, who late on election night magically produced just enough of a massive margin in Chicago to overcome Nixon's large lead in the rest of the state. (Thanks to a 319,000-vote advantage in Chicago, Kennedy won a paper-thin victory of 8,858 out of more than 4.7 million votes cast in the state—and thus captured all twenty-seven Illinois electors.)

The loss of Illinois would have reduced Kennedy's Electoral College majority edge to just six, and had he lost Texas as well, the election would have been Nixon's. In Texas, too, substantial voter fraud may well have occurred, though it is impossible to say whether fraud accounted for Kennedy's entire 46,242-vote majority out of over 2.3 million votes cast. One thing is for certain, though: Kennedy's running mate, U.S. Senator Lyndon B. Johnson of Texas, knew where all the votes were buried, and he had practiced electoral skulduggery before.[9] Having lost an agonizingly close U.S. Senate race in 1941 to former Governor Pappy O'Daniel, whose supporters may have stolen it, Johnson was determined to turn the tables when he ran again in 1948. LBJ's alliance with South Texas's political boss, Judge George Parr, known as the "Duke of Duval County," helped him do it. As in 1941, the Democratic primary battle between Congressman Johnson and former Governor Coke Stevenson was as tight as a tick, and the vote was so close it all came down to Voting Box 13 in Alice, Texas, in the heart of Parr's territory. Several days after the election, Parr's precinct man in charge of Box 13, Luis Salas, "found" 203 more votes, 202 of them for Johnson.[10] Amazingly, these good citizens had voted in alphabetical order, with the same handwriting and blue pen.[11] Moreover, the discovered ballots gave the victory to LBJ by a statewide margin of only 87 votes. Thus was a U.S. senator created by corruption and sent on his path to the Oval Office.

While there is little to admire in the low standards Johnson set, his sins must be interpreted in context. Voting fraud was a way of life in parts of Texas in the 1940s, just as it has been, at various times, in Chicago, Louisiana, West Virginia, New Jersey, and many other places. For much of our history vote fraud has been as American as (sour) apple pie. This is a humbling and sobering reality, and we need to remember this whenever we feel the urge to sanctimoniously condemn wide-scale fraud in other countries' elections. Election reformers still have a full plate right here in the United States.

The Philadelphia Story

The city where the American democracy was born is now proof of America's continuing corruption of the electoral process.[12] In 1993, a special election was held to fill the vacated 2nd Senatorial District seat in Philadelphia, Pennsylvania. The contestants for the seat, which would determine the balance of power in the state Senate, were Republican Bruce Marks and Democrat William Stinson. Even though the district was substantially Democratic, Marks had come close to winning it in 1990 against veteran state senator Francis Lynch, and after Lynch's death in May 1993, Marks decided to try again. His new opponent, Stinson, was often described as a classic Philly Democratic pol, a deputy mayor who lost a 1991 Democratic primary for a city council seat by a mere seventeen votes.

The battle was fierce, and the campaign attracted statewide attention because the Senate was then divided evenly, twenty-four Democrats to twenty-four Republicans. With a pro-GOP, anti-

Clinton tide running across the country in fall 1993, Marks appeared to surge. Sure enough, Marks received more Election Day votes (those cast in polling places on the day of the election) than his opponent—19,691 to Stinson's 19,127. Yet Stinson garnered an extraordinary proportion of the absentee ballots to turn the tide—1,396 to Marks's 371, yielding totals of 20,523 and 20,062, respectively. The Philadelphia County Commissioners (Democrats Margaret Tartaglione and Alexander Talmadge Jr., and Republican John F. Kane), sitting in their capacity as the County Board of Elections, certified Stinson as the victor of the race on November 18, 1993. State Democrats arranged for Stinson to be sworn into office quickly, before a court could issue an injunction to stop it.

While the board's imprimatur ordinarily would have marked the conclusion of the election, in the case of the Second District it marked the beginning of a lengthy inquiry, by the end of which Stinson was indicted (though not convicted) and Judge Clarence Newcomer of the U.S. District Court for the Eastern District of Pennsylvania condemned the commissioners for permitting blatant violations of state election law and overturned the result of the special election. Stinson was eventually cleared of criminal charges of absentee ballot fraud, but in the civil proceedings, Newcomer found sufficient proof to implicate Stinson in a conspiracy to steal the election, and Stinson was ousted from office. (Several Stinson staffers were even less fortunate; their involvement in the fraud resulted in criminal prosecution and conviction.[13]) *Marks v. Stinson,*[14] the conclusion of candidate Marks's civil challenge to Stinson's victory, marked an extraordinary but necessary intervention of a federal judge into the state's political process to redress claims of civil and voting rights violations. Newcomer's order to certify Marks as the winner on the basis of the machine vote total without considering the absentee ballots cast appears to be unprecedented in modern times.[15]

The vote fraud was documented beyond question.[16] Despite Pennsylvania's strict laws regarding application for, completion, and return of absentee ballots,[17] the Stinson campaign and related organizations engaged in the systematic distribution and collection of absentee ballots, which circumvented the normal process. More remarkably, the Democratic members of the Board of Elections themselves were implicated in the conspiracy, despite the procedural safeguards they were legally required to observe in order to prevent absentee voting fraud. The electoral process was corrupted not just by a campaign but by those charged with overseeing it.

The competition for the Second District seat was tight enough to convince members of the Stinson organization that fraud was required to ensure victory. In both predominantly white and minority areas, Stinson's campaign and related Democratic Party organizations engaged in a widespread effort to file fraudulent applications for absentee ballots and then ensure the proper choice was made when applicants returned their ballots. Some of the applicants did not realize what they were doing, some were not even registered, and others were browbeaten and intimidated. The Democratic commissioners played a key role in the plot; as Marks recalled, they and their staffs "illegally [gave] absentee ballots directly to my opponent's campaign and to [Democratic] committee people."[18]

Absentee voting in Pennsylvania is not unlike that of most states: exacting statutory guidelines determine the method of application, completion, return, and processing of an absentee ballot. Absence from the state or county of residence, or disability, are legitimate reasons to vote absentee. An absentee ballot cannot be requested more than fifty days prior to the election and must be requested at least seven days before the election. A voter is required to submit an absentee ballot request to his or her local board of elections by the Tuesday prior to the election. Although the Philadelphia board's official policy required a check of each applicant's signature against the file copy, in actual practice it did not do so. When any absentee application is approved, statutory language requires the board of elections to return an absentee ballot only to the applicant, who must mail or return the ballot to the board in person prior to the Friday preceding the election.

The Stinson campaign used two distinct ploys to put illegally obtained absentee votes in its column. First, from July through September of 1993, campaign workers solicited hundreds of absentee applications as part of a canvass and registration effort in predominately white Democratic precincts. Contrary to election law, "many persons who were hesitant to register because they simply did not want to go to the polls were told that they could fill out an absentee ballot application and obtain a ballot out of convenience."[19] The dates of the applications were left blank to conceal the fact that they were requested either before or after the filing deadline. When William Jones, a Stinson worker, approached the candidate to express his concern over the scheme, Stinson told him "that he was never going to lose another election because of absentee ballots."[20] Robert O'Brien, a campaign staffer, instructed subordinates to deliver the completed applications to the election board's office. As a result, the board sent over 500 ballots to the campaign, which O'Brien then distributed to workers, who proceeded to take them to homes of voters. As Stinson had instructed, the workers directed voters to "either check off the straight Democratic box, or to check off the individual Democratic names, and then to return the completed absentee ballot to O'Brien."[21] About 450 ballots supporting Stinson found their way back in this manner.

More dubious still was the Stinson effort to elicit absentee applications and "correctly" complete ballot packages in Hispanic and African-American precincts. Late in the campaign, polling results provided by the Democratic State Committee indicated Stinson was trailing Marks. The decision was made to target minority precincts in a last-ditch effort to turn the tide in his favor. In essence, the Stinson campaign workers convinced some minority voters that, in Marks's words, "if they wanted to vote from the convenience of their own home that they could do so, and they could just fill out the application and say that they were out of town or make up some medical reason."[22] Ruth Birchett, who directed the Stinson campaign in minority areas, was explicitly assured by both the candidate and one of the election board's Democratic commissioners that the scheme was legitimate, although others in the Stinson organization recalled that a hard-edged cynicism permeated the effort. For example, one staffer reported that the not-funny " 'joke' in the Stinson campaign was that the Hispanics would sign anything," a problem exacerbated by the fact that the absentee ballot application included no Spanish language instructions. Some Hispanics were apparently not even aware they were voting. Lydia Colon, for example, thought she was signing a form to request removal of a pile of refuse from her back yard. However, the Democratic canvasser who connived her into signing the ballot did not count on her subsequent decision to go to her polling place on election day and attempt to vote.[23]

The execution of the minority plan mirrored the one used for the majority white precincts: applications were solicited and submitted by the Stinson workers, who then received, distributed, and returned about 600 ballots. Likewise, campaign workers instructed voters to mark their ballots for Stinson. The special twist was that the field staffers were paid one dollar per correctly marked ballot returned. In other words, the Stinson workers distributing the applications and ballots took the supposedly neutral polling place to the voters while serving simultaneously as remunerated flushers and haulers.

The Stinson organization received the funds to implement this plan from several sources, including the Committee for a Democratic Majority PAC ($4,000) and a PAC associated with Democratic State Senator Vincent Fumo ($4,000).[24] The money also paid for a phone bank operated in English and Spanish, to inform voters of the "new way to vote." From direct testimony, the dates of the street money contributions, and the receipts retained for payments to workers, Judge Newcomer determined that the ballots—cast overwhelmingly for Stinson—could not have been returned prior to the absentee ballot deadline. Further, it was clear to the court that campaign workers aided completion of the ballots "in the homes of voters and often directed, coerced, and/or intimidated voters to vote for Stinson; . . . [and] the campaign workers had a political and financial interest in obtaining votes for Stinson."[25]

Compounding this disturbing pattern was the active assistance given the Stinson campaign by two election commissioners, both Democrats. These officials casually waived normal procedures, helped to process absentee applications for unregistered citizens, and permitted campaign workers to distribute ballots—all in contravention of the rules, and all consciously designed to result in a Stinson victory.[26] Judge Newcomer reserved some of his harshest language for Democratic commissioners Talmadge and Tartaglione, since they "could have prevented much of the illegal activity that occurred even if the Stinson campaign had acted illegally."[27] If the commissioners had required that existing written procedures be followed, for example, the wrongdoing that altered the outcome of the election could not have happened. As Republican election attorney Jack Connors, who worked on this case, suggested, "You had built-in arrogance of power in a local board of elections that had been in one party's control for over twenty years. The reason why this case is so outrageous . . . was that they thought they were going to get away with this."[28]

This particular instance of fraud, unlike so many others, had a just ending that served as a powerful warning to vote-tamperers. After concluding that nearly 600 absentee ballots had been cast after the deadline by unregistered people, Judge Newcomer stated firmly that "Bruce Marks would have won the 1993 Special Election in the Second Senatorial District" had it not been for the Stinson organization's violation of state election law.[29] Newcomer then evicted Stinson from the state Senate, gave his seat to Marks, and with it, control of the Senate to the Republican Party.

But we need to remember that the Philadelphia fraud was widespread, well established, relatively easy to accomplish, and stayed hidden for a good while. Only an aggressive, generously financed, and thoroughly politicized legal assault on the system that stole an election managed to right the balloting wrong. Most candidates are not so well positioned to pursue suspected fraud—and as a consequence, one suspects, similar or more subtle shenanigans elsewhere may go undetected and unexposed.

Sweet Home Alabama:
Southern Fried Voting Fraud

As Philadelphia's state Senate election suggests, it is the close election that often leads to revelations about voting fraud. (The candidates in close or disputed races are almost inevitably involved in court brawls, and their investigations can turn over rocks that hide sleazy shenanigans.)

Such has recently proved to be the case in Alabama as well. The 1994 election for chief justice of the state Supreme Court yielded a dead heat, with Democratic incumbent Sonny Hornsby losing to Republican Perry Hooper Sr. by fewer than 300 votes out of 1.2 million cast. It had been a high-stakes race, with the trial lawyers backing their former association president (Hornsby) with at least

$198,519 in campaign expenditures and Alabama business persons and groups spending many tens of thousands of dollars on their favorite son (Hooper).[30] To maintain his narrow lead, Hooper and his supporters launched a preemptive legal challenge after suspecting widespread fraud. Hooper's legal maneuvers were aimed at preventing the counting of 1,700 disputed absentee ballots—ballots that came disproportionately from solidly Democratic counties. The litigation was ultimately successful, permitting Hooper to finally be sworn in as the state's chief justice on October 20, 1995—eleven months after the election.[31] And along the way to this belated victory, the Hooper forces uncovered some disturbing facts about Alabama's electoral process.

Once again, it is the absentee ballots that present an occasion for sin. In Greene County, a heavily Democratic part of Alabama's "black belt," almost a third of the vote was cast absentee, compared to well under 10 percent just about everywhere else. Dozens of absentee ballots were mailed by elections officials to a nonexistent post office box, with many of the ballots allegedly being picked up at the post office by an unknown individual.[32] Local resident Paul Harrington readily observed the telltale signs of absentee fraud. During a meeting with the clerk of the Circuit Court of Greene County (who served as the manager of absentee ballots), Harrington found the clerk had discovered that

> approximately 60 applications for absentee ballots were received requesting that the absentee ballots be sent to Post Office Box 115, Eutaw, Alabama, 35462. According to [the clerk], however, she later learned that no such post office box existed. However, as absentee election manager, she was unable to recover all the ballots.... Approximately 10 to 20 were ... picked up by someone from the post office and the post office was unable to identify the individual or individuals retrieving the ballots.[33]

Several dozen other absentees were sent to two Democratic officials, with the party chairman's home listed as the "permanent address" for many of the absentee voters.[34] Other absentee ballots went to the local sewer and water authority, a woman who had moved out of the county six months earlier, and a man who had died well before the absentee balloting period began. This dead man somehow voted, by the way, while other legitimate voters showed up at Greene County polls on Election Day only to be told they were ineligible because they had supposedly already voted by absentee.[35]

Similar problems cropped up in other Alabama localities. In Houston County, in the far southeast corner of Alabama, a man "dead for seven years," according to his wife, has regularly been recorded as voting by absentee,[36] despite the difficulties in delivering a ballot to the afterlife. Reportedly, political activists would also provide absentees to eligible persons and then take them away after the ballot had been signed, with candidate choices marked only in pencil (or not marked by the presumed voter at all).

Then there were the helpful visits to nursing homes in Montgomery and elsewhere. For example, a young woman observed with absentee ballot materials showed up at the capital city's Tyson Manor Nursing Home shortly before the 1994 elections and "assisted" incapacitated and even comatose patients with their ballots. As one visitor reported: "I had seen [a particular patient] in the bed many times in the past . . . [and] I thought she was comatose . . . [she] was incapable of filling out the forms or even making a mark on the papers. She died three days after this event, which would have been before the election on November 8, 1994."[37] A patient with severe Alzheimer's disease supposedly cast a ballot in another nursing home even though her daughter testified that this was not possible and the woman had been removed from the voting rolls at the family's request the previous summer.[38] As the daughter recalled, "her name still appeared on the list in November, 1994," even though "no member of the family" had applied for an absentee ballot.[39]

Suspicious circumstances were identified all over the Alabama map. Some voting machines were apparently programmed to facilitate voting for Democratic candidates and to discourage GOP votes,[40] according to an affidavit of John Russell Campbell:

> You could vote the straight Republican ticket by punching one button at the top of the Republican column and it would light up all of the officials' names in the Republican column. And

then you could reach over and punch the button of individual Democratic candidates or independent candidates and it would light up and cancel the [individual] light on the Republican side and then . . . the votes would be cast. You could not do that if you were voting the straight Democratic ticket. If you punched the light at the top of the Democratic ticket, it would light up the entire Democratic ticket. But if you reached over and tried to vote individual Republican candidates, nothing would happen. The light wouldn't come on and it wouldn't cancel the light on the individual Democratic candidate.

Many absentee ballots from unregistered individuals and other unqualified people were counted by local election officials even though the ballots were challenged by authorized poll workers. Under state law, these suspect ballots are supposed to be separated out from unchallenged ballots so that they can be carefully reviewed; instead, the signed cover sheets were removed and they were mixed in with all other ballots—so it was impossible to identify and retrieve them.[41] The situation apparently approached the proportions of a parody, Campbell said:

> Despite my requests (over about a thirty-minute period of time), the Committee continued to open affidavit envelopes and separate them from the ballots at a feverish pace. Whenever I was able to stop the process of opening the affidavit envelopes at one end of the table, the Committee members at the other end would frantically begin ripping envelopes open and separating the ballots.

And despite the closeness of the election, which was obvious to everyone on election evening, the ballots were not secured in many counties. Some ballot boxes were missing, votes from one precinct were combined with another, seals on various containers of votes had been broken, and ballot boxes were openly available in unwatched public rooms.[42]

John Campbell, the dumbstruck Alabama poll watcher, summed up his reactions after a long election day of observing arbitrary, capricious, and downright illegal actions by local officials charged with safeguarding the electoral process: "When I was asked to serve as a Ballot Security Attorney, I could not believe that the election officials in Wilcox County would be capable of tolerating, much less participating in, the type of activities that were described to me as having occurred in the past. Not only was it as bad as it had been described to me, it was worse. I was shocked."[43]

Somewhat surprisingly, Campbell's description of Wilcox County's elections received backing from Dan Warren of the county's own Board of Registrars. When we contacted Warren, he refused to address Campbell's specific allegations but said they were "the tip of the iceberg" and that "there will never be a fair election in Wilcox County."[44]

Of course, there is no mystery about the systemic source of Alabama voting corruption. Election laws and procedures are followed—or ignored—in each county at the discretion of a board comprised of the local sheriff, the probate judge, and the circuit court clerk. Frequently, these individuals are all members of the same political party. An experienced Alabama attorney, currently involved in the search for voting fraud in his state's 1994 elections, offered us an overview of the state's election system:

> Do y'all understand how the system is rigged to begin with?
> Basically what happens is that you're not going to second-guess
> elections in the absence of strict proof. And then what you do
> is make sure the people who control the proof are in the inner
> circle of your party. And therefore, as the process unwinds in
> the wee hours of the [election] night, based on the information
> that's available from the media outlets, the inner circle comes
> up with what [votes] they need. Who's going to rat on them?
> Who's going to tell on them? Well, everybody knows that election officials never cheat, and after all, nobody can prove they
> cheat. The only thing that we know is that they're all from the
> same political party. And nobody would ever think that they
> would dare violate their oaths of office. And if I sound cynical
> about it, I am.[45]

All in all, the Alabama electoral process does not seem likely to be included in the state's promotional brochures. Vote fraud seems to be another deeply ingrained custom in a traditional state slow to change.

California: The Golden State for Vote Fraud

If mega-state California, as advertised, is the trendsetter for the rest of America, voting fraud will truly be a Malibu-sized wave of the future. For the Golden State has exceptionally serious difficulties in its system of registration, absentee balloting, and election-day voting.

The fundamental difference between California and Philadelphia or Alabama is that the breakdown of the electoral process begins at a much earlier stage than absentee balloting. The voter registration setup is the first source of trouble; not to put too fine a point on it, it is nothing short of a disgraceful mess. California has not thoroughly purged its voting rolls of those who are no longer eligible to vote since 1979, when advocates of greater political participation secured passage of a law permitting the removal of voters' names from the rolls only by means of an inconclusive "negative purge." Voters who have not cast a ballot in two consecutive general elections are sent a postcard asking whether they still live at the listed address. Only if the card is returned as undeliverable is the name stricken. So long as the card is not returned, for whatever reason, the name stays.

Many voters who have died or moved are thus retained on the registration rolls, and as a result there are literally millions of inaccurate or wrongful registrations on file. Many voters have moved out of California but remain on the rolls. Some have simply changed addresses within the state and have duplicate registrations (one each in the new and old locations). In many localities of California, a duplicate registration is recorded if a voter who has moved within a city or county makes the slightest addition or deletion (for example, of an initial or nickname) when he re-registers. A sample of 940 voters requesting absentee ballots in Tulare County discovered, for example, that 92 people had relocated (according to other voters currently residing at each address). Partial voter files showed 20 of this group were recorded as voting in the 1994 general election at their old address. It is not clear whether they returned to vote there, or they had voted twice (at an old and new address), or there was some other explanation.[46] Other voters have died or been convicted of felonies; either condition normally makes a person ineligible (though a Chicagoan might disagree). And at least a few individuals register twice in order to vote twice. In 1994, there were cases of people (1) voting both absentee *and* on Election Day, (2) voting two absentee ballots, and (3) voting at two different polling places on Election Day.[47]

Phony registrations encourage shenanigans in any place, and California's massively erroneous voter list is an engraved invitation to commit fraud. Incredibly, the most recent official estimates of the "deadwood" on the California voter rolls range from 14 percent to 24 percent of the more than 14 million registered voter total— meaning between 2 million and 3.4 million phony registrations crowd the books.[48] Every election cycle, deadwood voters cause state and local governments to waste $5 to $8 million of taxpayers' money printing and mailing voter pamphlets, unneeded ballots, and the like.[49]

Among the many factors responsible for this monumental ineptitude is the failure of bureaucrats at various levels to share death and incarceration records with registrars, as they are supposed to do;[50] the appalling lack of a centralized statewide voter registration list that could at least reduce or eliminate the extraordinary number of duplicate registrations; and most important for our purposes, the existence of a burgeoning, legal campaign industry whose raison d'être is the registration of citizens. Political parties, individual campaigns, and ideological interest groups contract with the consulting organizations to find and register eligible persons at a per-head price that ranges from $1 to $10. The profit incentive demands a large volume of registrants, obviously, and so the paid solicitors avariciously sign up whoever they can find, often without regard to the legal niceties, including illegal and legal aliens, some juveniles and infants, fictitious individuals, companion animals (known in less sensitive states as "pets"), and even the dead (or "life-challenged" voters). As one California elections official asserted, "You're just asking for trouble. . . . Anytime you pay to register people, you're going to have fraud."[51]

Because California registrars have "a ministerial duty to accept a registration without investigation, absent any challenge to its validity," the state's registration system is "a system of self-certification, [with no] certainty that a registrant is who he or she claims to be."[52] Since it is widely acknowledged that prosecution for registration fraud is given a very low priority by law enforcement agencies, this is yet another green light to sloppy or unethical work by paid voter solicitors.[53]

The lamentable results of widespread registration solicitation are to be found all over California. In the city of Los Angeles, paid solicitors added over 4,000 fraudulent registrations just in 1992.[54] In Glendale, bounty hunters "found" 190 unregistered voters in a single apartment building, and signed them up (along with a dog)—even though many were apparently already registered.[55] Jailed felons have registered while incarcerated, and other new voters have illegally listed business addresses (including department stores) as their supposed place of abode.[56] Illegal and legal aliens are, without question, on the rolls in many areas. A single precinct in San Diego County was found to have 30 verifiable legal aliens out of just 313 registered voters.[57] Illegals voted in Fresno and Tulare County in November 1994;[58] and a prominent legal alien—a Mexican businessman and a publisher of a Spanish language newspaper—registered to vote in 1987, while in the United States on a tourist visa, and cast a ballot in both 1992 and 1994 despite his lack of American citizenship.[59] Even Mario Aburto Martinez, the Mexican citizen who assassinated the ruling party's 1994 presidential nominee Luis Donaldo Colosio in Tijuana, was a registered voter in San Pedro.[60]

The use of paid solicitors for partisan registration efforts has plagued California for a decade or longer. The Republican Party, finding its share of the registration rolls lacking, engaged in a year-round registration drive as early as 1986. During that year, the party employed approximately 2,000 bounty hunters and paid them $1 to $4 per Republican registrant as part of its centralized, coordinated registration campaign. The simultaneous Democratic Party registration drive, though less organized, also utilized paid workers, employing 250 bounty hunters in Orange County alone.[61] In one recent case of bounty hunter abuse, two workers retained by political consultant Michael Long for Republican Brooks Firestone's campaign for the state assembly were arrested for registering the inhabitants of a graveyard and were actually charged with election fraud. Long's firm paid the two, and approximately fifty others, about $3 per completed Republican registration card. Unlike their companions, the two copied names from tombstones and submitted the cards to their employer, who reviewed the cards and then forwarded them to the Firestone campaign, which in turn submitted the cards to county officials.

Neither Firestone nor Long's firm was apparently aware the registration cards were fraudulent, and Firestone noted, "We had no intention of engaging in fraudulent registration whatsoever. . . . It wouldn't do us any good, because dead people don't vote."[62] Of course, while the dead logically cannot vote, neither should they be able to register. No evidence suggests that the Firestone campaign intended to capitalize on the life-challenged registrants, but less scrupulous candidates may not find the legal or ethical principles involved very compelling.

The tried-and-true fraud associated with absentee balloting is part of the California picture, too, mirroring the conditions already identified in Philadelphia and Alabama. Jim Boren, reporter for the *Fresno Bee,* described the bold and "sophisticated" pattern of activity by campaign staffers and candidates: "They know what the exact turnaround should be in neighborhoods. The campaigns mail the absentee requests to the elections office, and then they literally follow around the postmen and women as they deliver the absentee ballots back to the residences. They go up to the residences, offer people a stamp, and make sure they vote."

This harvesting of absentees (sometimes called "ballot farming") may simply seem like savvy politics, but violations of law are involved.[63] A recent *San Francisco Chronicle* investigation of one county's elections found that signatures on dozens of absentee ballot request forms did not match the registration signatures on file, yet the ballots were still mailed; and that 1,500 suspect absentee ballots were simply filed away and never referred to the district attorney for investigation.[64] At times, local candidates have directly obtained absentee ballots from the elections office and personally delivered the ballots to voters, entering their homes while the voters were casting them. Campaign workers have also punched holes in the ballots for voters, instructed people who to vote for, handed out free postage stamps, or simply taken the completed ballots away with them, and occasionally engaged in intimidation of voters during the balloting process.[65] All of these activities can result in misdemeanor or felony charges under existing law. Two recent city council elections in Stockton and Inglewood have been overturned because of absentee ballot hanky-panky of this sort.[66]

Of course, the ultimate form of absentee balloting is voting by the dead. Many years ago, if you planned to remain politically active once deceased, you had to arrange burial in Chicago or Louisiana. Now, apparently, California is an acceptable alternative. For example, in Alameda County a deceased woman's 1994 absentee ballot was cast—the registrar suspects that either her daughter or roommate did it,[67] and in San Francisco one Lazarus who had passed away twelve years earlier (in April 1982) came back to vote in 1994.[68]

The dead are not the only unexpectedly energetic voters on election days in California. Some registered Golden Staters are such good citizens they vote twice—this a result of the widespread duplicate registrations mentioned earlier. In one study of five Central Valley counties following the 1994 general election, 3,300 voters were found to have registered twice. With only very partial records available on some of these voters, 90 were identified as having cast at least two ballots.[69] (Had all data been accessible, the number of "vote-early-and-often" citizens would almost certainly have been higher.) A number of people may also be voting under the names of registered voters who, for whatever reason, are not expected to show up at the polls. On general Election Day 1994 at a Kern County precinct, for instance, a woman was in the process of casting her ballot when another women (with two female friends) entered the polling place and requested a ballot under the name of the woman who by chance was already in the voting booth. As the legitimate voter objected and stared in disbelief, the impersonator and her accomplices fled the area.[70]

As if all this were not enough to malign California's unsecured electoral system, the record-keeping and vote certification are so sloppy that almost nothing adds up correctly. When the state's Fair Elections Foundation, a nonprofit watchdog group, examined the November 1994 returns from seven counties, the county registrars inexplicably reported totals that differed by many thousands from the vote totals certified by the California secretary of state.[71] In Orange County, the registrar claimed 627,223 votes had been cast but the secretary of state's office released a final count of 618,448. To make matters worse, the tallies by poll workers of votes cast in each precinct frequently differed from the tallies recorded by the county registrars. In Los Angeles County, fully 40 percent of the 6,104 precincts showed a disparity between the counts of the poll workers and the registrars.[72]

Computer software glitches may well account for some (though not all) of these errors. Still, the mistabulations add to the seeming haphazardness of the laid-back California elections process. When combined with the abundant evidence of voter fraud (both potential and actual), there is but one reasonable conclusion: let honest California elections officials beware, and let concerned citizens be about the business of reform.

These recent California experiences also point to a noteworthy irony that applies to other states and the nation as a whole: laws intended to encourage voting have sometimes become an entrée for vote fraud. The last quarter-century has seen an opening up of the electoral process almost everywhere, as regulations concerning registration and balloting were eased to maximize convenience and turnout. But undeniably there is a hidden cost to these benefits: the resurgence of fraud apparent around the country. Remedies that neatly cure one ill frequently and surprisingly cause another. Just as with well-intentioned campaign finance schemes, the "law" of unintended consequences prevails—and it is a rule rarely given much thought when many reforms are first designed.[73]

Vote Fraud in Texas: The Wild, Wild Southwest

As we have already demonstrated in this chapter, the Lone Star state—whatever the extent of its electoral hijinks—will never walk alone in the field of voting fraud. Nevertheless, fraud in contemporary Texas is still breathtaking in its boldness and scope, amply fulfilling the state's "bigger and better" stereotype. Reformers bent on cleaning up political excesses had best hope that the state's informal slogan, "Don't Mess with Texas," does not extend to the registration and voting system.

One region or another of Texas features almost every breed of fraud found in Philadelphia, Alabama, and California: voting by illegal aliens, ballots from the living dead, manipulation of the elderly, double voting, absentee ballot shenanigans, street money incentives, and so on. In addition, some traditions and laws unique to Texas create conditions that spawn even more corruption.

The most egregious of the state's election law provisions permits people to come to the polls on Election Day, and without a recorded registration, to cast a ballot as long as they sign a sworn statement swearing that they are in fact registered in that precinct.[74] These ballots are *not* kept separate so that they can be challenged or checked later. Just in Harris County (the Houston area), *6,707* individuals *who were actually ineligible* voted this way in the 1992 presidential election.[75] Of this substantial total, 1,262 had *never* been registered *anywhere,* and twenty-five of the illegal voters were *convicted felons* not permitted to vote because of their crimes.[76] It took Harris County seven months to conduct the check, long after the election results had been certified. And of course, once again no one knows whether the illegal ballots affected the election since these provisional votes were not segregated from the clearly legal ones. Incidentally, even though it is a felony for a person to "vote or attempt to vote in an election in which the person knows he is not eligible to vote," no punishment is designated for those who "unintentionally" violate the law. Surprise: not a single one of the 6,707 illegal voters was prosecuted because it is very difficult to prove criminal intent.[77] Nor was this merely a localized problem affecting Houston. In the same 1992 general election, over 3,000 unregistered, ineligible people cast a ballot in Tarrant County (the Fort Worth area).[78]

Moreover, Texas has an extraordinarily generous "early voting" system[79] that permits *anyone* age 65 or older, for instance, to use a mail-in ballot (the same kind of ballot as the absentee, except that senior citizens need not be away from home on Election Day or incapacitated to use it). Generally, as Texas examples will show, the more substitutes there are for in-person voting, and the more frequently they are used, the greater the opportunities for voter fraud. To make matters worse, Texas does not require mail-ins and absentee ballots to be accompanied by a witness or notary signature on the sealed envelope that actually contains the completed ballot.[80] Nor is even a full signature by the *voter* necessary on this envelope, even though a space is provided. Many elections officials permit any mark (an "X" or a check) to suffice—making it impossible to verify the voter's signature and easing fraudulent efforts by people who come into possession of absentee or mail-in ballots. In addition, some registrars do not seem to match and carefully compare the signatures on the mail-in ballot application and the actual ballot envelope. One watchdog group counts over 200 instances of apparently differing signatures on the applications and envelopes in the 1994 Democratic primaries just in Galveston County; several races were decided by fewer than 200 votes.[81] A follow-up investigation by the Galveston district attorney's office found "some violations of the Texas Election Code," including a mentally and physically incapacitated voter's ballot being cast by a caretaker who lived in the voter's home.[82]

Some of the elderly—especially the infirm and the poor—are vulnerable to manipulation under this Texas regime. A Lone Star state form of street money pays individuals to organize absentee and mail-in voters.[83] (In Hispanic areas these activists, each paid around $100 per week, are referred to as the *politiqueras.*) Typical of these activists' targets in recent elections was Edward Taylor of Houston, a seventy-nine-year-old retiree. Prior to a 1993 municipal election, a woman Taylor had never met before arrived at his home and presented him with an absentee ballot *application,* which she mailed after Taylor signed it. Very shortly after the postman delivered the ballot to Taylor's mailbox, the woman returned. Taylor related the events that followed in a sworn affidavit:

> Shortly after I received the ballot, the same woman, in the company of a man, came to my house. . . . She used a hole punch to vote my ballot. She then told me to sign my ballot. This woman then put my ballot in the envelope as I was not allowed to mail in my ballot. The woman then took my ballot with her when she left.[84]

As is needless to point out, this entire procedure is not just unorthodox but blatantly illegal.[85]

Compared with some others, Taylor was well treated, and actually given a role—however inferior—in the requesting and casting of his ballot. One married couple, Maria and Jesus Casteneda, were misled when a "helper" showed up at their house.[86] Instead of aiding them in marking their ballots for an independent candidate for city clerk, David Pena, as the couple requested, the helper tricked them into checking the "straight Democratic" ticket box. As Jesus Casteneda recalled, "I later found out that I had not actually voted for David Pena and that [the helper] made me believe I did."[87] Another "helper" aided a husband and wife, Charles and Gloria Scott, by voting their ballots and falsifying the certificate signatures on the carrier envelopes.[88] Even more remarkable was the story of Mr. and Mrs. Jim Cheney Jr.[89] Neither of the Cheneys applied for an absentee ballot in 1993, but two arrived anyway. (Someone unknown to them did the application paperwork.) Soon after, Mrs. Cheney received a woman visitor who offered to take her to the polls on Election Day. She declined, indicating she did not plan to vote; she also pointed out the two unrequested ballots, which the visitor cheerfully took off Mrs. Cheney's hands. Of course, the ballots were cast and counted in the election. This was particularly noteworthy in the case of Mr. Cheney, who had died in September 1992. Mr. Cheney came back again to his old home in March 1994, when he seemingly could not resist applying for an absentee ballot to vote in the federal and state primary elections. (Fortunately, the bogus application was rejected this time by an alert registrar.)

In South Texas, meanwhile, remarkably little has changed politically since the days of LBJ's vote stealing. The sheriff is still the premiere power in most counties, with great influence over the electoral process. Some public officials (especially sheriffs) are again on the take, with drugs rather than moonshine being the source of their ill-gotten gains.[90] And all kinds of fraudulent shenanigans remain a staple of political life there. In recent elections, substantial charges included voting by non-citizens, the mailing of blocks of absentee ballots directly to a political party's headquarters, voting twice, intimidation of voters at the polling places, and campaign workers following around postal delivery persons in order to take mail-in ballots from voters' mailboxes shortly after they were delivered.[91] Poll workers have also observed official election judges—supposedly neutral arbiters—exhorting voters in line at the polling places to support a favored candidate or party.[92] And the beat goes on. . . .

To paraphrase John Donne, no state (except Hawaii) is an island, so Texas shares vote abuse practices with other parts of America. As in Philadelphia, fraud in Texas is bold. As in Alabama, Texas fraud is traditional and institutionalized. As in California, vote fraud in the Lone Star state is assisted by lax state laws that practically invite trouble. But as long-time residents of the state are fond of bragging to outsiders, everything is bigger in Texas, where vote fraud combines all of the polling problems observed elsewhere on our American journey.

Election Fraud in Perspective

What conclusions are reasonable, now that this electoral tour of some diverse precincts is over? As we asserted at the outset, contrary to the belief of some that voter fraud is a thing of the past existing today only in isolated pockets, if at all, the evidence accumulated in this chapter's case studies strongly suggests a persistent pattern of criminal fraud that is well organized and a continuing part of the political culture in some areas. The fact that fraud is generally not recognized as a serious problem by press, public, and law enforcement creates the perfect environment for it to flourish.

The role played by the news media deserves a special comment. Many of the stories we have just reviewed received little or no national press attention, even when the local media carried news accounts. Perhaps they were seen merely as "isolated" incidents of interest only to the citizens directly affected. Remarkably, though, some of these cases of fraud attracted amazingly light attention from the local news organizations themselves. Partly, as noted at the outset, this results from the mistaken belief among journalists that vote fraud is no longer a serious problem. But it also reflects a lack of knowledge even among opinion makers about vote fraud's resurgence. Less charitably, the coverage vacuum may also be another indication of a disease some reporters may have contracted from extended contact with political professionals: a blasé attitude about some unsavory aspects of the electoral sausage-making process.

In contrast to the absence of the press, the alert reader has probably already noticed that Democrats feature prominently in almost all of the instances of voter fraud featured in this chapter. Before

Democrats take umbrage, and the Republicans mount a high horse, an explanation is in order. First, the GOP is fully capable of voting hijinks when circumstances permit. For example, the two Ventura County workers who were arrested in October 1994 for collecting the names of newly registered voters from tombstones were working on behalf of a Republican candidate for the legislature.

Another hotbed of Republican vote fraud is rural southeastern Kentucky, where a sizable number of GOP local candidates, consultants, and precinct workers have recently been caught paying off voters to cast their absentee ballots "correctly," among other offenses.[93] Several decades later, the price of a vote was still reasonable—five dollars or a half-pint of whiskey—but by the 1980s and 1990s a combination of inflation and candidate competition had driven the per-vote cost to about $50.[94] Despite the substantial increase, various local Republican politicians and their absentee-ballot "brokers"—frontmen who give people cash in exchange for their marked and signed absentees—were more than willing to pay the price.[95]

"It's a way of life," commented former assistant state attorney general Dale Wright, who was assigned to the vote fraud hotline in his office. "It is basically conceded in Kentucky that people have a constitutional right to sell their vote. We laugh about there being three Kentucky cash crops: tobacco, marijuana, and votes."[96] Wright describes a particularly blatant form of vote-buying in some Kentucky precincts:

> Sometimes the buying or selling [of votes] is done right at the door of the polling place. The [vote-buyers] are stationed at the end of the road leading to the [precinct], and trucks stop and the drivers are given a kind of business card. Then these [bought] voters go into the polls and the [partisan] election judges see the card, know exactly where it came from, and watch to see that the voter votes correctly . . . Then one of the judges will tear off a certain corner of the card. When the voter drives off, he stops to see the vote buyer at the end of the road, presents the torn card, and is paid.[97]

Moreover, in some parts of the state, says Wright, "The patriarch or the matriarch of a very large family may commit the whole damn family to the highest bidder, and once [he or she's] been paid, [all family members] file for absentee ballots, sign them, and turn them over" to the party or candidate's agent. By the way, Wright knows whereof he speaks, and not just because he worked in law enforcement. "Hell, I was part of it. My first year out of law school, in 1971, I hauled half-pint whiskey bottles all [election] day around the polling places, and I took the money to the family patriarchs" at a time when he was active in partisan politics.

Kentucky and a few other places aside, Republicans have fewer opportunities for vote fraud available to them. In many states, particularly in the South and some border states, the GOP has rarely if ever controlled the local and legislative offices necessary to set the rules and manipulate the election process. Alabama and Texas clearly demonstrate this, although in those states and elsewhere in Dixie, Republicans are beginning to make the necessary gains at the ballot box that will change the balance of power in many localities.

In and out of the South, another factor is also at work: the hard reality of economic and class politics. In most areas, the Republican base consists primarily of white-collar, managerial professionals, as well as Christian conservatives. Neither group is easily induced to commit fraud; community standards, cultural values, "clean government" orientation, high education level, and/or the lack of a financial incentive to commit fraud for just a few dollars work against any Republican Party operative who seeks to draft them into any illegal schemes.

By contrast, the pool of people who appear to be available and more vulnerable to an invitation to participate in vote fraud tend to lean Democratic in their partisan predisposition, such as low-income minorities.[98] The usual turnout among African Americans and Hispanics is disproportionately low, and Democratic organizers are often desperate to boost their participation rate. Some liberal activists have even partly justified fraudulent endeavors on this basis; those making this case say it is unfair that the voices of the poor and dispossessed are muted at the ballot box, and therefore extraordinary measures (for example, stretching the absentee ballot or registration rules) are required to compensate.[99] To most observers, though, the rationalization that the end justifies the means is not very convincing. The 1993 passage of the "motor-voter" bill that dramatically eased voter registration requirements also considerably reduced whatever cogency such an argument possessed. (This bill, which also potentially increases the opportunities for vote fraud, is discussed in chapter 11.)

Less partisan readers might wonder more about the breadth of election fraud. Are polling problems restricted just to the four hot spots we investigated, or do they characterize the American electoral process generally and range more widely? Our strong suspicion—based on dozens of unexplored tips from political observers and interviewees—is that some degree of vote fraud can be found almost everywhere, and serious outbreaks can and do occur in every region of the country. In New Jersey, for instance, nearly 1,000 illegal votes were cast in Hudson County (Jersey City) in a 1989 election, including some by people who were unregistered and others who were dead.[100] In addition, several dozen psychiatric patients—some of whom believed Franklin Roosevelt or Harry Truman was still president—managed to cast absentee ballots in a local 1993 election in Secaucus.[101] And, one of our interviewees, Republican political consultant Ed Rollins, claimed in a session with us that in the 1993 New Jersey gubernatorial election, there were precincts with 100 to 200 votes recorded for the Democratic candidate, Governor James Florio, before the polls opened. Rollins blamed "Democratic sheriffs in control of the machines."[102]

Granted, vote fraud has been a staple of New Jersey's history; as one chronicler wrote, "What Renaissance Italy was to art, the old-time Garden State was to vote fraud."[103] However, places with relatively spotless records, where the authorities are convinced that the electoral process is clean, may be especially vulnerable to fraud. Virginia is a perfect example. Though administratively well run, the elections process in the prideful Old Dominion may be too reliant on an outdated "honor system" and sense of civic security. One can cast a ballot in Virginia on Election Day without displaying any identification. All one must do is give a name and an address to a poll worker who then checks the official voter list—a procedure potentially wide open to fraudulent manipulation.

Whether fraud is Democratic or Republican, or located in the North or the South or the West, the effect on American democracy is similar. While electoral hanky-panky affects the outcome in only a small proportion of elections (mainly in very tight races), even one fraudulent ballot is too many. The superstructure of any representative democracy ultimately rests on the soundness and integrity of the elections that produce its governors. Most important of all, citizens must have complete confidence that the declared winners are the actual winners; otherwise, the motivation to participate in elections is destroyed. Millions of citizens are already convinced that their one vote matters too little to exercise the franchise. Once the pattern of election fraud becomes too obvious for the media to ignore, and the public begins to suspect or believe elections can be stolen, then American democracy's currently tenuous hold on many individuals may well dissipate.

Therefore, the need for reform is urgent and clear. Voter turnout in the United States is traditionally too low, and cynicism among citizens too high, to permit the malodorous malady of election fraud to continue unchecked—or to spread. Fortunately, some simple procedural changes, combined with newly advanced technology, can make a real difference in this corrupt province, and proposals in both categories will be set forth in chapter 11.

PART III

Remedies

11

A Program of Reform

Every government degenerates when trusted to the rulers of the people alone. The people themselves, therefore, are its only safe depositories and to render even them safe, their minds must be improved to a certain degree.
—*Thomas Jefferson,* Notes on the State of Virginia

I n the end, we return to first principles. As Jefferson understood, the governors in any society are unlikely to check their appetites unless pressured to do so by the governed. Corruption exists because we the people permit it, either by silence, inattention or misunderstanding. If the persistence of corruption in American politics is going to be reversed, the public—and their tribunes in the press—will have to demand it.

Over the centuries Americans have demonstrated an amazing capacity to reinvent their political system, to counteract the corruptions that inevitably accumulate in each generation. But wise reinvention requires a clear-headed understanding of the system's ills. And to overcome the many obstacles placed in the path of change, to actually achieve that reinvention, a cynical public's capacity to feel outrage must be restored. We have written *Dirty Little Secrets* with Jefferson in mind, hoping that our efforts here will secure an important place in the national debate for campaign finance reform. Although in June of 1995 President Bill Clinton and Speaker Newt Gingrich made headlines by pledging to form a bipartisan commission to craft a solution to the problems that bedevil our electoral system, no such commission has been formed, and the promise has been allowed to evaporate. Although the experiences of coauthor Sabato on the last government-sponsored campaign finance reform panel (in 1990) suggest that the House and Senate are acutely aware that commission reports are not binding upon them, we have been disappointed at the remarkable lack of attention the disappearance of the Clinton/Gingrich pledge into the ether has provoked in the national press.

The goal of this book is not to feed the public's cynicism but to stoke the fires of reform. To judge by history, only public anger will turn the key to reform's motor. It is our belief that a public fully informed of the scurrilities detailed in this volume will become, if not enraged, then engaged enough to generate support for change. Not just any change, of course: what is needed is fair reform that focuses on real corruption but at the same time recognizes that parts of the American system are working well and do not need an overhaul; targeted reform that surgically removes the cancers while leaving healthy organs alone; and future-oriented reform that identifies core deficiencies and anticipates evolving circumstances rather than merely reacts to a current manifestation of a larger problem.

Taken individually, many of the corruptions we report in this book might seem minor, or at least local. Many readers may be familiar with some of these accounts because they appeared in local newspapers, or will know of stories like them from their own regions. But the fact that tales like these do come from all parts of the country, in a profusion far greater than we have the resources or the space to include, is proof that larger forces are at work. Take them all together, and it is indisputable that corruption is polluting our Republic.

Corruption can always be dismissed as the domain of the relatively small number of people who are not impressed by the laws and standards that are meant to prevent it. It is nearly impossible for any one person, or most news organizations, to get a bird's-eye view of the true state of our politics, because perspectives are always limited by time and distance. But the portfolio of abuses we have assembled in *Dirty Little Secrets* is meant to show Americans how widespread corruption is, today, here in our own country. Corruption in Mexico may be more dramatic. Italy's continuing corruption scandal may be a perversely entertaining set piece capping a centuries-long tradition of political accommodation. Singapore and Thailand are renowned for their corrupt brutality, and Russia may find that corruption prevents it from securing easy entry into the world economy. But the persistence of corruption in America, which rightly prides itself in its role as a beacon of democracy, is no less a disgrace. Ignoring corruption here, or refusing to recognize it as a national phenomenon that must be combated will ensure only that it spreads, mutates, and grows more toxic.

We understand that as a reflection of the undeniable darker side of human nature, corruption has been, and is, a staple of every society. But the form of government chosen by a people dramatically affects the *extent* of corruption. Dictatorships and oligarchies institutionalize corruption for the ruling families or classes. Democracies offer considerable checks against corrupt practices, including frequent elections, a free press, and (in the American Republic) divided power that encourages constant scrutiny of authority at every level and in each branch of government.

But even in a relatively favorable anticorruption environment such as ours, a disturbingly widespread pattern of abuses can be found, as we have seen in the pages of this volume. Just two decades after a Watergate-generated wave of reform, we have descended in some ways to pre-Watergate standards. How did reform's effects ebb and corruption's evils flow so swiftly after an earthshaking event like Watergate, in the aftermath of which nearly everyone pledged to change political practice fundamentally and forever?

First, the public's recall is very short; the press's institutional memory is not much longer; and generational replacement in the population may mean the political duration of "forever" is only ten or twenty years. Second, there are hundreds of moving parts in a piece of machinery as complex as our democracy. Defective parts are replaced quickly, but unplanned obsolescence means a part or two is always on the verge of going bad, especially when we are looking the other way. Third, in a very free country like the United States, liberty is a stricture against stricture; that is, First Amendment rights such as free speech and association make it exceedingly difficult to design airtight, loophole-free reforms that can truly end many nefarious activities. Finally, those loopholes are found and relentlessly broadened by the extraordinarily clever people who tend to be attracted to politics. The best and brightest gravitate to candidacy, campaign consultancy, staff work, and associated professions because, to paraphrase bank-robber Willie Sutton, that's where they keep the power. It is hard to outsmart this ambitious class of people who are steely determined to win and will bend whatever rules they must to do it.

As we noted in the introduction, American history is dotted with reform movements initiated and powered by a massive scandal (Crédit Mobilier, Teapot Dome, Watergate). The press exposes the wrongdoing, the public becomes outraged, the political elites respond with legislation, and once passed, the immediate problem is "solved." For a few years a sensitized press remains on the alert for violations of the new ethical standards, and politicians and consultants modify their behavior to conform with these standards, out of fear of retribution from the voters if they do not. This pattern was clearly observed during and after Watergate. By most accounts, campaigns in the mid-to-late 1970s were exceptionally clean, with more election controversies arising from gaffes by the candidates than from dirty tricks by the consultants.

From 1980 on, though, the spotlight moved to matters of more pressing concern: American hostages in Iran, high inflation and interest rates, recession, a foreign policy scandal (Iran-Contra), the end of the Cold War, a hot war in the Persian Gulf, another recession, health care, and an Oklahoma bombing. These blockbuster stories overwhelmed the hints of reemerging systemic corruption; moreover, substantive scandals such as the savings and loan fiasco of the 1980s seemed to interest press and public less than titillating tales emanating from the bedrooms of political celebrities. Campaign finance reform, which had engaged the news media and the politically active citizenry in the 1970s, became a guaranteed MEGO (my-eyes-glaze-over) nonstarter a decade later. By the 1990s, repeated mini-scandals about political excesses of various sorts and overweening special-interest influence on government appeared only to deepen cynicism and broaden the torpid apathy about corruption.

Reforms that work are the only cure for this cynicism and apathy. Some reforms necessarily involve statutory revision, though we understand that this is an antiregulatory age and legally, "less is more." And it is true that virtually every new law opens up possibilities for ingenious innovations in corrupt practice. Moreover, overpromising, which frequently accompanies the passage of legislation, contributes to public cynicism after the disappointing reality dawns. Because of the limitations of law, we must instead rely on the press to redress some flaws and grievances. In order for the media to accommodate this request, they must be willing to redirect their energies from the coverage of personal scandals and horse race politics to systemic corruption, even though the former is often easier to do and more rewarding (in terms of ratings points). This brings us to the citizenry, which after all supplies the readership and ratings points that drive the media. In a democracy, the ultimate responsibility for curing the ills of the political system must inevitably and appropriately rest with the body politic. By means of the ballot box and their political parties and organizations, not to mention the television remote control, citizens must hold their elected representatives *and* the news media to high standards.

Even if all this is done, we need to acknowledge—and the public must understand—that there are no final solutions. The ebb and flow of corruption, described at the outset, is a predictable, continuous part of politics. As the sea of corruption rises over time, the ethical dikes created by anticorruption laws will spring leaks and must be repaired or even rebuilt entirely. As a consequence, in a decade or two's time, many or most of the concerns we have outlined in this book will probably have been dealt with, but new ones will have arisen in their place, some perhaps unintentionally created by the statutory correctives enacted to resolve current abuses. This is the natural course of events in a free society, and it is no cause for despair. *The logical response is not cynicism but eternal vigilance against misuse of power, and a vigorous, unceasing search to expose old and new forms of corruption.*

We suggest that such a reformist campaign should begin with these remedies to the specific ills we have identified in this study.

Tax-Exempt Organizations

The use of tax-exempt organizations to aid political campaigns is not a new phenomenon, although it is becoming a commonplace and increasingly worrisome practice.

It is important to distinguish between different types of tax-exempt groups. The most objectionable are the 501(c)(3) organizations, such as Americans for Limited Terms and Newt Gingrich's Progress and Freedom Foundation. Because contributors to these groups receive a tax deduction for their gifts, the taxpayers are indirectly subsidizing campaign activity. The law on 501(c)(3) organizations is vague and contradictory, and experts in the field disagree about the legality of such activity. However, the weight of the evidence suggests that such conduct is highly questionable. It may also fail the reengineering test—if we were to build our political system over again from scratch, would we invent 501(c)(3) organizations?

The record of the Internal Revenue Service on this issue, to be kind, has been inadequate. As detailed in chapter 4, for example, Pat Robertson blatantly used a 501(c)(3) to aid his presidential campaign in 1987.[1] While the IRS opened an investigation that year, by late-1995—a full eight years later—there had been no resolution of the case. Is it too much to ask of the IRS either to prosecute such cases with reasonable speed, or alternatively to declare openly that the current laws are unenforceable?

We should recognize that the use of 501(c)(3) organizations amounts to partial public financing of campaigns. The government should make a consistent decision one way or the other: either everybody gets a tax exemption for making political contributions, or no one does. A special case is the Christian Coalition's use of 501(c)(3) organizations, that is, churches, as a distribution network for its political propaganda. Clearly, churches are not political groups masquerading as charities: rather, they are true charities. As detailed in chapter 5, however, they have been led to believe by the Christian Coalition that distributing the group's materials has no legal implication for their tax status. Given the information supplied in this book on the partisan nature of those communications, we believe this is not the case.

Less objectionable but still troubling is the use of 501(c)(4) "social welfare" organizations—such as the Christian Coalition itself. Contributions to C(4) organizations are not tax-deductible, and such groups consequently enjoy more freedom to play roles in politics. Yet C(4) groups are not supposed to have as their "primary" purpose involvement in political campaigns or lobbying. We are not lawyers, but any layman looking at the Christian Coalition could fairly conclude that its primary purpose is to engage in lobbying and campaigning. Here again the IRS has been derelict: some five years after the Christian Coalition was founded, the IRS has failed to determine whether it is a bona fide social welfare organization.

For tax purposes, C(4) organizations, when used in political campaigns, are largely indistinguishable from ordinary campaign committees—which are also largely tax-exempt.[2] The primary political advantage of setting themselves up under the "social welfare" section of the code rather than the "political organization" section is that they are not required to comply with the Federal Election Campaign Act. Thus, the C(4) groups—even though they are highly political organizations—have not been subject to FECA's limits on sources of funds, limits on sizes of funds, and disclosure requirements. In our view, these distinctions make little sense, and as we discuss in the section on campaign finance reform, they frustrate the goal of fuller disclosure.

Concerning the tax issue, it is understandable that the IRS is leery of vigorously prosecuting political actors; the abuse of the IRS in the Watergate scandal is certainly instructive on this point.[3] Yet the obvious result of continuing on the current course is that in a few years, much more—perhaps most—political activity will be conducted through tax-exempt organizations, a de facto, pure, regulation-free market. Clearly, current law is insufficiently precise to permit the IRS to handle the political exploitation of our nonprofit laws, and Congress needs to provide the statutory guidance.

Subcommittee Government

The elaborate baronial structure of subcommittee government, created with the best intention as a way of democratizing Congress, has perversely had the unforeseen effect of producing a cadre of immensely powerful mandarins whose concerns appear largely parochial or oriented toward the interests of their financial backers. Rather than truly opening up the congressional system, the creation of subcommittee government has simply multiplied the points at which special interests can exercise influence and ambitious legislators can tend to their own concerns (typically, getting reelected). A heretical suggestion: perhaps we were better off with committee government, where there were only a dozen barons to keep track of, rather than two hundred.

The Republican leadership in the House and Senate went some distance in 1995 toward eradicating subcommittee government by placing limits on the terms of committee and subcommittee chairmen. The advantages of such a scheme are clear and substantial. Term limits on all chairmanships will reduce the incentives for overly long service in a public office, and they may encourage senior legislators to retire at irregular intervals—thus accomplishing the Founders' desired rotation in office without the meat-ax approach of absolute constitutional limits on the number of terms a person can serve in Congress. Undoubtedly, some senior officeholders will nonetheless choose to stay on Capitol Hill, and their expertise and institutional memory can be freely tapped by colleagues. The difference is that senior members will not automatically enjoy an ever-increasing concentration of power, and they will not be able to develop subcommittee fiefdoms that in times past could sometimes be run autocratically for decades at a stretch. (How odd, and regrettable, that the seniority-based, non-term-limited subcommittee system stymied representatives of districts and states that are most sensitive to swings in the national mood, and thus most reflective of popular opinion.) Rather, power will be spread more evenly over time to many members of Congress, including those from politically competitive areas of the country where frequent seat turnover (via defeat at the polls and early retirement) has often prevented legislators from gaining influence.

However, term limits for committee and subcommittee chairs are only a partial solution. Recall that Bob Carr began capitalizing on his newfound position of influence virtually the day he assumed it. In just two years, he collected tens of thousands of dollars from a large number of favor-seekers, many of whom appear to have gotten what they were looking for. Already, a greatly empowered Speakership under Newt Gingrich has clearly placed committee and subcommittee chairmen on a shorter leash, but this may be a product of Gingrich's unique situation and therefore short-lived. More could be done institutionally to reduce the power of subcommittee chairmen. A fairly simple solution would be to modify many of the reforms of the 1970s by placing limits on the autonomy of subcommittees to set their own agenda, schedules, and staff appointments. Another important reform would be to formally vest in party leaders the right to recommend committee and subcommittee chairmen. This was done on an ad hoc basis in the House in 1995 for full committee chairmen only, while the Senate clung strictly to its seniority-based selection system. To give such authority to the House Speaker and Senate Majority Leader is to allocate to them an enormous cluster of carrots and sticks that they can use to enforce discipline and achieve passage of the party's legislative agenda—the central goal of all reformers who seek to strengthen so-called party-responsible government.[4]

Finally, there is ample reason to reduce the number of subcommittees in both House and Senate. While the House made a major reduction in the number of subcommittees in early 1995, the legislative landscape is still littered with obscure but powerful (and lucrative) redoubts. To give but one example, the House Judiciary Committee has retained its Patents and Trademarks Subcommittee, a little-watched warren in which special interests seek to manipulate intellectual property laws to their advantage.

None of these steps would eliminate the potential for abuse, but that is not a realistic goal. It is ultimately the duty of the public and the media to uphold high standards. To that end, by reducing the points of access to the system, the watchdogs would have fewer sites to scrutinize and thus could be more effective.

Dirty Tricks

Some simple, partial remedies spring to mind in retracing our steps down the backroads of dirty politics. As we will also suggest with street money, all campaigns should be required to disclose fully all subcontractors to which their treasury flows directly or indirectly. This will prevent a candidate from hiring a private detective in secrecy by funneling the money through a law firm and listing only the law firm on the campaign finance report. Where feasible, controls also ought to be tightened on access to credit reports, because at present it is entirely too easy for information brokers to tap into private databanks. All candidates should be aware of the dangers of privacy invasion, and they should check at regular intervals to see whether unauthorized scanning of their records has occurred. Agencies such as Equifax must be sensitive to the problem as well, and procedures for accommodating requests from wary candidates should be streamlined. At the least, every credit agency should establish a permanent toll-free number for the use of candidates. And the privacy laws in such matters ought to be vigorously enforced by police and prosecutors to discourage credit snooping. Similar safeguards in the health care industry need to be put into place. From hospitals to health maintenance organizations to individual physicians' offices, special security precautions should be taken with the files of public figures, wherever such protections are not already standard procedure.

These commonsense solutions are barely adequate to stem the burgeoning abuses outlined in chapter 6. As we noted there, campaigners will generally employ whatever techniques will bring them victory—unless the political costs of using those techniques can be made to exceed the benefits. Only the news media and the electorate have the power to change the cost–benefit ratio for today's dirty tricks: the media by means of investigation and bad publicity, and the voters via ballots on Election Day. If civility is ever to be a watchword of American campaigning, then the press and the public must make campaigns pay dearly for meanness and malpractice.

Street Money

As we have fully acknowledged, some aspects of street money are completely legitimate, including small election day payments to flushers and drivers and phoners. And many, probably most, minority political activists and ministers are well-motivated, hardworking individuals who participate in party politics because they believe in it. But few will even try to justify some of the outrageous practices we identified earlier in this volume: large unaccountable "tribute" payments to some black ministers, the gravy train for certain minority entrepreneurs, the political money shell game that defeats the purposes of disclosure laws, the offering of near-bribes such as free gasoline as an inducement to vote, and so forth. Neither should any GOP hijinks and dirty tricks to suppress the black vote escape public notice.

The natural impulse is to hope that Democratic leaders, who expressed deep unhappiness to us about the development and drift of street money, would begin to just say no. After all, one senior consultant termed it a "racket"; another said "the underlying principle is abhorrent to me. . . . Why should we be paying lots of money to people to participate in politics when it's in their own self-interest to do so anyway?"

But this "just say no" campaign is likely to be as ineffective as the one targeting drug use in the 1980s. A Democratic veteran put it bluntly: "Street money will continue because it works. And it is now a deeply rooted custom in the African-American community, where you need incentives to combat a general apathetic attitude that it doesn't matter who you elect, you're going to get screwed anyway." Whatever the truth of that, it seems rudely ironic for a community that shed much blood to secure a right so wrongly denied its members for centuries to now acquiesce in the selling or renting of that right—or even callously treat it as a mere business proposition.

Republicans angry about street money have called for outlawing it or even withdrawing the tax-exempt status of churches whose ministers aid and abet it. But the former is impractical—how should we statutorily distinguish between legitimate and illegitimate GOTV work, for instance?—and the latter is extreme. Rather, some relatively simple reforms in election disclosure law perhaps can do what human nature will not: reduce the chances that major street money fraud will pass undetected. At the least, the rest of the country can follow the New Jersey legislature, which, in the wake of the Rollins affair, passed a law requiring that all street money payments be made by check instead of in cash, thereby creating a disclosable record.[5] It is also essential that campaigns file a complete list (with mailing addresses) of all subcontractors, so that community organizers who receive large lump sums from campaigns and claim to be distributing the money to others will be forced to catalogue their subsidiary supervisors and flushers.[6] Also necessary are substantial civil fines and criminal penalties for violations of these new requirements, as well as some reasonable program of random auditing of the campaign finance reports so that illegalities can come to light in a timely fashion.

In addition, all states need to enact a statute similar to the current federal law banning voter inducements, that is, goods or services (such as gasoline, food, money, postage stamps, tickets to events, or anything of value) offered voters to induce them to cast a ballot.[7] In this way, state and local authorities across the country would be on firmer ground to prosecute nefarious street money schemes for their elections, just as federal law enforcement can already do for presidential or congressional contests.

Even if these suggested statutes are enacted everywhere—an unlikely "if"—their rigorous enforcement will depend upon a vigilant press. To judge by past practice, optimism would not always appear to be justified on this front. Political correctness, or the affirmative action tensions in some newsrooms, may have caused some journalists to avert their eyes from street money abuses. But these are poor excuses, not good reasons. The corruption is real, the information is readily available to established journalists with reliable sources, and readers and viewers have every right to expect full coverage of this unsavory electoral subject.

Franking

Free mail for incumbents is a perk that appears impervious to reform. The temptation to abuse it has been so great as to overwhelm the many reforms that have been enacted over the last century. There is now a substantial body of rules and regulations concerning franking on the books—one going so far as to limit the number of reflexive personal pronouns a legislator can employ per page—yet the misuse continues.

The money at issue, while considerable, is perhaps of less concern than the stifling effect of the frank on political competition. The body of knowledge now available leaves little question about the electoral consequences of the frank.[8] Even conscientious users of the mail privileges receive what would appear to be inordinate political benefits. But the worst of it is that the minority of true abusers tend to be the very legislators who, in a more competitive election system, might well be defeated. Thus a seemingly marginal matter has a disproportionate impact, overstabilizing the system. Thanks to the frank, other perks, and noncompetitive redistricting, even elections with relatively high turnover (such as 1974, 1980, and 1994) see more than 85 percent of all incumbents who seek another term reelected.

Republicans, who railed against the frank in their years out of power as an illegitimate tool of the majority to sustain itself in office, validated their own criticisms in 1995 when, as the new majority, they refused to do away with or even seriously curtail what they had previously called a gross waste of taxpayer funds.[9]

Obviously, legislators should be permitted to respond at government expense to any mail they receive. Yet the subsidization of unsolicited mailings by politicians is more difficult to justify today than ever. With the advent of cable television and the proliferation of other information channels from talk radio to computer bulletin boards, the argument that mail is the only way to reach constituents—already feeble—grows weaker by the day. Nonetheless, should defenders of the frank somehow successfully make the case that unsolicited mailings are still needed, despite all the evidence of misuse, there is a less radical solution than a simple ban: allot some mailing privileges to nonincumbent general election candidates for Congress. This is not a new idea and has been denounced in the past as too costly, but this issue can be framed as a simple choice: Do we want to give taxpayer-financed mailings to political candidates or not? If no, let us not do so at all. If yes, let us be fair and give them to all candidates.[10]

Staff

The same calculus applies to congressional staff who work in campaigns: while the misappropriation of taxpayer funds is objectionable, government subsidization of incumbents unfairly tilts the playing field, reducing electoral competitiveness.

As with the frank, the new Republican majority has seemed less than eager to tackle the staff problem. While they aggressively chopped away at the committee staffs they perceived to be an essential part of the liberal bureaucratic state, they left unscathed the large personal staffs allotted to each legislator. As our investigation showed, while committee staff is modestly involved in electioneering, most of the taxpayer-subsidized manpower for incumbent campaigns comes from the legislator's personal office.

Does anyone believe that citizens (as opposed to congressmen) would be worse off if every personal staff was cut a modest 10 percent, or even 25 percent? Yet the staff problem is thornier than franking in that a substantial staff is clearly necessary to perform the constituent service the public demands. It is important to recognize the effects the public's expectations can have on our government. The staff are there because they satisfy constituents' needs and give politicians tremendous political mileage as a result. It is a potent demonstration of how remarkably self-adjusting our system is. And it gives hope to the reformers—the people will get what they want when they apply the proper force in the proper place.

One way to reduce the potential for abuse would be to dramatically reduce personal staffs by turning over the whole constituent service role to a congressionally controlled ombudsman agency that would act as an advocate for citizens having problems with the bureaucracy. In theory, this would satisfy the ostensible reason for having so many employees while removing the potential for abuse. However, we are realistic about the small likelihood that either party would consent to such a radical solution so obviously against the political interests of legislators. There is a less dramatic but perhaps just as effective remedy: sustained media attention to abuses and better enforcement of existing criminal statutes on the use of staff for campaign activities. While the media rarely raise the issue and prosecutors have never been known to pursue the matter in this fashion, our investigation showed that ample public-record information exists to enable investigators from both camps to ask some very pointed questions.

In our examination of this issue, we encountered a pervasive "everybody does it" ethic. But it ought to be remembered that theft of government property is a crime, and as former Congressman Carroll Hubbard (Democrat of Kentucky) found, it is one that you can go to jail for. There also is precedent for citizens to bring civil actions against members of Congress who misuse congressional staff, which holds abusive lawmakers up to public shame and requires them to reimburse the federal treasury.[11] Media exposure, and civil and criminal prosecution, are immediate steps that can be taken to curb this practice; no congressional hearings are required, and no new laws need be passed.

Push-Polling

The last thing our already overly negative politics needed was a new technique guaranteed to increase the acidity of campaigning. But that is exactly what push-polling, especially the persuasive phoning variety, does. In addition to making politics even less attractive to the citizenry, it sullies the field of public opinion research and damages the credibility of honest polling practitioners. As one pollster put it, "Push-polling threatens legitimate survey research. Every project we do banks on the public's trust in our project, that when we call people we are not doing a number on them, or conducting campaigning in the guise of research."[12]

It would certainly be in the interests of both the public and survey professionals to blow the whistle on push-polling. But as with almost all the subjects covered in this volume, hard-and-fast remedies are elusive. For First Amendment reasons, push-polls certainly cannot be banned. And it is exceedingly difficult to craft rules that distinguish between the destructive forms of push-polling and the more acceptable survey research manifestation of the technique.

Once again, strengthened disclosure may be the best option; it does not directly solve the problem but gives the press and the public the tools to uncover wrongdoing and punish the guilty. Currently, all federal campaign print publications and electronic advertising must reveal their sponsorship. Similarly, then, pollsters and telephone bank operators conducting any type of survey or message delivery should be required by federal and state law to reveal the firm's name and every paying sponsor at the end of the survey.[13] At the specific request of any respondent,[14] the interviewer should also be obligated to send a copy of the questionnaire to the respondent and to give the address and phone number of the firm and sponsor.[15] Failure to fulfill these requirements, once proven in court, should trigger a substantial civil fine, and willful violators who are in supervisory and managerial positions in the firm or sponsoring organization should incur a misdemeanor criminal penalty.

What does this simple, consumer-empowering reform accomplish? Mainly deterrence, generated by fear of public backlash following disclosure. Every consultant will know in advance that any poll may be made public, and the firm and sponsor may be clearly identified if even one alert respondent requests the information. (The news media ought to encourage citizens to do precisely that, and then share it with reporters!) Also, since every paying sponsor must be revealed, phony shell organizations will do a campaign no good.

There will be some sacrifice by legitimate pollsters—fifteen seconds or so of interviewer time and long-distance charges will be tacked onto each call—but the requirements are hardly too burdensome given the threat to their own credibility. The quality of survey research will not be much affected, because disclosure is not necessary until the interview's conclusion—thus avoiding the biasing of respondents (who might give "expected" answers if they knew the poll sponsors at the interview's start).[16] It is true that the interviewers will know the sponsorship, thereby eliminating "blind" interviewing (where, to avoid bias on their part, interviewers are not told about the poll's sponsorship). But most pollsters fully realize that intelligent interviewers are often able to guess the sponsorship anyway, from the wording of the questions. Finally, potential candidates who are "testing the waters" for a candidacy will run the risk of public exposure under these proposed requirements. Yet again, most possible contenders are well known in advance, and the sacrifice of a bit of their strategic planning privacy is a small price to pay for a cleaner political system.

Incidentally, other reformers have already proposed more intrusive remedies than our own, ranging from the mandatory disclosure of all polling and telephone questionnaires (attached to regular contribution and expenditure filings with the Federal Election Commission and state boards of election) to outright registration and direct regulation of polling firms and telephone-bank organizations.[17] We do not believe that such steps are yet necessary, but if moderate measures such as the ones we suggest are not possible or successful, the more drastic remedies may have to be tried in some form.[18]

Legal niceties are not likely to temper all boiler-room telephone operations, so it would be helpful if each major state and local news organization established and publicized a toll-free "campaign corruption hotline" telephone number for citizens to use during the final month of election campaigns. It is far easier to piece together the story of corrupt practices while the phones are still warm than after Election Day, when the boiler-rooms have been dismantled. As we will discuss shortly, these hotlines can do double-duty, allowing citizens to report their suspicions of voter fraud as well.

Vote Fraud

Philadelphia, Alabama, California, and Texas make it obvious that the solutions required for voter fraud must necessarily be adapted to each locality's culture and practice. But one imperative unites all the cases: while registration and voting should be as easy as possible, the process ought also to be as fraud-proof as possible.

With the enactment of the federal "motor-voter" law in May 1993, ease of registration was guaranteed.[19] The major provisions of the legislation required states to permit people to register when applying for a driver's license or using other governmental offices that provide public assistance.[20] Few would argue with the intent of this aggressive approach to increasing America's abysmally low levels of registration and voter turnout.

However, some aspects of the motor-voter law also augment the potential for fraud. Registration by mail is mandated for every state; thus, the safeguards that can be present during in-person registration (such as the showing of picture identification cards) are removed. Workers at governmental offices are forbidden from challenging any registrant, even if they have good reason to suspect an individual is ineligible to vote. Under the motor-voter law, it has become more difficult to keep the voting rolls clean of "deadwood" voters who have moved or died, making fraudulent voting easier and therefore more tempting for those so inclined.[21] A "fail-safe" provision in the law also permits voters who have moved within the same county and congressional district to vote at either their old or new address—potentially inviting "extra-diligent" citizens (or their unknown substitutes) to cast a ballot at both locations.[22]

Motor-voter is not the only new wrinkle in the election process that could complicate the system's integrity. In its December 1995 party primaries and January 1996 special election for the U.S. Senate held to fill the unexpired term of the disgraced Robert Packwood, Oregon became the first state to hold a congressional contest entirely by mail. Ballots were mailed to registered voters about three weeks before both the primaries and general election, with citizens able to return them by mail or drop them off at designated sites in each locality up until the technical "election day." Officials went to considerable lengths to prevent fraud, including checking every single ballot signature against the registration card original. A progressive state with a history of clean elections, Oregon was not a likely site for voting irregularities in any event. But it is easy to imagine the potential for electoral mischief in states with less squeaky-clean traditions or careful procedures. Mail-in-balloting—which by definition includes everyone on the registration rolls, rather than the fraction voting by mail absentee in regular elections—exponentially increases the chances for fraud.

Add these ingredients to the already boiling pot of fraud in parts of America, and the cooling balm of reform becomes absolutely essential. So what can reasonably be done to minimize, if not eliminate, voter fraud? No system is absolutely foolproof, but one long-term solution made possible by advanced technology stands out from all others: the use of thumbprint scanners to record and identify each voter.[23] At the time of registration, an individual's thumbprint—unique to every human being—could be scanned by this reliable machine (which is already used at motor vehicle offices in some states). If registration is being done by mail, a print-sensitive adhesive square (covered by a thin removable plastic sheet) can be affixed to the form for the same purpose. The print information would be digitized and stored statewide, and transferred regularly to each locality so that registered citizens can be instantaneously scanned and cleared to vote at their precinct on Election Day. The same thumbprint technology can also make safe the absentee and early-voting/mail-in ballot process; in addition to current certification requirements, every absentee and early-voting/mail-in ballot should be sealed with a thumb imprint that can be scanned before counting.

Obviously, before this high-tech vision comes to pass, financial investment in the scanner hardware and a lengthy transition period to convert from the current system will be required. But since the most costly election in a democracy is a stolen one, the scanner-secured polling place ought to be the goal everywhere.

Until that objective is reached, other measures should be instituted. At the very least, a photo identification card (of any sort) ought to be produced by each voter at the polls. While phony photo IDs can certainly be manufactured, it takes time, trouble, and money to do so by any organization attempting to generate a sizable number of fraudulent votes. Second, voters should also be asked at registration to give a number unique to them—a social security number, a driver's license number—that can be prerecorded on the voter list provided each precinct's workers.[24] Third, every voter should have to sign his name on the voting roll at the polls, so that the signature can be compared to the one on the registration form to see if they match up.[25] This comparison would probably be made only in the event the results of a close election were challenged (although again, the computer technology already exists for instantaneously scrolling, side by side, the poll signature and the registration signature).[26] Finally, all potential voters ought to be advised at the polls, whether orally by an elections official or by means of a printed statement, of the eligibility requirements for voting and the penalties for fraudulent voting.[27] (A similar warning should be prominently featured on all absentee and early-voting/mail-in ballots.) These four overlapping safeguards are not too burdensome for voters or pollworkers, but they would go a long way toward discouraging fraud at the precinct stations on Election Day.

Many other commonsense remedies are also available to help neutralize voter fraud, all of which should be universally employed. No early-voting/mail-in and absentee ballot should ever be separated from its cover sheet and counted until the voter's signature has been carefully checked against the registration file signature. Every envelope containing the marked absentee or early-voting/mail-in ballot should also be signed by an adult witness whose address should also be listed. (Ideally, these ballots would be notarized, but this involves too much trouble and expense.) And full signatures ought to be written; the Texas "mark" is clearly unacceptable. Also, the number of absentee ballots mailed to a single address should not exceed the number of voters registered at that address. It might also be a good idea to require that an absentee ballot be mailed to the voter's official registration address and no other, unless the voter swears that he will be absent from his locality for the entire duration of the absentee voting period. Every state should have a meticulously maintained, centralized list of registered voters that is frequently purged of duplicate registrations, the deceased, those who have moved out of the district and out of the state, felons, and legal or illegal aliens. (The vital statistics offices, corrections departments, post offices, and other appropriate government agencies should provide this information to each state's elections board at least twice a year.)[28] If, as in Texas, voters are permitted to vote without record of registration—a dubious practice—then at least the ballots ought to be cast provisionally, segregated from the clearly legal ones until their status can be determined. Election laws should always provide stiff penalties for candidates or campaign workers who remain present while a voter casts an absentee ballot. While the outright banning of paid voter registration solicitors is constitutionally untenable, states can eliminate per-person payments to these bounty hunters (thus taking away some of the incentive to register ineligible individuals and animals). States also can and should require regular disclosure filings by all such solicitation groups; the disclosures might include the names and addresses of both the persons employed and the individuals registered. Lastly, the ballots need to be counted in the full view of all interested parties, then professionally secured, sealed, and stored. And any precinct showing a substantial discrepancy between the voter sign-up total and the actual tally of ballots needs to be visited within a day of the election by supervisory officials. Surely, all this is not too much to ask as we prepare to enter the twenty-first century.

These regulations, even if followed to the letter, will be insufficient if (1) registrars and elections offices are not staffed and funded adequately; (2) the statutes do not punish fraud severely—major felonies are required, not minor misdemeanors; (3) law enforcement

authorities do not make voter fraud a priority and press for substantial legal penalties against those found violating the fraud
statutes; and (4) the news media do not begin to look for evidence of
voter fraud—a probable prerequisite to their finding it. A good first
step would be for every news organization to establish and publicize
a "campaign corruption hotline," mentioned earlier in the context of
the media's exposing push-polling.

We believe that these reforms will help to counteract the individual
corrupt practices that have been our focus in the chapters of this
book. But we have more fundamental concerns about the current
operation of the country's political and governmental system that
the targeted remedies do not address. The big-picture reform plan
must necessarily be greater than the sum of the specific targeted
reforms.

This is usually the point at which our fellow academic or journalistic idealists call for the creation of a parliamentary system in the
United States, or rigid term limits for all elected officials, or four-
year terms for the House of Representatives, or full public financing
of congressional elections. But in our view, these solutions are either
(for now) impractical pipe dreams, unwise alternatives, or both. The
parliamentary system's unitary executive-legislature is alien to two
centuries of American tradition, and there is no serious popular or
elite movement to undertake such a drastic change. In our opinion,
many good arguments against legislative term limits remain unan-
swered by their proponents, including the inevitable power shifts
that limits on legislative tenure bring to lobbyists, experienced
staffers, bureaucrats, and the executive branch generally. Four-year
terms for the House, with elections coinciding with the one for president, eliminate useful midterm course corrections by the voters.
And while we favor certain forms of public financing, such as free
mailings for congressional challengers and tax credits for small political contributions, there is enormous opposition in Congress and
the electorate to initiating full taxpayer funding of House and Senate campaigns in an era of large budget deficits and cuts in governmental services.

We prefer more realistic macro-remedies that will be explained in
the next section.

Campaign Finance Reform

One of the broad problems with our campaign financing system, highlighted by this book, is that our complex campaign regulatory structure—administered by the Federal Election Commission—has become catastrophically overburdened. That is why we see declining compliance with the law and the opening of ever-wider loopholes. Regulators are simply unable to keep up. As one knowledgeable critic of the current system has noted, the current state of affairs is corrosive:

> The FEC's weak enforcement has made the campaign finance laws a fraud on the public. Such sham reform not only breeds contempt for those laws among the lawmakers themselves, but also produces in turn contempt among the voters for politicians and the political process. This should not be surprising, since even the most honest candidates, seeing violations by their opponents going unpunished, feel tremendous pressure to cheat. This leads to a competitive cycle in which a loophole opened by one side is widened by the other, so that eventually there is little left of the original intent of the law.[29]

Undoubtedly, part of the situation has been a willful effort on the part of Congress to hamstring the Federal Election Commission, starve it of resources, and block any statutory improvements in the Federal Election Campaign Act. Yet a powerful new agency equipped with vast new funds administering a slew of new legal provisions might not make things any better. The system is already monstrously complex. As House Speaker Newt Gingrich fairly observed, "We've created all sorts of Mickey Mouse rules."[30] The 1995 edition of the Federal Election Commission's code of regulations stretches to 264 pages of dense legalese, virtually indecipherable to the layman.[31] It makes sense to ask whether we really want to complicate the law further and vest greater powers in a political regulatory agency.

There is a good argument to be made that in many respects, the FEC should be a weak agency. As the veteran election attorney Jan

Baran suggests, it is perhaps too idealistic and naive to suppose that the FEC can be "the first benign political police in the history of mankind." The United States has thrived on unfettered political activity; it is a core national value. Practically speaking, it may also be unrealistic to think that political participants—and the courts—will ever abide the draconian new restrictions on political activity contemplated by some reformers. Finally, there is a simple question of efficacy. The last two decades have produced greater regulation of politics than occurred in all of the preceding two centuries, and yet many critics contend that the problems are worse now than they have ever been. Is the logical step really more regulation?

The Real Ills

A critical symptom (and disturbing product) of the system's ills has been the growth of shadow campaign organizations allegedly outside the purview of the campaign laws, such as the Christian Coalition and GOPAC. As we have previously pointed out, anyone who visits the Federal Election Commission to learn more about the groups that were among the most important in the 1994 elections— the Christian Coalition, the term limit advocates, GOPAC—will be sorely disappointed. The Christian Coalition and term limit groups have not registered at all, while GOPAC discloses only about 10 percent of its activity. The failure of these groups to comply with campaign laws was the subject of FEC-inspired lawsuits as this was being written, but it appeared likely that the FEC would lose one or more of the cases. Regardless, the 1994 elections are over, and these organizations have already accomplished much of what they sought. If one were to perform a cost–benefit analysis, one would likely conclude that the potential political gains of refusing to comply with the campaign laws far outweigh the potential cost of running afoul of the FEC. As an agency asked to do far too much with far too little, the FEC lacks the authority to compel corrective actions promptly.

A similar and related problem at the federal level is the blurring of distinctions between the relatively unrestricted funds known as "soft" money (used to finance a party's general overhead and generic "get out the vote" appeals) and the tightly limited "hard" money (direct contributions to individual candidates). All hard money counts against the federal contribution limits (for example, $1,000 per candidate per election for an individual citizen), whereas only a portion of the soft money gifts do so. Yet the distinction between hard and soft money is increasingly artificial, part of the larger blurring of lines we sought to depict earlier in the book. Political operatives believe soft money can affect election outcomes just as directly as hard money, and they do not hesitate to use it in this manner.

The Keating Five case, a touchstone for all of the system's flaws, featured both a "non-federal" political action committee and huge amounts of soft money (as well as a 501(c)(3) foundation). Indeed, some 80 percent of the money at issue in that case was not subject to federal reporting requirements, prompting the Senate Ethics Committee to conclude that any campaign finance reform "will have to address these mechanisms for political activities, as well as campaign fundraising and expenditures directly by candidates, in order to deal effectively with the issues presented in these cases."[32]

The final major defect of the American system of campaign finance is its potent pro-incumbent bias. Since the 1970s, a declining sense of ideological and party loyalty has generally led political action committees and other special-interest contributors to gravitate with abandon toward incumbents of all persuasions, a trend that congressional Democrats both encouraged and exploited to maintain themselves in power for decades. Since the 1994 election, Republican legislators have done much the same, with the new majority party continuing the PAC shakedown. This practice reeks of cynical, principle-free influence-peddling, where lobbyists unashamedly try to secure access to powerful legislators with whom they usually disagree.

Phony Cures versus a Workable Solution: Deregulation Plus

The system's problems, then, are vexing. Indeed, is it possible to fashion a solution to all of them simultaneously? Over the years, the reformers' panacea has been taxpayer financing of elections and limits on how much candidates can spend. Public financing is a seductively simple proposition: if there is no private money, presumably there will be none of the difficulties associated with private money. But in a country such as ours, which places great emphasis on the freedoms of speech and association, it is unrealistic to expect that the populace at large or even many of the elite activists will come to support greater federal subsidization of our election system at the cost of their individual and group political involvements. Spending limits are also enticing. Are politicians raising and spending too much money? Let's pass a law against it! Yet such a statute may be difficult to enforce in an era when politicians and the public seek less regulation, not more—not to mention the serious, maybe fatal, problem of plugging all the money loopholes (the C(4)s; Supreme Court-sanctioned, unlimited "independent expenditures" by groups and individuals unconnected to a campaign, and so on). Once again, the biggest, the original, and the unpluggable loophole is the First Amendment.

Public financing and spending limits are both also objectionable on the basic merits: the right to organize and attempt to influence politics is a fundamental constitutional guarantee, derived from the same First Amendment protections that need to be forcefully protected. To place draconian limits on political speech is simply a bad idea. (The call for a ban on political action committees suffers from the same defect.)

Once again, even if candidates could be persuaded to comply voluntarily with a *public financing and spending limits scheme*, such a solution would fail to take into consideration the many ways that interest groups such as the Christian Coalition and labor unions can influence elections without making direct contributions to candidates. Even if we passed laws that appeared to be taking private money out, we would not really be doing so. This is a recipe for deception, and consequently—once the truth becomes apparent—for still greater cynicism.

In our opinion, there is another way, one that takes advantage of both current realities and the remarkable self-regulating tendencies of a free-market democracy, not to mention the spirit of the age.

Consider the American stock markets. Most government oversight of them simply makes sure that publicly traded companies accurately disclose vital information about their finances. The philosophy here is that buyers, given the information they need, are intelligent enough to look out for themselves. There will be winners and losers, of course, both among companies and the consumers of their securities, but it is not the government's role to guarantee anyone's success (indeed, the idea is abhorrent). The notion that people are smart enough, and indeed have the duty, to think and choose for themselves, also underlies our basic democratic arrangement. There is no reason why the same principle cannot be successfully applied to a free market for campaign finance.[33] In this scenario, disclosure laws would be broadened and strengthened, and penalties for failure to disclose would be ratcheted up, while rules on other aspects—such as sources of funds and sizes of contributions—could be greatly loosened or even abandoned altogether.

Call it *Deregulation Plus*. Let a well-informed marketplace, rather than a committee of federal bureaucrats, be the judge of whether someone has accepted too much money from a particular interest group or spent too much to win an election. Reformers who object to money in politics would lose little under such a scheme, since the current system—itself a product of reform—has already utterly failed to inhibit special-interest influence. (Plus, the reformers' new plans will fail spectacularly, as we have already argued.) On the other hand, reform advocates might gain substantially by bringing all financial activity out into the open where the public can see for itself the truth about how our campaigns are conducted. If the facts are really as awful as reformers contend (and as close observers of the system, much of what we see is appalling), then the public will be moved to demand change.

Moreover, a new disclosure regime might just prove to be *the* solution in itself. It is worth noting that the stock-buying public, by and large, is happy with the relatively liberal manner by which the Securities and Exchange Commission regulates stock markets. Companies and brokers (the candidates and consultants of the financial world) actually *appreciate* the SEC's efforts to enforce vigorously what regulations it does have, since such enforcement maintains public confidence in the system and encourages honest, ethical behavior, without unnecessarily impinging on the freedom of market players. Again, the key is to ensure the availability of the requisite information for people to make intelligent decisions.

Some political actors who would rather not be forced to operate in the open will undoubtedly assert that extensive new disclosure requirements violate the First Amendment. We see little foundation for this argument. As political regulatory schemes go, disclosure is by far the least burdensome and most constitutionally acceptable of any political regulatory proposal. The Supreme Court was explicit on this subject in its landmark 1976 *Buckley v. Valeo* ruling. The Court found the overweening aspects of the Federal Election Campaign Act (such as limits on spending) violated the Bill of Rights, but disclosure was judicially blessed. While disclosure "has the potential for substantially infringing the exercise of First Amendment rights," the Court said, "there are governmental interests sufficiently important to outweigh the possibility of infringement, particularly when the free functioning of our national institutions is involved."

The Court's rationale for disclosure remains exceptionally persuasive two decades after it was written:

> First, disclosure provides the electorate with information "as to where political campaign money comes from and how it is spent by the candidate" in order to aid the voters in evaluating those who seek federal office. It allows voters to place each candidate in the political spectrum more precisely than is often possible solely on the basis of party labels and campaign speeches. The sources of a candidate's financial support also alert the voter to the interests to which a candidate is most likely to be responsive and thus facilitate predictions of future performance in office.
>
> Second, disclosure requirements deter actual corruption and avoid the appearance of corruption by exposing large contributions and expenditures to the light of publicity. This exposure may discourage those who would use money for improper purposes either before or after the election. A public armed with information about a candidate's most generous supporters is better able to detect any post-election special fa-

vors that may be given in return. And . . . full disclosure during an election campaign tends "to prevent the corrupt use of money to affect elections." In enacting these requirements [the Congress] may have been mindful of Mr. Justice Brandeis' advice: "Publicity is justly commended as a remedy for social and industrial diseases. Sunlight is said to be the best of disinfectants; electric light the most efficient policeman."[34]

A new disclosure-based regime, to be successful, would obviously require more stringent reporting rules. *Most important, new reporting rules would require groups such as organized labor and the Christian Coalition to disclose the complete extent of their involvement in campaigns.* Currently, such groups rely on a body of law that holds that under the First Amendment, broadly based "nonpartisan" membership organizations cannot be compelled to comply with campaign finance laws, nor can groups that do not explicitly advocate the election or defeat of a clearly identified candidate.[35] However, expert observers of the current system, such as former Federal Election Commission chairman Trevor Potter, believe the Court has signaled that constitutional protection for such groups extends only to limits on how much they can raise or spend, not to whether they are required to disclose their activities.[36] The primary advantage of this step is that it would formally bring into the political sphere groups that clearly belong there. By requiring organizations such as GOPAC and labor unions to disclose, their role in elections can be more fully and fairly debated.

Another possible objection to broadening the disclosure requirements would be the fear that the rules would drag a huge number of politically active but relatively inconsequential players into the federal regulatory framework. Clearly, no one wants the local church or the Rotary Club taken to court for publishing a newsletter advertisement that indirectly or directly supports candidates of their choice. To our mind, this is easily addressed by establishing a high reporting threshold—something between $25,000 and $50,000 in total election-related expenditures per election cycle.[37] After all, the concern is not with the small organizations, but the big ones. GOPAC, the Christian Coalition, the term limits groups, and organized labor have all raised and spent millions of dollars annually and operated on a national scale. It is not hard to make a distinction between groups such as these and benign small-scale advocacy.

Another necessary broadening of disclosure would involve contributions made by individuals. While most political action committees already disclose ample data on their backers and financial activities, contributions to candidates from individuals are reported quite haphazardly.[38] New rules could mandate that each individual contributor disclose his place of employment and profession, without exception. The FEC has already debated a number of effective but not overly oppressive means of accomplishing this goal (although to date it has adopted only modest changes). The simplest solution is to *prohibit* campaigns from accepting contributions that are not fully disclosed. Disclosure of campaign *expenditures* is also currently quite lax, with many campaign organizations failing to make a detailed statement describing the purpose of each expenditure. It would be no great task to require better reporting of these activities as well.

The big trade-off for tougher disclosure rules should be the loosening of restrictions on fundraising. Foremost would be liberalization of limits on fundraising by individual candidates. This is only fair and sensible in its own right: there is a glaring disconnection between the permanent and artificial limitations on sources of funds and ever-mounting campaign costs. One of the primary pressures on the system has been the declining value in real dollars of the maximum legal contribution by an individual to a federal candidate ($1,000 per election), which is now worth only about a third as much as when it went into effect in 1975. This increasing scarcity of funds, in addition to fueling the quest for loopholes, has led candidates (particularly incumbents) to do things they otherwise might not do in exchange for funding. Perversely, limits appear to have increased the indebtedness of lawmakers to special interests that can provide huge amounts of cash by mobilizing a large number of $500 to $1,000 donors. By increasing contribution limits, candidates would enjoy more freedom to pick and choose among their contributors. Given the option, we hope more candidates would turn primarily to those contributors whose support is based on values and ideological beliefs, spurning the favor-seekers. Most candidates are not eager to sell their offices: they do it because they feel they must. For all their ambition, able politicians such as Bob Carr and Frank Lautenberg—so typical of the current system—are certainly not evil people. Each has expressed with genuine feeling a distaste for what the system forces him to do, as have many other members of Congress. By lifting disclosure and contribution levels at the same time, politicians' access to "clean" funds would rise at the same time that scrutiny of "dirty" funds would be increased. The idea is to concede that we cannot outlaw the acceptance of special-interest money, but the *penalties* for accepting it can be raised via the court of public opinion. So at the very least, the individual contribution limit should be restored to its original value, which would make it about $2,800 in today's dollars, with built-in indexing for future inflation. We would actually prefer a more generous limit of $5,000, which would put the individual contribution limit on a par with the current PAC limit of $5,000 per election.

For political parties, there seems little alternative to simply legitimizing what has already happened de facto: the abolition of all limits. When the chairman of a national political party bluntly admits that millions of dollars in "soft money" receipts mean that the committee will be able to spend millions of dollars in "hard money," it is time for everyone to acknowledge reality (see chapter 5). Moreover, such an outcome is not to be lamented. Political parties *deserve* more fundraising freedom, which would give these critical institutions a more substantial role in elections.

How would the new disclosure regime work? While the FEC has already moved to impose some tighter disclosure requirements, it lacks the resources as currently constituted to enforce the new rules across the board. However, the solution does not necessarily require a massive increase in funding. Under a disclosure regime, the agency could reduce efforts to police excessive contributions and other infractions, devoting itself primarily to providing information to the public. The commission's authority to audit campaigns randomly would have to be restored to ensure compliance, and sanctions for failure to disclose would have to be increased substantially. In addition, the commission should be given the power to seek emergency injunctions against spending by political actors who refuse to comply with disclosure requirements. And to move the FEC away from its frequent three-to-three partisan deadlock, the six political party commissioners (three Democrats and three Republicans) ought to be able to appoint a seventh "tie-breaker" commissioner. Presumably anyone agreeable to the other six would have a sterling reputation for independence and impartiality. Another remedy for predictable partisanship on the FEC would be a one-term limit of six years for each commissioner. Freed of the need to worry about pleasing party leaders in order to secure reappointment, FEC commissioners could vote their consciences more often and get tough with election scofflaws in both parties.

Finally, in exchange for the FEC relinquishing much of its police powers, Congress could suspend much of its power over the FEC by establishing an appropriate budgetary level for the agency that by law would be indexed to inflation and could not be reduced. Another way of guaranteeing adequate funding for a disclosure-enhanced FEC is to establish a new tax check-off on Form 1040 that would permit each citizen to channel a few dollars of her tax money directly to the FEC, bypassing a possibly vengeful Congress's appropriations process entirely. The 1040 solicitation should carefully note that the citizen's tax burden would not be increased by his designation of a "tax gift" to the FEC, and that the purpose of all monies collected is to inform the public about the sources of contributions received by political candidates. It is impossible to forecast the precise reaction of taxpayers to such an opportunity, of course, but our bet is that many more individuals would check the box funding the Federal Election Commission than the box channeling cash to the presidential candidates and political parties. In today's money-glutted political system, the people's choice is likely to be reliable information about the interest groups investing in officeholders.

Supplementary Improvements

One reform that would be essential to heightening the political peril a legislator would face when doing favors for big contributors: increased disclosure of congressional contacts with regulatory agencies. In the wake of the Keating scandal five years ago, Senate Majority Leader Bob Dole proposed just such a reform, which he dubbed the front-page test. With the knowledge that all of their telephone calls and letters to regulators would be placed on the public record, legislators would be forced to consider before each and every contact how the intervention would look on the front page of a newspaper. Reporters have been immeasurably aided in the effort to step up policing by public interest organizations that have devoted greater resources to campaign finance analysis.[39] Rather than pushing for public financing and spending limits, perhaps reformers would do better to concentrate their energies on performing their role as corruption watchdogs by seeking out and spotlighting instances of inappropriate conduct.

One final step to combat influence-peddling would be to alter the federal statutes that cover bribery and conflict of interest. Despite many examples of seemingly indictable campaign finance offenses (the Keating case being the most prominent), prosecutions for campaign finance bribery and conflicts of interest are exceedingly rare. At the same time, Congress has shown disinclination in the extreme to police such misconduct in-house (again, as shown by the Keating case). One thoughtful observer of the campaign finance system, attorney and former FEC official Kenneth Gross, has suggested that there are few prosecutions because influence-peddling statutes require proof of criminal intent and provide only for criminal prosecutions with severe penalties.[40] Putting someone in prison for doing favors in exchange for campaign contributions (but not personally profiting) is arguably disproportionate to the offense. Were such cases to be prosecuted in *civil* court instead, the stakes could be lowered considerably while the primary goal of such prosecutions—deterrence—would be preserved.

The purpose of all of these reforms is to make regulation of campaign financing more rational. Attempts to outlaw private campaign contributions or to tell political actors how much they can raise and spend are simply unworkable. Within broad limits, the political marketplace is best left to its own devices, and when those limits are exceeded, violators should be punished swiftly and effectively.

Regarding the pro-incumbent bias of contributors, there is unfortunately no obvious practical solution. It is impossible to predict how a deregulated system would affect the existing heavy bias toward incumbents by contributors, both PAC and individual. In truth, there may be no way to eliminate pro-incumbent financial bias.[41] However, it is possible that expanding private resources through deregulation will actually end up helping challengers more than incumbents. A substantial body of research shows that the amount an incumbent spends is less determinative of election outcomes than the amount a challenger spends.[42] Simply put, challengers do not need to match incumbent spending, but need merely to reach a "floor" of financial viability. Deregulation's greatest impact could actually be in helping challengers reach this floor. If fears about the effects a free market will have on competition prove warranted, however, a modest federal subsidy in the form of discounts on mail or broadcast time—so that every nonincumbent candidate could at least reach the floor—would seem reasonable and might be acceptable even to some conservatives as long as it was tied to deregulation.

If Deregulation Plus proves too radical, perhaps it is time to revive the sensible scheme proposed in 1990 by the U.S. Senate's Campaign Finance Reform Panel, which attempted to bridge the gap between partisans on the basic issues by suggesting many ideas, including so-called flexible spending limits.[43] These are limits on overall campaign spending by each candidate, with exemptions for certain types of expenditures by political parties (such as organizational efforts), as well as small contributions from individuals who live in a candidate's own state. Since the Supreme Court has ruled that spending limits must be voluntary, incentives such as reduced postal rates and tax credits for the small individual donations mentioned above should be offered.[44] The flexible limits scheme represents a reasonable compromise between the absolute spending limits with no exceptions favored by Democrats and the opposition to any kind of limits expressed by Republicans.

Flexible limits or Deregulation Plus ought to be supplemented by free broadcast time for political parties and candidates, as well as strengthened disclosure laws that cover every dollar raised and spent for political purposes.[45] Detailed free-time proposals have been made elsewhere but ignored by a Congress fearful of alienating a powerful lobby, the National Association of Broadcasters.[46] Yet no innovation would do more to reduce campaign costs or help challengers than this one. Fortunately, technological advances such as "digital" television—which will multiply available "analog" TV frequencies by a factor of about six once it is available in 1997—are creating new opportunities to implement an old idea. Federal Communications Commission chairman Reed E. Hundt has recently endorsed the provision of free time for candidates and parties once digital TV comes into being, noting that free time was "not practically achievable in an analog age [but is] entirely feasible with the capacity and band width explosion of the digital era."[47]

We cannot leave this subject without bringing up the fact that reform is needed not only at the federal level. While researching several of our chapters, particularly the investigation into vote fraud, we were struck by the inadequacy of many states' campaign finance lobbying and disclosure laws. At the very minimum, every state ought to provide broad disclosure of all political money, a computerized public disclosure system for campaign finance data, reasonably high caps on individual and political action committee contributions to candidates, and some kind of random auditing process to check the reports submitted.[48] Also useful for each state would be provision for tax credits for small individual contributions; a ban on honoraria (speaking fees) and strict gift limits for elected officials; full, year-round disclosure of lobbyist expenditures; tight supervision of the "revolving door" that finds state employees leaving government to take lucrative jobs with special interests they have previously been regulating; and the establishment of an ethics office or commission to handle complaints, educate public officials, and issue advisory opinions about relevant subjects. There is much work to be done here; for instance, only about half the states currently have any kind of ethics board.[49]

Conclusion

One final, vital question needs to be posed as we consider the subject of corruption and reform: *Where will we be in ten years if the problems identified in this volume are not addressed?* Historically, it is clear that corruption inexorably grows like a slow cancer unless checked. Practices once deemed unthinkable become commonplace, and the burning desire of ambitious politicians and consultants to guarantee victory leads them to go where no electionauts have gone before, to conquer and pillage additional ethical territory with each passing campaign. In short, experience in and around political circles leads to an inescapable conclusion: politicians and the people who run their campaigns will do what they must do to win and will try to get away with as many electorally profitable shenanigans as possible. Not all candidates or consultants fit this description; maybe most do not. But standards are often defined by the lowest common denominator, and if some are "getting away with it," most others will follow in order to remain competitive.

At regular intervals, the American press and public have interrupted this degenerative cycle by blowing the whistle on corruption and making the cost of these practices higher than their gain on Election Day. If corruptus interruptus can be engineered now, the rollback and cleanup can begin. But if corruption is not exposed and the reformist impulse delayed or extinguished, many of the practices described in these pages will become bolder and more widespread.

If no price is to be paid for push-polling, or misuse of congressional mailing and staff, or vote fraud, then why should its practitioners cease and desist? If the public does not care about dirty tricks on the campaign trail, or street money, or the misappropriation of nonprofit group privileges, then why should politicians and consultants? The stakes are high, and the call for reform must be heard and answered soon lest the citizenry sink further into the stupor of cynicism that is already apparent.

Appendix: List of Interviews

The authors and their research team conducted a total of 303 interviews, mainly by telephone but some in-person. Fifty-seven of the interviews were off the record, and these names are *not* included below. Representatives and senators are listed with their district and the dates of the interview, and the remaining individuals are listed with their titles and the dates of the interview. A few interviewees requested prior approval of any direct quotations from their sessions, and we complied; however, a substantive change in a quotation was subsequently made in only one minor instance. We took the liberty of correcting interviewees' grammar, but in no case did we alter the meaning of their words. The vast majority of interviews were tape-recorded, and the tapes have been preserved.

Former Representatives

Barlow, Tom
D-Ky.-1
1/16/95

Byrne, Leslie
D-Va.-11
1/10/95

Cantwell, Maria
D-Wash.-1
1/20/95

Cooper, Jim*
D-Tenn.-4
1/31/95

Coppersmith, Sam*
D-Ariz.-1
1/18/95

English, Karan
D-Ariz.-6
1/13/95

Fingerhut, Eric
D-Ohio-19
1/23/95

Hoagland, Peter
D-Nebr.-2
1/17/95

Huffington, Michael*
R-Calif.-22
4/14/95

Inslee, Jay
D-Wash.-4
1/18/95

Johnson, Don
D-Ga.-10
1/23/95

Klein, Herb
D-N.J.-8
1/17/95

Kreidler, Mike
D-Wash.-8
2/3/95

LaRocco, Larry
D-Idaho-1
2/6/95

McCloskey, Frank
D-Ind.-8
2/13/95

Price, David
D-N.C.-4
1/31/95

Shepherd, Karen
D-Utah-2
1/8/95

Strickland, Ted
D-Ohio-6
1/27/95

Synar, Mike
D-Okla.-2
1/27/95

Unsoeld, Jolene
D-Wash.-3
1/20/95

*Denotes ran and lost Senate race in
    1994.

Former Senators

Durenburger, Dave
R-Minn.
1/25/95

Wofford, Harris
D-Pa.
2/13/95

Current Representatives

*Baldacci, John***
R-Maine-2
1/6/95

Bass, Charles
R-N.H.-2
1/18/95

Bilbray, Brian
R-Calif.-49
1/23/95

Burr, Richard
R-N.C.-5
1/26/95

Chabot, Steve
R-Ohio-1
11/30/94

Coburn, Tom
R-Okla.-2
12/1/94

Cubin, Barbara
R-Wyo.-at large
1/24/95

Davis, Tom
R-Va.-11
1/17/95

Ehrlich, Bob
R-Md.-2
1/17/95

Ford, Harold
D-Tenn.-9
2/15/95

Fox, Jon
R-Pa.-13
1/27/95

Funderburk, David
R-N.C.-2
1/25/95

Goodlatte, Bob
R-Va.-6
3/3/95

Graham, Lindsey
R-S.C.-3
3/23/95

Hastings, Doc
R-Wash.-4
11/30/94

LaHood, Ray
R-Ill.-18
11/30/94

Metcalf, Jack
R-Wash.-2
1/24/95

Ney, Bob
R-Ohio-18
1/23/95

Salmon, Matt
R-Ariz.-1
1/20/95

Sanford, Mark
R-S.C.-1
1/24/95

Seastrand, Andrea
R-Calif.-22
1/27/95

Thornberry, William
R-Tex.-13
1/25/95

Tiarht, Todd
R-Kans.-4
12/5/94

**Italicized names indicate freshman
representatives.*

343

General List

Alper, Jill
Deputy Political Director
Democratic National Committee
7/17/95

Anderson, Robert
Republican Candidate 1994
North Carolina 7th District
2/15/95

Appell, Keith
Senior Account Executive
Creative Response Concepts
12/18/95

Arnold, Bill
Clerk
Texas House Elections Committee
4/17/95, 4/18/95

Ashenfelter, Orley
Professor of Economics
Princeton University
11/30/94

Attlesey, Sam
Reporter
Dallas Morning News
4/4/95

Ballenger, William
Editor
Inside Michigan Politics
2/14/95

Baran, Jan
Attorney
Wiley, Rein, and Fielding
6/12/95

Barbour, Haley
Chairman
Republican National Committee
2/26/95, 5/31/95

Barren, Jeff
Executive Director
New York Christian Coalition
3/9/95

Bauer, Robert
Counsel
Democratic Congressional
    Campaign Committee
4/23/95

Begala, Paul
Democratic Political Consultant
8/3/95

Bennett, Rick
Republican Candidate 1994
Maine 2d District
11/23/94

Berlin, George
Projects Director
Turnberry Associates
1/27/95

Bernard, Beth
Campaign Manager
Wynia for Senate 1994
11/29/94

Bernick, Bob
Reporter
Deseret News
1/25/95

Bernstein, Alan
Political Writer
Houston Chronicle
4/18/95

Billmeyer, Richard
Consultant
National Republican Congressional
  Committee
12/12/95

Bishop, Kevin
Press Secretary
Steve Stockman (R-Tex.-9)
12/16/95

Black, Charles
Republican Political Consultant
8/10/95

Bocscor, Nancy
Republican Political
  Consultant
3/8/95

Boesey, Alex
Executive Director
Michigan Asphalt Paving
  Association
1/31/95

Boren, Jim
Reporter
Fresno Bee
3/27/95

Boyd, Michael
Airline Consultant
Aviation Systems Research
  Corporation
1/24/95

Brown, Jeffrey
President
Campaigns Plus
4/26/95

Bunch, Gary
Executive
Bank of Kingston
1/12/95

Bury, Blair
Midwest Asphalt Corporation
2/2/95

Cahill, Mary Beth
Executive Director
Emily's List
2/2/95

Callahan, Bill
President
Unitel, Inc.
12/16/95

Carrick, Bill
Democratic Political Consultant
8/2/95

Carter, Kip
Campaign Treasurer (1974–78)
Newt Gingrich for Congress
1/10/95

Carville, James
Democratic Political Consultant
8/14/95

Cerrcll, Joseph
Democratic Political
  Consultant
7/28/95

Churchill, Jane
President
Across the Aisle
4/26/95

Connorly, Mitt
Former Campaign Manager

Newt Gingrich for Congress
12/4/95

Connors, Jack
Deputy Legal Counsel
Republican National
    Committee
7/18/95

Cooley, Dave
Partner
McNeely, Pigot, and Fox
5/18/95

Cooper, Terry
Republican Political Consultant
Terry Cooper Research
12/9/95

Cottington, Scott
Republican Political
    Consultant
12/17/95

Cox, Claudine
Former GOPAC Contributor
12/14/94

Cox, James
Partner
Morrisard & Rossi
1/19/95

Cross, Al
Reporter
Louisville Courier-Journal
6/29/95

Culnan, Mary
Associate Professor
Georgetown University
School of Business
5/3/95

Cuscla, Kristen
Press Secretary
Phil English (R-Pa.-21)
12/1/94

Dail, Jack
Staff Director
Congressional Commission on
    Mailing Standards
2/24/95

Diddel, A. Glenn
Attorney
The Diddel Law Firm (owner)
4/24/95

Didier, Jodie
Congressional District Coordinator
Illinois Christian Coalition
3/14/95

Dunn, Anita
Democratic Media Consultant
11/28/95

Dutton, Leslie Carol
Executive Director
Citizens Protection Alliance
4/11/95

Edgell, John
Former Democratic Congressional
    Staffer
11/18/95

Edmonds, Thomas
Republican Political Consultant
8/2/95

Ellison, Donald
President
Advanced Paving Corp.
1/30/95

Ellison, Wayne
Assistant District Attorney
Fresno County
4/14/95

Fazloloah, Mark
Reporter
Philadelphia Inquirer
7/18/95

Flader, Joe
Administrative Assistant
Rep. Thomas Petri (R-Wis.- 6)
4/7/95

Fierce, Don
Director, Strategic Planning &
  Congressional Affairs
Republican National
  Committee
2/28/95

Fowler, Donald
Chairman
Democratic National Party
3/15/95

Fraser, Barry
Legal Research Advocate
Privacy Rights Clearinghouse
5/5/95

Frederick, Keith
Democratic Political Consultant
8/7/95

Freeman, Matt
Director of Research
People for the American Way
12/23/94

Gans, Curtis
Director

Committee for the Study of the
  American Electorate
5/12/95

Garin, Geoff
President
Garin-Hart Strategic Research
4/13/95

Gartland, Patrick
State Director
Georgia Christian Coalition
3/8/95

Gillespie, Edward
Congressional Staff
Representative Dick Armey
  (R-Tx.-26)
6/10/95

Gold, David
President
Gold Communications Company
4/27/95

Goodman, Adam
Republican Political Consultant
7/28/95

Gordon, Mike
President
Gordon & Schwenkmeyer
7/20/95

Ginsberg, Ben
Partner
Patton Boggs LLP
6/20/95

Grabinski, Tom
State Director
Arizona Christian Coalition
3/10/95

Grant, Kari
Political Director
Aristotle Industries
2/17/95

Greene, Lyn
Owner
Greene & Associates/
Adjunct Professor of Political
    Science
California State Polytechnic Uni.
2/17/95

Groff, Neal C.
President
The Madison Group
1/18/95

Gross, Kenneth
Former Enforcement Officer
Federal Election Commission
6/20/95

Guterboch, Thomas
Associate Professor
University of Virginia, Department
    of Sociology
2/10/95

Haaland, Doug
Political Consultant
Haaland Communications
3/29/95

Hales, Eddie
Legal Counsel
National Association for the
    Advancement of Colored People
4/10/95

Hanauer, Jill
Executive Director

Interfaith Alliance
12/4/95

Hansbrough, Charles "Mac"
President
National Telecommunications
    Services
4/14/95, 4/19/95

Harris, Joshua
Former Employee
Southern Education Council
11/30/94

Heller, David
Democratic Political Consultant
Politics, Inc.
11/29/94, 8/3/95

Hendricks, Evan
Publisher
Privacy Times
5/11/95

Henshaw, Mark
Director of Finance
Tennessee Democratic Party
2/15/95, 2/16/95

Hickman, Harrison
Democratic Political Consultant
8/5/95

Hiltachk, Tom
Counsel
Michael Huffington, R-Calif.
4/5/95

Horn, Steve Jr.
Campaign Director
Steve Horn for Congress 1994
2/17/95

Hopkins, Bruce
Attorney, Author
Specializes in Representation of
Tax-Exempt Organizations

Hunter, Bob
Attorney
Patton Boggs LLP
4/17/95

Imhoff, Walter
Principal
Hanifen, Imhoff Inc.
1/23/95

Ingels, Kirk
Chairman
Capital City Christian Coalition
(Austin, Texas)
3/17/95

Innocenzi, Jim
Republican Political Consultant
8/2/95

Jensen, Jean
Executive Director
Virginia Democratic Party
2/15/95

Johnson, David
Executive Director
Virginia Republican Party
2/14/95

Johnson, John
Investigator
Tulare District Attorney's Office
5/8/95

Jordan, Albert
Partner

Wallace, Jordan, Ratliff, Byers, &
Brandt
3/27/95

Kamber, Vic
Democratic Political Consultant
8/3/95

Kane, Dennis
Former Staffer
House Banking Committee
11/28/94

Kane, Robert
President
Intrusion Detection
5/3/95

Keene, David
Republican Political
Consultant
8/3/95

Keating, David
President
National Taxpayers Union
2/15/95

Klaus, Christopher William
President
Internet Security Systems Inc.
5/2/95

Kogovsek, Ray
President
Kogovsek & Associates
1/20/95

Kompa, Michael
President
Corum Real Estate
1/17/95

Kopp, Mike
Press Relations
Jim Cooper for Senate 1994
4/25/95

Kortz, Donald
President/CEO
Fuller & Co.
1/19/95

Kubiak, Gregg
Former Congressional Staffer
Senator David Boren (D-Okla.)
2/14/95

Laquidara, Cindy
Partner
Laquidara & Edwards
1/25/95

Larson, Reed
President
National Right to Work Committee
3/3/95

Luke, Colin
Chairman
Ballot Security Attorneys for the
    Alabama Republican Party
3/24/95

Luntz, Dr. Frank
President
Luntz Research & Companies
5/5/95

McConville, Tim
Vice President of Communications
    and Development
National Right to Work Committee
12/10/94

McClung, Dan
Managing Director

Campaign Strategies, Inc.
1/7/95

McLemore, David
Staff Writer
Dallas Morning News
4/18/95

MacNett, Steve
General Counsel
Republican Majority, Pennsylvania
    State Senate
7/18/95

Mahe, Eddie
Republican Political Consultant
7/28/95

Maloney, Gary
President
The Jackson-Alvarez Group
5/9/95

Mangum, Michael
President
C. C. Mangum Inc.
1/27/95

Marks, Bruce
Former Pennsylvania State Senator
2d District, Philadelphia
7/18/95

Marshall, Debbie
Senior Legislative Assistant
Representative Vernon J. Ehlers
    (R-Michigan-3)
2/16/95

Mellman, Mark
Democratic Political
    Consultant
8/14/95

Meredith, Michael
County Chairman/District Director
  (Rockingham)
Virginia Christian Coalition
3/15/95

Milo, Anthony
Deputy Director
Michigan Asphalt Paving
  Association
2/6/95

Montgomery, Pam
Citizen activist
Greene County Alabama
8/21/95

Morgan, John
Strategist/Political Demographer
Republican National Committee
12/10/94

Morgan, Olivia
Former campaign aide, 1994
Pennsylvania Democratic Party
8/9/95

Morgan, Tim
California Attorney
Private practice
3/30/95

Mulligan, Anne
Director, Legislative Affairs
New York Christian Coalition
3/14/95

Murphy, Mike
Senior Partner
Murphy, Pintak, Gautier
6/27/95

Newhouse, Neil
Partner

Public Opinion Strategies
4/20/95

Nordlinger, Gary
Democratic Political Consultant
8/7/95

O'Connor, Jeannette
Woman Vote Project Coordinator
Emily's List
3/4/95

Parker, Tony
President
The Parker Group
4/28/95

Pauls, William
President
E. F. International
1/20/95

Payne, Dan
Political Consultant
7/28/95

Pena, David
Former Candidate, County Clerk
Starr County, Texas
4/20/95

Pepple, Randy
Campaign Consultant
Rick White (R-Wash.-1)
11/30/94

Potter, Trevor
Chairman (former)
Federal Election Commission
4/15/95

Prescott, Douglas
Project Manager

HNTB Corporation
1/26/95

Reed, Dr. Joe
Chairman, Montgomery Office
Alabama Democratic
    Conference
4/10/95

Reed, Ralph
Executive Director
Christian Coalition
5/4/95, 5/11/95

Riddle, Kay
Former Executive Director
GOPAC
11/28/95

Ritchie, Tom
President
Ritchie Paving
2/1/95

Roach, David
Press Secretary
Pat Williams
4/24/95

Roberts, John
Republican Political Consultant
11/28/95

Robinson, Richard
Chairman, CEO
Robinson Dairies
1/23/95

Rodriguez, Juan
Legislative Correspondent
Rep. Luis Gutierrez (D-Ill.-4)
2/14/95

Rollins, Ed
Chairman
Rollins International
5/26/95

Russo, Sal
Republican Political Consultant
8/3/95

Saranita, Karin
Chairperson
Fair Election Foundation
4/14/95

Scheckler, Lew
Coordinator, Southwestern
    Virginia
Virginia Christian Coalition
3/14/95

Schenker, Rick
Executive Director
Pennsylvania Christian
    Coalition
3/10/95

Segal, Michael
President
The Advance Research Group
5/3/95

Sellers, Fred
Chairman
Oklahoma Christian Coalition
3/16/95

Settle, James
Former Director
National Computer Crimes Unit,
    Federal Bureau of
    Investigation
12/5/95

Severin, Jay
Republican Political Consultant and
   Talk Show Host
12/17/95

Shea, Wev
Former U.S. Attorney
State of Alaska
3/9/95

Shepherd, Lee
Reporter
Tax Analysis, Inc.
12/9/95

Sherbert, Bruce
Electon Administrator
Dallas County
4/20/95

Sherman, Bob
Vice President
Computer Assisted Research On Line
5/1/95

Shinay, Michael
Director
House Post Office
3/9/95

Shirley, Craig
Republican Political Consultant
8/7/95

Shulem, Jeff
Chief Financial Officer
Data + Imagination Incorporated
2/13/95

Siegal, Mark
Democratic Political Consultant
8/2/95

Smoot, Samantha
Regional Field Director
Democratic Congressional
   Campaign Committee
12/9/94

Sontag, Frederick
President
Unison Industries
1/25/95

Spillane, Kevin
Opposition Researcher
The Stonecreek Group
5/10/95

Spohrer, Bill
President
Challenge Air Cargo
1/24/95

Stirton, Ian
Press Officer
Federal Election
   Commission
5/18/95

Stockmeyer, Steve
Executive Vice President
National Association of Business
   PAC
12/12/94

Stohler, Sally
Press Secretary
David Price Campaign 1994
2/17/95

Struble, Karl
Democratic Political
   Consultant
8/3/95

Svendson, Paul
Campaign Manager 1994
Karen Shepherd (D-Utah-2)
1/20/95

Sweeney, John
Commissioner of Labor
State of New York
7/18/95

Sweitzer, Thomas "Doc"
Democratic Political Consultant
7/28/95

Tobe, Amy
Campaign Manager 1994
Mike Synar (D-Okla.-2)
3/6/95

Tomkins, Tim
Campaign Manager
David Price Campaign 1994
2/9/95

Tomkins, Warren
Administrative Assistant
Governor Caroll Campbell, S.C.
3/10/95

Torano, Maria
President
Maria Elena Torano Associates
1/26/95

Towery, Matt
Georgia State Representative
(R-Vinings)
4/5/95

Trippi, Joe
Democratic Political Consultant
8/2/95

Van Schaack, H. C.
General Partner
Van Schaack Associates

Vargas, Clark
President
C. Vargas & Associates
1/26/95

Varoga, Craig
Political Consultant
12/16/95

Vigilante, Kevin
Republican House Candidate, 1994
12/12/95

Watson, Bobby
Deputy Executive Director
Democratic National Committee
3/7/95

Watterson, Russell
Partner
Watterson & Fair Inc.
1/18/95

Weiner, Rick
Former Chairman
Michigan Democratic Party
2/15/95

Weinhold, Dick
Chairman
Texas Christian Coalition
3/8/95

Welchert, Steve
Democratic Political Consultant
The Welchert Company
1/7/95

Weyrich, Paul
President
Free Congress Foundation/
    National Empowerment
    Television
5/16/95

Wice, Jeff
Counsel
Democratic Legislative Leaders
    Association
3/6/95

Wilcox, Clyde
Professor
Georgetown University
11/28/95

Williamson, Julie
Democratic Political Consultant
11/29/94

Winters, Ron
Minister
Resurrection Baptist
    Church
3/9/95

Worley, David
Attorney
1/20/95

Wright, Dale
Former Assistant Attorney
    General
Kentucky
7/18/95

Zemsky, Calvin
President
Florida Engineering
    Consulting
1/24/95

Notes

PREFACE

1. Out of the many thousands of books written by political scientists or journalists, the experts and publishers we contacted could identify only a handful produced by joint authorship. Among the works cited were Susan and Martin Tolchin, *Selling Our Security: The Erosion of America's Assets* (New York: Knopf, 1992); Linda Witt, Karen Paget, and Glenna Matthews, *Running as a Woman: Gender and Power in American Politics* (New York: Free Press, 1994); and Neal R. Peirce, Curtis Johnson, and John Stuart Hall, *Citistates: How Urban America Can Prosper in a Competitive World* (Washington, D.C.: Seven Locks Press, 1993).

INTRODUCTION

1. There is a wealth of material documenting this point. Of particular interest are Stephen Pizzo, Mary Fricker, and Paul Muolo, *Inside Job: The Looting of America's Savings and Loans* (New York: McGraw-Hill, 1989); Kathleen Day, *S&L Hell: The People and Politics Behind the Savings and Loan Scandal* (New York: W. W. Norton, 1993); and Brooks Jackson, *Honest Graft: Big Money and the American Political Process* (New York: Alfred A. Knopf, 1988). Press accounts and House Ethics Committee investigations detailing the entanglements of House Banking Chairman Fernand St. Germain and Speaker James C. Wright provide additional evidence.
2. This is particularly true of Cranston. See Senate Select Committee on Ethics, "Investigation of Senator Alan Cranston," 102 Cong., 1 sess., 1991, S. Rept. 102-223, pp. 8–12.

3. The committee issued a reprimand containing no substantive sanction.

4. Senate Committee, "Investigation of Senator Alan Cranston," pp. 8–12.

5. *Congressional Record,* November 20, 1991, p. S17174.

6. Ibid., p. S17175.

7. A useful one-volume survey of American corruption is Nathan Miller, *Stealing from America: A History of Corruption from Jamestown to Reagan* (New York: Paragon House, 1992).

8. See Nelson Trottman, *History of the Union Pacific* (New York: Ronald Press, 1923), pp. 30–54, 71–91; Robert G. Athearn, *Union Pacific Country* (Lincoln: University of Nebraska Press, 1976), pp. 123–27; and John P. Davis, *The Union Pacific Railway* (Chicago: S. C. Griggs, 1894), pp. 163–202.

9. In 1874 a piece of special legislation was attached to an appropriations bill, which permitted the Justice Department to prosecute culpable Crédit Mobilier and Union Pacific executives so as to recover excess capital. The U.S. attorney general brought suit against 170 individuals in a circuit court, but the court threw out the suit for technical reasons. On appeal, the circuit court decision was upheld in the Supreme Court in *United States v. Union Pacific Railroad Company et al.* (98 U.S. 569 [1879]). See Trottman, *History of the Union Pacific,* p. 88.

10. See Lincoln Steffens, *The Shame of the Cities* (New York: Hill and Wang, 1904, 1968). The book was largely a reprinting of Steffens's earlier articles in *McClure's.*

11. 18 U.S.C. 610.

12. George Thayer, *Who Shakes the Money Tree?* (New York: Simon and Schuster, 1973), pp. 61–65. See also Alexander Heard, *The Costs of Democracy* (Chapel Hill: University of North Carolina Press, 1960), pp. 352, 357–59.

13. Frank J. Sorauf, *Money in American Elections* (Glenview, Ill.: Scott, Foresman/Little, Brown, 1988), p. 33.

14. For more information about the Teapot Dome scandal, see Burl Noggle, *Teapot Dome: Oil and Politics in the 1920s* (Baton Rouge: Louisiana State University Press, 1962); James L. Bates, *The Origins of Teapot Dome: Progressives, Parties and Petroleum, 1909–1921* (Urbana: University of Illinois Press, 1963); and Charles L. Mee Jr., *The Ohio Gang: The World of Warren G. Harding* (New York: M. Evans, 1981).

15. The Senate acted in 1924; Fall was convicted in 1929, and he entered prison in 1931—a full decade after his original misdeed.

16. Incredibly, even though he had already been warned about Fall's activities, Harding actually told the press he offered to appoint Fall to the Supreme Court when Fall resigned as interior secretary on March 4, 1923. Fall declined the appointment, which of course would have required Senate confirmation.

17. For a detailed description of the Watergate scandal, see Carl Bernstein and Bob Woodward, *All the President's Men* (New York: Simon and Schuster, 1974); Bernstein and Woodward, *The Final Days* (New York: Simon and Schuster, 1976); Theodore White, *Breach of Faith: The Fall of Richard M. Nixon* (New York: Atheneum, 1975); Richard Ben-Veniste and George Frampton, *Stonewall* (New York: Simon and Schuster, 1977); and Sam J. Ervin, *The Whole Truth: The Watergate Conspiracy* (New York: Random House, 1980).
18. Public Law 92-225, 86 Stat. 3 (1971). See also 2 U.S. Code 431-455.
19. Public Law 93-443, 88 Stat. 1263 (1974).
20. The 1971 FECA had first established the checkoff fund, but the 1974 amendments wrote the rules of primary and general election public funding.
21. 424 U.S. 1 (1976).
22. Expenditure limits were upheld for presidential candidates who voluntarily accept public funding.
23. Public Law 94-283, 90 Stat. 475 (1976).
24. Public Law 96-187, 93 Stat. 1339 (1979).
25. The Iran-contra affair, the House of Representatives "House bank" scandal, and financial controversies involving many Cabinet officers would certainly qualify. For a review of many of these incidents see Suzanne Garment, *Scandal: The Crisis of Mistrust in American Politics* (New York: Times Books, 1991); and Larry J. Sabato, *Feeding Frenzy: How Attack Journalism Has Transformed American Politics* (New York: Free Press, 1993).
26. Or at the state level, a governor and his aides; or at the local level, a mayor and her inner circle.
27. From Merrill D. Peterson (ed.), *The Portable Thomas Jefferson* (New York: Penguin Books, 1977), p. 198.
28. A superb overview of this many-splendored subject is provided by Arnold J. Heidenheimer, Michael Johnson, and Victor T. LeVine (eds.), *Political Corruption: A Handbook* (New Brunswick, N.J.: Transaction Publishers, 1989). See also the bibliography in ibid., pp. 1007–14. Among many dozens of books on the subject of political corruption, two of our favorites are John T. Noonan Jr., *Bribes* (New York: Macmillan, 1984); and Bruce L. Felknor, *Political Mischief: Smear, Sabotage, and Reform in U.S. Elections* (New York: Praeger, 1992). See also Peter DeLeon, *Thinking about Political Corruption* (Armonk: M. E. Sharpe, 1993).
29. V. O. Key Jr., *The Techniques of Political Graft in the United States* (Chicago: University of Chicago, 1936), esp. pp. 386–400.
30. For a defense of patronage, see Larry J. Sabato, *The Party's Just Begun: Shaping Political Parties for America's Future* (Glenview, Ill.: Scott, Foresman/Little, Brown, 1988), pp. 229–32.

31. For a defense of PACs, see Larry J. Sabato, *PAC Power: Inside the World of Political Action Committees* (New York: W. W. Norton, 1984).

32. For a discussion of real and pseudo corruption, see Larry J. Sabato, *Paying for Elections: The Campaign Finance Thicket* (New York: Priority Press, 1989), pp. 1–5.

33. See Heidenheimer et al., *Political Corruption,* pp. 213–1006; and Noonan, *Bribes,* pp. 3–424.

34. See Noonan, *Bribes*, pp. 427–680.

35. Glenn R. Simpson, "Frosh May Be Republican, But They Aren't Very Rich," *Roll Call*, November 14, 1994, p. 1.

36. *Congressional Record,* November 20, 1991, p. S17175.

PART I. REVOLUTION

1. Committee for the Study of the American Electorate, "GOP Gains First Vote Plurality since 1946, Turnout Rises Modestly, Democratic Troubles, Volatility Predicted" (Washington, D.C., June 23, 1995), pp. 1–8.

2. Craig C. Donsanto, *Federal Prosecution of Election Offenses,* 6th ed. (Washington, D.C.: U.S. Department of Justice, Criminal Division, Public Integrity Section, January 1995), p. 97.

CHAPTER 1. THE EDUCATION OF A HOUSE-WRECKER

1. Howell Raines, "Prof Eyeing House Race," *Atlanta Journal-Constitution,* December 25, 1973, p. A9.

2. Ibid.

3. Gingrich for Congress Executive Committee Meeting, September 30, 1974, p. 1. This document and many of the other original Gingrich campaign materials cited in this section were obtained indirectly from an archive at West Georgia State College kept by Gingrich and curated by his long-time associate and biographer Mel Steely. While the archive is not open to public access today, some of the materials kept there were obtained by the authors from other sources.

4. Ibid. These are quotations from the meeting's minutes, rather than direct quotations of Gingrich.

5. Newt Gingrich, "America's Real Problems—Rough Draft," Steely Collection, 1974.

6. "Notes from Newt," circa July 1974, p. 1.

7. Cliff Green, "Congress," *Atlanta Journal-Constitution,* July 22, 1974, p. A12.

8. The precise provenance of these charges is unclear. Gingrich does not appear to have dredged them up himself, but he clearly was responsible for

making them a major issue in the campaign. In a November 3, 1974 article, the *Atlanta Journal-Constitution* said Gingrich had been "releasing a series of charges against Flynt in the Atlanta news media." Cliff Green, "Gingrich Is Tough One for Rep. Flynt," p. B15.

9. Brad Cutts, "Gingrich 'Appalled' Flynt Took Ford Money," *Atlanta Journal-Constitution,* September 21, 1974, p. 3.

10. Flynt complained that the farm was barely operational and asserted that the staff member spent little time there. His response to the Ford allegations was far less convincing.

11. Rex Granum, "Gingrich Hits Flynt Fund Use," *Atlanta Journal-Constitution,* October 16, 1974, p. A10.

12. Sam Hopkins, "Gingrich Scoffs at Ford Land Statement," *Atlanta Journal-Constitution,* September 27, 1974, p. A10.

13. "Newt Gingrich for Congress," Speech Text, November 3, 1974, p. 3.

14. John M. Barry, *The Ambition and the Power* (New York: Viking, 1989) p. 532.

15. Minutes of Key Leaders meeting, Hapeville Headquarters, October 20, 1974, p. 1. Steely Collection. For reasons that are unclear, a key portion of this document, "Newt's Summary," on page 8, has apparently been blotted out in the copy obtained by the authors.

16. Interview with L.H. "Kip" Carter, January 10, 1994.

17. The minutes indicate that he was present during this discussion.

18. Former Gingrich campaign treasurer L. H. Carter said that the campaign often engaged in this practice.

19. Carter is clearly a Gingrich antagonist, and thus his assertions about the Speaker should be regarded with caution. However, the authors have independently confirmed many of Carter's assertions and ultimately found him to be a credible source.

20. "Notes from Newt," p. 2.

21. Minutes of Key Leaders meeting, Hapeville Headquarters, October 20, 1974, p. 1.

22. "Newt Gingrich for Congress," p. 4

23. This sentence is the first recorded use by Gingrich of the adjective "grotesque," later to become a favored grenade in the Gingrich rhetorical arsenal.

24. Interview with Steven Stockmeyer, December 9, 1994.

25. "Gingrich Speaks to Young Republicans," August 24, 1976, p. 2.

26. Ibid, p. 2.

27. Dave Hamrick, "Gingrich Flies to Washington, Attacks Flynt on Home Ground," *Fayette Sun,* September 30, 1976, p. 1.

28. Ibid.

29. Gingrich News Conference Statement, October 14, 1976, p. 1.

30. Prepared remarks, Newt Gingrich Fundraising Dinner, Holiday Inn, Atlanta, October 29, 1977.
31. Gingrich flier.
32. An article in the *West Georgia News,* published on October 27, just a week before the election, reported that the Shapard campaign had misdated by about two weeks two loans Shapard made to her campaign. The errors were of little consequence, but Gingrich's aide hinted darkly that they were scandalous and illegal.
33. *Atlanta Journal-Constitution,* "Labor Support Gave Gingrich Victory in 6th," November 21, 1978.
34. Gingrich letter to Robert Claxton, March 16, 1979.
35. *West Georgia News,* June 24, 1978, p. 8.
36. Ann Woolner, "Gingrich Fights to Build Party," *Atlanta Journal-Constitution,* November 27, 1979, p. C1.
37. O'Neill was chastised for calling Gingrich's remarks "the lowest thing" he had seen in his career.
38. John E. Yang, "Gingrich's Fiery Fight to Prove Wright Is Wrong Has GOP House Colleagues Scurrying for Cover," *Wall Street Journal,* May 20, 1988.
39. *Congressional Record,* June 22, 1987, p. H5345.
40. *Congressional Record,* May 19, 1988, p. H3422.
41. Associated Press, April 27, 1989.

CHAPTER 2. THE OLD ORDER

1. It is possible to find political scientists on both sides of the question of whether a partisan gerrymander is effective. Gary King and Andrew Gelman argue that it is possible to promote a partisan bias in an electoral system through redistricting, and also that redistricting generally promotes responsiveness (see King and Gelman, "Enhancing Democracy through Legislative Redistricting," *American Political Science Review* 88 [September 1994]: 541–59). Likewise, Peverill Squire describes the correlation between declining competitiveness in congressional races during the 1980s and partisan redistricting (see Squire, "The Partisan Consequenses of Congressional Redistricting, *American Politics Quarterly* 23 [April 1995]: 229–40). Donald Ostdiek argues that partisan gerrymanders in the 1980 congressional redistricting were accomplished by diluting the strength of dominant parties in safe districts (see Ostdiek, "Congressional Redistricting and District Typologies," *Journal of Politics* 57 [May 1995]: 533–43). However, this view is by no means unchallenged. Richard G. Niemi and Alan I. Abramowitz accept that redistricting can offer short-term partisan benefits under conditions of one-party dominance but pre-

sent evidence from the 1992 election to show that party control at the state level did not, on average, bring benefits to the ruling party (see Niemi and Abramowitz, "Partisan Redistricting and the 1992 Congressional Elections," *Journal of Politics* 56 [August 1994]: 811–17). Following a similar approach, Mark Rush argues that demographic variability over time frustrates would-be gerrymandering efforts and that the theoretical models of voting behavior that political scientists use fail to capture the nuances of actual voting and therefore fail to explain the behavior (see Rush, *Does Redistricting Make a Difference? Partisan Representation and Electoral Behavior* (Baltimore, Md.: Johns Hopkins University Press, 1993).

2. Terry Catchpole, *How to Cope with COPE: The Political Operations of Organized Labor* (New Rochelle, N.Y.: Arlington House, 1968), p. 59.

3. J. David Greenstone, *Labor in American Politics* (Chicago: University of Chicago Press, 1977), p. 177.

4. Jonathan Cottin and Charles Culhane, "Washington Pressures COPE's Political Craftsman: Build Smooth Organization," *National Journal,* September 12, 1970, p. 1965.

5. Catchpole, *How to Cope with COPE,* p. 352.

6. National Education Association, *Budget: Fiscal Year 1994–95* (Washington: National Education Association, 1995), p. iv.

7. Ibid., p. 1-1.

8. Ibid., p. 3-6.

9. Ibid.

10. Ibid., p. 1-5.

11. U.S. Federal Election Commission, *Federal Election Commission's Top 50 PAC's by Receipts 1993–94,* June 7, 1995.

12. The authors arrived at these figures by analyzing contributor lists and identifying trial lawyers, their relatives, and employees of their law firms using a list of members of the Association of American Trial Lawyers, as well as newspaper articles and other published material.

13. This figure includes only contributions of $200 or more.

14. Alexander P. Lamis, *The Rise of the Two-Party South* (New York: Oxford University Press, 1984), p. 22.

15. Summary page of Receipts and Expenditures, Friends of Bob Carr, 1989–90, Federal Election Commission. Campaign contribution data were retrieved from the Federal Election Commission's computerized database.

16. Summary page of Receipts and Expenditures, Friends of Bob Carr, 1991–92, Federal Election Commission. To be fair, it is also true that Carr faced a tough opponent in 1992 and was unopposed in 1990. Some of the increase in contributions undoubtedly resulted from stepped-up fundraising efforts by Carr, but the comparison remains valid. In 1986

and 1988, when he had strong opponents, Carr's fundraising was similar to that in 1990. In any case, most modern politicians raise money at a frenetic pace even when they do not have opposition.

17. Itemized contributions, Friends of Bob Carr, 1991–92, Federal Election Commission.

18. Anne Rackham, "Construction Management Firms Watch Billings Rise," *Los Angeles Business Journal,* August 29, 1994, p. 13.

19. See "Pulse," *Engineering News-Record,* July 12, 1993, p. A28, and "Three MBE/WBE Firms Chosen to Provide Construction Management Services for the MTA," *PR Newswire,* February 26, 1993.

20. House Transportation Appropriations Subcommittee, *Hearings,* April 28, 1992, pp. 148–49.

21. Department of Transportation and Related Agencies Bill, Report 102-639, p. 153.

22. Tara Parker Pope, "Off to a Flying Start; Metro's Better Bus Plan Well Recieved by Key House Panel," *Houston Chronicle,* April 29, 1992, p. 1. This issue is discussed in greater detail below.

23. House Transportation Appropriation Subcommittee, *Hearings,* April 28, 1992, p. 186.

24. Eve Lubalin, *Presidential Ambition and Senatorial Behavior: The Impact of Ambition on the Behavior of Incumbent Politicians,* Ph.D. diss. (Johns Hopkins University, 1981), p. 5.

25. Four senior current and former Lautenberg staff were interviewed about the fundraising practices of Lubalin and Lautenberg on condition of anonymity, and the authors established the reliability of all four. We rely on their commentary primarily for context, background, and confirmation of documentary evidence. With a few minor exceptions, we base specific allegations about fundraising and legislative activity on publicly available documents.

26. Senator Lautenberg's willingness to tap his private funds, crucial in his 1982 victory over opponent Millicent Fenwick, significantly decreased in his 1988 and 1994 campaigns for reelection.

27. Memorandum from Eve Lubalin to Mimi Walsh and Jennifer Cohen, July 2, 1993, p. 1. Portions of this memo and other Lubalin writings were originally published in *Roll Call* on March 31 and April 11, 1994. The authors established beyond doubt the authenticity of the materials, obtained from a confidential source.

28. Memo from Lubalin to Walsh and Cohen, July 2, 1993, p. 1.

29. Memo from Lubalin to Walsh and Cohen, July 2, 1993, p. 1.

30. Itemized receipts, Lautenberg for Senate, 1993–94, Federal Election Commission.

31. See Glenn R. Simpson, "Cash and Aid Linked in Lautenberg Memo; Transportation Industry Targeted for Gifts," *Roll Call,* March 31, 1994, p. 1.

32. Letter from Senator Frank Lautenberg to Acting Federal Aviation Administrator Joseph M. Del Balzo, July 9, 1993.

33. "Senate DOT Appropriations Bill Includes $1.8 Billion for Airports," *Airports* 10, (October 1993): 393. The bill also directed the FAA to send $10 million to Chicago's O'Hare Airport and the San Juan, Puerto Rico Airport.

34. Memo from Lubalin to Walsh and Cohen, July 2, 1993, p. 1.

35. Laura Parker, "FAA Shops Used Car Lots and Finds a 'Cadillac,' " *Washington Post,* September 26, 1988, p. A13.

36. Memo from Lubalin to Walsh and Cohen, July 2, 1993, p. 2.

37. Ibid.

38. Simpson, "Cash and Aid Linked in Lautenberg Memo," p. 1.

39. "Infrastructure: Appropriations Panel Said Developing Tough Criteria for Project Selection," *BNA Washington Insider,* April 23, 1993.

40. Itemized contributions, Friends of Bob Carr, 1993–94, Federal Election Commission.

41. See Peter Mitchell, "Lynx Added to Lobbyists' List of Clients," *Orlando Sentinel,* March 26, 1993, p. B3.

42. Van den Berg later retired but was retained as a consultant for the Greater Orlando Airport Authority. At the time, Arkin was named as a possible successor for the legal counsel position. See Roger Roy, "Van den Berg May Stay as a Consultant to GOAA; Attorney, Associates Will Continue to Advise Authority," *Orlando Sentinel,* May 15, 1995, Central Florida Business, p. 17.

43. Interview with Douglas Prescott, January 26, 1995.

44. Interview with Carl Vargas, January 26, 1995.

45. Michael Griffin, "House Panel Approves $7 Million for LYNX-Trolley System Left Out," *Orlando Sentinel,* June 25, 1993, p. B1. The grant was later scaled back to $2.5 million at the insistence of the Senate.

46. Committee Report 103-543, June 9, 1994, pp. 66, 139.

47. Alan Byrd, "Orlando Airport Gets Millions From Feds," *Orlando Business Journal* 11 (October 7, 1994): 20.

48. Interview with Maria Torano, January 26, 1995.

49. John Williams, "All Funds Are Fungible, Except . . . ," *Houston Chronicle,* September 27, 1994, p. A27.

50. House Transportation Appropriations Subcommittee, *Hearings on Department of Transportation and Related Appropriations for 1994, Testimony of Members of Congress and Public Witnesses,* 103 Cong., 1st sess., part 7A, p. 728.

51. John Williams, "Congressional Panel OKs Most Metro Funds," *Houston Chronicle,* October 16, 1993, p. A40.

52. The fundraiser was hosted by attorney Jonathan Day of Mayor, Day, and Caldwell.

53. "Hands Off Metro: Taxpayers Must Be Weaned from Transit Fund," *Houston Post,* March 31, 1994, p. A28.
54. Rosalind Jackler and Karen Weintraub, "Federal Transit Agency Looking at Metro; But Not on Official Basis," *Houston Post,* May 27, 1994, p. A31.
55. Rosalind Jackler and Karen Weintraub, "Metro's Spending Plans Attract Federal Scrutiny," *Houston Post,* May 26, 1994, p. A1.
56. T. R. Goldman, "Asphalt Pavers Roll Back Tire Recycling Program," *Legal Times,* October 19, 1994, p. 5. The only published account of Carr's connections to the asphalt lobby, Goldman's piece understandably missed the massive campaign donations flowing into Carr's coffers from the roadbuilders.
57. Interview with Bill Ballenger, February 14, 1995.
58. "Why a PAC Decided to Pack It In," *Nation's Business* 71 (December 1983): 17.

CHAPTER 3. A SPECIAL REVOLUTIONARY ORGANIZATION

1. Gingrich cited Mao's observation (fully, "War is politics with blood; politics is war without blood") in explaining his philosophy in a May 26, 1995, speech.
2. Walter Dean Burnham, *Critical Elections and the Mainsprings of American Politics* (New York: Norton, 1970), pp. 6-7.
3. David Pace, "Gingrich Says Almost All of His PAC's Money Went to Pay Mail Costs," Associated Press, January 27, 1988.
4. "Notes from Newt," circa July 1974, p. 2
5. This part of Gingrich's story is already well known, and there is little we can add. We recommend to the reader John M. Barry's masterful *The Ambition and the Power* (New York: Viking, 1989), an inside account of Wright's fall.
6. As Barry noted, Gingrich cultivated the press, planting "seeds" with reporters—true or untrue charges about Wright. Then Gingrich used the anti-Wright stories that resulted from his labors as proof of the charges. One blatant example of a Gingrich-planted falsehood involved an allegation regarding the developing savings and loan scandal. While in Miami in 1987, Gingrich met with Tom Fiedler, political reporter for the *Miami Herald*. As Barry recounts, Gingrich sought out Fiedler for the interview; regarding Fiedler's story, he notes: "The story also said that 'Wright, according to published accounts, used his influence to block federal investigations into the lending practices of friends and supporters.' That statement was false. The article added, 'Gingrich said his charges are based on numerous news accounts.' Many of those news accounts Gingrich had generated" (from Barry, *The Ambition and the Power,* p. 532).

7. Larry Margasak, "Gingrich Used Wright Case as Fund-Raising Tool," Associated Press, June 14, 1989.

8. Ibid.

9. Barry, *Ambition and the Power,* p. 243.

10. One account captures the significance of the relationship of public opinion and Congress succinctly: "In 1973 when Gallup first asked Americans how much confidence they had in seven institutions, Congress ranked fourth; 42 percent of respondents expressed a 'great deal' or 'quite a lot' of confidence in it. It followed the church and organized religion (66 percent), public schools (58 percent), and the Supreme Court (44 percent). In 1994, of those same seven institutions, Congress ranked last; only 18 percent of Americans expressed a great deal of confidence or quite a lot in it." (Karlyn Bowman and Everett Carll Ladd, "Public Opinion toward Congress: A Historical Look," in Thomas E. Mann and Norman J. Ornstein, *Congress, the Press, and the Public* [Washington, D.C.: American Enterprise Institute and Brookings Institution, 1994], p. 53).

11. Newt Gingrich, "The Gingrich Manifesto; The New GOP Whip Says It's Time to Clean House," *Washington Post,* April 4, 1989, p. B1.

12. David Mould, "Gingrich Denounces Congressional Corruption," United Press International, August 16, 1988.

13. Susan F. Rasky, "Representative Newt Gingrich: From Political Guerrilla to Republican Folk Hero," *New York Times,* June 15, 1988, p. A24.

14. Ibid.

15. E. J. Dionne, "G.O.P. Keeping Up Ethics Pressure on the Democrats," *New York Times,* May 29, 1989, p. A1.

16. Newt Gingrich, "Driving Realignment from the Presidency Down to the Precincts; How Realignments Occur: Six Historic Principles," delivered February 9, 1989. While the source of the document requested anonymity, its authenticity has been confirmed beyond question.

17. Burnham, *Critical Elections and the Mainsprings of American Politics.*

18. Burnham himself, it should be noted, acknowledged (on pages 26-27 of *Critical Elections*) that "the precise timing of the conditions which conduce to realignment is conditioned heavily by circumstance, of course: the intrusion of major crises in society and economy with which 'politics as usual' in the United States cannot adequately cope, and the precise quality and bias of leadership decisions in a period of high political tension, cannot be predicted in specific time with any accuracy."

19. Newt Gingrich, "Driving Realignment from the Presidency Down to the Precincts; How Realignments Occur: Six Historic Principles."

20. Burnham, pp. 7–8.

21. All further Gingrich quotations in this section are from "Driving Realignment."

22. Other projects included "demanding a Capital City Americans can be

proud of," "developing a conservative doctrine on drugs and crime," "developing a 'reform slate' of referenda to be placed on state ballots," and "opening the Republican Party up to minorities, especially in urban areas." Most of these are familiar Gingrich projects.

23. Interview with Kay Riddle, November 28, 1994.
24. Letter by Newt Gingrich, "Campaign for Fair Elections: A Project of GOPAC," June 1989.
25. 2 U.S.C. 431 (8)(a).
26. 2 U.S.C. 431 (9)(a).
27. Remarks of Newt Gingrich before the Heritage Foundation, Federal News Service, August 22, 1990.
28. Letter of Newt Gingrich to Jack Kemp, January 3, 1991.
29. Letter of Richard Pomboy to Newt Gingrich, December 4, 1990.
30. Jeff Gerth and Stephen Labato, "The Local Forces That Helped Shape Gingrich as a Foe of Regulation," *New York Times,* February 12, 1995, p. 22.
31. Michael Hinkelman, "Newt's Patron Reaps Harvest," *Atlanta Business Chronicle,* October 23, 1989, p. 1A.
32. Jeff Gerth and Stephen Labato, "The Local Forces That Helped Shape Gingrich as a Foe of Regulation."
33. Letter of Newt Gingrich to Robert A. Mosbacher, November 1, 1989.
34. Letter of Newt Gingrich to L. Joyce Sampers, assistant secretary, Economic Development Administration, June 13, 1991.
35. Gerth and Labato, "Local Forces," p. 22.
36. Gingrich's role in setting up the meeting is reflected in a September 27, 1991, letter from Associate Chief Accountant John M. Riley of the Securities and Exchange Commission to Gingrich.
37. "Renewing American Civilization Draft," n.d.
38. Exempt Organization Tax Review, January 1995, vol 11., no. 1, p. 44.
39. Letter of Michael F. Anton to Newt Gingrich, June 2, 1992.
40. Letter of James R. Hunt to Michael F. Anton, May 19, 1992.
41. Letter of Newt Gingrich to William K. Riley, June 22, 1992.
42. *Atlanta Journal-Constitution,* July 10, 1993, p. B2.
43. Letter of Newt Gingrich and GOPAC to potential contributors, n.d., circa September 1994.
44. Letter of Newt Gingrich to Leon Panetta, September 2, 1994.
45. Authored by political scientist Douglas Kooperman, an aide to Representative Richard Armey.
46. David Broder, "Monopoly on Congress," *Washington Post,* August 10, 1994, p. A19. Broder said the issues raised by the report "ought to engage both scholars and political journalists," which we interpret as a gentle chiding of each group for its failure to do so previously. The notion that

Democrats established a political monopoly over Congress by question-able means remains an unpopular one in both academia and journalism.

47. Jonathan Rauch, *Demosclerosis: The Silent Killer of American Government* (New York: Times Books/Random House, 1993); Mancur Olson, *The Rise and Decline of Nations: Economic Growth, Stagflation, and Social Rigidities* (New Haven, Conn.: Yale University Press, 1982).

48. Even this figure depends upon the survey one wishes to cite. The figure quoted (18 percent) is from the 1994 Gallup Poll; a similar question in the National Opinion Research Center survey for 1993 found only 7 percent of respondents willing to say they had a great deal of confidence in Congress. See Bowman and Ladd, "Public Opinion Toward Congress," p. 54.

CHAPTER 4. THE LORD'S WORK

1. For simplicity's sake, we identify religious conservatives as evangelicals. The religious conservative movement embraces a wide variety of de-nominations, but "evangelical" is the most widely accepted term.

2. "Preachers in Politics," *U.S. News & World Report,* September 24, 1979, p. 37.

3. Paul Edwards, "Survey Confirms Liberal, Conservative Party Images," *Washington Post,* July 6, 1978, p. D2.

4. James Mann, "Preachers in Politics: Decisive Force in '80," *U.S. News & World Report,* September 15, 1980, p. 24.

5. Michael Isikoff and Mark Hosenball, "Pat Robertson: Hawking Vita-mins—and Skin Cream from the Holy Land," *Newsweek,* October 3, 1994, p. 42.

6. Allan J. Mayer, "A Tide of Born-Again Politics," *Newsweek,* September 15, 1980, p. 28.

7. John Herbers, "Ultraconservative Evangelicals a Surging New Force in Politics," *New York Times,* August 17, 1980, p. 1.

8. "Preachers in Politics," *U.S. News & World Report,* September 24, 1979, p. 37.

9. Mayer, "A Tide of Born-Again Politics," p. 28.

10. Thomas B. Edsall, "TV Preacher Eyes GOP Nomination," *Washington Post,* August 19, 1985, p. 1.

11. See, for example, Thomas B. Edsall, "GOP Fund-Raiser Plans 'Nonpar-tisan' Vote Drive," *Washington Post,* June 6, 1984, p. A10.

12. Thomas B. Edsall, "Fundraising Methods of Pat Robertson Council Questioned," *Washington Post,* June 6, 1986, p. A1.

13. Ibid.

14. Thomas B. Edsall, "High-Stakes Fundraiser Benefits Robertson," *Washington Post,* May 17, 1986, p. A6.
15. Ibid.
16. Edsall, "Fundraising Methods," p. A1.
17. Thomas B. Edsall, "Pledge Made to IRS to Avoid Campaign," *Washington Post,* June 21, 1986, p. A4.
18. Jeff Gerth, "Tax Data of Pat Robertson Groups Are Questioned," *New York Times,* December 10, 1986, p. B11.
19. Charles R. Babcock, "Robertson's $11 million in Spending Leads Rivals," *Washington Post,* October 16, 1987, p. A3.
20. Charles R. Babcock, "Robertson Computer Sold to Firm above Cost," *Washington Post,* October 22, 1987, p. A1.
21. Charles R. Babcock, "Robertson: Blending Charity and Politics," *Washington Post,* November 2, 1987, p. A1.
22. Benjamin Hart, "Abbie Hoffman's Nightmare," *Policy Review* (Fall 1987): 72.
23. Interview with Ralph Reed, May 4, 1995.
24. Bruce R. Hopkins, *The Law of Tax Exempt Organizations* (New York: John Wiley and Sons, 1987), p. 549.
25. "Introduction to Christian Leadership School," Christian Coalition Leadership Manual (Chesapeake, Va.), p. 1.1.
26. Ibid., p. 1.2. As a fourth reason, Reed also listed the Supreme Court's *Webster* decision, which returned some decisions on abortion laws to the states.
27. Ibid., p. 1.4.
28. Ibid., p. 3.3.
29. Ibid., p. 3.1.
30. Interview with Ralph Reed, May 11, 1995.
31. Interview with Ralph Reed, May 4, 1995.
32. "Introduction to Christian Coalition Leadership School," p. 36.
33. Ibid., p. 3.23.
34. Ibid., p. 3.26
35. Interview with Ralph Reed, May 11, 1995.
36. Ibid.
37. "Introduction to Christian Coalition Leadership School," p. 6.17.
38. Ibid.
39. Ibid., p. 6.18.

CHAPTER 5. INSURRECTION

1. Interview with Haley Barbour, who related Dole's words, February 24, 1995.

2. Glenn R. Simpson, "Republicans Step Up Pressure on PACs as November Gains Seem More Certain," *Roll Call,* October 6, 1994.

3. Charles Babcock and Ann Devroy. "Gingrich Foresees Corruption Probe by a GOP House; Party Could Wield Subpoenas against 'Enemy' Administration," *Washington Post,* October 14, 1994, p. A1.

4. For example, see Peter Stone's analysis of soft money, "Labyrinth of Loopholes," *National Journal,* November 25, 1995, p. 2912.

5. Interview with David Durenberger, January 25, 1995.

6. Charles R. Babcock, "Amway's $2.5 Million Gift to GOP, the Largest Ever," *Washington Post,* January 11, 1995, p. A1.

7. A coalition of thirty-seven corporate telecommunications managers wrote to Senate Majority Leader Bob Dole urging him to support these amendments, which would allow for a quick and simultaneous entry of all would-be competitors into all communications markets ("Corporations Lobby Dole on Telco Bill," *National Journal Congress Daily,* June 6, 1995). Officials from Amway cosigned the letter.

8. Gingrich is regarded as the "Godfather" of FDA reform (Peter H. Stone, "Ganging Up on the FDA," *National Journal* 27 [February 18, 1995]). He has publicly denounced the agency as "the leading job killer in America" and branded FDA Commissioner David A. Kessler "a thug and a bully."

9 Interview with Kay Riddle, November 28, 1994.

10. Interview with Brian Bilbray, January 23, 1995; interview with Kevin Vigilante, December 12, 1995.

11. Interview with Claudine Cox, December 14, 1994.

12. Ruth Marcus, "GOP Donation Aided Right to Life Group; Money Was Not Earmarked, Sen. Gramm Explains," *Washington Post,* February 12, 1995, p. A27.

13. Pat Robertson, remarks at the Christian Coalition "Road to Victory" conference, September 1994.

14. Interview with Don Johnson, January 23, 1995.

15. Ibid.

16. Interview with Sam Coppersmith, January 18, 1995.

17. Interview with Karan English, January 13, 1995.

18. Interview with Leslie Byrne, January 10, 1995.

19. Interview with Eric Fingerhut, January 23, 1995.

20. Ibid.

21. Interview with Ralph Reed, May 4, 1995.

22. Interview with Ted Strickland, January 27, 1995.

23. Interview with Ralph Reed, May 4, 1995.

24. Interview with Tom Barlow, January 16, 1995.

25. Interview with Leslie Byrne, January 10, 1995.

26. Interview with Don Johnson, January 23, 1995.

27. Interview with Ralph Reed, May 4, 1995.

28. Interview with Jeff Barren, March 9, 1995.

29. Interview with Eric Fingerhut, January 23, 1995.

30. Interview with Kevin Bishop, December 16, 1995.

31. A National Public Radio reporter happened to be doing a story on Inhofe and recorded the exchange, though she did not realize the significance of what she had picked up. Linda Killian, "Oklahoma Senate Race Focuses on Negative Ads," National Public Radio's *All Things Considered,* November 7, 1994.

32. Matt Campbell, "Freeman Campaign Spreads Literature of Christian Coalition," *Kansas City Star,* November 4, 1994, p. C3.

33. The authors obtained from the Christian Coalition a set of 193 voter guides for House and Senate contests. While there were some 470 races, the set provided by the coalition covers most of the races considered "competitive" and is thus, for our intents, an almost complete set and certainly representative of the voter guide program as a whole.

34. *Congressional Record,* March 30, 1994. There were several votes on various term limits measures in the House in early 1995, but the overall pattern for Republicans was 75–25 percent, and for Democrats, 25–75 percent.

35. Interview with Ralph Reed, May 4, 1995.

36. Ibid.

37. Memo from Ralph Reed to the authors, August 8, 1995.

38. See 26 USCS at 501(c)(3) (1994).

39. Probably a conservative estimate.

40. See, respectively, Josh Sugarmann, *NRA: Money, Firepower, Fear* (Washington, D.C.: National Press Books, 1992), p. 88; and Federal Election Commission, Communications Cost Index, 1993–94 (Washington, D.C., April 8, 1995), p. 51.

41. The only news accounts of which we are aware were written by coauthor Simpson for the Capitol Hill newspaper *Roll Call.*

42. Paul South, "NRA Endorses Walter Jones," *Virginian-Pilot,* October 27, 1994, p. B1.

43. Conservative estimate based on authors' calculations. There are an average of 10,000 to 12,000 NRA members per congressional district, and the bumper stickers went to some 240 House races.

44. Doug Monroe, "Southerners Have Something to Say," *Atlanta Journal-Constitution,* January 27, 1995, p. G2. The figure is from the *Journal's* polling; nationwide about 17 percent of drivers have bumper stickers.

45. Interview with Kenneth Gross, June 20, 1995.

46. According to internal GOPAC records, ALT supporters Fred Sacher and K. Tucker Anderson together have given GOPAC in excess of $350,000.

47. David Rogers, "Conservatives Fund Campaign to Limit Terms," *Wall Street Journal,* November 4, 1994.
48. These scripts were obtained from a confidential source.
49. These scripts were obtained from a confidential source.
50. Letter of Charles Mack to Washington association executives and PAC directors, January 12, 1995.
51. Tim Curran, "House GOP Claims Fundraising History," *Roll Call,* May 29, 1995, p. 1. At the same point in 1994, the NRCC had raised just $3.4 million.

CHAPTER 6. DIRTY TRICKS REDUX

1. Interview with Joseph Cerrell, July 28, 1995.
2. Interview with James Carville, August 14, 1995.
3. Interview with Bob Sherman, August 7, 1995. Sherman is vice president of Computer Assisted Research On Line in North Miami, Florida.
4. Interview with Gary Nordlinger, August 7, 1995.
5. John F. Persinos, "Gotcha!" *Campaigns and Elections* 15 (August 1994): 20–23, 56–58.
6. "The Political Pages, 1995–96," *Campaigns and Elections* 17 (February 1995): 47.
7. Interview with Eddie Mahe, August 7, 1995.
8. Interview with Doc Sweitzer, July 28, 1995.
9. Interview with Sal Russo, August 1, 1995.
10. Interview with Jane Churchill, April 26, 1995. Churchill is president of Across the Aisle in Austin, Texas.
11. Diana Walsh, "Databases Used to Dig Up Dirt on Candidates," *San Francisco Examiner,* May 6, 1994, p. A1.
12. Katie Kerwin, "Files Reveal Benson's Nasty Divorce," *Rocky Mountain News,* September 23, 1994, Local News, p. 5A.
13. Interview with Gary Maloney, May 9, 1995. Maloney is president, The Jackson-Alvarez Group, McLean, Virginia.
14. Ibid.
15. Editorial, "Private Life of Bruce Benson: Should Voters Care?" *Rocky Mountain News,* September 25, 1994, p. 102A.
16. Interview with Bob Sherman, April 28, 1995.
17. Ibid.
18. Interview with Kevin Spillane, May 10, 1995. Spillane is a managing partner of The Stonecreek Group.
19. Ibid.
20. See Jack Germond and Jules Whitcover, *Whose Broad Stripes and Bright*

Stars? The Trivial Pursuit of the Presidency, 1988 (New York: Warner Books, 1989) pp. 10–12, 157.

21. Tom Precious, "Cuomo vs. Pataki: Going Negative Goes High-Tech in the Information Age, Politicians Are More Vulnerable Than Ever," *Albany, N.Y., Times-Union,* October 2, 1994, p. A1.

22. Dwayne Yancey, "Scribbler Sought Goods on Goodlatte," *Roanoke Times,* October 28, 1992, p. A1. We have examined a photocopy of the original legal pad. Detailed material about Zach Wamp, a 1992 GOP U.S. House candidate in the Third District of Tennessee, was also included. In his youth, Wamp had had a self-admitted addiction to cocaine and various legal problems, such as bad checks written in college. All of this was duly noted on the legal pad, along with other actual or suspected sins. Wamp narrowly lost his race in 1992—his past transgressions were controversial—but he won the Chattanooga-based seat in the Tennessee Republican landslide of 1994.

23. Interview with Robert Goodlatte, March 3, 1995.

24. Interview with Dan Payne, July 28, 1995.

25. Interview with James Carville, August 14, 1995.

26. G. Gordon Liddy, *Will: The Autobiography of G. Gordon Liddy* (New York: St. Martin's Press, 1980), p. 237.

27. Interview with Michael Segal, May 3, 1995. Segal is president of The Advance Research Group in Cambridge, Massachusetts.

28. Ibid.

29. Interview with Bill Carrick, August 2, 1995.

30. Frank Phillips, "Detectives Probe Romney for Kennedy Campaign," *Boston Globe,* August 19, 1994, p. 1.

31. Michael Isikoff and Mark Hosenball, "Snooping for Pols," *Newsweek,* September 5, 1994, p. 73.

32. Ibid.

33. Ibid.

34. Reed Branson, " 'Gumshoe' Asks about Bredesen, Supporters Accuse GOP of Hiring Spy," *Commercial Appeal,* October 7, 1994, p. 9B.

35. Reed Branson, "State Warns Private Eye: Halt Probe of Bredesen," *Commercial Appeal,* October 15, 1994, p. 13A.

36. All together, the Clinton campaign spent $93,000 on Palladino. Michael Isikoff, "Back Doing the Wright Stuff for the President; In Reprise of Campaign Role, Former Clinton Aide Joins Fight against Latest Sex Allegation," *Washington Post,* December 25, 1993, p. A4.

37. Michael Isikoff, "Clinton Team Works to Deflect Allegations on Nominee's Private Life," *Washington Post,* July 26, 1992, p. A18.

38. Interview with Ian Stirton, press officer, Federal Election Commission, Washington, D.C., May 18, 1995.

39. Interview with Kevin Spillane, May 10, 1995.

40. Ann Devroy, "GOP Aide Probed Party Candidate," *Washington Post,* January 3, 1990, p. A4.

41. Bill Thomas, "Heard on the Hill," *Roll Call,* January 22, 1990, p. 1. Maloney went from research director to deputy director for strategy.

42. Michael Isikoff, "Perot Unit Hired Private Eyes to Probe Volunteers; California Firm Was Paid More than $78,000 for Security and 'Background Checks,' " *Washington Post,* October 1, 1992, p. A10.

43. Interview with Dan Payne, July 28, 1995. In addition, Stephen Esack refers to the 1993 race in "Appellate Candidates Sign Fair Ad Pledge," *Pennsylvania Law Weekly,* April 24, 1995, p. 30.

44. The consultant who related this incident permitted us to use it on the condition that all names were deleted.

45. Interview with David Keene, August 3, 1985.

46. Chris Burritt, "Spy Scandal Snares N.C. Democrats," *Atlanta Journal-Constitution,* November 17, 1993, p. 3.

47. Danny Lineberry, " 'Scannergate' Was No Trifling Matter," *Durham Herald-Sun,* April 17, 1994, editorial, p. A16.

48. The first was the interception of Virginia Lieutenant Governor Douglas Wilder's phone conversation by an associate of Virginia Senator Charles Robb. See Donald P. Baker, "Wilder Says He's Bugged: Rivals Have Secret Tapes, Governor Claims," *Washington Post,* June 8, 1991, p. A1; and Larry J. Sabato, *Feeding Frenzy* (New York: Free Press, 1993), pp. 292–94.

49. Interview with John Roberts, November 28, 1994.

50. Dan Harrie, "Shepherd, Cook Join to Condemn Investigation of Donor Records in 2d District; Shepherd, Cook Condemn Search," *Salt Lake City Tribune,* October 28, 1994, p. B1.

51. Tony Semerad, "Waldholtz Acknowledges Hiring a Private Eye, 2d District Candidate Cites Death Threats; Opponents Are Critical Waldholtz Hired an Investigator," *Salt Lake City Tribune,* October 27, 1994, p. C1.

52. Interview with Karen Shepherd, January 8, 1995.

53. "Magnum P.I., Check Your Messages," *Kansas City Star,* November 5, 1994, p. A14.

54. Interview with John Roberts, November 28, 1994.

55. Interview with Sal Russo, August 1, 1995.

56. See 15 USCS at 1681b (1994). The "Consumer Credit Protection" section of the statute clearly specifies the situations in which, and to whom, consumer reporting agencies (such as Equifax or TRW) may provide credit information.

57. Interview with Paul Begala, August 3, 1995.

58. "When Politics Hits Bottom," *Atlanta Journal-Constitution,* October 30, 1994, editorial, p. R4.

59. Celia Sibley, "Checking Up on Campaign Rivals; Crews Search Puts Issue in Spotlight," *Atlanta Journal-Constitution,* October 20, 1994, p. J1; Sibley,

"'Withdraw from Race,' County GOP Urges Crews Opponent," *Atlanta Journal-Constitution,* October 29, 1994, p. J1.

60. "When Politics Hits Bottom," p. 4.

61. Richard Whitt and Mark Sherman, "GOP-Hired Info Peddler Known as 'Loose Cannon,' " *Atlanta Journal-Constitution,* November 5, 1994, p. B7. Viator denied all these allegations.

62. Mark Sherman, "Marietta Man Pleads Guilty to '94 Credit File Snooping," *Atlanta Journal-Constitution,* June 16, 1995, p. D2.

63. Interview with Barry Fraser, May 5, 1995. Fraser is a legal research associate with the Privacy Rights Clearinghouse, Center for Public Interest Law, University of San Diego.

64. Interview with Evan Hendricks, May 11, 1995. Hendricks is the publisher of *Privacy Times.*

65. Source confidential at request of interviewee.

66. Interview with Mike Murphy, June 28, 1995.

67. Sometimes these searches turn up valid information. Recalls Murphy: "I was in one campaign where the brother-in-law had run a credit check on the opponent without any permission from any of us. He didn't know that it was illegal, he had just done it. He had found out that this guy had nine credit cards with a different social security number, off by one digit, and a different middle initial on each card. He was out doing real estate deals with these phony credit cards. That guy is now a U.S. congressman."

68. Phillips Business Information, Financial Services Report, October 14, 1992, p. 4.

69. Tracy Everbach, "Probe of Allegations on Perot Camp Ends," *Dallas Morning News,* June 11, 1993, p. A29. Less than two weeks before the 1992 general election, Ross Perot revealed the reason he had dropped out of the campaign in July, only to reenter it a few months later. The GOP was plotting against him, he said, planning a campaign of "dirty tricks," which included releasing phony, doctored photographs of his daughter with another woman. The release was to coincide with his daughter's summer wedding, embarrassing him and his family. This seemingly bizarre claim was followed by another: that the Bush campaign had hired a CIA contract worker to break into Perot's computerized trading program, thus sabotaging his ability to finance his revived campaign. Finally, Jim Oberwetter, the Texas chairman for Bush's reelection effort, said two men appeared in his office one day offering him tapes of phone conversations from Perot headquarters received by illegally tapping the phones. Oberwetter rejected the offer and later said he believed the offer was part of an FBI sting operation instigated by Perot.

70. Pete Bowles, "Pol Sues Hospital over Leak of Record," *Newsday,* May 14, 1994, p. 4.

71. Paul Basken, "Lawmaker Tells Colleagues of Violation," United Press International, April 20, 1994.

72. Interview with Barry Fraser, May 5, 1995.

73. Associated Press, "Congresswoman Sues over Patient's Privacy," *The Record,* May 14, 1994, p. A7. The suit was pending at the time this was written.

74. Interview with Barbara Cubin, January 24, 1995.

75. Interview with Adam Goodman, July 28, 1995.

76. Interview with Dan Payne, July 28, 1995.

77. Interview with David Keene, August 3, 1995.

78. Interview with Mark Mellman, August 14, 1995.

79. Interview with Doc Sweitzer, July 28, 1995.

80. Glenn R. Simpson, "Allegation of Eavesdropping, Moles Take Center Stage in Hutchison-Fisher Race," *Roll Call,* August 1, 1994, p. 1.

81. Ibid.

82. Interview with Leslie Byrne, January 10, 1995.

83. Interview with Joe Trippi, August 3, 1995.

84. Interview with Karan English, January 13, 1995.

85. Mike Oliver and Michael Griffin, "Plot Thickens as Politicians Resort to Pulling Dirty Tricks," *Orlando Sentinel,* October 11, 1992, p. B1.

86. Interview with Paul Begala, August 3, 1995.

87. Interview with Olivia Morgan, August 9, 1995.

88. "Overlooked: Guess Who's Not Coming to Breakfast," *The Hotline,* June 29, 1995, Volume 8, item 193.

89. This prank works in reverse, too. Democratic consultant Joseph Cerrell told of a call he received from a hotel "wanting to know where everyone was for my big luncheon. They had phony reservations for a 200-person prime-rib lunch on behalf of my candidate." Interview with Joseph Cerrell, July 28, 1995.

90. Aired on June 29, 1995.

91. Interview with James Carville, August 14, 1995.

92. For a good overview of Segretti's activities, see Carl Bernstein and Bob Woodward, *All the President's Men* (New York: Simon and Schuster, 1974), pp. 115–29.

93. Jonathan Alter, "When Tricks Turn Dirty," *Newsweek*, July 18, 1983, p.18.

CHAPTER 7. STREET MONEY

The quotation at the beginning of the chapter is from an interview with Ernest Edwards that aired on CNN's *Inside Politics* on March 9, 1995. Mr. Edwards may well be correctly summarizing his personal experiences in Arkansas, but as this chapter will show, reality (at least in some areas) is the opposite of that suggested by Mr. Edwards.

1. Actually, there are classical antecedents. Forms of street money existed in ancient Greece and Rome. See Louise Overacker, *Money in Elections* (New York: Macmillan, 1932), pp. 5–13. Similarly, various kinds of so-called treating—giving voters some reward (money, liquor, food-stuffs) in exchange for their ballots—were common in Great Britain from the fifteenth to at least the late nineteenth centuries. Ibid., pp. 14–18, 34–35.

2. Paul F. Boller, Jr., *Presidential Campaigns* (New York: Oxford, 1984), p. 6.

3. Ibid. From the *Gazette of the United States* (New York), November 24, 1792, 1.

4. Bruce L. Felknor, *Political Mischief: Smear, Sabotage, and Reform in U.S. Elections* (New York: Praeger, 1992), pp. 156–58. See also Matthew Josephson, *The Politicos 1865–1896* (New York: Harcourt, Brace, 1938), pp. 407–33; and Matilda Gresham, *The Life of Walter Quintin Gresham* (New York: Rand McNally, 1919), vol. 2, p. 605.

5. Josephson, *The Politicos,* p. 433.

6. An exit poll conducted by the television networks on Election Day 1992 gave Bush a thin 40 percent to 39 percent edge over Clinton among whites (with Perot at 21 percent). But Clinton garnered 83 percent of the votes of blacks and 62 percent among Hispanics.

7. Interview with Jean Jensen, February 15, 1995.

8. See "Not a Pretty Picture," *Campaigns and Elections* 15 (March 1994): 58–59. Eighteen percent answered "hardly ever," 2 percent "never," and 5 percent "don't know." The wording of the question was imprecise and may have confused some respondents, since "legal, reported" street money can be misused as readily as "illegal, unreported money," as the discussion in this chapter makes clear.

9. Fifty-five percent said "hardly ever," 20 percent "never," and 6 percent "don't know."

10. Rollins's consultant-partner for the Whitman race, GOP television ad-man Mike Murphy, insists, "Rollins was just spinning bullshit. . . . Not a friggin' dime went to [street money] because I sucked it all up for viewer TV." Telephone interview with Mike Murphy, June 28, 1995.

11. According to reports on the 1993 campaign filed with the New Jersey Election Law Enforcement Commission, the Democratic State Committee spent $544,526 and the GOP State Committee $43,320. These committees are not the only sources of street money, but according to state political observers, they are the primary ones.

12. Actually, some candidates do pay poll workers in white neighborhoods. For example, Illinois Democrat Al Hofeld gave each of his poll workers in white precincts the princely sum of about $350. But this is a relatively rare case. See Jim Merriner, "Hofeld Paid Election Day Help Top Dollar," *Chicago Sun-Times,* January 19, 1994, p. 3.

13. Sue Schmidt and Sharon LaFraniere, "Starr Probes Payments in Arkansas," *Washington Post,* January 29, 1995, p. A1.

14. Theodore won the runoff narrowly, but this issue dogged him throughout the general election, which he lost to Republican David Beasley. See "Riley Accuses Theodore of Paying Official," *Greenville Piedmont,* August 19, 1994, p. A1; and Schuyler Kropf and Tony Bartelme, "Tisdale Resigns after Riley Suit," Charleston (South Carolina) *Post and Courier,* August 23, 1994, pp. A1, 9.

15. See Larry J. Sabato, *Paying for Elections* (New York: Priority Press, 1989), pp. 40–42, 80 n. 34.

16. Mark Sherman, "Campaign '94 Street money: Both Parties Spread It among Black Voters," *Atlanta Journal-Constitution,* November 5, 1994, p. B5.

17. Interview with Mark Henshaw, February 16, 1995.

18. Interview with Harold Ford, February 18, 1995.

19. See brief of appellants, *Danereau et al. v. Ulmer et al.,* Alaska Supreme Court No. S-6894, filed February 24, 1995.

20. The vouchers permitted voters to request *up to* ten gallons, but not surprisingly, almost all asked for the maximum amount.

21. See brief of appellants, pp. 21–34, esp. p. 30. Additional information was provided by Wevley W. Shea, former U.S. attorney for Alaska. The "Gas for Votes" program is a new form of the age-old practice of "treating." See n. 2, this chapter.

22. Brief of appellants, p. 30.

23. Telephone interview with Frank Luntz, May 5, 1995.

24. Interview with Keith Frederick, August 7, 1995. Frederick said that GOP-financed telephone banks generated intimidating calls to black voters, asking: "Are you sure where your precinct is? You can only vote at your designated precinct, and if you are not sure where that is, you should not try to vote."

25. See Jack Wardlaw, Bill Lynch, and Ed Anderson, "Cover-up Is Charged in Vote Purge," *Times-Picayune,* October 28, 1986, pp. B1, 2; and Allan Katz, "Black Voters Purge Target, Memo Shows," *Times-Picayune,* October 25, 1986, pp. A1, 4.

26. According to Frederick, Republicans telephone "people with foreign sounding names, especially Mexican, and say: 'We are calling from Washington. Are you aware that you can only vote if you have previously registered to do so?' "

27. Interview with Karl Struble, August 1, 1995.

28. Ben Smith III, "Brooks' firm is paid $52,000 by state GOP," *Atlanta Journal-Constitution,* October 27, 1994, p. C1. According to Republican state Representative Matt Towery, who assisted Millner with his campaign,

first-time candidate Millner "was somewhat naive in the sense that he didn't even expect that he was ever going to have to pay anyone to do anything." When Towery explained to Millner that his Democratic opponent was "going to dump a half million dollars or more on the street, Millner responded that he was 'not real wild about doing that.' And then we said, 'Don't worry, we don't have the network to [spend a half-million] even if we wanted to.' " However, Millner's alliance with Brooks and some other African-American leaders may well have paid some dividends. Millner received about a tenth of the black vote, according to his own exit poll, and black turnout was down in some areas (depriving Miller of needed votes). Black voting patterns are one reason why the election was as close as it turned out.

29. See reports from the Associated Press Political Service, dateline Charleston, S.C., October 5, 1994; and the Associated Press, "Blacks Blast S.C. Democrat," dateline Columbia, S.C., October 7, 1994.

30. Neal later left the Beasley administration to join Riley's mayoral campaign team. See Herb Frazier, "Beasley Executive Rejoins Riley team," *Charleston (South Carolina) Post and Courier,* September 2, 1995, p. A1.

31. William Bunch, "Ballot Bedfellows: 'Street money can paper way to City Hall," *Newsday,* December 6, 1993, p. 3.

32. This contretemps was reminiscent of earlier disputes about GOP "ballot security programs" in other locales, such as the 1981 New Jersey gubernatorial contest. During this contest between Republican Thomas Kean and Democrat James Florio, the National Republican Party funded a "National Ballot Security Taskforce." The taskforce, headed by Jack Kelly of the Republican National Committee, took precautions to prevent voter fraud in what eventually proved to be a razor-thin Kean victory. However, Florio challenged the outcome, requesting a recount and alleging Kelly's fraud-prevention tactics, which included posting threatening signs warning of the penalties for fraudulent voting in largely black and Hispanic precincts, as well as "poll guards" who patrolled the polling sites on the day of the election, amounted to little more than outright intimidation of minority voters. When it was revealed that some of the armband-wearing patrol members were armed off-duty police officers, the controversy ballooned into investigations at the state and county level. (See Richard J. Meislin, "Jersey Controversy Widens over G.O.P. Patrols at Polls," *New York Times,* November 7, 1981; and "Jersey Vote Controversy Moves Further in Courts," *New York Times,* November 8, 1981.) In a bizarre turn of events, Kelly was revealed to have falsified his biography, and was characterized by then assistant to President Reagan Ed Rollins as "a con man and it's becoming increasingly evident." Rollins continued, ironically, to lament the challenge to Kean's victory, saying

"Anything that taints victory is sad." (See Jane Perlez, "Kelly Reported on Reagan's Appointees," *New York Times,* November 13, 1981, p. B3.)

CHAPTER 8. PERKS

1. "A Vital Highway Project Hits Another Roadblock," *Bergen Record,* May 15, 1994, p. A22.
2. "A Finger-Pointing Game," *Bergen Record,* May 20, 1994, p. C6.
3. *Department of Transportation and Related Agencies Appropriations Bill of 1995,* 103 Cong., 1st sess., S.R. 103-310, July 14, 1994, p. 132.
4. "Unclogging the Log Jam at Route 4 and Route 17," *Bergen Record,* July 12, 1994, p. B6.
5. Like other incumbent abuses, the misuse of staff has received some coverage, just not enough. (See, for example, Frank Greve, "Good Help Isn't Hard to Find," *Atlantic Monthly,* November 1993, p. 32). One reason for this is that the records necessary to document cases of possible abuse only become publicly available several months after the election, when the media's attention has shifted elsewhere.
6. Morris P. Fiorina, *Congress: Keystone of the Washington Establishment* (New Haven, Conn.: Yale University Press, 1977 and 1989). With Gary Jacobson's *The Politics of Congressional Elections* (New York: Harper Collins, 1992) and David Mayhew's "Congressional Elections: The Case of the Vanishing Marginals," (*Polity* 6 [Spring 1974]: 295–317), Fiorina's highly original discussion of congressional staff and other "perks" of office formed the basis for much subsequent research about incumbency. Here, we intend to supplement his thesis and provide empirical data that substantiates his argument.
7. Norman J. Ornstein, Thomas E. Mann, and Michael J. Malbin, *Vital Statistics on Congress, 1991–1992* (Washington, D.C.: Congressional Quarterly, Inc., 1992), p. 119.
8. Ibid., p. 126. Committee staffs grew at the same rate. For example, House standing committees employed 167 individuals in 1947, compared with nearly 2,000 throughout most of the 1980s. Senate committee staffs grew at a slightly slower rate, from 232 individuals in 1947 to close to 1,000 in 1989.
9. *Congressional Record,* 1992, S9762.
10. The House Committee on Standards of Official Conduct, *Ethics Manual for Members, Officers, and Employees of the U.S. House of Representatives,* 102 Cong., 2d sess., 1992, pp. 200–201.
11. On Capitol Hill, it is often difficult to determine any one staffer's yearly salary because staff salaries and titles often change from quarter to quarter. The authors used the first quarter as a baseline standard. Slevin earned $27,058 for his legislative duties during this quarter.

12. Glenn R. Simpson, "Hubbard Pleads Guilty in Complex Plot Tied to Bank Flap," *Roll Call,* April 7, 1994, p. 1.

13. He also admitted guilt in connection with other serious charges, including obstruction of justice and conspiracy to defraud the United States, but prosecutors emphasized the gravity of the theft charge.

14. This is on a pro-rata basis. John Ralston's official salary did decrease, but only because he stopped working for Young on December 2.

15. Glenn R. Simpson, "Different (Pen) Strokes for Different Folks," *Roll Call,* December 2, 1991, p. 11.

16. In 1989, for example, the average House office received about 2,353 pieces of mail a day, while the average Senate office received about 1,584 pieces. John Pontius, "U.S. Congress Official Mail Costs: FY 1972 to FY 1991," Congressional Research Service, Library of Congress, Washington D.C., July 20, 1990, tables 3, 4, CRS-29, CRS 37. Pontius reports that in fiscal year 1989, the House received 262,300,000 pieces of mail, and the Senate received 40,393,063 pieces. These figures are discussed and critiqued later in the chapter.

17. *The Encyclopedia of the United States Congress,* vol. 2 (New York: Simon and Schuster, 1995), p. 884.

18. American National Election Study, Center for Political Studies, University of Michigan, 1990. Analysis by Professor James Gimpel, University of Michigan. Cited in Roger H. Davidson and Walter J. Oleszek, *Congress and Its Members* (Washington, D.C.: Congressional Quarterly, Inc., 1994), p. 109.

19. Sara Fritz and Dwight Morris, *Gold Plated Politics: Running for Congress in the 1990's* (Washington, D.C.: Congressional Quarterly, Inc., 1992), p. 14.

20. Charles L. Clapp, *The Congressman: His Work As He Sees It* (Washington, D.C.: Brookings Institution, 1963), p. 84.

21. Richard V. Benson, *Secrets of Sucessful Direct Mail* (Savannah, Ga.: Benson Organization, Inc., 1987), p. 6.

22. Conservative Richard Viguerie was among the first to found a direct mail company, in 1965. See Larry J. Sabato, *The Rise of Political Consultants: New Ways of Winning Elections* (Basic Books: New York, 1981), p. 221.

23. Irwin B. Arieff, "Computers and Direct Mail are Being Married on the Hill to Keep Incumbents in Office," *Congressional Quarterly* 37 (July 21, 1979): 1446–47.

24. Common Cause lost the original lawsuit filed in the U.S. District Court for the District of Columbia (see *Common Cause v. Bolger,* 574 F. Supp. 672 [1982]). Judge John H. Pratt, writing for the lower court, did not contend that the frank was politically ineffective, nor that it was not used as a campaign instrument; rather, he wrote that "the level of impact has not been

shown to be sufficient in this case for us to assume the responsibility of re-drafting a statute or promulgating regulations to govern the congres-sional use of the frank" (at 685). More interesting was the court's second "prudential consideration," namely that "to grant the relief which plain-tiffs seek would in effect require us to issue rules of behavior superseding those that Congress, a coordinate branch of government, has responsibly set for itself" (at 685). In other words, in addition to avoiding the political thicket and definitional problems of distinguishing between "official" and "unofficial" mailings, the district court simply declined to challenge the power of Congress. Judge Pratt's opinion for the district court was af-firmed by the Supreme Court without comment (see *Common Cause v. Bolger,* 461 U.S. 911 [1983]).

25. *Common Cause v. Bolger,* 461 U.S. 911 (1983).
26. Irwin B. Arieff, "Franking Law Revisions Approved by Congress; Senate Mass Mailings OK'd," *Congressional Quarterly* 39 (October 18, 1981): 2030.
27. John Pontius, "U.S. Congress Official Mail Costs: FY 1972 to FY 1991," Congressional Research Service, Library of Congress, Washington D.C., July 20, 1990, table 1, CRS-11.
28. Postal Reorganization Act, U.S. Code, vol. 39, sec. 3210 (a)(2) 1995.
29. Ibid., sec. 3210 (c).
30. Interview with Jack Dail, February 24, 1995.
31. "Congressman Dan Burton Reports to 6th District Hoosiers," 1994 Newsletter.
32. Ibid.
33. Newsletter by Congressman Elton Gallegly, 1994.
34. Weston Kosova, "Congress's Mail Prostitution Ring," *Washington Monthly* 22 (September 1990): 32.
35. "Congresswoman Helen Delich Bentley Reports," Summer 1994, p. 3.
36. Interview with Jeff Shulem, February 13, 1995.
37. Interview with David Keating, February 15, 1995.
38. Letters from Representative Dan Burton to his constituents, June 30, 1994, and July 5, 1994.
39. Ibid.
40. This information comes from a variety of sources, including interviews with computer and database vendors who sell on Capitol Hill.
41. Timothy J. Burger, "House Rejects Move to Cancel Controversial CD-ROM Voter Registration List Deal, 231-182," *Roll Call,* October 31, 1991.
42. Interview with Kari Grant, February 17, 1995.
43. Burger, "House Rejects Move." The member was Representative John Boehner.
44. See Anne Willette, "House Members Buy Lists to Help Them Target

Mail," Gannett News Service, September 27, 1992; and "House Administration Committee Authorizes $250,000 for CD-ROM Data Bases," *Roll Call,* July 23, 1992.

45. See Timothy J. Burger, "GOP Seeks to Bar Members from Purchasing Voter Lists," *Roll Call,* November 21, 1991; and Burger, "Controversial CD-ROM Franked-Mail System Is Approved Over Recess," *Roll Call,* January 21, 1993.
46. Interview with Jeff Shulem, February 13, 1995.
47. Prices for constituent mail manager systems can vary greatly, from about $25,000 to $60,000 for computer software and hardware. Sophistication varies with price.
48. Interview with Debbie Marshall, February 16, 1995.
49. Interview with Juan Rodriguez, February 14, 1995.
50. Interview with Jeff Shulem, February 13, 1995.
51. Ibid.
52. Alan C. Miller, "Congress' Mailbag; Constituents Put in Their $.22 Worth," *Los Angeles Times,* February 1, 1988, p. 1.
53. Interview with Michael Shinay, March 9, 1995.
54. Ibid.
55. To its credit, the National Taxpayers Union has consistently pointed this out in a variety of creative ways; the media are at fault for rarely taking much notice.
56. Price Waterhouse Audit, p. 110.
57. Jennifer Senior, "Western Freshmen Worry about Losing Franking; New Efforts to Stamp Our Free Congressional Mail," *The Hill,* February 22, 1995, p. 10.

CHAPTER 9. REACH OUT AND SLIME SOMEONE

The first quotation at the beginning of this chapter is from an interview by Jacki Lyden with Luntz and Democratic consultant Don Rose on National Public Radio's *All Things Considered,* aired on November 6, 1994. The second quotation is from an interview with the authors on August 3, 1995.

1. We are grateful to Professor Thomas Guterbock, director of the Center for Survey Research at the University of Virginia, for his help in crafting this definition.
2. From "Background Information on Frederick/Schneiders," April 1995, given by the firm to a Democratic candidate-client.
3. See Matt Campbell, "Poll Results Stir Skepticism: 'Push' Survey Indicated Freeman Held Lead over McCarthy, but Experts Say It Is Not a Reliable One," *Kansas City Star,* October 11, 1994, p. B1. Note that in this case, the reporter was properly suspicious of the pollster's spin.

4. A plethora of scholarly articles on the subject exist; to cite a small sample, see: "The Vanishing Marginals, the Bandwagon, and the Mass Media," *Journal of Politics* 56 (August 1994): 802; Ian McAllister and Donley Studlar, "Bandwagon, Underdog, or Projection? Opinion Polls and Electoral Choice in Britain, 1978–1987," *Journal of Politics* 53 (August 1991): 720; William J. Baumol, "Interactions between Successive Polling Results and Voting Intentions," *Public Opinion Quarterly* 21 (1957): 318–23; Stephen J. Ceci and Edward L. Kahn, "Jumping on the Bandwagon with the Underdog: The Impact of Attitude Polls on Polling Behavior," *Public Opinion Quarterly* 46 (1982): 228–42; Philip D. Straffin, "The Bandwagon Curve," *American Journal of Political Science* 21 (1977): 695–709; Herbert A. Simon, "Bandwagon Effects and the Possibility of Election Predictions," *Public Opinion Quarterly* 18 (1954): 245–53; Robert Novazio, "An Experimental Approach to Bandwagon Research," *Public Opinion Quarterly* 41 (1977): 217–25; Daniel W. Fleitas, "Bandwagon and Underdog Effects in Minimal Information Elections," *American Political Science Review* 65 (1971): 434–38; and Catherine Marsh, "Back on the Bandwagon: The Effects of Opinion Polls on Public Opinion," *British Journal of Political Science* 15 (1984): 51–74.

5. Actually, this horse race question is usually asked twice—once in the survey's beginning so an unbiased match-up can be measured, and then at the conclusion, as described here. Of course, the results of the first horse race question are only for internal campaign consumption and are not released publicly (unless favorable to the client).

6. This is particularly true when the contenders are little known and the respondents do not have much prior knowledge of them on which to base a judgment.

7. Veteran journalists at the national and state levels are experienced enough to discount internal campaign poll data; they are well aware of frequent manipulation of survey findings, and some are sophisticated enough to ask about question order. But it is remarkable how often younger, local press persons can be hornswoggled into trumpeting these bogus polls.

8. For a general discussion of polling techniques, see Herbert Asher, *Polling and the Public: What Every Citizen Should Know,* 2d ed. (Washington, D.C.: Congressional Quarterly Press, 1987); and Albert H. Cantril, *The Opinion Connection: Polling, Politics, and the Press* (Washington, D.C.: Congressional Quarterly Press, 1991). For a contemporary look at prominent pollsters and the development of their art, see David W. Moore, *The Superpollsters* (New York: Four Walls Eight Windows, 1992). Some innocuous antecedents to research push-polling can be found on pp. 98–101 and 184–85.

9. See Stephen E. Ambrose, *Nixon: The Education of a Politician, 1913–1962* (New York: Simon and Schuster, 1987), pp. 138–40. See also Paul Bul-

lock, *Jerry Voorhis: The Idealist as Politician* (New York: Vantage Press, 1978), p. 276.

10. Bullock, *Jerry Voorhis.*

11. Ambrose, *Nixon,* p. 138.

12. See, for example, two *Washington Post* articles: Thomas E. Edsall, "GOP's Cash Advantage Failed to Assure Victory in Close Senate Contests," November 6, 1986, p. A46; and Paul Taylor, "Social Security Overhaul Finds Advocates in GOP; IRA-Type Proposals Aim for Younger Voters," November 26, 1986, p. A4.

13. It is impossible to quantify the effects of such tactics, but the political professionals believe that the social security charge swung many elderly voters to Democratic Senate candidates—or at least this is the lesson taken away from the election by the pros, which clearly affected their future behavior (such as propensity to use persuasive phoning).

14. See also *Hotline* 6 (April 30, 1993), 560-word report on social security persuasive phoning in a special U.S. House election in Wisconsin.

15. "The Political Pages: 1995–96 Guide to Political Consultants, Products, and Services," *Campaigns and Elections* 17 (February 1995): 74–79.

16. We interviewed political consultants at seven telephone marketing firms in researching this section.

17. See Larry J. Sabato, *The Rise of Political Consultants: New Ways of Winning Elections* (New York: Basic Books, 1981).

18. Mac Hansbrough, "Dial N for Negative—Using Phones to Make Your Attacks Heard but Not Seen," *Campaigns and Elections* 13 (April 1992): 58–61.

19. Telephone interviews with Mac Hansbrough on April 14 and April 19, 1995.

20. See William Booth, "Chiles Admits Campaign Made 'Scare Calls' in Florida Gubernatorial Race," *Washington Post,* November 10, 1995, p. A4. See also *Hotline* 10 (November 9, 1995): item 20.

21. Hansbrough, "Dial N for Negative," p. 61.

22. Telephone interview on January 17, 1995.

23. Interview with David Heller, November 29, 1994.

24. The only national focus on the topic during the 1994 elections came in a syndicated column by David S. Broder, first published in the *Washington Post* on October 9, 1994 ("Beware the 'Push-Poll,' " p. C7). The day after the election, the *Wall Street Journal* also published a story on push-polls: John Harwood and Daniel Pearl, "In Waning Campaign Hours, Candidates Turn to Phone 'Push-polling' to Step Up the Attack," November 9, 1994, p. A24. The Associated Press sent out a feature story on the subject, "Phone 'Polls' Used Politically," on May 29, 1995, "as legitimate polling starts getting under way in the 1996 presidential race." This piece also noted that the technique had apparently been exported. In March 1995

the Australian prime minister accused the opposition party of using this "grubby and sinister" method.

25. Interview with Joshua Harris, November 30, 1994.
26. Officials in all the Democratic campaigns mentioned here confirmed to us that they had received reports from the field about these antiabortion calls. Joshua Harris also specifically recalled that the identified campaigns were targeted for calls.
27. Dennis J. McGrath, "Wynia, Grams Pull Out Stops for Final Push," *Star-Tribune* (Minneapolis), November 7, 1994, p. B1.
28. Quoted in ibid.
29. See chapter 5.
30. Interview with Ted Strickland, January 27, 1995.
31. Interview with Matt Salmon, January 20, 1995.
32. Interview with Rick Bennett, November 23, 1994. See also Susan Young, "Candidates Make Push-polling Claims," *Bangor Daily News,* October 27, 1994, p. A1.
33. Young, "Candidates."
34. Chairwoman Victoria Murphy claimed the Democrats conducted only voter identification polls with no push-polling questions. She was responding to charges by independent gubernatorial candidate and now-Governor Angus King that the Democrats were also running a push-poll operation against him. See John Hale, "Push-poll, Flier Complaints Filed," *Bangor Daily News,* October 25, 1994, p. A1.
35. Interview with David Heller, November 29, 1994.
36. Interview with Rick Bennett, November 23, 1994.
37. Interview with Tom Barlow, January 16, 1995.
38. This example is taken from a report aired on National Public Radio's *All Things Considered,* October 30, 1994. The correspondent was Peter Kenyon of Alaska Public Radio.
39. Interview with Beth Bernard, November 29, 1994. Prior to election eve, Bernard says the push-poll calls focused on other issues, such as abortion and taxes.
40. Without a doubt, the calls had an impact on her narrow loss to Republican Rod Grams.
41. Interview with Eric Fingerhut, January 23, 1995.
42. See Bob Gibson, "GOP Takes Issue with Polling Firm's Presentation of 'Facts,' " *Daily Progress,* August 8, 1993, p. B1; and Gibson, "Local Poll Contrasts with Others," *Daily Progress,* August 15, 1993, p. B1. See also Tyler Whitley, "Polling Described as 'Dirty Tricks,' ": *Richmond Times Dispatch,* August 14, 1993, p. B1; and John F. Harris, "Va. Republicans Say Democrats Are Slinging a Little Mud in Their Poll Questions," *Washington Post,* August 18, 1993, p. D1. Incidentally, the president of Cooper & Secrest, Alan M. Secrest, did not take kindly to Gibson's efforts.

In a letter to Gibson dated August 9, 1993, Secrest accused the reporter of "a pattern of very disturbing behavior . . . potentially including . . . receipt of stolen materials, . . . fraudulent means to acquire propriety [sic] trade materials, and . . . harass[ment of] employees in a dark parking lot as they left work." No action followed, and the facts of Gibson's reporting were never convincingly challenged or refuted.

43. The average population of registered voters per district was approximately 30,000, so as many as one of every twenty *households* containing a registered voter was being reached—a sizable proportion if one's goal was to spread rumors.

44. Nine separate questions in the poll posed negative arguments about Orrock. The respondent was asked to state whether each argument was "a very persuasive reason not to reelect him," "an only somewhat persuasive reason," or "a not at all persuasive reason."

45. Wisconsin Republicans have also been targeted in state legislative races. These push-polls were reportedly conducted by the National Education Association's Wisconsin affiliate. See Harwood and Pearl, "In Waning Campaign Hours." See also Judy Williams, "5th District Candidates Pull Plug on Phone Calls," *Appleton (Wisconsin) Post-Crescent,* October 9, 1994, p. B8; and Judy Williams, "Candidates at Odds Over Phone Tactics," *Post-Crescent,* October 29, 1994, p. B1.

46. See Phil Porado, "A Case Study: How Negative Phoning Didn't Work in Two State House Races," *Campaigns and Elections* 13 (April 1992): 62; Buddy Nevins, "Many Undecided about Candidates in Upcoming Primary," *Fort Lauderdale Sun-Sentinel,* August 28, 1994, p. B4.

47. Telephone interviews with Haley Barbour, February 26 and May 31, 1995.

48. Barbour noted, "At one point, we considered a script saying, 'If the Democrats contact you, would you call [the following] 800 number.' But we ended up not doing that because it was kind of complicated."

49. The information in this section is taken from Maloney's testimony before the Federal Election Commission on March 8, 1995.

50. See Scott Lehigh, "Kennedy Camp Reacts Angrily to 'Push-poll,' " *Boston Globe,* November 5, 1994, p. B18.

51. The calls also tied North to the Reverend Jerry Falwell and U.S. Senator Jesse Helms (Republican of North Carolina). See Laurie Kellman, "Robb callers tie North to David Duke," *Washington Times,* October 28, 1994, p. A14; Laurie Kellman, "North Says Recent Troubles Won't Keep Him out of the Senate," *Washington Times,* October 29, 1994, p. A1; and Margaret Edds, "Get-Out-the-Vote Efforts Crucial in Close Senate Race," *Virginian-Pilot,* October 30, 1994, p. A2.

52. News Staff, "Bird Says Benson 'Survey' Is Just a Dirty Political Trick," *Rocky Mountain News,* July 23, 1994, p. A8.

53. See Harwood and Pearl, "In Waning Campaign Hours."

54. See R. H. Melton, "Poll Firm That Irked Voters Paid by Coleman," *Washington Post,* November 1, 1989, p. A1.
55. Interview with Mark Sanford, January 24, 1995.
56. Interview with Geoff Garin, April 13, 1995.
57. Interview with Karan English, January 13, 1995.
58. Telephone interview with Steve Horn Jr., campaign manager for his father, February 17, 1995. Horn Jr. suggests that the push-polling for his father's 1994 Democratic foe, Peter Mathews, was done by a prominent Democratic telephone bank firm, Gordon and Schwenkmeyer. Indeed, Mathews's filings with the Federal Election Commission show two late payments to the firm, $10,000 on November 6, 1994, and an additional $3,270 on November 13, 1994. Mike Gordon, president of the firm, declined to comment on the substance of the allegation, citing his firm's policy of "not discuss[ing] clients with anyone." Telephone interview with the authors, July 20, 1995.
59. Telephone interview with Tim Tomkins, February 2, 1995.
60. Interview with Steve Chabot, November 30, 1994.
61. Interview with Herb Klein, January 17, 1995.
62. Interview with Mike Synar, January 27, 1995. Also interview with Amy Tobe, Synar's campaign manager, March 6, 1995. According to our interviewees, computer-automated calls are often made when the message is brief and no response from the listener is required. The technology exists for computer-automated phoning that includes listener response, but it can be clumsy or off-putting to those at home.
63. See Mike Oliver and Michael Griffin, "Plot Thickens as Politicians Resort to Pulling Dirty Tricks," *Orlando Sentinel Tribune,* October 11, 1992, p. B1.

CHAPTER 10. VOTE FRAUD

1. In the 1994 general elections there were several well-publicized close contests in which vote fraud was alleged, including the Maryland gubernatorial race, won by Democrat Parris Glendening over Republican Ellen Sauerbrey by 5,993 votes out of more than 1.4 million cast; a North Carolina U.S. House contest in District 7 won by incumbent Democrat Charles G. Rose over Republican Robert Anderson by 3,821 votes out of 121,519 cast; and a California U.S. House race in District 36 between incumbent Democrat Jane Harman and GOP challenger Susan Brooks, which Harman won by only 812 votes of 195,808 cast. In this chapter, however, we have chosen to focus on less well-known examples that are indicative of systemic corruption.
2. Bruce L. Felknor, *Political Mischief: Smear, Sabotage, and Reform in U.S. Elections* (New York: Praeger, 1992), p. 160; see also pp. 155–82.

3. For a classic treatment, see Paul Leland Hayworth, *The Hayes-Tilden Disputed Election of 1876* (Cleveland: Burrows Brothers, 1906).

4. Louise Overacker, *Money in Elections* (New York: Macmillan, 1932), p. 31.

5. Many "floaters"—individuals who would roam from precinct to precinct, casting a ballot at each one—were imported from other cities and towns to perform this extraordinary civic "duty." The practice may be the origin of the old aphorism, "Vote early and often."

6. J. J. McCook, "Venal Voting: Methods and Remedies," *Forum* 14 (September/October 1892): pp. 1, 159; as cited in Overacker, *Money in Elections,* p. 32.

7. A. Z. Blair, "Seventeen Hundred Rural Vote-Sellers," *McClure's* 38 (November 1911): 33; as cited in Overacker, *Money in Elections,* p. 33.

8. For further details on the 1960 election, see Theodore C. Sorensen, *Kennedy* (New York: Harper and Row, 1965), chap. 8, pp. 211–23; Stephen E. Ambrose, *Nixon* (New York: Simon & Schuster, 1987), chap. 26, pp. 584–608; and Theodore White, *The Making of the President 1960* (New York: Pocket Books, 1961).

9. As Johnson underling L. E. Jones later reported, LBJ had an early introduction to the (under) world of voter fraud. Working for the left-leaning Maury Maverick in his winning 1934 congressional campaign, Johnson sat at a table covered with money and paid barely bilingual Mexican-Americans in multiples of $5 bills. Jones realized that Johnson was paying each man $5 for each eligible voter in his family. See Robert A. Caro, *The Years of Lyndon Johnson: The Path to Power* (New York: Alfred A. Knopf, 1982), pp. 276–77. Johnson put this experience to good personal use in 1937, campaigning in his successful bid to fill Texas's Tenth Congressional District seat, which had been vacated by the death of James P. Buchanan. Caro reports that Johnson bought votes in African-American and Czech communities.

10. Parr ordered Salas to come up with the needed votes in a meeting attended by Johnson himself, according to Salas. Decades later, Salas admitted that two deputy sheriffs added the extra names to the voter list, at his direction. Most observers at the time strongly suspected this skulduggery, but efforts in the Democratic state committee and in the courts to change the results failed. See James W. Mangan, Associated Press interview, July 30, 1977. For a more extensive account of Johnson's Box 13 shenanigans, see Caro, *The Years of Lyndon Johnson,* chaps. 14 and 15, pp. 318–412.

11. The hundreds of previous signatures were written in different color inks, and were clearly signed by each individual voter separately.

12. The first draft of the Philadelphia section was researched and written by University of Virginia graduate student Charles H. Woodcock.

13. See "Stinson Cleared of Election Fraud," United Press International regional news, June 22, 1994. There was insufficient evidence to tie Stinson directly to the fraudulent efforts made on his behalf. The Democrat had been specifically charged with unsealing and counting absentee ballots, as well as unlocking voting machines in his own precinct. For a description of the pretrial proceedings, see Marc Duvoisin, Daniel Rubin, and Henry Goldman, "Stinson, 2 Aides Are Indicted; Charges Center on Absentee Ballots," *Philadelphia Inquirer,* March 13, 1994, p. A1.

14. Newcomer's final opinion in the *Marks v. Stinson* case (1994 U.S. Dist. LEXIS 5273; hereafter, *Marks v. Stinson*) was actually the second time he ordered Stinson stripped of the seat and certified Marks. The proceedings occurring prior to his April 26, 1994, decision are complicated, and an accounting of the entire obstacle course Marks was forced to run in order to gain redress would require a chapter in itself.

    Marks's appeal through the state court system proved futile. The Marks campaign was actually aware that absentee malfeasance had occurred prior to election night. Even so, Steve MacNett, a Pennsylvania lawyer who worked on Marks's appeal, explained that at each of several stages of the appeal process, "the apparent over-politicization of the Pennsylvania Courts, especially in Philadelphia," prevented successful action. MacNett continued, "[The] three judges he was before in Philadelphia, each of them has deep ties to the Democratic party establishment" (interview with Steve MacNett, July 18, 1995).

    Marks's inability to gain redress quickly was compounded by the actions of the County Board of Elections, which prompted Judge Clarence Newcomer to note that "the actions of the board [of Elections] were designed to, and did in fact, prevent any realistic opportunity to appeal the certification in the State court system.... Defendants allege plaintiffs consistently failed to avail themselves of the proper appeal procedures. Plaintiffs were never given the opportunity to present their claims because the safeguards failed at every level" (1994 U.S. Dist. LEXIS 5273, 58).

    With his appeal to the State Supreme Court pending, Marks filed for redress in federal court. Judge Newcomer found his claims compelling, and on February 18, 1994, delivered his initial injunction stripping Stinson of the seat, threw out all absentee ballots, and ordered the Board of Elections to certify the victor of the machine vote, that is, Marks. While federal judges have in the past overturned the results of state elections on civil and voting rights grounds, this was the first occasion a federal judge simply installed the opposing candidate in office rather than ordering a new election.

    However, Newcomer was found to have exceeded his authority by the court of appeals. (See his original opinion, *Marks v. Stinson,* 1994 U.S. Dist.

LEXIS 1586, order overturned.) The Third Circuit Court of Appeals upheld the portion of Newcomer's order stripping Stinson of the seat, but vacated his order to install Marks. While the Circuit Court agreed the District Court was correct to claim jurisdiction, proof of voter fraud was not sufficient to award the seat. Writing for the court, Judge Stapleton, stated, "The district court should not direct the certification of a candidate, unless it finds, on the basis of record evidence, that the designated candidate would have won the election but for wrongdoing" (19 F.3d 873, 889 [3d Cir. 1994]). The appellate judges relied on *Griffin v. Burns* (570 F.3d 1065 [1st Cir. 1978]) to suggest that Newcomer's order to install Marks might be unconstitutional, creating an opportunity for voters to challenge the decision under the Federal Voting Rights Act. Because Newcomer's order voided *all* absentee ballots cast, it inevitably voided some that were lawfully and properly cast. The First Circuit in *Griffin* "concluded that rejection of a ballot where the voter has been effectively deprived of the ability to cast a legal vote implicated federal due process concerns" and possible Fourteenth Amendment violations (*Marks v. Stinson,* 19 F.3d at 889).

The second opinion, which we discuss in the text, was the result of the circuit court's remand to Newcomer. See particularly Newcomer's analysis of the number of illegal absentee ballots and the statistical tests used to corroborate his findings. Newcomer went to great pains to show that the Stinson campaign's "dollar a ballot" drive produced approximately 600 fraudulent votes (greater than the 461 needed to change the election results). He also found via expert testimony that Stinson received approximately 1,000 more absentee votes than expected.

The story does not end here, however. Stinson unsuccessfully appealed Newcomer's second opinion to the Third Circuit in August 1994, and then in January 1995, to the U.S. Supreme Court, which declined to overturn or comment upon the judgment. In the (presumably) final chapter of the story, Marks ironically lost his hard-won seat in the regular 1994 general election to Nina Tartaglione, the daughter of Democratic County Commissioner Margaret Tartaglione, who had been implicated in the scandal that denied Marks the seat to begin with. (See "Recount Shows Marks Still a Loser," United Press International regional news, November 14, 1994.)

15. See, for example, *Griffin v. Burns* (570 F.2d. 1065, 1st Cir. 1978), the case cited by the Third Circuit panel to justify remanding the case to the district court. In this case, Providence election officials distributed absentee ballots for a primary city council contest, although Rhode Island law only provides for absentee voting in general elections. The Rhode Island Supreme Court found the statutory omission precluded the use of absen-

tees in primary elections, decertified the primary victor, and ordered re-certification based only on machine votes—which also changed the outcome of the election. However, the circuit court agreed with absentee voters' claims that the lower court ruling effectively disenfranchised them, vacated the order to certify on the basis of the machine count, and ordered a special election. Note, however, that the *Burns* case did not involve fraud per se, and the Third Circuit left Newcomer the option to certify Marks if he found the Republican would have been elected but for the wrongdoing.

16. See "Improper Ballots Turned Election," *Philadelphia Inquirer,* March 25, 1995, p. A1. The *Inquirer's* investigation, which required a massive effort, indicated that at least 540 absentee ballots cast for Stinson were tainted, a number that exceeded his margin of victory.

17. PA Stat. Tit. 25, 3146.1–3146.6 (1994).

18. Interview with Bruce Marks, July 18, 1995. In addition, several hundred rejected applications (some of which were for unregistered individuals, and some of which were simply fraudulent) were covertly returned to the Stinson campaign to prevent their discovery. These documents are public records, and should have been preserved for two years.

19. *Marks v. Stinson,* 1994 U.S. Dist. LEXIS 5273 p. 23.

20. Ibid., p. 26. As noted above, Stinson had narrowly lost an election for a Philadelphia city council seat in a June 1991 Democratic primary. For a fuller account of Jones's recollections of his work for Stinson, see also Henry Goldman and Sergio Bustos, "Campaign Worker Says Stinson Ignored Warning on Ballots," *Philadelphia Inquirer,* February 8, 1994, p. A1. Stinson, on the other hand, challenged Jones's credibility and claimed that he deliberately maintained his ignorance of many details of his campaign, including the absentee ballot program. See Mark Fazlollah, "Stinson Said He Stayed Clear of Details," *Philadelphia Inquirer,* February 8, 1994, p. A1. Stinson's argument, however, contradicts the testimony of many of those who worked on his campaign; see Marc Duvoisin, "Absentee-ballot Quest Described as Obsessive; Aides Say Stinson Discussed It Frequently," *Philadelphia Inquirer,* March 13, 1994, p. A1.

Ironically, Marks later recalled that Daniel McElhatton, Stinson's opponent in the 1991 city council primary, was one of the sources who suggested he investigate Stinson's use of absentee ballots: "I ran into [Daniel McElhatton] who had run against my opponent in a 1990 primary, . . . and he just recommended to me that I look into the absentee ballots" (interview with Bruce Marks, July 18, 1995).

21. *Marks v. Stinson,* p. 23.

22. Ibid. See also *Marks v. Stinson,* p. 31, where Judge Newcomer notes the scheme; Hispanic and black voters were also told "that the law had been

changed and there was a 'new way to vote' from the convenience of one's home."

23. For a more complete account, see "Voters Say Ballots Were Forged," *Philadelphia Inquirer*, November 21, 1993, p. A1; and John F. Dickerson, "Is This Seat Stolen? Angry Republicans Contend That Dirty Tricks at the Polls Tipped the Balance of Power in Pennsylvania," *Time*, February 7, 1994, p. 34.

24. *Marks v. Stinson*, p. 36.

25. Ibid., p. 39.

26. One of the Democratic commissioners even gave an order to "stay out of it" to an elections board employee who ascertained that unregistered citizens had applied for absentee ballots and so informed the commissioner.

27. *Marks v. Stinson*, p. 55.

28. Interview with Jack Connors, July 18, 1995.

29. *Marks v. Stinson*, p. 47.

30. Office of Alabama Secretary of State, Elections Division. As was the case with the Philadelphia story, where party control of the Pennsylvania state senate was at stake, the significance of the Alabama election was tied to a larger issue current in the state at the time. Tort reform, which gained national prominence in the Republican Party's "Contract with America," is an especially significant issue in Alabama, as in many states where judges are elected. Plaintiff trial lawyers categorically oppose regulatory efforts to limit jury awards for punitive damages and pain and suffering in civil liability suits. Alabama is distinguished by the large dollar amounts that juries award to plaintiffs, and by the fact that the state appeals courts, including the Supreme Court, often maintain the amounts set by juries. Hornsby is the past president of the Alabama Trial Lawyers Association and is critical of tort reform. Hooper and the Alabama Business Council are outspoken proponents of reforming tort award limits. The Hornsby–Hooper race is therefore symbolic of the wider issue.

31. The United States Court of Appeals for the 11th Circuit requested that the state Supreme Court clarify the status of the 1,700 absentee ballots under Alabama electoral law prior to ruling on the merits of Hooper's supporters' claims. A five-judge panel of the state Supreme Court (not including Hornsby), all Democrats, ruled on March 15, 1995, that by Alabama Code 17-10-7, the ballots were in substantial compliance with Alabama electoral law and should be counted despite the fact that the affidavits attached to the ballots were not notarized or witnessed by two individuals, as required. This ruling would place their colleague Hornsby back on the bench. The circuit court is currently considering the panel's opinion, and as Hooper noted, "This isn't even close to being over." (See

Ronald Smothers, "Court Orders Votes Counted in Alabama," *New York Times,* March 16, 1995, p. A23.) However, in September 1995 a U.S. district court judge in Mobile threw out the disputed absentee ballots, and the U.S. Court of Appeals then upheld the judge's decision, thereby clearing the way for Hooper's swearing-in, at long last. (See "Chief Justice Takes Office in Alabama," *New York Times,* October 22, 1995, p. A25.)

32. Affidavit of Paul J. Harrington, November 20, 1994. All affidavits cited in this section are public record, and were submitted as documentation for *Larry Roe et al. v. Mobile County Appointing Board et al.* (Civil Action 94-885-AH-S).

33. Affidavit of Paul J. Harrington, November 20, 1994.

34. Affidavit of Pam Montgomery, November 11, 1994.

35. Affidavit of H. O. Kirksey, November 21, 1994.

36. Affidavit of Anthony J. Keith, November 14, 1994. See also affidavit of Juanita Crawford, November 1994.

37. Affidavit of Jacquelyn Gandy, November 22, 1994.

38. Testimony of Helen Watts, from transcript of Civil Action 94-885-AH-S, *Larry Roe et al. v. Mobile County Appointing Board et al.* (preliminary injunction hearing before Judge Alex Howard [U.S. District Court, Southern District of Alabama]), pp. 122–28.

39. Ibid.

40. Affidavit of John Russell Campbell, November 15, 1995.

41. Ibid. See also affidavit of John Modris Grods, November 14, 1994.

42. Testimonies of William Moulton and Murphy Gewin, from transcript of Civil Action 94-885-AH-S, *Larry Roe et al. v. Mobile County Appointing Board, et al.* (request for temporary restraining order before Judge Alex Howard [U.S. District Court, Southern District of Alabama]), pp. 48–63 and 109–11.

43. Affidavit of John Russell Campbell, November 15, 1994.

44. Telephone interview with Dan Warren, July 20, 1995. Warren is a member of the Board of Registrars.

45. Telephone interview with attorney Albert Jordan (of Wallace, Jordan, Ratliff, Byers, & Brandt), March 27, 1995.

46. See Doug Haaland and Doug Swordstrom, "A Report on Election Law Irregularities: California 16th Senate District," personally published report, January 27, 1995, p. 8.

47. See "Report of the Fair Elections Foundation (II)" (Costa Mesa, Calif.: self-published, winter 1995), pp. 34–48.

48. See "Report of the 1995 Elections Summit" (Sacramento, Calif.: Office of the California Secretary of State, April 18, 1995), pp. 11–14. Karen Saranita, of the nonpartisan watchdog group Fair Elections Foundation, estimated that the deadwood clogging the registration rolls was in the

range of 14–17 percent, while Trudy Shaffer, of the California League of Women Voters, cited an estimate of 24 percent from a study conducted in the 1980s.

49. Secretary of State Jones estimated "deadwood" costs for the state of California at between $3 and $5 million. Similarly, Associated Press reporter Doug Willis estimated that registration inaccuracies cost the state government $5 million and local governments an additional $3 million. See "Report of the 1995 Elections Summit," p. 14; and Doug Willis, "Deadwood on Voter Registration Rolls Wastes Millions for Taxpayers," AP News Analysis, May 1, 1995.

50. The lists have apparently been lost in the shuffle of bureaucracy, and the names of dead voters who passed away in the early 1980s are still on the rolls in good standing. This problem was discussed at length at the Election Summit. (See the "Report of the 1995 Elections Summit," p. 13.)

51. Ventura County elections head Bruce Bradley, as quoted in the *Los Angeles Times,* October 28, 1994, p. B1.

52. See "Report of the 1995 Elections Summit," p. 16.

53. Ibid.

54. See "Report of the Fair Elections Foundation (I)," p. 4. The Los Angeles County registrar's office disputes this figure. In an interview with the authors on July 20, 1995, Wendell Patterson, manager of the records division, said there is "no positve proof" that 4,000 people illegally registered to vote, and he stressed that under California law, when a person signs the affidavit on the registration card, the registrar cannot challenge its authenticity or any information on the card. Of course, this provision of the law in itself may be a problem.

55. Robert B. Gunnison, "Registrars Seek Voting Reform," *San Francisco Chronicle,* February 23, 1995, p. A16.

56. See Haaland and Swordstrom, "A Report on Election Law Irregularities," p. 9.

57. See "Report of the Fair Elections Foundation (I)," p. 61.

58. Haaland and Swordstrom, "A Report on Election Law Irregularities," pp. 7, 9. In a letter to us dated July 13, 1995, Norma Logan, assistant registrar in Fresno County, wrote that while she has "no direct knowledge or proof that illegal aliens are voting," there are "many allegations about it, and the possibility is that some may be voting."

59. See "Report of the Fair Elections Foundation (I)," p. 62. The man in question is Eduardo Rivera, who publishes *Nuestra Gente.*

60. See Shawn Hubler, "County Ordered to Tighten Rules for Voter Registration," *Los Angeles Times,* March 30, 1994, p. B3. He registered in September 1990, when he was nineteen years old, and re-registered in 1993, changing his address and his party affiliation from American Indepen-

dent to Democrat. There is no record of Martinez actually casting a ballot. His intention may have been to gain documentation in order to qualify for welfare benefits, as Congressman Steve Horn pointed out. (See *Congressional Record,* April 20, 1994.) Or like other illegals, he could have been seeking a voter registration card in order to obtain a separate border-crossing card that facilitates transit across the border and qualifies the holder for a California driver's license. (A notarized voter card can be used to secure the border document—see the "Report of the Fair Elections Foundation [I]," p. 4.)

Ironically, Luis Donaldo Colosio, the man Aburto assassinated, had pledged to depart from the fraudulent electoral practices that have severely damaged the credibility of the Institutional Revolutionary Party (PRI), including massive, systemic voter fraud. To his credit, as president of the PRI, Colosio conceded his party's loss to the right wing National Action Party (PAN) candidate in the gubernatorial race in Baja California Norte, the first such defeat in 60 years. (See Larry Rother, "Mexico's Ruling Party Concedes First Defeat in a Governor's Race," *New York Times,* July 6, 1989, p. A1.) However, Colosio was also the campaign manager of former President Carlos Salinas's 1988 presidential campaign, the conclusion of which was marred by widespread evidence that the PRI stole the election from Salinas's opponent, Cuauhtemoc Cardenas. See David Gardner, "Mexico's New Man Bows to the Past; Mexican Elections," *Financial Times,* May 22, 1988, p. 4.

61. See Lanie Jones, "Veteran GOP Director Leads Charge in Voter Registration Campaign," *Los Angeles Times,* October 5, 1986, pt. 2, p. 1.

62. See Matthew Mosk, "Two Accused of Voter Registration Fraud," *Los Angeles Times,* October 28, 1994, p. B1. This case is also mentioned later in the chapter. In another example of registration excess, twenty-six transient residents of a Salvation Army shelter were registered and requested absentee ballots, but left before the election. See Robert B. Gunnison and Susan Yoachum, "Abuses Cast Doubt on State Voting System," *San Francisco Chronicle,* February 22, 1995, p. A1; and Robert B. Gunnison, "Registrars Call for State Voting Reform," *San Francisco Chronicle,* March 27, 1995, p. A15.

63. Under California election law, a "helper's punching holes in other people's absentee ballots, his or her instructing voters in their choice of candidates, or handing out free stamps are misdemeanors, and his or her handling or mailing of another individual's absentee ballot is a felony offense." Now a sophisticated process, absentee "farming" skirts the law, and in some cases violates it.

64. See Gunnison and Yoachum, "Abuses Cast Doubt on State Voting System," p. A1.

65. Ibid.
66. Ibid. According to the article, although it is illegal for a candidate to elec-
    tioneer "while in the residence or in the immediate presence of the voter,
    and during the time he or she knows the absentee voter is voting," candi-
    dates have admitted on the record to engaging voters completing absen-
    tee ballots. As explained by Fresno City Council candidate Dan
    Ronquillo, "there was nothing wrong with entering voters' homes and
    answering their questions while they voted." (Quoted in Ibid.) However,
    evidence existed that Ronquillo did more than answer questions; as Gun-
    nison and Yoachum found, "Some voters said in interviews that they felt
    pressured by Ronquillo. 'He wanted to help me fill out my ballot,' said
    one elderly voter. 'You know, that's as private as my purse.' "

    Ronquillo's actions certainly had precedents in Fresno. City council-
    man Homero Espinoza, elected in 1992, was found guilty of voter fraud
    in 1995. Among other offenses during his campaign, Espinoza personally
    took and cast other people's absentee ballots, in some cases having the un-
    marked ballots mailed to his own post office box. Espinoza won by just
    thirty-four votes in an election where an extraordinarily high 35 percent
    of the ballots were cast by absentee voters. (Probation report of Homero
    Espinoza, Fresno County Superior Court Case No. 503088-7, released to
    us by letter on May 30, 1995, by County Counsel Phillip S. Cronin.)
67. Letter to the authors from Bradley J. Clark, Registrar, County of
    Alameda, dated July 31, 1995. Mr. Clark pointed out two loopholes in the
    California process for removing the deceased from the voting rolls:
    "Alameda County residents who die outside the county have their death
    records reported in the county of death. These records are then for-
    warded to the state registrar of vital statistics who in turn sends reports
    back to the county of residence. There can be a lag of six months to a year
    to receive this information. Alameda county residents who die outside the
    state have their death recorded in the state of death. Due to confidential-
    ity laws in many states, these records are never provided to us."
68. See "Report of the Fair Elections Foundation (II)," p. 15. This San Fran-
    cisco man somehow awoke from a severe case of methadone poisoning,
    which left him in rigor mortis on April 1, 1982. But he stiffly registered
    as a Democrat on September 29, 1991, and cast his ballot via coffin in the
    1994 general election.
69. Haaland and Swordstrom, "A Report on Election Law Irregularities," p. 6.
70. Ibid., p. 10. The legitimate voter was interviewed and signed an affidavit
    for the report's authors.
71. See "Report of the Fair Elections Foundation (II)," p. 51.
72. Ibid., p. 24.
73. This "law" is applied to the world of campaign finance in Larry J. Sabato,

Paying for Elections: The Campaign Finance Thicket (New York: Priority Press, 1989), pp. 19–24.

74. Texas election law permits "election officers, watchers, or any other person lawfully in the polling place" to challenge any voter's eligibility, including absence from registration rolls. Following the challenge, the voter is given the opportunity to rebut the reasons given by executing an "affidavit that states the facts necessary to support the voter's eligibility to vote." If such an affidavit is produced, the voter may proceed to vote and his or her ballot is not separated from those of unchallenged voters. If the voter refuses to execute the affidavit, he or she is simply not permitted to vote. See Tex. Elec. Code Ann. 63.010 (West, 1994).

75. See Alan Bernstein, "Thousands Voted in 1992 Sans Registration," *Houston Chronicle,* October 24, 1994, p. A1. The total voter turnout in Harris County (including the 6,707 ineligible persons) in November of 1992 was 958,234.

76. Note that 5,277 registrations had expired, and 143 were living in another county.

77. As Alan Bernstein of the *Houston Chronicle* explained it to us in a telephone interview on April 20, 1995, "The registrar's office took [the 6,707 illegal cases in Harris County] en masse to the district attorney's office, who took them to a grand jury, and the grand jury said, 'To hell with that, we have got [serious crimes] going on to worry about.' "

78. See Selwyn Crawford, "Vote Fraud Allegations are Probed; Registration of 3,000 in Tarrant Doubted," *Dallas Morning News,* May 27, 1993, p. A33.

79. Early voting is available to all voters twenty days before Election Day, although most voters must appear at a designated polling site in person. Exceptions are made for certain individuals and groups, such as the elderly; this is explained in the text following. In 1992, over 40 percent of the registered voters cast an early ballot in some of Texas's most populous counties. See Edwina Rogers, "Election Daze: Is Early Voting Coming to a State Near You?" *Campaigns and Elections* 15 (September, 1994): 36–37.

80. The signature of a witness is required on the mail-in-ballot application and the certification on the carrier envelope only if another signs for the voter, perhaps if he or she is illiterate or otherwise incapacitated. See Tex. Elec. Code Ann. § 87.041.(b)(2) (West, 1994).

81. See Kevin Moran and Bob Sablatura, "Mail-in Fraud Allegations Probed," *Houston Chronicle,* October 5, 1994, p. A1.

82. Press release, Office of the Criminal District Attorney, Galveston County, Texas, December 20, 1994, pp. 1–3.

83. For example, the campaign of U.S. Representative Craig Washington of Houston made five separate payments in February and March 1994 total-

ing $22,505 to the "Acres Home Community Relations" group for an "early voting drive" (Federal Election Commission). This group has been suspected of orchestrating some of the mail-in abuses involving early voters, according to reporter Alan Bernstein of the *Houston Chronicle,* but "nobody has ever proved anything on them." (Telephone interview with Alan Bernstein, April 20, 1995.)

84. Affidavit of Edward Taylor, subscribed December 7, 1993, by R. M. Simmons, Harris County, Texas.

85. According to Texas elections law, it is a misdemeanor to "prepare the voter's ballot in a way other than the voter directs," or "suggest by word, sign, or gesture how the voter should vote." (See Tex. Elec. Code Ann. § 64.036, [a][2-3] [West, 1994].) These stipulations apply to both the polling place and early voting by mail.

86. Affidavits of Maria Gloria Casteneda, subscribed by Debra Ann Garza, October 27, 1992, and Jesus Casteneda, subscribed by Debra Ann Garza, October 28, 1992. Mr. and Mrs. Casteneda, who intended to vote for David Pena, were told by "helper" Federico Pilon that marking the ballot in the straight Democratic ticket oval would cast their vote for Mr. Pena. Pena was an independent candidate.

87. Affidavit of Jesus Casteneda, subscribed by Debra Ann Garza, October 28, 1992.

88. Affidavit of Celia Seymour, subscribed by Henry Rodriguez, December 3, 1994. Ms. Seymour interviewed Mr. Charles Scott and his son and discovered that Mr. Scott and his wife did not prepare the ballots, nor did they sign the carrier envelopes as required. Mr. Scott had signed his mail in application, and his wife placed her "mark" on the signature line, which would have been appropriate only if she were visually disabled or if a language barrier existed. The interloper, a neighbor, requested the Scotts' absentee ballots and indicated which candidate should be selected. Once the ballots were sealed in the carrier envelopes, the "helper" signed Mr. Scott's name on the envelope certification and requested that the Scotts' son sign for Mrs. Scott. The discrepancy in signatures *should* have rendered the ballots invalid.

89. Affidavit of Curley Cheney, subscribed by Catherine A. Platz, December 17, 1994; interview with A. Glenn Diddel, April 24, 1995; the death certificate of James Cheney Jr., dated September 17, 1992; and the falsified applications for mail-in ballots for both Curley and James Chaney Jr., dated November 23, 1993, and February 17, 1994. Although the spellings of the names differ by one letter, the applications were matched to the Cheneys by address.

90. In the past two years, sheriffs in two South Texas counties have been implicated, and other counties' officials are undergoing investigation.

Brigido Marmolejo, sheriff of Hidalgo County for twenty years, was prosecuted and convicted for accepting bribes from a drug dealer. (See James Pinkerton, "Bribes Cost Sheriff His Job, Respect," *Houston Chronicle,* November 13, 1994, p. 1.) In Zapata County, Judge Jose Luis Guevera, Sheriff Romeo Ramirez, and County Clerk Arnoldo Flores were either convicted of or pleaded guilty to drug related charges. Interestingly, Judge Guevera's opponent alleged vote fraud in a primary election, the results of which were overturned by a state judge. See David McLemore, "Fallout from Drug Sting Has County in Quandary; Zapata Officials Going to Prison, Who'll Lead?" *Dallas Morning News,* July 3, 1994, p. A1; also, James Pinkerton, "Trafficking and the Long Arm of the Law," *Houston Chronicle,* July 31, 1994, p. 1.

91. See David McLemore, "Starr County Denies Election Irregularities," *Dallas Morning News,* August 21, 1994, p. A47. Also, telephone interviews with David McLemore, April 18, 1995; Bruce Sherbert, Dallas County election administrator, April 20, 1995; and David Pena, April 20, 1995. Pena was an unsuccessful candidate for city clerk in Starr County. These kinds of fraudulent activities, it should be noted, are not limited to South Texas in the Lone Star state. See Sylvia Martinez and Frank Trejo, "Hopefuls, Backers Accused of Fraud, Document Tampering in Two Districts," *Dallas Morning News,* May 5, 1995, p. A30; and Todd J. Gillman, "Dallas JP Loser Alleges Voting Fraud," *Dallas Morning News,* May 17, 1994, p. A21. Also see the affidavit of Victor Cantu, August 25, 1992, regarding favoritism in the mailing of absentee ballots.

92. Affidavits of Mary Ramirez, November 12, 1992; and of Sonia Garza, November 15, 1992.

93. Political scientist Louise Overacker, in her *Money in Elections* p. 34, explained the Kentucky operation this way: "The Republican organization in Louisville, Kentucky, has worked out a novel method of payment [for votes]. In the local election of 1925 aluminum discs the size of a half dollar bearing the imprint of a bulldog were distributed to the faithful by precinct workers. These bulldog checks were then taken to a district paymaster and redeemed for $2.00. By this plan the use of money around polling places was avoided and only a few persons were entrusted with cash."

94. These estimates were given by veteran Kentucky journalist Al Cross of the *Courier-Journal* in an interview with the authors, June 29, 1995. Another prosecutorial source told us the usual price was "more like $20 . . . but the highest that I heard was $150. . . . It depends on the market and how tight the race is."

95. The absentee ballots were either sent directly to the voters, who marked them in the presence of the broker, or were sent to the broker, who then

simply had the voter sign pre-marked ballots. Once the voters signed off, they would receive the payoff.

The Kentucky legislature had attempted to curb vote fraud by passing reform legislation in 1988 that made purchasing or selling votes a felony offense. (Rigging election machinery and electioneering within 500 feetof the polls were also severely punished.) (See Kentucky Revised Statutes, Title X, at 117.235.) The new law apparently did indeed stem fraud at the polling places, where illicit activity is easily observable, but it may simply have channeled more fraud into the relatively hidden absentee process. As a result of the recent disclosures of absentee fraud, the legislature has passed still more reforms, including two mandates directly affecting absentee voting. Now, no individual is permitted to assist more than two voters, and citizens are allowed to vote by mailed absentee ballot only if they are certifiably disabled, or living outside their county, or serving in the military. (Kentucky Revised Statutes, Title X, at 117.075.) Other people who wish to vote prior to the election day must do so *in person* at their county courthouse. (Kentucky Revised Statutes, Title X, at 117.077.)

Unlike some of the other states we have investigated, Kentucky has taken vote fraud seriously. As George Russell, executive director of the State Board of Elections commented, "I think you'll find that the Attorney General, Secretary of State, and the General Assembly are completely committed to eliminate vote fraud. Of course, that's the *present* Attorney General, Secretary of State, and General Assembly" (interview with George Russell, July 27, 1995). The state election system is well administered; statewide registration records are computerized, and voters are identified by a unique number to prevent duplicate registration. Sources differed on whether the revisions of the election code, or a more active, aggressive approach to combating electoral abuses on the part of the State Board of Elections, secretary of state, and the state attorney general have contributed to a decrease in election fraud. In any case, there was a significant decrease in the number of calls made to the attorney general's statewide vote fraud hotline in 1994 and 1995. See, for example, John Voskuhl, "Primary '95: State's Vote-Fraud Hot Line Rings Only Three Times," *Courier-Journal,* May 24, 1995, p. B5.

96. Interview with Dale Wright, July 19, 1995.

97. Ibid.

98. The same class and economic distinctions can explain the presence or absence of "street money" in any community.

99. A couple of our Democratic interviewees alluded to this reasoning in off-the-record comments.

100. United Press International, "Election Officials: Four Dead People Cast Ballots in Hudson," January 12, 1989.

101. Peter J. Sampson, "Judge's Ruling Leaves Secaucus Mayorless: Chal-

lenge to Just's Victory to Proceed," *Bergen Record,* January 22, 1994, p. A4.

102. Interview with Ed Rollins, May 26, 1995.
103. The author of the observation is journalist Marc Mappen. See the retelling of a classic 1889 ballot-box stuffing in Hudson County in Marc Mappen, "Jersey-ana," *New York Times,* November 13, 1994, section 13, p. 17.

NOTES TO CHAPTER 11

The quotation at the beginning of the chapter is from Merrill D. Petersen (ed.), *The Portable Thomas Jefferson* (New York: Penguin Books, 1977), p. 198. We have now come full circle. The first part of this Jefferson citation appeared in the introductory discussion of corruption.

1. As did a number of other candidates, none of whom was ever called to account by the IRS.
2. Title 26, Internal Revenue Code, Sec. 527.
3. President Nixon and high-ranking members of his administration attempted to use the Internal Revenue Service to retaliate against critics and opponents. As John Dean explained in a memo made public during his explosive testimony before the 1973 Senate Watergate hearings between June 25 and 27, the goal was to "maximize the fact of our incumbency with persons known to be active in their opposition to the administration. Stated a bit more bluntly—how we can use the available federal machinery to screw our political enemies." Grants, contracts, litigation, prosecution, and audits were possibilities Dean raised.

   In addition, attempts were made to gain access to IRS information for use against "enemies." When initial attempts to gather the "dirt" failed, Nixon brought pressure to bear on both Internal Revenue Service Commissioner Johnnie Waters (who was later replaced) and Treasury Secretary George Shultz.

   Another document Dean made public was the actual "priority list" of opponents (compiled by then-special White House counsel Charles Colson), which included prominent corporate executives (such as Arnold M. Picker of the United Artists Corporation), labor union officials (such as Alexander Barkan of AFL-CIO COPE and Leonard Woodcock of the UAW), Democratic congressmen (such as Ronald Dellums and John Conyers), and media figures and entertainment personalities (such as Daniel Schorr, Mary McGrory, and Paul Newman).

   For a fuller account, see Bob Woodward and Carl Bernstein, *The Final Days* (New York: Simon and Schuster, 1976), p. 89; and Mercer Cross and Elder Witt (eds.), *Watergate: Chronology of a Crisis* (Washington, D.C.: Congressional Quarterly, 1975), pp. 151–53.

4. All those who study the tenets of party-responsible government inevitably return to the landmark report of the Committee on Political Parties of the American Political Science Association (APSA), *Toward a More Responsible Two-Party System* (New York: Rinehart, 1950). Essentially, this APSA Committee urged the parties to be more issue-oriented by offering the voters clear policy choices at election time, then following up once in power to see that these policies were enacted.

5. See "No More Cash in New Jersey," *Political Finance and Lobby Reporter* 15 (February 9, 1994): 8. See also Bruno Tedeschi, "Pascrell Paid Out $14,360 in Street Money, by Check," *Bergen Record,* June 1, 1994, p. C1. This latter story reports that the new check requirement worked well in its first test. See also the well-written New Jersey statute, C.19:44A-11.

6. Lists of subcontractors should be appended to all campaign finance disclosure filings sent to the appropriate federal and/or state election commissions as currently scheduled.

7. 18 USCS at 597.

8. In addition to our own examination of this issue, a 1982 study convincingly demonstrated the political utility of the frank. See Albert D. Cover and Bruce S. Brumberg, "Baby Books and Ballots: The Impact of Congressional Mail on Constituent Opinion," *American Political Science Review* 76 (June 1982): p. 347.

9. While Republicans limited mailings in the ninety days before an election and trimmed the budget somewhat, we do not count these reforms as the major surgery that is required.

10. We believe the major party candidate should be entitled to one or two mass mailings for the general election, and only independent candidates who received (or whose party received) at least 10 percent of the vote in at least one of the previous three general elections should be eligible for the same privilege.

11. Former Senator Howard Cannon (Democrat of Nevada) and Representative William Clay (Democrat of Missouri) were both the subject of private civil suits alleging misuse of staff. Clay lost the suit; Cannon won.

12. Interview with Thomas Guterbock, director of the University of Virginia Survey Research Center, February 10, 1995. The National Council on Public Polls issued a statement in May 1995 calling push-polling "thoroughly unethical." See "Beware of Push-Polls," Press Release of the National Council, May 22, 1995.

13. Many respondents hang up before a survey is completed. Pollsters should not be required to recontact them to reveal sponsorship.

14. Pollsters should *not* be required to ask all respondents whether they would like a copy of the questions. This must be initiated and volunteered by the respondent.

15. The Supreme Court ruled in a recent Ohio case on April 19, 1995, that anonymous political pamphleteering was protected free speech, and that mandatory disclosure was a violation of the First Amendment. But a close reading of the justices' varying opinions in this fractious 5-4 ruling indicates that it is unlikely that the anonymity privilege will be expanded beyond this narrow exception. Required sponsorship disclosure for TV ads, radio spots, and—one would presume—telephone persuasion messages would all probably pass constitutional muster. See *McIntyre v. Ohio Elections Commission,* 61 LW 4279.

16. Respondents who request sponsorship information at the start of or during the interview can be told it will be revealed at the end.

17. Two members of Congress, U.S. Representatives Thomas E. Petri (Republican of Wisconsin) and Carolyn Maloney (Democrat of New York), are among those urging strong action. Maloney favors pollster sponsorship disclosure, while Petri wants political poll information, including the questionnaires, filed with the FEC.

18. In addition to the general remedies for push-polling that we discuss here, there may be two specific legal remedies that can be applied. First, in 1994, Congress enacted the Telemarketing and Consumer Fraud and Abuse Prevention Act (P.L. 103-297, 103d Cong., 2d Sess., 1994, published in 1994 USCAAN [108 Stat.] 1545 [1994]). Designed primarily to limit commercial telemarketers, the law instructs the Federal Trade Commission to enact rules that include, among other things, "a requirement that telemarketers may not undertake a pattern of unsolicited telephone calls that the reasonable consumer would consider coercive or abusive of such consumer's right to privacy," and "restrictions on the hours of the day and night when unsolicited telephone calls can be made to consumers" (sec. 3[a] [3][A]-[B]). These restrictions presumably would apply to push-polling, and they ought to be upheld by the court because they do not significantly affect the content of the polling, or unduly restrict candidates' ability to disseminate their message. Such rules should prevent the worst abuses, such as the midnight phone calls discussed in chapter 9.

    Moreover, some affected candidates may be able to pursue a successful tort legal claim of defamation against push-poll telemarketers (assuming the telephoners are identified). In order to establish any private tort claim for defamation against the maker of a statement, the allegedly defamed party must prove that the statement has been disseminated to a third party and is defamatory. (*Prosser and Keaton on Torts,* 5th ed. [St. Paul, Minn.: West Publishing, 1984], pp. 797–802.) In order to establish a cause for action for slander (verbal statements, as opposed to libel, involving written statements), actual damages must be proven, except in the case of a few narrow classes of cases. Among those exceptions, however, are statements "affecting the plaintiff in his business, trade, profession, office or calling."

Under the standard of *New York Times v. Sullivan* (376 U.S. 254 [1964]), any defamatory statements made about public officials relating to their conduct in office must be made with "actual malice" for there to be any knowledge of its falsity or reckless disregard in determining its truth; as "actual malice" has been applied in the case law, it has proved an exceedingly difficult threshold to cross. For political candidates, the courts seem willing to find a valid claim for defamation in only the most egregious cases and would require outright lies, and not simply innuendo or twisting or misrepresentation of the facts.

19. The act was officially termed the "National Voter Registration Act of 1993" (Public Law 103-31, 103d Cong., 1st sess., May 20, 1993). See Richard Sammon, "Senate Kills Filibuster Threat, Clears 'Motor-Voter' Bill," *Congressional Quarterly Weekly* 51 (May 15, 1993): 1221.

20. Besides the motor vehicle agencies, these offices include those providing food stamps, Aid to Families with Dependent Children (AFDC), the Women, Infants, and Children (WIC) food program, disabilities assistance, armed forces recruitment, and the like.

21. Under the provisions of the motor-voter law, states are prohibited from purging eligible voters from the registration rolls for federal elections because of the person's failure to vote (P.L. 103.31 § 8[b][2]). Thus, the primary tool traditionally used by registrars to remove "deadwood" voters has been stripped away for federal elections. This is in spite of recent research indicating that the antipurging provisions of the motor-voter law may be among the least useful in increasing voter registration. See Stephen Knack, "Does 'Motor-Voter' Work? Evidence from State-Level Data," *Journal of Politics*, 57 (August 1995): 796–811 at 804–5.

States may remove deceased registrants (§ 8 [a][3][B]), as well as those ineligible under state law because of criminal conviction or mental incapacity (§ 8 [a][3][B]). Voters may also be removed at their own request.

However, in order to remove voters who have moved from the jurisdiction, registration officials now must follow an exceedingly complicated notice procedure. After receiving changes of address information from the post office, the registrar must send the voter by forwardable mail a notice including a postage prepaid, preaddressed return card for the voter to confirm his new address. (If the voter has moved out of the jurisdiction, he must be told how to remain eligible). Any voter not returning the card still must be permitted to vote at either his past or present address (upon discretion of state officials) provided he makes an oral or written verification of his new address (8 [a]). Voters who have moved from the registration area may only be stricken from the rolls if they (1) confirm their new address in writing via the reply card, or (2) they do not confirm their new address and fail to appear to vote for two federal general elections. In the latter case, approximately four to five years could elapse from the time of a voter's relocation to the removal of his or her name.

As one commentator noted, "The provisions of the federal law have caused acrimony and confusion in many states. Six states—California, Louisiana, Michigan, Mississippi, Pennsylvania, and South Carolina—were sued by the Justice Department and voter-advocacy groups to force compliance with the act. All of these states had failed to pass corrective legislation to bring their voting regulations into compliance with the federal law." (See Ann Scott Tyson, "Illinois Court Drives Motor-Voter Debate," *Christian Science Monitor,* May 8, 1995, p. 3.) Federal judges in several states sided with the federal government, and all of the renegade states eventually agreed to comply.

In California, Governor Pete Wilson issued an order forbidding state agencies from complying with the act's provisions until the federal government agreed to put up the money to pay for the changes, estimated to cost $1 million per year in one county alone. (See Brad Hayward, "Battle Looming as State Snubs 'Motor-Voter' Law," *Sacramento Bee,* December 4, 1995, p. A1; and Gary Pitzer, "Voter Law Could Cost County $1 Million a Year," *Sacramento Bee,* November 117, 1994, p. N1.) None fought harder than Pennsylvania, which claimed that the act was unconstitutional because the states—and not Congress—have the power to regulate voter registration. Federal Judge Ronald L. Buckwalter rejected this argument on March 30, 1995, becoming the third federal judge to find the act constitutional. (See *U.S. v. Pennsylvania,* PICS Case No. 95-3055 [E.D. Pa., March 30, 1995]; "Pennsylvania Loses Constitutional Claim, Motor-Voter Law Held Valid," *Pennsylvania Law Weekly,* April 10, 1995, p. 3).

Meanwhile, Pennsylvania's failure to conform its voting regulations to federal law caused conflict for county registrars, who were left with the option in early 1995 of purging voters in violation of federal law, or violating state law by refusing to purge (see Frank Devlin, "Candidates Want 60,000 Back as Voters," *Allentown Morning Call,* May 10, 1995, p. B1, and Bob Laylo, "Federal Law Keeps 2,300 Non-Voters on Carbon Rolls," *Allentown Morning Call,* April 14, 1995, p. B.3). The confusion continues, because as of May 1995 Pennsylvania had complied with the motor-voter provisions for federal elections but retained the old rules for nonfederal elections. Thus a voter could be purged for state and local elections but remain eligible to vote in federal races. These potentially Byzantine consequences are hardly what congressional drafters had in mind with the motor-voter act.

22. See "Report of the 1995 Elections Summit," April 1995, p. 40, also 38–41.

23. See "Report of the 1995 Elections Summit," p. 14. See also Doug Haaland and Doug Swordstrom, "A Report on Election Law Irregularities: California 16th Senate District," personally published report, January 27, 1995, p. 11.

    Fingerprint scanning technology has advanced quickly since the 1980s and has become available for a wide range of relatively inexpensive identification and fraud prevention applications. The scanners rely upon sophisticated laser scanners (such as supermarket barcode scanners) and computer databases and can be more accurate than ink and paper prints (which can smudge) and the human eye. Some government agencies at the federal, state, and local level already use fingerprint scanners, and others have conversion plans in the works. Scanners have obvious applications in the field of law enforcement and are being implemented at all levels of government as a means of positively identifying suspects or inmates. The Federal Bureau of Investigation is in the process of creating a central fingerprint database, which would vastly reduce the time required to find print matches. Some state and municipal departments have already converted to the new fingerprinting technology, as in California, including San Diego and Los Angeles. (See Ronald J. Ostrow, "FBI Nabs New Technology for Fingerprint System," *Los Angeles Times,* April 3, 1995, p. A1; and J. Harry Jones, "Now Its Harder to Hide; Computer Net Checks Prints at the Touch of a Key," *San Diego Union-Tribune,* February 1, 1994, p. B1.) California also uses a fingerprint scanning system to verify identity for drivers' licenses. The Secret Service has recommended a similar system to prevent fraudulent use of the experimental welfare debit card. (See Associated Press, "Crooks Devise Ways to Defraud Welfare Debit-Card System," *Rocky Mountain News,* January 11, 1995, p. A41.) Others are experimenting with this technology for use with credit or debit cards and automatic teller machines.

    Interestingly, Mexico has implemented a sophisticated fraud prevention program to enhance the legitimacy of its electoral system. One of the safeguards was a laminated identity card sealed with a hologram, computer bar code, and thumbprint. (See Mark Fineman, "Anxious Mexicans Await Day of the Vote," *Los Angeles Times,* August 21, 1994, p. A1.)

    Conceivably, costs could be minimized through developing a multiple application system in conjunction with motor-voter provisions requiring registration at welfare offices and motor vehicle departments. A single system could establish a rate fingerprint file for entitlement eligibility, vehicle registration, or registration to vote (as long as separate databases were established).

24. A recent federal case may prevent the use of voters' social security numbers. To comply with *Greidlinger v. Davis,* (988 F.2d 1344 [4th Cir. 1993]),

it would not be lawful to distribute any list containing voters' social security numbers except to precinct workers and elections officials. This ruling would make the proposal above difficult to enact in a state such as Virginia, where social security numbers are in fact used as drivers' license numbers.

25. Those unable to sign their names, for reasons of illiteracy or physical inability, should be required to give their mark, so that it can be compared with that witnessed and attested on their registration form. When done in conjunction with a requirement to show a photo identification, this should not create a significant potential for fraud.

26. Haaland and Swordstrom, "A Report on Election Law Irregularities," p. 11. This technology, known as signature recognition, utilizes a computer pad and pen to recognize the size, pressure, and direction of a signature for identification. Although any one individual's signature may vary for a number of reasons, such as natural change over time, signature recognition is a generally reliable means of determining authenticity. (See Betsy Pisik, "'Smart Card' Security: High-Tech ID System for Future Consumers," *Washington Times,* April 16, 1995, p. A11.)

This technology "captures" the user's signature on the pressure-sensitive pad, and converts it into a graphic file that can easily be stored in a computer database. One application for which signature recognition is already used is the familiar UPS clipboard, on which package recipients record their signature on a small pressure-sensitive pad. A similar system is currently available for retail merchants and has been used by companies such as booksellers Barnes & Noble. (See Lisa A. Spiegelman, "Executive Update, Computers & Automation," *Investor's Business Daily,* August 10, 1994, p. A4.)

27. Haaland and Swordstrom, "A Report on Election Law Irregularities," p. 16. Although this mechanism has been used in the past by Republican "ballot security" programs, it is necessary to note several crucial differences that distinguish this proposal from knowing attempts to intimidate or coerce potential voters. First, the statement would appear on official documents, and would disclose requirements which are, after all, the law of the land (and are to be provided with mail registration forms as per § 7 [a][6][a]. While offering a disincentive to fraudulent voters, such a notice would not cause the law-abiding citizen concern. Second, any oral notification would be delivered by officials of the election board in the neutral polling zone. While we are aware that, in extreme cases, even elections officials could be implicated in attempts to intimidate voters, the public nature of the forum would prevent most mischief (and crooked officials do not need to openly intimidate voters in any case). Further, oral notification could be carefully monitored in areas with poor civil rights or

voting rights records, to prevent discrimination against minority groups. Finally, it would eliminate the ostensible justification for ballot security programs intentionally aimed at decreasing minority group turnout, and would expose the less savory goals actually behind such programs.

28. Under § 8 (c)(B) of the motor-voter act, names can be removed from the registration list on the basis of death (§ 8 [a][4][A]), or criminal conviction or mental incapacity (§ 8 [a][3][B]). Removal of duplicate registration would probably be allowed by § 8 (c)(B)(ii), which permits "correction of registration records pursuant to this act." However, it would be necessary to show a convincing, clear indication of duplication, such as the use of a number unique to the registrant, as suggested above.

   Changes of address fall under the complicated procedures of § 8 (d)-(e), and anyone moving within the jurisdiction must have his or her address corrected automatically by the registrar. Any regular effort to purge must be ninety days before the federal election (primary or general) (§ 8 [c][2][A]). Aliens are a different matter entirely. Potential registrants are to be notified of citizenship requirements and attest that they fulfill all obligations, under the penalty of perjury (§ 7 [a][6][A]), but the information gathered for voter registration purposes *must not* be used for other purposes. Therefore, if the registrar discovers the person is registered illegally because he or she fails to meet citizenship requirements, the registrar cannot forward this information to other agencies for which citizenship is a concern (such as Immigration and Naturalization, Aid to Families with Dependent Children, or Women, Infants, and Children).

29. Brooks Jackson, *Broken Promise: Why the Federal Election Commission Failed* (New York: Priority Press Publications, 1990), p. 2.

30. Address to the National Press Club, July 5, 1995 (Federal Document Clearinghouse, Inc.).

31. *Code of Federal Regulations, Federal Elections* (Washington, D.C.: Government Printing Office, 1995).

32. *Statement of the Committee Following Hearings Involving Senators Cranston, DeConcini, Glenn, McCain and Riegle,* Senate Select Committee on Ethics, 102d Cong., 1st sess., 1991.

33. We are indebted to attorney Jan Baran of the law firm Wiley, Rein & Fielding for this analogy.

34. *Buckley v. Valeo,* 424 U.S. 1, at 66-7 (1976).

35. This is among the many fundamental decisions made by the Supreme Court in *Buckley v. Valeo.*

36. Interview with Trevor Potter, July 12, 1995.

37. Indexing for inflation should be provided for.

38. The exception are some so-called nonconnected PACs, that is, PACs not formally associated with a trade or interest group.

39. Most notably the Washington-based Center for Responsive Politics.
40. Kenneth A. Gross, "The Enforcement of Campaign Finance Rules: A System in Search of Reform," *Yale Law & Policy Review* 9 (1991): 279.
41. Frank Sorauf, one of the most astute students of campaign finance, has raised the possibility that "voluntary funding of campaigns for public office is intrinsically committed to the support of incumbents and likely winners." Frank J. Sorauf, "Competition, Contributions, and Money in 1992," in James A. Thurber and Candice J. Nelson (eds.), *Campaigns And Elections American Style* (Boulder, Colo.: Westview Press, 1995), p. 81.
42. For a cogent review of the literature, see Frank Sorauf, *Inside Campaign Finance: Myths and Realities* (New Haven, Conn.: Yale University Press, 1992), pp. 215–16. There is an increasing number of dissenters to this view. For instance, Christopher Kenny and Michael McBurnett argue that those who say that the level of incumbent spending has no effect neglect the interrelationship of challenger and incumbent spending in producing the outcome of the election. Incumbent spending is at least partially a function of challenger spending, that is, when challengers spend more, incumbents respond to the increased competition with greater outlays. When this interrelationship is taken into account, both challenger and incumbent spending levels affect the outcomes of the races; Kenny and McBurnett provide empirical evidence to show the effect is statistically significant. (See Kenny and McBurnett, "An Individual Level Multiequation Model of Expenditure Effects in Contested House Elections," *American Political Science Review* 88 (September 1994): 699–707).
43. See "Campaign Finance Reform: A Report to the Majority Leader and Minority Leader, United States Senate, by the Campaign Finance Reform Panel," March 6, 1990, p. 41. Coauthor Sabato was one of the panel's six members, appointed by then Senate Majority Leader George Mitchell (Democrat of Maine) and then Senate Minority Leader Robert Dole (Republican of Kansas).
44. *Buckley v. Valeo,* 424 U.S. 1 (1976).
45. See Larry J. Sabato, *Paying for Elections: The Campaign Finance Thicket* (New York: Twentieth Century Fund/Priority Press, 1989), esp. pp. 25–42, 61–64. For example, disclosure laws do not currently cover contributions to foundations that presidential candidates sometimes form. These foundations often pay for pre-campaign travel, and openly promote their candidate-creator.
46. The Campaign Finance Reform Panel mentioned above endorsed the free broadcast time proposal in ibid., pp. 25–42.
47. Remarks delivered at the Nieman Foundation, Harvard University, May 5, 1995, p. 7. Hundt has proposed making these new frequencies

available under two government-imposed restrictions: (1) some broadcast time must be devoted to educational programming for children, and (2) free broadcast time must be given to political candidates and parties. See also Max Frankel, "Airfill," *New York Times Magazine,* June 4, 1995, p. 26; and Mary McGrory, "The Vaster Wasteland," *Washington Post,* June 4, 1995, p. C1.

48. Given the importance of the data, as well as their complexity, a computerized database for campaign finance reports is an essential component of a fair, accountable electoral finance system. Most state agencies that oversee campaign finance have entered the computer age (as the Council of State Government reports, in 1992 virtually all state election boards or ethics boards already had some computing capacity). In addition, states should provide public access to their computerized reports, or in the optimal case, follow the lead of the Federal Election Commission and make an on-line database available for public access (as Alabama, Alaska, Hawaii, Texas, and Washington already have). The FEC database, for instance, made possible much of the authors' research into campaign contributions. It must be noted, however, that any on-line system is limited by the data made available by the provider. A frequent criticism of the FEC is that expenditure reports are not available on the on-line system, although tracking where candidates spend their war chests is frequently as interesting as, and in some cases more interesting than, where their funding originates.

   Council of State Governments listed sixteen states (Alabama, California, Colorado, Idaho, Indiana, Iowa, Illinois, Nebraska, North Dakota, Ohio, Pennsylvania, Tennessee, Texas, Utah, Virginia, and Washington) as having no contribution caps for any state or local offices. The council also listed twenty-five states that have at least some limits, which vary by primary or general election and office: Alaska, Arkansas, Connecticut, Delaware, Georgia, Florida, Hawaii, Kansas, Louisiana, Maine, Massachusetts, Michigan, Minnesota, Montana, Nevada, New Jersey, New York, Oklahoma, Rhode Island, South Carolina, South Dakota, Vermont, West Virginia, Wisconsin, Wyoming. Puerto Rico also has contribution caps for general elections. One state actually does perform random audits on campaign finance reports—California. The Franchise Tax Board randomly audits lobbyists and campaign finance reports.

50. The Council of State Governments listed twenty-eight states as having ethics commissions as of 1992: Alabama, Arkansas, California, Connecticut, Florida, Georgia, Hawaii, Illinois, Indiana, Kansas, Louisiana, Maine, Maryland, Massachusetts, Minnesota, Mississippi, New Jersey, New York, North Carolina, Ohio, Oklahoma, Oregon, Pennsylvania, Rhode Island, South Carolina, South Dakota, Utah, and Wisconsin.

Index